Man of the House

Man of the House
The Life and Political Memoirs of Speaker Tip O'Neill
with William Novak

THE BODLEY HEAD
LONDON

British Library Cataloguing
in Publication Data

O'Neill, Tip
Man of the house.
1. O'Neill, Tip 2. United States. *Congress
House of Representatives* — Biography
I. Tite II. Novak, William
328.73'0762 E840.8.054

Grateful acknowledgment is made to E. P. Dutton for permission to
reprint the poem "Around the Corner" by Charles Hanson Towne from
Selected Poems of Charles Hanson Towne by Charles Hanson Towne.
Copyright 1925 by D. Appleton & Co. Copyright renewed 1953 by Ara
Searle. A Hawthorn book. Reprinted by permission of E. P. Dutton, a
division of N.A.L. Penguin Inc.

ISBN 0 370 31220 1

Printed in Great Britain for
The Bodley Head Ltd,
32 Bedford Square, London WC1B 3EL
by
the Alden Press, Oxford

*First published in the United States by Random
House, New York in 1987
First published in Great Britain in 1988
Reprinted 1988*

For Millie
The Speaker of My House

A loving wife and mother,
and my partner through so many triumphs and trials

ACKNOWLEDGMENTS

I'd like to thank the many people whose help and support during the writing of this book meant so much, starting with my beloved Millie and our children: Rosemary, Tom, and his wife, Jackie, Susan, Kip, and his wife, Stephanie, and Michael.

In my Washington offices: Susan Athy, Roger Brooks, Deborah Cabral, Leo Diehl, Sally Ericsson, Mary Ann Green, Pam Jackson, Billie Larson, Chris Matthews, Frank McLaughlin, Lee Pendergast, Kevin Peterson, Dolores Snow, Christine Sullivan, Barbara Sutton, Dessa Vrtikapa, and Ari Weiss.

Eleanor Kelley, Kirk O'Donnell, and Jacob Lew were especially helpful, and I greatly appreciate their contributions.

In my district offices: Lewis Armistead, Herb d'Arcy, John Carver, Mary Fahey, Jim Ferguson, Francine Gannon, Helen Harvey, Dorothy Kelly, Leonard Lamkin, Mike Ralph, Jim Rowan, and Isabelle Sylvester.

Special thanks to my literary agent, Jay Acton, and his associate, Larry Moulter, and to Taren Metson in Newton.

Peter Osnos, our editor, was intimately involved with this book from the start, asking all the right questions and keeping us firmly on track. Thanks, too, to Nina Ryan, Peter's assistant at Random House, and to Virginia Avery, our copy editor.

William Novak wishes to thank the following individuals for their time and their recollections: Chick Artesani, Lud Ashley, Richard Bolling, Leo Diehl, Frank Fitzgerald, Barney Frank, Doris Kearns Goodwin, Ralph Granara, Bob Griffin, William Hamilton, John Harris, Robert Healy, Gary Hymel, Eleanor Kelley, Leonard Lamkin, Jacob Lew, Mary McGrory, Chris Matthews, Mary Mulcahy, Martin Nolan, David Nyhan, Kirk O'Donnell, Jackie O'Neill, Kip O'Neill, Millie O'Neill, Rosemary O'Neill, Stephanie O'Neill, Susan O'Neill, Tom O'Neill, John Parker, David Powers, William Ragan, Jim Rowan, Billy Sutton, Martin Tolchin, and Ari Weiss.

Special thanks to Colleen Mohyde and Ronnie Friedland for their editorial assistance, and to Donald Altschiller for research.

We are also grateful to three writers whose work made ours easier: Jimmy Breslin, author of *How the Good Guys Finally Won*; and Paul Clancy and Shirley Elder, who coauthored *Tip: A Biography of Thomas P. O'Neill*.

Finally, a tip of the hat to Linda Novak and Steve Axelrod.

Contents

Man of the House

Prologue

On October 18, 1986, as the Ninety-ninth Congress drew to a close, my long career in politics finally came to an end. I had served in public life for fifty years, including thirty-four as a member of Congress. I was also completing ten years as Speaker of the House of Representatives—the longest continuous term for any Speaker since Congress first met in 1789.

Believe me, it wasn't easy to walk off the floor of the House that day. My colleagues were generous with their tributes, but as I listened to their words, my thoughts kept wandering back to other moments in this city.

More than half a century had passed since the day in 1934 when, as a sophomore in college, I had the political thrill of my life. I had come to Washington to visit relatives, and Missy LeHand, the president's secretary, who came from our neighborhood, had once said, "If you ever come to Washington, give me a call at the White House."

When I contacted her, she invited me over to see the place. I took the bus downtown, and Missy was waiting for me at the gate.

When we were inside, she said, "Would you like to meet the president?"

I was speechless. Franklin Delano Roosevelt was like God to me.

"Cordell Hull is with him now," she said. "But as soon as they're finished talking, I'm going to bring you in."

When I saw the president sitting in a wheelchair, I was so shocked that my chin just about hit my chest. Like most Americans, I had absolutely no idea that Franklin Roosevelt was disabled. It's hard to imagine in this age of television, but in those days the president's handicap was kept secret out of respect for the office.

Nineteen years later, on January 3, 1953, I cast my very first vote as a member of Congress—for Sam Rayburn as Speaker. But the Republicans had gained control of the House in the Eisenhower landslide of 1952, so Joe Martin of Massachusetts won the job.

I arrived in Washington at the age of forty, fresh from four years as the first Democratic Speaker in the history of the Massachusetts legislature. Back home, I had worked my way up until I was the second-most-powerful man in the state. But now, as a lonely freshman member from the minority party, my status was about as low as you could get. I knew that my lights were to be dimmed for some time.

At the first caucus I ever attended, Sam Rayburn addressed the House Democrats. "We're in the minority, now," he said. "But we're still going to be helpful and constructive. Remember, any jackass can kick over a barn door. It takes a carpenter to build one."

A few days later, Harry Truman, who was finishing out his term, invited the freshman Democrats to the White House. Old Harry was as feisty as his reputation, and that day he really lit into President-elect Eisenhower. I loved old Harry, not only for all he had accomplished, but because he was so down-to-earth. He was an underrated president in his time, but history is making him look greater every day.

In the Eisenhower era, the nation was in its glory and the economy was booming. Ike will be remembered more for his great military ability than for his political leadership, but he served his purpose. And he was absolutely right when he warned the nation about the growing dangers of the military-industrial complex.

Jack Kennedy was a great friend of mine, with a glamour and a charisma that people loved. Not just in our own country, either; during his three years in office, Kennedy inspired the entire world. I remember the first time I met Jack. He was a skinny, bashful kid, and it was hard to imagine him as a schoolteacher, let alone president. But he grew like nobody I've ever known, and he went on to become one of the great political leaders of our time.

From then on, I knew them all—Lyndon Johnson, Richard Nixon, Gerald Ford, Jimmy Carter, and Ronald Reagan. I worked with each of them, and had a close-up look at their strengths and their weaknesses.

But on my final day in the House, it was Congress I was thinking about. Over the years, I had cast so many votes in this great hall. As a freshman member, I had opposed additional funding for the House Committee on Un-American Activities. That was a tough one, because my home district was fairly conservative and the majority of my constituents supported the anti-Communist crusade of Senator Joe McCarthy.

But most of the votes I cast were easy, because I came to Washington as a New Deal liberal who believed that government has a moral responsibility to help people who can't take care of themselves. Although so much has happened in thirty-four years, I still feel that way today.

It was very difficult for me to bang that Speaker's gavel for the last time, but my final day in office was made easier by a tremendous outpouring of friendship and support from my fellow members, and from the thousands of people who wrote from across the nation, thanking me for all I had stood for and wishing me well in my retirement.

Leaving was a slow process, as there were so many friends to say good-bye to in Congress—not only Democrats, but Republicans as well. Over the years, I've traveled to many other countries, and in most of them the members of opposing parties barely speak to each other. They're always amazed to see that in our society, Democrats and Republicans can be friends.

That, to me, is the special greatness of our political system. There's no rancor or hatred—only the energetic clash of conflicting ideas. Your views may be different from mine, but we can still respect each other and work together, which is what the Congress is all about.

During my years in Washington, I participated in hundreds of debates, including more than a few that were tough and bitter. But I left with no malice in my heart. Instead, I felt a tremendous love and affection for the Congress, and for the system it represents.

I will always be proud to call myself a man of the House.

1

★★★★★

All Politics Is Local

It was at Harvard University in 1927 that I first decided to go into politics.

No, I wasn't a Harvard man. But I was born and raised in North Cambridge, Massachusetts, a stable, mostly Irish, working-class neighborhood a mile or two from the university. At the age of fourteen, I landed a summer job as a groundskeeper, cutting the grass and trimming the hedges at Harvard. It was tough work, and I was paid seventeen cents an hour.

On a beautiful June day, as I was going about my daily grind, the class of 1927 gathered in a huge canvas tent to celebrate commencement. Inside, I could see hundreds of young men standing around in their white linen suits, laughing and talking. They were also drinking champagne, which was illegal in 1927 because of Prohibition.

I remember that scene like it was yesterday, and I can still feel the anger I felt then, almost sixty years ago as I write these words. It was the illegal champagne that really annoyed me. Who the hell do these people think they are, I said to myself, that the law means nothing to them?

Although I could walk home from my Harvard job in twenty minutes, North Cambridge might just as well have been on the other side of the moon. My own neighborhood was relatively well off by working-class standards, but you didn't have to go very far to find pockets of real poverty. Every town had its poorhouse, and in those days, of course, there was no such thing as health insurance or Social Security. When you turned sixty-five, your family had to take care of you, and if they couldn't you were out of luck.

We had our street people, too, like old Barber Burke, an alcoholic who was a fixture in the neighborhood. One cold winter morning he stopped me on my way to high school and said, "Tip, could you give me a nickel for a cup of coffee?"

I had ten cents with me for lunch, and I gave him a nickel. "Where did you sleep last night?" I asked him.

"In the city barns," he said.

"Jesus, Barber," I said, "it must have been cold in there. How did you cover yourself?"

I'll never forget his answer as long as I live. "Newspapers," he said. "But they ain't making them out of the stuff they used to."

On that commencement day at Harvard, as I watched those privileged, confident Ivy League Yankees who had everything handed to them in life, I made a resolution. Someday, I vowed, I would work to make sure my own people could go to places like Harvard, where they could avail themselves of the same opportunities that these young college men took for granted.

I knew I was Irish even before I knew I was American. Back in 1845, my grandfather and his two brothers had been brought over from Ireland by the New England Brick Company. I still have a deed for the plot that my grandfather bought in the Cambridge cemetery. The immigrants had seen so much death during the potato famine that the first thing they did when they came to America was to buy a plot to be buried in—just in case.

My grandfather settled in North Cambridge and worked in the brickyards, where they made bricks with nothing more than picks, shovels, and wheelbarrows. They would mix the clay, soften it, throw it in the kiln, and then bake the bricks. My father was born in 1874, and as a young man he, too, worked in the brickyards— digging with a pick and an ax and loading the clay on a tram, with a horse to pull it up the slope from the pit.

But the Irish didn't want their kids in the clay pits, and by around 1900 these jobs were taken over by the French Canadians. Twenty years later it was the Italians, with each successive generation moving their own kids out and getting them educated as clergymen, lawyers, or doctors. Banking and insurance, however, remained closed to the ethnics. The old aristocracy, the Brahmins of Boston, the Yankees, held those for themselves.

There was one section of our neighborhood, around Clay Street and Montgomery, where some of the old-timers still spoke Gaelic. But they never encouraged their kids to speak it, because we in the younger generation were expected to be "real" Americans.

Still, at the age of seven I was sent to Gaelic school, which met on Sunday afternoons. We learned a few Gaelic phrases and a couple of songs and step dances, but my Irish education didn't last very long. In 1920 Terrence MacSweeney, the lord mayor of Cork, died of a hunger strike. Our teacher was MacSweeney's sister-in-law, and on the following Sunday she wouldn't allow me back. Because my parents had been born in America, I was considered a "narrowback"—somebody who wasn't really fit for good labor. And narrowbacks were no longer welcome at the MacSweeneys'.

We had a tremendous hatred of the English. In addition to our fierce Irish pride, there was our American heritage as well. Kids in other cities were playing cops and robbers, or cowboys and Indians, but with us it was patriots and redcoats. During the Revolutionary War there had been skirmishes right in our own neighborhood between the British soldiers and the colonials. There was a store on Massachusetts Avenue on the spot where the redcoats had cut through as they rode into Cambridge from Arlington, and every day we passed by the stone markers that commemorated the dead. Bunker Hill, the Old North Church, the U.S.S. *Constitution*, Paul Revere's house, the site of the Boston Tea Party—these were familiar landmarks, and we felt a firsthand connection to the brave men and women who fought the American Revolution. This wasn't just history; it was real life.

One of the favorite topics in our neighborhood was how the Yankees in Boston had burned down the Ursuline Convent over in Charlestown, just a few miles from where we lived. People would talk about that terrible deed, about what the Protestant Yankees had done to those poor Irish Catholic nuns, and they'd stir themselves up into a frenzy.

I heard so much about that incident that one day, when I was in my teens, I decided to look it up in a book. To my shock, the burning of the convent had occurred back in the summer of 1834! But to hear people talk about it, you would have thought it happened the day before yesterday.

But not all of our problems with the English were in the past. There were businesses in Boston that needed employees but put up signs in the windows saying NINA, which, as we all knew, meant No Irish Need Apply. And each year on Easter Sunday, men in our neighborhood would go from door to door, collecting money for the Irish Republican Army. On the front window of almost every house you would see a sticker: "I gave to the Army." In those days, of course, the IRA was a very different organization from what it is today; back then, it simply stood for the united freedom of Ireland.

More than any other group I know of, the Irish in this country have used the ballot box to improve their lives. When I was growing up, one of the real powers in Boston politics was an Irishman named Martin Lomasney, who worked out of the Hendricks Club in the West End. It was said that Martin would meet the new immigrants at the boat and take them straight over to register to vote. Then he'd bring them over to the gas works and get them a job. Finally, he'd take them to the West End and he'd show them where they were going to live until they had earned enough money to find their own place.

The old-timers used to tell stories of how Martin would greet them at the polls on election day. "Here's your ballot," he'd say. "I've already marked it for you. When you get in there, pick up the ballot they give you and give them back this one." When you came out you'd give Martin the clean ballot, and he'd mark it off and give it to the next guy in line.

In the 1930s, when I first entered politics, all the financial institutions in the city of Boston were closed to my people. Today, of course, that's only a bad memory. It was the politicians who made the difference, who took their people out of the menial jobs and gave them better opportunities.

I'm proud that I was able to play a role in that process. Although it happened gradually, there was one occasion when I literally used my political power to force a change in the system. In 1950, when I was Speaker of the Massachusetts Legislature, I had business to attend to one day in the North Avenue Savings Bank in North Cambridge. As I was climbing the stairs, I saw a fellow coming down with tears in his eyes.

"What's the matter?" I asked him.

"You're Tip O'Neill, aren't you?" he said. "Then you probably know my father, Billy Askin. We're from Worcester, and he used to be in the State House."

"Sure I know your father," I said. "But what happened to you?"

"Last week I gave up my job at another bank because this place promised to make me a vice president. But this morning, when I came in, they found out I was a Catholic and now they won't hire me. So instead of a promotion, I'm out of a job!"

I was furious. I ran up the stairs and into the office of the bank president, a German fellow named Karstein, whose family had run the local coal-and-oil company back when Cambridge was a Yankee town.

"Mr. Karstein," I said, "my name is Tip O'Neill."

"Yeah? What do you want?"

"I'm the Speaker of the Massachusetts legislature and I'm also your local representative. I grew up around here, and when I went to St. John's Grammar School, every Tuesday we'd put a dime in the bank. Today, all my children have accounts in this bank, and so do most of the people in North Cambridge. Our St. Vincent de Paul fund at the church has thirty-three thousand dollars on deposit here.

"Now I understand that you just refused to hire a man because he's Catholic. I can't believe it, and I'm going to give you until Monday to change your mind. If my friend doesn't get the job, I'm going to walk the streets from here to Fresh Pond Parkway, and I'm going to tell every person I meet along the way that you're a bigoted son of a bitch who won't hire Catholics. And I can guarantee you'll have the biggest run on your bank that you've ever seen in your life!"

When I returned to the bank a few days later, Billy Askin's son was sitting in his office as the new vice president. There was also a new teller named O'Connor, and a third Catholic whose name I no longer remember. A lot had changed since that commencement day at Harvard in 1927.

I never knew my mother, who died of tuberculosis when I was nine months old. Years later, one of the nuns from our parish told me how, when I was an infant, she had come to our house to take care of me so that my father, my brother, and my sister could attend the funeral. All through my childhood, the nuns, knowing I didn't have a mother, kept watch over me.

After my mother's death, my father hired a French-Canadian housekeeper from Nova Scotia named Rose Le Blanc. Rose did everything for us, and she became a second mother to me, and to Bill and Mary, my older brother and sister. She stayed with us for six years, and I grew up speaking with a French accent.

When I was eight, my father married a lady named Mary Cain. It wasn't a happy union, and Bill and Mary, who were teenagers, never really got along with her. But I was the youngest, and my stepmother was always very kind to me—even if she did try to dress me up and make me wear a straw hat, which I hated.

By this time, people were already calling me Tip—a nickname that came from a popular baseball player of my father's generation. The Irish were infatuated with baseball, which they believed the Americans had stolen from the Irish game of rounders. In 1887, Edward O'Neill, who played for the old St. Louis Browns, finished the season with an astounding batting average of .492. That year, however, walks were counted as base hits, so today's record books list his average as .435—which is still the second highest in the history of the game. Edward O'Neill was a master at drawing walks, and he would foul off pitch after pitch until the pitcher finally missed the strike zone. Because of his many foul tips, he became known as Tip O'Neill.

When I was growing up, there were many Irish families with a boy named Tip, and I've met people named Tip O'Neill all over the country. My own brother, Bill, was known as Tip for a while, but for some reason the name stuck with me. In my family, however, I've always been known as Tom.

My father, Thomas P. O'Neill, was always interested in politics, and in 1900 he was elected to the Cambridge City Council. In those days, local politics boiled down to one thing—jobs. Because of the elaborate patronage system, my father was in a position to control such jobs as teacher, policeman, city clerk, fireman, and trash collector.

In 1914, he took a civil service examination and became superintendent of sewers. That may not sound very glamorous, but it was a very important office in those days because the superintendent of sewers controlled over a thousand jobs in the community. My father's new position, together with his political experience and his energetic personality, made him a powerful man in our neighborhood.

He was known as the Governor, and people were always coming to our house to ask him for advice or a favor. He was a generous man, and although he didn't have much money, he would do what he could for people who needed help. During the Depression, they flocked to him to ask if he could get them on the public payroll, putting in sidewalks or reconstructing streets. These jobs didn't pay much, and they were only part-time, but for many families they brought in enough to keep the wolf from the door.

You don't get rich working for the city, but we always had enough to eat. Still, we never threw anything away, because there was always somebody in the neighborhood who could use your old shirt, your hat, your coat—even your old shoes. My father used to form organizations to collect food and clothing, and to distribute it secretly so that poor people could be helped without being embarrassed. At Christmas and Easter we would prepare food baskets for the needy, which we'd leave at their doorsteps in the dark of night. There was a lot of goodwill in our neighborhood; in those days people really looked out for one another.

My father was also a teetotaler, and was president of the St. Matthew's Temperance Society. His brother Jack, who died from alcohol before I was born, had been a vagabond and a hobo. My father used to say that my uncle Jack had broken his mother's heart, and that he, Thomas P. O'Neill, would never take a drink. Many years later, at a party to celebrate his seventy-fifth birthday, we finally got him to break that oath with a glass of champagne.

My father lived by the clock. He would leave the house at precisely ten minutes to eight, when a fellow from the sewer department would pick him up with a horse and wagon. He would always return home at five minutes past five, and every night before supper he would shave. In church, he always sat in the same seat.

I've never been a teetotaler, and I've never been a man of precise habits, either. But in other respects, I'm a lot like my father. He taught me four big lessons, and I've tried to live up to each one of them. The first lesson was loyalty. The second was to live a clean and honest life. The third was to remember my responsibilities to my fellow man—I *am* my brother's keeper. The fourth lesson was to remember, always, from whence I came. When people say that I'm like my father, I always take it as a great compliment.

It wasn't until I was writing this book that I understood that my father had taught me a fifth lesson—a lesson that seemed so natural at the time that I didn't appreciate it until much later. Boston had a bad reputation with regard to political corruption. But my view, which came from my father, was that politics was a profession that depended on your honesty and integrity. In our family, public service was considered a great honor—and it still is.

On December 9, 1912, the day I was born, my father was putting his principles into action by walking a picket line at Harvard because the university had dared to hire nonunion bricklayers. He was a bricklayer himself, who was loyal to his friends, to the Irish, the Catholics, the Democrats, and of course the union. Nobody in our house was allowed to wear anything that didn't have a union label.

My father had a friend named Peter Stiller, who was a bricklayer for the city. Peter Stiller was an "oval man," which meant he laid the brick in the round sewers. Years later, my father went to see the civil service commissioner, a fellow named Lupien, to see if he could get Peter's rating changed from "laborer" to "specialist," which would mean a pay raise.

"A specialist?" sneered Lupien. "Why, anybody can lay brick. Back in 1912 I did it myself at Harvard University to help pay my tuition."

My father glared at him and said, "You bastard, you. I was on a picket line while you were laying bricks. You weren't a bricklayer, you son of a bitch. You were a scab!"

Lupien couldn't get him out of the office fast enough. But Peter Stiller got his raise.

My father's great love was sports. He loved the Red Sox, but he loved amateur baseball just as much. "Let's go over to Somerville High on Saturday," he would say. "Danny McFadden is pitching for Somerville, and this kid Munroe is pitching for Everett High. Should be a hell of a game."

It was, too. The game lasted eighteen innings, and Everett won, 1–0. Danny McFadden went right to the big leagues, and Munroe would have, too, if they had allowed blacks in those days.

I still remember the first major league game he took me to. It was at Fenway Park on July 1, 1920, when I was seven and a half. My father paid thirty-five cents to get in, and fifteen cents for me. The program was a nickel. It was Boston against Washington that day, and little did I imagine that I would be spending thirty-four years of my life commuting between these two great cities.

The Washington Senators were a terrible team, but the legendary Walter Johnson was on the mound, and from our seats in the center-field bleachers we saw Johnson pitch the only no-hitter of his career, as the Senators defeated the Red Sox, 1–0. At one point, I watched in amazement as Walter Johnson retired six Boston batters on six consecutive pitches. I've always wondered whether that was some kind of record, but this turns out to be one of the few statistics in baseball that nobody kept track of.

I also counted the number of pitches thrown by each pitcher. I had read that baseball managers did this, and that when a pitcher reached a certain quota—maybe 115 pitches—it was time to bring somebody in from the bullpen. I've always loved working with numbers, and throughout my career in politics I was known as a guy who knew how to count. Who knows? Maybe it all began with counting Walter Johnson's pitches at Fenway Park.

My father couldn't get enough of baseball, and as head of the North Cambridge Knights of Columbus he organized a semiprofessional baseball team that became the lifeblood of the community. You'd go to a game on a Sunday and there would be twelve thousand fans there. The crowds were so big that some of the players were actually making more playing semipro ball than they would have in the major leagues. Our team was composed of local men, but some of the other players in our league were major leaguers who signed up for the final weeks of our season, after their own had ended.

You weren't allowed to charge admission for baseball on a Sunday, so to get around the blue laws, there would be a band concert at one in the afternoon, and you'd pay fifty cents to get in. Admission was free after two o'clock, but if you didn't pay for the concert, you wouldn't get a seat for the game. For the less important games, the price of admission was an ice-cream stick for a quarter.

My father liked to tell a baseball story to explain the fine art of compromise. He was watching a group of kids play on a Sunday afternoon when the batter hit a line drive over second base and tried to stretch an easy single into a double. After the umpire called him out, all his teammates jumped off the bench to protest. Then the umpire changed his mind and called him safe, at which point everybody on the other team started to holler.

Finally, after ten minutes of this yelling and arguing, the umpire sent the batter to first base. When the inning was over, my father went up to the umpire and said, "Son, I've been watching baseball my whole life, and I've never seen a call like that one. First you called him out. Then you called him safe. Then you sent him to first base. Why did you do that?"

"I'll tell you," said the umpire. "When I saw that we weren't getting anywhere, I asked, 'How many of you think the runner was safe?' Nine guys raised their hands. Then I asked, 'How many of you think he was out?' Here, too, nine guys raised their hands. Then I asked, 'How many of you say he was safe when he rounded first base?' All eighteen players raised their hands, so I sent him back to first."

"And that," my father used to say, "is what compromise is all about—finding areas where both sides can agree."

My father died in 1953, a few months after I was sworn in as a member of Congress. He had spent the day on the living-room couch, watching a Red Sox game on television. I was in Boston that day, and when I came home, he said, "Well, I saw Ted hit one today." My father loved Ted Williams. A few hours later, the priest came to administer the last rites, and gone was a great man.

We were good Catholics, but for my friends and me, baseball was almost a second religion. If you gave us the initials of any player in the major leagues, we could tell you his name and his batting average. Growing up in the Boston area, we were lucky enough to have two major league teams, the Red Sox and the Braves, so we got to see quite a few games. (The Braves, of course, later moved to Milwaukee, and then Atlanta.)

The Boston Braves had a special deal for kids called the Knothole Gang, which allowed you to get in for free and sit in the left-field bleachers as long as you had a membership card, which sold for a nickel. Most days, there would be only a few hundred fans—along with an equal number of gamblers, who sat out in right field and placed bets on every pitch. The Braves played at Braves Field, just a few blocks from Fenway Park, and there was always a truckload of kids going over from North Cambridge.

But I was an American League fan, so I followed the Red Sox. The Sox didn't have a knothole club, but they offered something even better—they played in the same league as the mighty New York Yankees, the team of Babe Ruth and Lou Gehrig.

Babe Ruth, of course, had started out as a pitcher for the Red Sox. That was before my time, but I did see him pitch once in an exhibition game. There had been a terrible fire in the town of Everett, and to raise money for the families of the victims, the local Everett team played a benefit game against the Red Sox at Glendale Park in Everett. The special attraction was that Babe Ruth would pitch for Everett, and Lou Gehrig would play first base.

A pitcher named Pat Simmons was on the mound for Boston, and in the first inning he struck out Babe Ruth.

I was sitting right behind the Red Sox bench, and when Simmons came back at the end of the inning, I could hear the manager yelling at him. "Listen, Simmons, do you think these people are here to watch you pitch? Throw one down the pike so the Babe can hit it."

"The hell I will," said Simmons. "He'll knock my head off!"

But in the bottom of the fourth, Simmons threw him a fat one and Babe Ruth smacked that ball clear out of the park. It was an amazing hit, and the crowd was so excited that they ran out onto the field and pulled the Babe's shirt off. It was hard to believe how much that man was idolized.

When we weren't going to games, we followed the teams on the radio. When I was younger, in the days before radio, the evening ritual in North Cambridge was to go over to Lynch's drugstore on Massachusetts Avenue to check out the day's scores on the *Bulletin Board*, which was a newspaper sheet that certain stores subscribed to. Every evening around nine o'clock, a kid would ride by on a bike and deliver the paper, which they'd post in the window. You'd find that day's box scores, along with a couple of ads.

During the World Series, we'd all go up to Tupper's drugstore on Yorktown Street. Tupper had a wireless set and a megaphone, and there would be two or three *thousand* people standing in front of the store, listening to Tupper announce every pitch. I can still hear it: "Frankie Frisch is at the bat. Strike one!" At the end of each half inning, Tupper would post the score.

All through my teenage years and well into my twenties, my life revolved around a neighborhood gang known as Barry's Corner, which got its name from the fact that we had our headquarters in an abandoned barbershop downstairs from where the Barry family lived. When the barber moved out, we all chipped in fifty cents a month for rent and used the place as a clubhouse.

On a warm spring or summer evening, we would sit out on the Barrys' front steps—in order of seniority. If Bob Kane came along, and I was the new guy, I'd get up and give Bob my place, and I'd sit back out on the curbstone. When we stayed too late, or made too much noise, old man Barry would open up a window and holler, "Hey, gang, it's getting late. How long are you going to hang around here?" If we were still there five minutes later, he'd toss down a bucket of water.

There was always a card game in the back room, where we played a version of gin called 500 rummy. Most weeks, we'd play on Sunday afternoons, after church. Nobody had much money, so the games were for a few pennies, or a nickel at most. I've always been a pretty good cardplayer, because I pay attention and concentrate on the cards. Here, too, I soon learned how to count. Most of the game is luck, but if you play long enough, the luck factor eventually evens out. In the end, it's skill that makes the difference.

I was a very sociable kid. Even as a youngster, I knew everybody in our neighborhood. I'd be walking with Bill or Mary, and they'd be amazed at how many people I greeted.

"Who was that lady?" Mary would ask.

"Don't you know Mrs. Murphy from the next street? Gee, you ought to know her."

My brother, Bill, was just the opposite. If he was walking down the street and a neighbor came along, he'd cross the road to avoid the awkwardness of having to say hello.

I used to walk to high school, which was about half a mile away, and I knew every person at every house—Red Fitzgerald, Sheik Sheehan, Toddy Megan, Wee Wee Burns, Skinny McDonald, Ike

Kelly, the Moose, Potatoes Labo, Big Red, and all the rest. In Barry's Corner, I was kind of a back-room pol: if you wanted to be elected to a position of leadership in the club and you had my support, you would probably win. But the actual leader of the club was Jack Barry, who lived upstairs.

We all looked up to Jack because at a very young age he became a sportswriter for the Boston *Globe*. One of his responsibilities was to compile the batting averages of all the players, and there wasn't a kid in Barry's Corner who wouldn't sit in the back room with Jack on a Sunday night, dividing the times at bat into the number of hits. Somebody would say, "Jimmy Foxx. Hits, one-one-five. At bats, two-nine-seven." A few seconds later, a voice would call out, "Three-eight-seven." It was all done by hand, of course, so we became very adept at long division.

The fellows at Barry's Corner all had great respect for women and for the clergy. We weren't prudes by any means, but there was never any loose talk around that place. Another striking thing about Barry's Corner was how loyal we were to each other. We still are. To this day, we have a reunion every year in North Cambridge, when we get together to talk over old times.

We were mostly Irish Catholics, with a scattering of French Canadians. There was one black kid in our group, a big fellow named Henry Owens, who was a hell of a boxer. One night he was fighting a guy from New York at the Knights of Columbus Hall in Somerville, the neighboring town. In the second round, Henry took a shot to the chin and he went down. Suddenly, all the lights went out. A moment later, when they came back on, Henry was standing up and ready to continue.

As soon as he hit the floor, one of our guys had turned out the lights while another had hit Henry with a bucket of water. We all thought that Henry Owens was going to be the next Joe Louis, but he went into the moving business instead and became a wealthy man.

Lenny Lamkin was the only Jewish kid in Barry's Corner, and when he came over to my house, my stepmother used to make him a garden salad and scrambled eggs without the ham. Lenny and I have always been close friends, and until I retired he ran one of my district offices. It's great to have a guy working with you who has known you all your life.

When I was twenty-one, Lenny and I took a trip to Washington together. On the way down, we stayed at the YMCA in New York. We had to keep quiet about that because Monsignor Blunt, our local pastor, wouldn't allow us to go to the Y, which was run by Protestants—not even during the Depression, when the Y gave out free memberships to the unemployed. Blunt spoke from the altar and proclaimed that anyone who went to the Y had to tell about it in confession, because it was a sin. He also chastised people who helped out the Salvation Army, until Archbishop Cushing told him to mind his own business.

So there we were, Lenny and I, a Jew and a Catholic, staying at the Sloane House, which was run by the Y. A night's lodging was sixty-five cents, which was a lot of money. But if you signed up for the Episcopal service, it was only thirty-five cents, with breakfast included.

We were nobody's fools, so we signed up for the thirty-five-cent deal and figured to duck out after breakfast and before the service. But apparently we weren't the first to think of this brilliant plan, because they locked the doors during breakfast, which meant that we were stuck. Although I was in my twenties, it was the first time in my life that I had ever listened to a Protestant minister.

We drove back to Cambridge right after Labor Day. Lenny was at the wheel when we got stopped for speeding by a state trooper. "Yes, I was speeding," Lenny told him, "but I'm Jewish and it's Rosh Hashanah tonight and I've got to be home before sundown."

The officer looked at Lenny and he said, "Son, you have nothing to worry about. It's raining. There'll *be* no sundown tonight." Lenny and I still laugh about that one.

Another story we still laugh about at Barry's Corner concerns a misadventure I once had as a golf caddy. It was a sunny afternoon in October, and I was caddying for a guy named Al Teevens, who was the golf pro at Bryan's Sporting Goods in Harvard Square. On the sixth hole, Al sliced a ball into the woods, and I went chasing after it with his bag of clubs. After a few minutes, I finally located the ball, but then I couldn't find the golf bag. I could have sworn that I had laid it down on the ground, but four golfers and four caddies searched for half an hour and nobody could find it. In the end, we figured that somebody must have run off with it.

The bag turned up about six weeks later. Apparently, I had hung it on the branch of a tree, where it blended in with the foliage. In November, when the leaves fell, another golfer spotted it easily. I took a lot of kidding over that one. People used to say that many a caddy lost a ball, but Tip O'Neill was the only one who ever lost a bag.

Compared with Barry's Corner, school was a minor part of my life. I started off at St. John's Grammar School in my parish, and continued at St. John's High. In grammar school the discipline was pretty strict, and if you were late or you didn't know your catechism, the nuns would hit you on the hand with a piece of rattan. I wasn't much of a student, although I did pretty well in math and in history. As I recall, I was also pretty good at playing hooky. When I graduated from high school, somebody wrote a little ditty about each student. Mine was "Never worried, never vexed, in one day and out the next."

Still, I was always well liked by the teachers and popular with my fellow students. Although I wasn't a great athlete, I was elected captain of both the football team and the basketball team. Apparently, people saw in me a quality of leadership that I myself didn't know I had.

The best thing about high school was a wonderful teacher named Sister Agatha. Actually, she was much more than a teacher, for whenever I had a problem, I would go to her. It was Sister Agatha who introduced me to Millie Miller, who was a grade behind me. She used to say that Millie was the girl for me, and she was certainly right about that. Millie and I were married in 1941, and we've been happy together ever since.

I graduated from high school in 1931 and went to work driving a truck for Warren Brothers, a big construction company. The money—three dollars a day—was pretty good during the Depression, and I worked six days a week. At night I'd play cards at Barry's Corner or go to a dance. I loved the job at first, but by the time the cold weather rolled around I quickly lost my early enthusiasm.

One November day I ran into Sister Agatha on the street. When she saw that I was driving a truck, she couldn't believe it. "Thomas," she said, "you should be going to college to make something of yourself." Now, if anybody else had told me this, I wouldn't have listened. But Sister Agatha was special, and if that's what she thought, well—maybe she was right.

Many years later, when I was a member of Congress, I came home from Washington one snowy day and found that my son Tommy had been crying his eyes out because he hadn't been accepted at Boston College. I tried to talk to him, but he just grabbed his coat and hat and ran out of the house.

A few days later, a letter came in the mail saying that a mistake had been made, and that Tommy was accepted by Boston College. Millie gave me a funny look, but I swore to her that I had absolutely nothing to do with their sudden change of heart.

About eight years later, I met Father Walsh, the director of admissions at Boston College. "Say, Tip," he said, "how's that little old nun over there in North Cambridge?"

"Do you mean Sister Agatha?" I asked.

"That's the one," he said. "I'll never forget the day she came to see me. We had eighteen inches of snow, but this nun came over on the streetcar, climbed up the hill, and came into my office. 'I taught Tom O'Neill's father,' she said. 'Maybe he wasn't the best student I ever had, but he was a fine young man, and today he's a member of Congress. Everybody at Boston College should be proud of him. I also taught Tom O'Neill's mother, and Millie's a wonderful woman. Young Tommy reminds me of his parents, and some day you're going to be proud of him, too. I'd like you to give him an opportunity to go to school here, because I know he can make the grade. He's already been accepted by three other colleges, but this is where he wants to be.'

"How could I say no to that little nun? So the following week I mailed your boy a letter telling him we had made a mistake."

So Sister Agatha was responsible for getting both me and my son into Boston College.

She also played a big part in convincing me not to run for governor of Massachusetts. When I was first elected to Congress, I didn't intend to stay there for more than two or three terms. My plan was to run for governor in 1958, so in 1956, at the end of my second term in Congress, I began accepting invitations to speak at dinners and political meetings all over the state.

Then one day I received a letter from Sister Agatha. "Dear Tom," she wrote. "I've been reading in the papers that you're thinking of running for governor. But I don't think that's a good idea. You have a certain softness about you which would make it difficult for you to say no to anyone. That's a fine quality, but it would get you into a lot of trouble if you were governor. I know in my heart that Washington is the place for you, where you can do so much good for people in need all over the country."

I showed the letter to Millie, who smiled and said, "Well, there goes my chance of being the first lady of Massachusetts."

Sister Agatha's letter wasn't the only reason I decided not to run. At the time, the polls weren't very encouraging, either. But there's no question in my mind that her letter had a lot to do with my decision to remain in Congress.

After I had been there for a number of years, I received an unusual letter from Sister Agatha. "Dear Tom," she wrote. "There's a special event coming up in my life, and I'd like you and Millie to play a part in it. I have no members left in my own family, and the two of you are my closest friends."

We guessed, correctly, that she was referring to the fiftieth anniversary of her entering the convent. She came to Washington, where I put her up in the presidential suite at the Alban Towers. At the time, Paul Young, who owned a popular restaurant in town, kept a Rolls-Royce to pick up special guests, and he agreed to lend me the car and his driver so I could show Sister Agatha around the city.

We were riding through town, and I said, "Is there anything I can do for you, Sister?"

"Tom," she said, "I'd really love an ice-cream soda. Is there a place around here where we could get one?"

I explained that I didn't know any ice-cream parlors, but that if she was interested in a couple of beers, I could definitely make a few suggestions.

That night I took her to dinner at Paul Young's restaurant. "Sister," I said, "will you have a drink?"

"Alcohol has never touched my lips," she replied. "But to be honest, I've been dying for a drink for years. Do you think it would be all right?"

"Absolutely," I said.

"Then I'll have a Southern Comfort," she said.

"You've got to be kidding," I told her. She didn't know one drink from another, but I guess she liked the name of that one. I took the liberty of ordering her a scotch, and she asked to have it brought in a teacup so nobody would raise an eyebrow.

I had to fly back to my district the next day, but I arranged for her and a friend to have dinner that night at Duke's Restaurant. I had called Duke Zeibert and told him to give Sister Agatha the royal treatment.

At seven o'clock, the Rolls-Royce pulled up to the restaurant. Duke himself was there to greet her, with a red carpet all the way up to the door.

"Good evening, Sister," he said. "I've been looking forward to meeting you. Tip tells me that if it weren't for you, he wouldn't have amounted to a hill of beans."

I certainly can't argue with that.

When I graduated from Boston College in 1936, I was voted "class politician." Actually, my political career had begun eight years earlier, when I worked for Al Smith's presidential campaign in 1928. Everybody in our neighborhood was enthusiastic about Smith, not only because he was a Democrat but because he was a Catholic. The nuns in school were praying for his success, and they urged all of us to make sure that our parents were registered to vote.

I was a freshman in high school, and together with my good buddy Red Fitzgerald, I helped out by getting voters to the polls. We would go to Mrs. Murphy's house to make sure that she was ready when the car came by to pick her up. Then on to Mrs. Sweeney's house, and Mrs. O'Brien's, and Mrs. McCarthy's—and so on down the line. Later, in the evening, when their husbands came home from work, we did the same thing all over again. As I recall, there were only four people in the precinct who didn't vote— and they were all out of town.

There were two sisters in our neighborhood named Haley, who happened to be cousins of Jack Haley, who later was to play the Tin Man in *The Wizard of Oz*. The Haley girls were both Radcliffe graduates but they didn't believe that women should vote. (The Nineteenth Amendment, giving women the right to vote, had been passed only eight years earlier, in 1920.) To deal with the Haleys, the Democrats got a fellow named Jack Kelleher to dress up as a Protestant minister with a clerical collar. He knocked on the Haleys' door and said, "The Catholics are all registering to vote. We were told that you were non-Catholics, and we know you'll want to register to keep the pope from coming to America."

It worked like a charm. The Haley girls were so outraged by this that they ran right out to register for Al Smith.

Come to think of it, I also worked on an earlier campaign—when Charley Cavanaugh from our neighborhood was running for the state house in 1927. To help him out, my friends and I ran around delivering posters to people's houses. Charlie later went on to become a state senator, but in that first election he lost by one vote.

The amazing thing about that campaign is that Charlie didn't even vote for himself! On election day, he was up at his father's farm picking apples with a couple of his pals. It was a powerful lesson for Charlie, and for me as well. In politics, you can't take anything for granted.

In 1932, I became deeply involved in another campaign when my friend Jed Barry from Barry's Corner ran for the Cambridge School Committee. Jed was a schoolteacher, but he couldn't find a job during the Depression, so he decided to run for office instead.

I was his campaign manager—despite the fact that Jed was three or four years older than I. He had an old Packard touring car with a loudspeaker, and I would introduce Jed at the street-corner rallies. I was speaking at a rally at the corner of Concord and Huron streets when a gust of wind swept the notes from my hand and, for the first time in my life, I was forced to wing it. Thinking on my feet, I stressed that Jed was a schoolteacher, that he was a graduate of Holy Cross and Harvard, and that we needed somebody in there with his ability and experience. Speaking off-the-cuff was a scary experience, but I seemed to have a knack for it, and I soon realized that I did better without notes.

My luck ran out a few days later, however, when Jed gave me a newspaper editorial and told me to be sure to quote from it at that night's rally in Central Square. As I was about to introduce Jed, I reached into my pocket—but the clipping wasn't there. So I pulled out a letter instead and told the crowd I was quoting from the

Cambridge Chronicle. Unfortunately, a kid standing in front noticed what I was up to.

"That ain't no newspaper!" he called out.

I turned to one of my workers and whispered, "Get that little bastard out of here!" Unfortunately, the microphone picked up every word I said. The crowd loved it.

In those days, street-corner rallies were very popular in Boston, and people would follow them from one corner to another over the course of an evening. They were also an important source of information, because nobody used campaign literature in those days, radio advertising was too expensive, and television hadn't been invented yet.

As a civil servant who was supposed to remain neutral, my father wasn't too happy about my involvement in Jed Barry's campaign. I was riding around town with Jed and talking over the microphone, but a couple of times, when I saw my father's car, I had to shut up and duck down on the floor so he wouldn't notice me.

Jed Barry didn't win, but politics was in my blood, and a couple of years later, during my senior year at Boston College, I decided to run for the Cambridge City Council. The main issue was jobs— for me, jobs would *always* be the main issue—and I came up with a plan: any business in Cambridge that hired more than a certain quota of local people would receive a tax exemption. My plan was unconstitutional, but I didn't know that at the time, and I squawked and hollered about "Cambridge jobs for Cambridge people" on every street corner in town.

Because of my tender age, I was considered a real long shot, and the *Cambridge Chronicle* didn't even mention that I was a candidate. I didn't really expect to win, but I came damn close, finishing ninth in a field of sixty candidates, of whom the top eight were elected. The day after the election, the *Cambridge American* ran a column that said that Tip O'Neill, a senior at Boston College, was a comer on the political scene because he had received a large number of votes even though he was virtually unknown.

This was the only race I ever lost in my life, but in the process I learned two extremely valuable lessons. During the campaign, my father had left me to my own devices, but when it was over, he pointed out that I had taken my own neighborhood for granted. He was right: I had received a tremendous vote in the other sections of the city, but I hadn't worked hard enough in my own backyard. "Let me tell you something I learned years ago," he said. "All politics is local."

It was good advice, and I've always adhered to it. My father wasn't referring to Congress, of course, but the lesson applies there, too. You can be the most important congressman in the country, but you had better not forget the people back home. I wish I had a dime for every politician I've known who had to learn that lesson the hard way. I've seen so many good people come to Washington, where they get so worked up over important national issues that they lose the connection to their own constituents. Before they know it, some new guy comes along and sends them packing.

The second political lesson I learned from my first campaign came from Mrs. O'Brien, our elocution-and-drama teacher in high school, who lived across the street. The night before the election, she said to me, "Tom, I'm going to vote for you tomorrow even though you didn't ask me to."

I was shocked. "Why, Mrs. O'Brien," I said, "I've lived across from you for eighteen years. I cut your grass in the summer. I shovel your walk in the winter. I didn't think I had to ask for your vote."

"Tom," she replied, "let me tell you something: people like to be asked."

She gave me the lesson of my life, which is why I've been telling that story for fifty years. But it's true: people *do* like to be asked—and they also like to be thanked.

Poor Millie is sick of hearing me tell that Mrs. O'Brien story, and I can't blame her. But during my long career in Congress, we would always go to the polls together on election day. Before leaving the house, I would say to her, "Honey, I'd like to ask for your vote."

"Tom," she would reply, "I'll give you every consideration."

2

★★★★★

James Michael Curley
and the State House Years

THE first night I sat down with Ronald Reagan in the White House, the president wanted to hear all about James Michael Curley, the four-time mayor of Boston who was immortalized in *The Last Hurrah*, Edwin O'Connor's famous novel about politics in Boston. The same was true of Jimmy Carter—and just about every other politician I've ever known. When they found out that I had known Curley, they couldn't wait to hear about him.

The Last Hurrah, as good as it is, doesn't begin to do justice to its subject. But what novel could? There are times when real life throws up characters who are more fantastic than any that are found in books. When the good Lord made James Michael Curley, He broke the mold.

For over five decades, between 1900 and 1955, Curley *was* politics in Boston, as he served a total of twenty-six years in public office. I grew up hearing stories about Curley, who was a member of Congress the year I was born. Later on, during the early part of my own career in public life, I came to know him fairly well.

He was a sight to behold, standing over six feet tall, with long gray hair and the ruddy good looks of a matinee idol. He was always handsomely dressed and well groomed, and he was quick to pass out whatever he had in his pocket to the poor as he walked along. He was the greatest orator I've ever heard—a man who could quote Scripture and Shakespeare with ease, although he claimed he never made it past the third grade. Whether he made it even that far I can't say for sure.

Curley was a great Irish folk hero, and to the working people of

Boston he was a beloved figure who could do no wrong. The Yankees, however, detested him so much that they passed a law in the state house that the mayor of Boston could not succeed himself. Curley hated *them* with a passion and campaigned for decades against what he called "our Brahmin overlords." He loved to pronounce that word "Brahmin," and he didn't mean it as a compliment. He used that word as a curse against the Yankees—especially the Harvard graduates who dominated the politics and the economy of the city.

The Yankees looked down on him as a shanty-Irish rogue, but Curley did a tremendous amount of good for the people of Boston. Years before the New Deal he was running on a platform of "work and wages." As mayor, he provided thousands of jobs while improving the schools and the playgrounds, paving streets, expanding the subway, establishing public beaches, putting up hospitals, tearing down slums, and doing favors for an untold number of people who needed his help.

He was continually running for office. Before he finally retired from public office, he had spent eight years in Congress, two more as governor, and sixteen as mayor. He also found time to serve two spells in jail. The first time, in 1903, he had taken a civil service exam for an Irishman, a recent arrival from the old country who couldn't read or write. When they saw that the poor fellow couldn't decipher the writing on an envelope, the truth came out and Curley was put away.

His second brush with the law came forty-five years later, when he was convicted of mail fraud. As Curley told the story—there are, of course, other versions—a contractor who had given him a campaign contribution sent out a letter saying that Curley, then a member of the House Appropriations Committee, would be helpful in securing government contracts.

By the time he was convicted the second time, Curley was serving another term as mayor. He spent five months in a federal prison, but he continued to draw his salary from city hall. He had tried to avoid serving time by showing up at his trial in a wheelchair, claiming he was in ill health and hadn't long to live. He also wore a collar that was too large for his neck, to give the impression that he had lost weight. But when he was released from jail, he had miraculously recovered.

There's no question that Curley looted the city, and that he was a latter-day Robin Hood who took from the rich and gave to the poor. Nor is there any doubt that he was corrupt—even by the ethics of his day, which were fairly loose. He liked to brag that he had never accepted a donation from a person who couldn't afford it, but that still leaves a lot to the imagination. It was said that nobody ever bribed him hand-to-hand, but the door was open, as the phrase went. He'd stand in his office and look in a mirror while you'd come in and open the drawer of his desk and drop in an envelope full of money. I never witnessed this myself, but that's what people said and I don't doubt it's true.

But I also know this: despite all the money that Curley was able to steal, he didn't have a quarter when he died. In fact, his friends had to take up a collection to bury him. Whatever ill-gotten gains he had, he gave away to the poor. Nor was there ever a personal scandal with regard to his family, or alcohol, or other vices. He was too busy with politics.

Whatever you could say about his methods, his heart was always in the right place. One winter, he called up Filene's, a major department store, and said to the owner, "I need five thousand sweaters this afternoon. And by the way, it's time to reassess your property." Curley got the sweaters, which went to the poor people of Boston.

In the mid 1950s, when Curley was no longer holding public office, I had a unique opportunity to see his generosity in action. It was a cold day in December, and the two of us spent a few hours together as volunteers for the Boston *Post* Santa. Back then, the prominent politicians of the day would be invited to appear at the newspaper office in a friendly competition to see who could raise the most money from his friends and supporters. Whatever we collected went into a Christmas fund to buy food for poor families and toys for their children.

I was a second- or third-term congressman at the time, and I wrote to all my supporters, asking them to come in on the day I'd be there. And many did. "Tip, I want to leave five dollars in memory of my father," they'd say, and they'd toss the money into a bucket. When Curley showed up, it seemed that all the broken-down people of the city were lined up to see him. "Jim, I love you, you're a good man. But I haven't eaten in two days." And Curley would reach into the bucket and hand the fellow a ten-dollar bill.

We were supposed to be there to *collect* money, and here was Curley
with his hand in the cookie jar! But when you saw the people he
was helping, who could argue?

After years of watching Curley, I did my best to emulate his good
qualities while staying away from his obvious faults. Seeing him in
action, I reinforced my own commitment not only to jobs and the
local economy but also to the more mundane and immediate details
of serving the people in my district. In 1937, when I was a freshman
in the Massachusetts state legislature, Curley, who had just completed his term as governor, invited me to his office and gave me
some excellent advice on dealing with constituents. "Over the
years," he said, "hundreds and hundreds of people will come to your
office and ask you for favors. Some of these favors may be great, and
some of them may be small. Some may be important, and some may
be trivial. Some will be easy, some will be difficult.

"But always remember, for the person who comes to you, that
favor is the most important thing in the world. If he could take care
of it himself, he wouldn't be here. So treat them all alike and try to
help everybody—no matter how big or how small the problem is."

I was inclined in that direction anyway, and I followed Curley's
policy all the way up the ladder. Years later, when I was a member
of Congress, my office had such a good reputation for helping
constituents with problems that we constantly received requests
from people in other districts who heard about our good name.

Curley gave me one other piece of old-fashioned advice that day,
and I've never forgotten that one, either. He said, "Son, it's nice to
be important. But remember—it's more important to be nice." It's
corny, but it's true.

He lived in a grand brick house overlooking Jamaica Pond, right in
the midst of the well-heeled Yankees. Curley's home was known as
"the house with the shamrock shutters" because of the purple sham-
rocks that had been painted on the blinds. The Irish used to drive
by that house with pride, and if you were visiting from out of town,
someone always took you over to see Jim Curley's place. Every
morning, people who needed help would come around to the back,
and Curley would talk to them through the window and try to lend
a hand.

He did so many favors. He helped unemployed men find jobs. He gave coats to people who were cold in the winter. He helped get mischievous boys out of jail. Whatever the problem, Curley tried to help with money, advice, or his connections. And he continued to do so long after he had retired from public life.

As mayor, he was a tremendously hard worker. It was said that he talked to two hundred people a day, and that by the end of each four-year term as mayor he had met every registered voter. At city hall, his hours were so long that newspaper reporters had to cover him in two shifts.

He often left the office so late that the night-shift cleaning ladies were already on the job. One night, he stopped to watch them and saw how they worked on their hands and knees. The next day, he ordered long-handled scrub brushes so they could work standing up. His mother had been a scrubwoman, and he wasn't going to let these ladies suffer the way she had. The story has the ring of legend to it, but I still remember the day it happened, and the articles about it in the papers.

The crowds came from all over New England to hear Jim Curley speak at his campaign rallies. One of his favorite techniques was to point out individuals in the crowd whom he had helped but who had abandoned him for another candidate. He'd say, "I see Danny Moynihan down there in the third row. Now where would you be today, Danny, if you hadn't come to see me when you were out of work and your wife was sick?" Curley had done favors for almost everyone, so people got the point.

In 1942, three decades after he had first served in Washington, he ran for Congress against Tom Eliot. Eliot was the incumbent in what was then the eleventh district, which included Cambridge, Charlestown, Somerville, East Boston, the North End, and Brighton. He was the epitome of the Boston Brahmin. His father was the Reverend Samuel Eliot of the Arlington Street Church in Boston, and his grandfather was Charles Eliot, a former president of Harvard. And yet he was a New Dealer who had the support of the Roosevelts and of labor. Still, Curley was so confident of winning that he went down to Washington to buy a house several weeks before the primary. It was a tough election, but Curley's optimism proved well-founded.

During the campaign, Eliot went on the radio and complained that Curley was trying to create an ethnic fight by making a separate pitch to each of the "newer races," by which he meant the Italians, the French Canadians, the Lithuanians, the Poles, the Jews, and the blacks. This approach, Eliot charged, was positively un-American.

The following day, a prominent Cambridge woman said to Curley, "I heard Tom Eliot on the radio, telling people you were un-American. That young Harvard pinko! Why there's more Americanism in one-half of the seat of your pants, Mr. Curley, than in the whole of that pink Mr. Eliot."

That night, I heard Curley speak before a huge crowd in Pemberton Square. "I want you to know," he said, "that Mrs. Clark told me that there was more Americanism in one-half of Jim Curley's ass"—he pronounced it "ahss," with a great flourish—"than in that pink body of Tom Eliot!" The crowd roared as he let those Brahmins have it. Curley would draw three thousand people a night, whereas poor Eliot would be happy to get a hundred.

Politicians in Boston played hardball in those days, and Curley had no qualms about attacking his opponent's religious faith. Tom Eliot was a Unitarian, which was a little unusual in our heavily Catholic district. At a rally in East Boston, Curley decided to give the audience a little lesson in comparative religion: "I don't believe that the God-fearing citizenry of East Boston understand the Unitarians," he said. "They are a curious sect who seem to believe that our Lord Jesus was a young man with whiskers who went around in his underwear."

At another rally during that same campaign, Curley showed up in an expensive raccoon coat. Just before he spoke, he took it off and laid it down carefully at the end of the sound truck where he was speaking. With the war on, Curley announced that he would start with a prayer for all the boys who were overseas. "Our Father who art in heaven," he began, "hallowed be thy name—*Leave that coat alone, you son of a bitch!*—Thy kingdom come . . ." He didn't miss a beat.

His political philosophy was "Do unto others as they wish to do unto you—but do it first." He was merciless with hecklers, and when he didn't take care of them himself, he relied on Paddy Hynes, a tough-talking little guy who worked for him and who later worked for Paul Dever, when Dever was governor. I was in Dever's office one day when the phone rang, and Paddy Hynes picked it up and dismissed the caller in six short syllables: "Da guv's too biz to buzz."

During one of Curley's campaigns, he was shadowed by a fellow who kept heckling him about a questionable real estate transaction in East Boston. Everywhere Curley spoke, the heckler would be there, shouting, "What about the land deal?"

This went on for some time, until finally, just before a big rally, Curley turned to Paddy Hynes and told him to take care of the heckler. That night, the man was silent. When the rally was over, Curley asked Hynes what had become of the man.

"Well, Mr. Mayor," Hynes replied, "I said to him, 'So it's land you want to talk about?' And he said, 'Yes.' So I had a fellow lean behind him, grab him by the balls, and give them a good squeeze. And then I said, 'If it's land you want to talk about, here's a couple of achers for you!'"

Incidentally, I saw a similar technique used many years later at a rally in Hawaii for President Lyndon Johnson. A group of hecklers had been giving the president a hard time, and a team of longshoremen was brought in to protect him. The longshoremen stood behind the hecklers, and as soon as one of them would open his mouth, a longshoreman would grab the guy's balls from behind and give them a little twist. They did that to three or four of the hecklers, which soon put an end to the disturbance. For all the changes I've seen in politics, I guess some of the old tricks are still pretty good.

Along with Paddy Hynes, Curley had a delightful staff man who was known as Up-Up Kelly. John Kelly was a handsome gentleman with gray hair who always wore a derby, and he functioned as an early advance man. He'd go into a hall where Curley was to speak, and he'd bow to everybody and charm them, all the while looking at his watch. Then, just before Curley came in, Kelly would start yelling, "Up, up, the governor." (In politics, it's customary to refer to a person by the highest office he has held.) And automatically, everybody would get up and join in the cheering. It was an amazing thing: Up-Up Kelly had that magic touch, so that even people who hated Curley would be applauding.

Curley liked to tell about the time he had received an invitation

to address a deaf audience, speaking alongside a sign-language interpreter. Kelly, who had not been informed, came in as usual and
started calling, "All up for the governor." This time, of course, there
was no reaction.

"What's the matter with these people?" he said to Curley. "Are
they all deaf?"

"Yes, John, they are," said Curley. "Now run along to the next
rally."

During one election campaign, Curley found himself running
against Ralph Granara. Now Ralph was one of the great political
characters in Boston. At one point he was registrar of veterans'
graves, but he held a variety of minor jobs at city hall and later in
Washington, where he worked for Speaker John McCormack and
eventually for me. Ralph was a man of many talents. Once, on the
Fourth of July, he won three one-mile races in three different cities:
Boston at ten-thirty in the morning, Providence, Rhode Island, at
one-thirty, and Woburn, north of Boston, at four-thirty the same
afternoon—a feat that earned him a mention in Ripley's "Believe It
or Not." Later, he became a professional boxer, and after that a
song-and-dance man under the name of George E. Faye. Ralph also
liked to chew tobacco, and we called him Juicy because of his
tendency to drip.

Ralph was a popular fellow, but he was never a serious candidate
for office. In the 1950 campaign, he was in as a stalking-horse for
John Hynes, who was running against Curley. Hynes was eager to
call attention to the scandals of the previous Curley administrations,
but he couldn't throw the mud around because if he attacked Curley
directly he would lose a lot of Irish votes. So he brought Ralph
Granara into the campaign for the sole purpose of criticizing Curley. Granara had no chance of winning, but if Hynes was successful
(which he was), Ralph would be given a job.

As soon as the campaign began, Ralph started putting ads in the
paper saying, "Mr. Curley, I will debate you on the City Hospital
scandal. J. Ralph Granara." And the next day, "Mr. Mayor, I will
debate you on the East Boston land deal. J. Ralph Granara." Every
day, on the front page of the Boston *Post*, there would be a prominent ad to remind the people of Curley's past misdeeds in office.

Finally, on the Sunday night before the election, Curley held a tremendous rally at the Blackstone School in the North End, the great Italian section of Boston. "I understand there's a young fellow who portrays himself as being of Italian ancestry who's running against me for mayor," said Curley. "Every day he's been challenging me to a debate. If Ralph Granara is in the audience tonight, I'd like him to come up here on the stage and I'll debate him."

A moment later a huge black man came up on the stage. He happened to be an air-raid warden, but the crowd didn't know that.

"Are you J. Ralph Granara?" asked Curley.

"Yes, boss, I is," he said. The whole place went into an uproar, as everybody knew that this fellow was definitely not Ralph Granara.

Poor Ralph was furious! He went to the Hynes people and demanded that they put him on the radio. And did he tear into Curley! "Mr. Curley," he said, "before you criticize any more people about their physical appearance, when you go home tonight to that beautiful mansion of yours on the Jamaicaway, and you climb those stately stairs to your bedroom, and you stop to admire yourself in that beautiful mirror, don't forget to take a good look at those cabbage ears of yours!"

Curley really blew his top when he heard that, as he was very sensitive about his large ears. Ralph also sued him for $60,000, but the suit was dropped after the election.

In office, Curley would do almost anything to get his way. On more than one occasion, the mayor spent so much money on public works that the city treasury was broke. The only way he could pay the city employees was to borrow money against future taxes. But the banks were all controlled by the Yankees, who hated Curley and abhorred his policies. They had no interest in lending money to the city so that Curley could piss it all away on public projects.

On one occasion, when he wasn't able to arrange a loan, Curley approached one of the big bankers in town and made a direct threat: "I want you to know that the city water main goes right under your building. If you don't know where it is, your architect can tell you. If I don't have that money by three o'clock, I'll open the valves and flood your bank and all your vaults." The fellow understood that Curley meant business, and by three o'clock the mayor had his loan.

Another time, Curley said to a bank president, "You know, I have a nice picture of you and a nice picture of that beautiful estate you have in the country. If I don't get the money for the payroll, I'm going to print those pictures in the newspaper. Under your picture it will say, 'This is the fellow who is responsible for payless paydays for city employees.' And under the picture of your house it will say, 'And this is where he lives.' If that happens, I would stay away from that house if I were you." Once again, James Michael Curley prevailed.

He was the first big-city mayor to support Roosevelt, and in 1932 he filmed an extemporaneous speech for FDR. The theme of Curley's speech was "the forgotten man," and it was so good that the Democrats arranged to have it shown in every motion-picture theater in the nation.

A few months earlier, however, most of the Massachusetts Democrats were supporting Al Smith, and Curley's slate of delegates to the Democratic National Convention was badly beaten in the preferential primary. Somehow, Curley showed up at the convention anyway—as Alcalde Jaime Miguel Curleo, an FDR delegate from Puerto Rico!

In return for his support of the president, Curley asked to be made secretary of the navy. When the administration turned him down, he asked to be ambassador to Italy. Roosevelt was willing, but there was said to be opposition from Cardinal O'Connell in Boston and from the Vatican, which didn't want a man with Curley's unsavory reputation to be named to the post.

When Curley walked into the president's office, Roosevelt came up with a new offer: ambassador to Poland. "Jim," he said, "I've been looking all over the country for the right man to send over there. It's a very important position, because the next world war could be fought over the Polish Corridor, and it will take all the skill of our ambassador to prevent it."

But Curley was outraged. "Poland?!" he said. "That's a job you should give to a Republican, or to someone you want to get rid of."

"Oh, no, Jim," said the president. "Poland is one of the most important nations in the world."

But not to Curley. "If Poland is so goddamn important, Mr. President," he said, "why don't you resign your office and go over there yourself?" Whereupon Jim Curley walked out of the president's office.

It's too bad that Curley said no, because he would have made one hell of an ambassador. The trouble with diplomats is that it can take them six months to come out and say what needs to be said. A politician can do the job in five minutes, and Curley was a master politician.

Naturally, his enemies were delighted that he wasn't given the post. One of them cracked that if Curley had been named ambassador, he would have paved the Polish Corridor.

While I watched Curley closely over the years, I always kept a certain distance from him—not only because I didn't approve of his ethics, but also because I was determined to be my own man. But before I could accomplish anything in politics, there was one little obstacle to overcome. I had to get myself elected.

After losing my first race for the Cambridge City Council, I started thinking about running for the state legislature. I had come pretty close in my campaign for a seat on the city council, and a lot of people in the neighborhood were telling me that I ought to try for the state house. There was even a vacancy because Joe Cleary, our representative, was running for the state senate.

When I ran for city council, my dad hadn't shown much interest in the fight. I was still in school, and I'm sure he was reluctant to see me getting involved in politics before I had completed my education. But when I ran as well as I did, his friend Bill McMinimen, the superintendent of streets in Cambridge, said to him, "Tom, your son's showing is quite a lavish endorsement of your career. You ought to be proud that he's done so well by capitalizing on the old man's name."

My father was taken by surprise, because he hadn't seen it that way. "I never encouraged the kid," he said, which was certainly true.

But when I ran for the state house in 1936, he more than made up for it. This time around, he did everything he could humanly do on my behalf. He went through his files and sent me out to see his many friends and acquaintances. I paid a visit to every one of these people, and then they sent me out to see *their* friends. Everybody I met gave me a warm greeting: "The Governor's boy is at the door," and the entire household would come downstairs to say hello.

Invariably, I would be told what my father had done for them:

"I work for the phone company, and your dad got me that job back in 1906 when he was on the city council." Or, "Your dad put me to work for the gas company. He saved my life." I knew my father had helped a lot of people, but I never realized just how many jobs he had given out and how many favors he had done until I started making the rounds and hearing these stories for myself.

Many years later, when my son Tommy was campaigning in Lexington for the office of lieutenant governor, a woman came up to him and said, "I'm going to vote for you because your grandfather gave my father a coat during the Depression." It warmed my heart to hear that my father's good name was alive for another generation.

The most important person my father sent me to see was Kitty Danehy, the chairman of our ward. My father had befriended her brother, who was blind, and had found him a job answering the phones in the complaint department of the municipal offices. Kitty was very grateful for what my father had done—this was back in the days when blind people had very few employment opportunities—and she was determined to help me succeed in my campaign.

She was one of the first women to be active in politics; everyone accepted her because she was outgoing, and because she was knowledgeable about the issues. She would take me out to visit her friends, and Kitty would always ask them who else they knew on the street whom we could speak to.

Pretty soon, I started ringing *every* doorbell to meet people and to introduce myself as a candidate. Until I ran for the state house, no office-seeker—at least not in our area—had ever done this. But I enjoyed the social part of campaigning, and I had already learned that people like to be asked for their vote. Although I continued to speak at all the rallies, this time around, instead of standing by and waiting for my turn to go on, I used the extra few minutes to visit all the houses on that street to ask the people for their support.

You never win a race on your own, and during that campaign I had a tremendous amount of support from the old Barry's Corner gang, as well as my friends from Boston College. The election took place during the height of the Depression, and only a handful of my volunteers had jobs. As a result, most of them were free to devote themselves full-time to my campaign. I've always been grateful to the old pals because without their hard work, I never would have been elected to public office.

This continued to be true sixteen years later, when I first ran for Congress. In 1952, I sent out a letter to all two hundred and fifty of my classmates from Boston College, telling them I was running and asking for their support in the campaign. I got back a huge sum—eight thousand dollars—at which point Freddy Roche, our class president, went out and raised another five thousand. For me, this was one more piece of evidence that all politics is local.

With eighteen candidates running for three seats, the state house race was basically a popularity contest. Like Curley's, my platform was work and wages, because I have always believed that people in our society are *entitled* to jobs. In those days, that was still a fairly radical idea, and even today, the Republicans still don't see it that way. But the Depression was on and President Roosevelt was running for reelection, and I was talking about the New Deal brought down to the local level. Specifically, I wanted to provide jobs by cleaning up the Charles River and the Alewife Brook.

I stood for what I called the O'Neill Family Plan, by which I meant that the breadwinner ought to be able to support his family with enough food, clothing, and shelter—and have a little extra to set aside for a rainy day. But money wasn't the only consideration; families also needed *time*. If a worker had to put in seventy or eighty hours a week to support his family, then when could he actually *be* with them? In those days, the postman delivered mail on Saturdays and even on Christmas Day. A fireman worked a hundred and four hours a week. A policeman worked eighty-four. A laborer worked six days a week. The families I knew had only one day a week to be together. I always thought that was wrong, and as soon as I got into the state house, I started fighting for a five-day week.

One of my seventeen fellow candidates was an unemployed comic named Russ Howard. Instead of giving a standard political speech, he used to perform vaudeville routines. We all loved him, and whenever he spoke at a rally, Russ drew tremendous crowds, which helped us all. "If you think Jim Curley is a thief," he would say, "you ain't seen nothing yet. Just send *me* to the state house." People laughed at his jokes, but he finished near the bottom of the list.

I finished third in that election, which was good enough to win a seat in the state house. And so, at the age of twenty-four, I found myself in one of the nation's great political institutions. I've always believed that anyone who serves in the Massachusetts legislature and then goes on to Congress is four or five terms ahead of most of his colleagues. Political life in Massachusetts is so tough, so competitive, and so sophisticated that you come out of there with a great deal of political skill and experience. It's no accident that so many of our national political leaders have come from Massachusetts, or that three presidents (John Adams, John Quincy Adams, and Calvin Coolidge) and no fewer than six Speakers of the House have served in the Massachusetts legislature. In 1832, by the way, the state house chaplain was a fellow named Ralph Waldo Emerson.

The Massachusetts General Court, as the state legislature is officially known, included some of the finest orators I have ever heard. There was nobody around to prepare their speeches, either; they wrote them on their own. I would never classify myself as a great orator, but I certainly improved my abilities as part of that crowd.

Ever since the Republican party had come into being, the Republicans had controlled the legislature, and in 1937, when I was sworn in, there were 178 of them and only 62 of us. The Republicans were mostly Anglo-Saxon Protestants, with a smattering of ethnics. They saw themselves as the guardians of the public purse and were especially interested in legislation affecting the banks and the insurance companies, which were completely dominated by Yankees. Roughly a third of the Republicans were older men, retired from the major financial institutions of Boston, who were there to protect the interests of big business.

The Democrats, on the other hand, were the New Deal party. Unlike the Republicans, about a third of our members had no outside job, so the two thousand dollars that legislators were paid was their entire income. Most of the Democrats, myself included, were small-business men or lawyers. I had recently opened a small insurance business in Harvard Square, in part because I didn't want to run for public office as an unemployed person.

Although politics always came first, I made out quite well in the insurance business. I've always had the ability to generate enthusiasm for what I do, and I used to visit newlyweds and sign them up for home and property protection. Later, when I went to Congress, I was no longer able to provide personal service, so business started falling off. In the 1970s, when I became Democratic whip, Common

Cause made a fuss about my insurance business, claiming it represented a conflict of interests. They were wrong, but by that point it was easier to give the whole thing up, which I did.

During my early years in the state house, the Speaker was Christian Herter, a tall, stately-looking, and articulate gentleman who always wore a bow tie. His mother's family was connected with Standard Oil, and his father was a great mural painter. Later, Herter went on to serve in Congress, and during the last two years of the Eisenhower administration, he served as secretary of state. The old-timers in Washington maintain that he was the real author of the Marshall Plan, although Senator Arthur Vandenberg received most of the credit.

Christian Herter was a brilliant man and a great Speaker. Although he wasn't a lawyer, he was a terrific legislator and an expert on parliamentary procedure. But he was also extremely partisan, as I learned one spring day when the Democrats were having a caucus and Johnny Aspell, the Democratic minority leader, told me to ask the Speaker to grant us an extra half hour to discuss the legislation.

No sooner did I make my request than Herter whacked the gavel and announced: "The clerk will lock the door and the house will be in order." I couldn't believe it. "You're not going to let me out?" I asked. "But I'm supposed to report to the caucus!"

Herter simply ignored me, and within five minutes and without any debate the Republicans passed the very bill we had been caucusing about. We didn't have enough votes to affect the measure in any event, but that wasn't the point. When it was all over, I approached the Speaker a second time. Although I was outraged by what he had done, I was also in awe of the man, so I made sure to restrain myself. "Mr. Herter," I said, "that wasn't a very fair thing to do."

"Son," he replied, "we already gave you half an hour. The Red Sox are opening today and we're getting out of here."

I was stunned. If the Democrats had ever tried something like that, the press would have crucified us. But that's the way the Republicans operated in the state house in those days, when Christian Herter simply trampled on the rights of the opposition. The Republicans actually had a rule that no Democratic member—not even the Democratic *leader*—could enter the Speaker's office. If you

wanted to see the Republican leadership, they met you at the door
and spoke to you there. They were so partisan that we weren't even
allowed to cross the threshold.

It's hard to believe, but in those days the Democrats didn't even
have an office. In 1948, when I became the first Democratic Speaker
of the house, I provided the Republican minority with a lavish suite
of rooms and offices. I said to myself: if my own party is ever again
in the minority, at least next time we'll have office space. Four years
later, in 1952, Eisenhower swept the country and the Republicans
once again won a majority in the state house. This time the minority
Democrats had office space. But we regained control in 1954, and the
place has been Democratic ever since.

Oddly enough, there was nothing personal about Christian
Herter's behavior. He was a perfectly nice fellow who believed he
was simply following the rules. And the rules, as he understood
them, said, Screw the Democrats!

Herter was a little aloof from the members, but he made a genuine
effort to be one of the boys. One year, when he was governor, he
decided to show up at the annual state legislative barbecue. He had
been campaigning all day and hadn't had time to eat, and when he
arrived, around five o'clock, he was famished. He stood in the food
line with everybody else, and when he reached the front, he said to
the serving lady, "Do you mind if I take a second piece of chicken?"

"I'm sorry," she said. "It's one to a customer."

"But I'm starving," said Herter.

"Sorry, mister," she said. "But that's the rule."

"Do you know who I am?" he said. "I'm Governor Herter."

"Do you know who *I* am?" she replied. "I'm the lady in charge
of the chicken. Now move along, because there are people behind
you."

Herter may have trampled over the Democrats in the house, but
the working people of Boston wouldn't put up with any nonsense—
and certainly not from a Republican governor.

Because the Democrats were so badly outnumbered, there wasn't
much we could do in terms of initiating legislation. Instead, we put
our efforts into patronage—getting jobs for the people in our districts. I had a particular talent in this area, in part because I always
followed the legislation closely enough to know where the jobs
were. I also made sure to be friendly with Johnny Canon, the

dispenser of patronage. During my eight terms in the state house, I probably sent more kids to college by finding summer jobs for them and got more of their fathers onto public works programs than any other member. I still remember going over to the Manhattan Market in Central Square, where I myself had worked during college, to ask how many summer jobs they had coming up for kids.

In those days, each legislator would draw up a list of constituents who were to be given jobs, and we'd get the forms approved in the governor's office. As I recall, we were allowed to fill twenty positions each. Jimmy Burke was a fellow state representative who later served with me in Congress; he and I would type out our twenty names and get our lists signed and approved by Johnny Canon. But we'd always make sure to double-space the names, and after the list was approved we'd go back and type twenty *more* names in the blank spaces. Everyone wanted to know how Jimmy and I were getting so many jobs for our people. But they never figured it out, and Johnny Canon just winked. That's how desperate we were to put people to work.

The Depression was bad enough everywhere, but for the unemployed people of Boston, the winters were almost unbearable. Part of the patronage system in those days consisted of snow buttons, which entitled you to shovel snow for one day. If you worked for the city or the state you were paid four dollars a day; if you shoveled snow for the transit authority, it was three dollars. When it snowed during the night, men would start lining up outside a legislator's house at five in the morning to get a button. We'd start by giving out the city and state buttons, and the latecomers would get transit buttons. I was still living at home, and my stepmother would be out there with me, helping me take down all the names.

Sometimes I would put aside a few buttons for my friends who had helped me in my campaign, so they wouldn't have to stand outside at five in the morning. But the men in line would be counting, and when we ran out of buttons, there would always be at least one fellow who would complain. "Hey, you only gave out forty-seven. You're holding back three." Which we were. That's how valuable those buttons were.

Now that I was in the state house, I tried to bring up the kinds of legislation I had been talking about in my campaigns, such as cleaning up the Charles River. At that time, a good amount of sewage and street drainage emptied into the river. You'd go swimming, and every now and then a piece of horse manure would float by. My plan was to put in a huge pipe all along the river for the sanitary drainage. It seemed so simple: Uncle Sam would pay for it under the WPA program, and it would provide jobs. But a bill like that had no chance during a Republican administration, because the quarter of a million dollars it would have cost the state seemed far too expensive.

Many years later, during the Kennedy administration, Stewart Udall, secretary of the interior, appropriated four million dollars simply to conduct a *study* on cleaning up the river, which by that time was considerably more polluted. Eventually the Charles did get cleaned up—at the cost of sixty or seventy million dollars. If my plan had been followed, we could have saved a lot of money.

The first bill of mine that became law was known in the press as "the newsboy's friend." As a kid, I had sold the *Saturday Evening Post* on a paper route. The customers paid a nickel, of which I got to keep two cents. I had thirty customers, and that sixty cents a week in pocket money was a lot for a youngster to be making.

But in 1937 I kept meeting kids who wanted to be newsboys but who couldn't afford the license, which sold for a quarter. I couldn't believe that there was a law requiring kids to have a license to deliver papers, but there was, and it was being enforced—presumably because the newsstands didn't want any competition. I filed a bill that did away with the licenses, and it sailed through the house.

Over time, I became known as a power in the legislature. I've always said that power accumulates when people think you have power, and in my case, this image came from my reputation for getting things done—especially for my constituents. Politics is also about people working together, and I was blessed with a gregarious and social personality. I've always enjoyed the company of other people, and during my years in the state house I made a lot of friends.

It helped enormously that I liked to play cards. There was always a game going on in the basement of the statehouse, and one of the local breweries used to bring in a barrel of cold beer. We referred to our hideout as the Alpine Club, so that when anybody inquired as to the whereabouts of a member, we could always say with a straight face, "Charlie's over at the Alpine Club." It sounded a lot better than "He's playing cards in the basement."

It was a nickel game, and the players came from both parties. From our seats in the Alpine Club we could hear the roll-call bells, and whenever there was a vote we'd all climb in the elevator and go up to the floor. During my state house years, and later, when I went to Congress, poker provided me with a great opportunity to meet my fellow legislators, which in turn enhanced my political career.

The members from the western part of the state used to stay at the old Manger Hotel, which was next to the Boston Garden, where they paid something like $2.15 a night for a beautiful room. Because there were so many of them, the hotel provided a special hospitality suite, which was also the site of many a card game. Here, too, there was always beer and camaraderie. Although I lived just over the river, I spent many an evening in that suite.

Each winter, on Washington's Birthday, a group of us from the state house would take the train down to New York for an insurance meeting. Silvio Conte was chairman of the Senate Committee on Insurance, and he'd always be there. We became great friends, and Sil later served with me in the Congress, where our friendship continued to flourish despite the fact that he's a Republican. Sil's memory is a little sharper than mine, and he swears that we used to spend most of the weekend in our suite at the Lexington Hotel, playing cards, with our shirts off and a bathtub full of beer.

I certainly recall our Sunday routine. In the morning, the Catholics would attend mass at St. Patrick's or at St. Malachy's, the actors' church, where we'd usually bump into a celebrity or two. Then we'd all head down to Grotta Azzurra in Little Italy for a tremendous dinner of fish, spaghetti, antipasto, and my personal favorite, lobster fra diavolo.

One year, shortly before the start of our annual trip to New York, a neighbor of mine suffered a heart attack and died. His young daughter clammed up and refused to utter a word, and somehow I ended up driving her to the hospital. But when we arrived, they turned us away because there were no empty beds.

When I returned home, Millie said to me, "You're not leaving for New York until you get that girl to a hospital. That's the least you can do. You're a big man in the legislature, and you should be able to take care of something like this." The following day, I found a hospital and the girl was admitted.

By this time, the rest of the gang had already taken the train to New York, so I flew down and joined them at the hotel. When I walked in, the poker game was well under way. "Tip," somebody shouted, "where the hell have you been?"

I told them the story about the little girl who lost her father. A rep named Louis Glazer said, "What a tragedy. Why don't we each chip in a deuce and we'll go over to F.A.O. Schwarz and send the kid a doll." Everybody gave me two bucks, and Glazer and I went out and bought the biggest doll in the entire store and had it shipped to the hospital where the girl was staying. When that doll arrived, I was told later, the girl lit up and started to talk again. Years later, after a speech I gave at a college in my district, a woman came up to me and said, "I'm the little girl you sent that doll to. It meant so much to me, and I've always wanted to thank you." So here's to you, Louis Glazer.

During my first term in the legislature, the only rough spot came over a piece of controversial legislation known as the teachers' oath bill. In 1935, at the instigation of the American Legion, the legislature had passed a bill that stipulated that every "professor, instructor or teacher at any college, university, teachers' college, or public or private school in the commonwealth shall, before entering upon the discharge of his duties, take and subscribe to . . . the following oath or affirmation: 'I do solemnly swear that I will support the Constitution of the United States and the Constitution of the Commonwealth of Massachusetts, and that I will faithfully discharge the duties of the position of _____ according to the best of my ability.' "

In 1937, during my first year in the house, I was one of the few representatives who supported a move to repeal the bill. My sister, Mary, was a teacher, as were many of my friends. Forcing these people—not to mention all the nuns and priests who were teachers—to swear a loyalty oath was an insult to some of the finest men and women I had ever known. Who the hell were we to require a loyalty oath? Was this Massachusetts or Nazi Germany? Any fool could see that making teachers swear an oath was no way to increase patriotism. If a teacher had an interest in being disloyal, he wasn't going to let an oath stand in his way.

It was a bitter fight, and I was one of only three or four Democrats to oppose the bill. Given the nature of my district, this was a difficult position for me to take, as both the Irish and the Catholics tend to be conservative on issues of patriotism. In 1938, when I ran for reelection, the American Legion took out prominent full-page ads against me in the newspapers. They also sent some of their members, in uniform, to demonstrate against me at the polls. To counter them, we sent our own Legionnaires—mostly old friends of my dad. I won that election easily.

Looking back, I can see that my vote against the teachers' oath marked an important step in my career. Despite the pressure I was under from the Legionnaires, the Veterans of Foreign Wars, the press, and the members of my own party, I made my decision and stuck to it. Naturally, I explained my position to my constituents.

In retrospect, I believe that my vote on that issue freed me up and gave me a tremendous independence that lasted through all my years in politics. I had gone against all the powers and I had survived. Because I had provided so much public service to my constituents, they were willing to give me the benefit of the doubt—so long as I took the trouble to explain my position.

My independence on that vote soon identified me as a potential leader in the legislature. "Here's a guy with guts," people said. "Here's a fellow who's going to call them as he sees them, and who can take criticism without giving in."

In the 1940 election, however, I almost lost my seat when a city councillor named Walter Madigan ran against me. Madigan was in the race at the instigation of Tansy Norton, a championship fighter who owned the liquor store where Walter Madigan worked. (Later, Tansy Norton and I became very close friends.)

Tansy was a good friend of Mike Ward, a political leader in Boston whose organization was famous for running in repeaters. Mike ran several organizations, including one in Chinatown. People used to talk about Mike Ward and his Chinese hat trick. The story was that Mike would hire ten Chinese men, pay them each five dollars for the day, and have them vote repeatedly under different names. Each time they came to the polls, however, they would be wearing a different hat, the idea being that to Caucasians, all Chinese people looked the same.

With the help of Mike Ward, Walter Madigan pulled a few fast ones, such as using the names of people who hadn't voted, and the old Boston practice of voting the dead.

"He's running them in," I said to my father.

"Tom," he said, "people know you, and everyone in the neighborhood likes you. You've got your own insurance business in Harvard Square. You've been in the legislature for four years. Your opponent is a city councillor who works in a liquor store. If you can't beat this guy, even with all the people he's running in, then you ought to get the hell out of public life."

Madigan gave me quite a fight, but I beat him by something like 4,400 to 4,000. As soon as I returned to the state house, I filed a bill that anyone caught repeating in an election would be given an automatic one-year jail sentence. Getting that bill out of committee was a cinch, because who could dare oppose it? Privately, however, some of the members let me know how disappointed they were, and that they hadn't expected I was the kind of guy who would rock the boat. But I didn't like people stealing elections—and I especially didn't like people stealing them from me! The bill passed easily, and that particular brand of corruption virtually disappeared from Massachusetts.

Until then, repeating and voting the dead had been facts of life in our state, which brings to mind the story of Beef Stew McDonough. Beef Stew was a friend of Leo Sullivan's, who was a friend of mine from the state house. He was also a friend of Major Lynch, president of the Boston City Council. The Major had another friend, named Jimmy Horihan, who in South Boston, naturally, was known as Jimmy the Whore. Jimmy had been a pal of Lynch's for years, but when the Major failed to take care of him with a job, Jimmy grew furious. He began going around to the Major's rallies, carrying a lantern and hollering, "Major, this is Diogenes! I'm searching for an honest man, you crook, you!"

Each year the Major would run for the city council, and each year, as more candidates entered the race, it became increasingly difficult for him to win. In the 1935 election, his supporters said, "We'll give the Major a break. Let's clear the field and give him a free ride. The guy deserves no less."

They managed to get every other candidate to withdraw, with the exception of a young man named Johnny Kerrigan. As a result, Major Lynch was left with just one opponent. But it was a hell of a fight, because all the Major's enemies, led by Jimmy the Whore, were now supporting Kerrigan.

The night before the election, Jimmy the Whore ran into Beef Stew McDonough. "Beef Stew," he said, "we're going to kick the bejesus out of you tomorrow morning. At eight o'clock, when the polls open, I'll be the first guy there. When I vote for Kerrigan, he'll be leading the ticket. And he'll lead all day—because I'm going to vote twenty-five times tomorrow."

The following day, Beef Stew showed up at five minutes to eight. At precisely eight o'clock, when the polls opened, he went inside.

"Name?" they asked him.

"James Horihan," he said. "I live at 35 O Street, South Boston."

After Beef Stew voted, he stood outside the polls. A moment later, Jimmy Horihan walked in. "You see," said Jimmy the Whore, "I told you I'd be the first to vote."

When Jimmy went inside, the woman at the polls said, "Name?"

"James Horihan, 35 O Street, South Boston."

"But you just voted!" she said.

Jimmy, of course, raised holy hell, and it took about nine cops to lock him up. And because Jimmy wasn't around that day, Kerrigan's supporters figure they lost about twenty-five votes.

In 1944 there was a battle among the state house Democrats for the position of minority leader. I supported Joe Rowan, a very popular old-timer, against John Flaherty, a younger fellow who was more articulate and more sophisticated. Rowan lost, but when it was over, some of the fellows came to me and said, "Tip, if you had been the candidate, we would have voted for you."

I kept that in mind, and two years later I ran for the job and won easily, 58 to 17. Now being elected minority leader of the Massachusetts legislature was no great honor, and the office that the Republican Speaker assigned to me was a former men's room. But at least we had an office—which I shared with Tommy Mullen, an old pal of mine from North Cambridge who became my legislative assistant.

Which brings me back to Jim Curley. One afternoon, in June of

1947, Tom Mullen came on to the floor of the house to give me a message: "The governor wants to see you tonight at seven o'clock in his office. He says it's a highly personal matter, and that you're to go in by the side door and not tell anyone about the meeting."

Governor Robert Fiske Bradford was a pipe-smoking Republican, a Brahmin who had been a great athlete at Harvard. As a tough district attorney, he had cleaned up a number of communities and sent several mayors to jail. One of his victims, the mayor of Marlborough, was so distraught at being indicted that on Christmas Day he cut a hole in the ice and drowned himself in a pond in the middle of town.

"Tip," the governor said, "on Thursday Jim Curley goes to jail." This was Curley's second conviction, and although he was the mayor of Boston, he was about to enter a federal prison for mail fraud.

"Now I have a choice," said the governor. "I can take the office away from Curley because of the felony. Or I could allow him to resume his term as mayor when he returns from jail. If I go the first route and strip him of the office, the Irish in this state will say that Bob Bradford is a no-good, bigoted bastard. But if I allow Curley to keep the job, my Republican friends in Newton and Melrose will never vote for me again, which means I won't be reelected.

"Still, I'd rather walk the streets with my head held high than retain the governorship and have people think I'm a bigot. So I'm going to send a bill to the legislature naming John Hynes as acting mayor until Curley is released." Hynes was the city clerk. (Normally the job would have gone to John Kelly, the city council president, but Kelly was under indictment.)

John Hynes was a dignified, soft-spoken fellow whose nickname was Whispering Johnny. He had worked his way up through the city government and was appointed city clerk in 1945.

"Tip," said the governor, "I'd like you to ask Hynes if he'll take the job. Come back and let me know because I have to write the legislation tonight."

I called Hynes.

"What can I do for you, Tip?" he asked.

"No, John," I said, "it's what can I do for you? How would you like to be mayor of the city of Boston?"

"What are you talking about?"

I outlined the governor's plan.

"Well," he said, "you catch me by complete surprise. I'm taken aback that such a position could be offered to me. Would you allow me to give the matter some consideration?"

I told him to call me back in ten minutes.

When he called, he said, "As you know, the city clerk is elected by the members of the city council. If I take Curley's job, I'm bound to disappoint a lot of the members. When Curley returns, they'll never vote for me again, and I could be out of a job. The only way I could accept this otherwise benevolent offer is if the governor can guarantee me that I can have the clerk's position for life."

"I can't speak for the governor," I said, "but I'll mention it to him and get back to you."

The governor quickly agreed to John's request. "I'll write it into the legislation," he said. "Now, would you go over to city hall to tell Curley he can keep the office."

Before leaving the statehouse, I called Millie to say I'd be home late for dinner. She was furious, because we were having company, and they had already arrived. But I was under orders from the governor, and I was determined to help Curley keep his job.

Tom Mullen and I drove down to city hall. We couldn't find a parking spot, but when I spotted Georgie Leary and Joe Scalpinetti, two of Curley's men, I jumped out of the car. With Millie and our guests waiting for me, I decided to save a few minutes by telling Curley's aides about the governor's offer. They assured me that they'd make sure the mayor heard the good news.

Curley was supposed to serve between six and eighteen months in jail, but John McCormack, the Boston congressman who was then minority whip in the House of Representatives, had circulated a petition asking President Truman to pardon Curley, which Truman did. As a result, Curley was out in five months.

After his first day back, he bragged to a reporter, "I accomplished more in eight hours than John Hynes did in his five months." John Hynes didn't much care for that remark, which was stupid on Curley's part. Hynes beat Curley in the next election, and twice more after that, and served as mayor of Boston for a total of ten consecutive years.

A few years later, when Curley was an older man and I was the Speaker of the state house, he used to come in to visit. Now that he was out of office, he was poor and lonely and had no place to hang his hat. "Tip," he would say, "can I make a few phone calls from your office?" I felt sorry for the guy, and we used to talk together about old times.

"You know, Governor," I said on one occasion, "I remember the time that Bradford called me in to his office and told me he was saving the job for you while you were in jail because he didn't want to be accused of being a bigot."

"That was *you?*" said Curley. "You're the fellow who accomplished that?"

"I was a party to it," I said. "But it was the governor who arranged it all."

"Now that's a funny thing," he said, "because I always thought it was done by Leary and Scalpinetti. They're the ones who came in and told me about it. You know, since that day I've probably sent them a million dollars in law fees because they took the credit for what you and the governor had done."

3

★★★★★

Speaker of the
Massachusetts House

As soon as Curley was out of jail and back at city hall, he and I became adversaries in a major political battle. As the highest-ranking Democrat in the state—at the time, the governor and our two United States senators were all Republicans—Curley controlled the Massachusetts delegation to the 1948 Democratic National Convention. But when the state house boys discovered that he had included only two of us on his slate of thirty-two—Tip O'Neill as delegate and Jerry Crowley as alternate—we were furious.

At our Monday morning caucus, Johnny Asiaf, the representative from Brockton and a real fighter, jumped up and said, "Who the hell does that son of a bitch think he is? *We* were the ones who were carrying on the fight while he was sitting in jail. And now he's naming the delegates? Tip, you better go down and tell Curley that we demand a better representation."

The motion carried, and as the Democratic leader in the legislature, I went over to city hall to see Curley. "Forget it," he said. "I'm running this state, and that's all there is to it. You're lucky to be a delegate yourself."

The state house members were so outraged at Curley's high-handed action that we decided to run our own slate of delegates against his slate. Our list supported Harry Truman for president, whereas Curley's slate claimed to be independent. Some people said that Curley was mad at the president for not getting him out of jail even sooner, but I don't believe that. Still, there's no question that he was furious at us, and especially at me.

Peter Allen, Curley's secretary, called me and said, "Listen, if you'll only drop this thing, we'll give the boys patronage, favors, whatever you need." But by then we were in too deep, and we held fast.

Then Curley himself called me. "Get out of the fight," he said.

"I'm sorry, Governor," I replied, "but there's no way I can do that."

"All right, you fat bastard," he said. "I'm taking you and Crowley off my slate. I'm going to put on a nigger and a Chinaman, and we're going to beat your ass off." The next day, Crowley and O'Neill were replaced with Shag Taylor, a black, and Frank Goon from Chinatown.

Suddenly I found myself involved in the biggest political fight of my life. On our side were the Young Turks in the state house. Lined up against us were Jim Curley, most of the mayors in Massachusetts, and John McCormack, the leader of the Massachusetts congressional delegation.

We campaigned all over the state. In Boston, our daily protest rallies in Scollay Square drew huge crowds. The public will always turn out to hear the young upstarts attack the leadership, and we attracted more people to these rallies than actually voted.

I was the one who did most of the haranguing: "These men haven't got the guts and the courage to come out for Harry Truman! Mr. McCormack, you've been in public life for thirty years. Mr. Curley, you've been there for over forty years, living like a Hindu prince. When are you going to get out and give us young fellows a chance to move up?"

Little did I realize, of course, that I myself would be spending fifty years in public life, and that one day younger people would be breathing down my neck in much the same way as we were doing to the leadership of our day.

The state house slate won most of the votes, but somehow we lost the election. The only possible explanation is that they stole it from us. Several years later, Joe Conners, the election commissioner, confirmed my suspicions. He told me that they were sitting around at five in the morning, counting the ballots. "Curley was licked," said Joe, "and we couldn't let that happen. So we transposed the figures."

"What the hell," Curley had said. "They're not going to protest it. It would mean a big fight, and that would hurt the party. They can't afford to raise a stink."

He was right. The next day, we were all set to go before the Ballot Law Commission and demand a recount. But before we could register a protest, Paul Dever, our candidate for governor, came to see me. "Listen," he said, "the party is already in bad shape. If we show people we're a bunch of thieves, it will destroy us. In the name of party unity, please drop the fight."

I had great respect for Paul Dever, and I knew he was right. Reluctantly, I agreed to his request.

Not long after this incident, John McCormack called and asked if I would come to see him at his district office in the Federal Building. I had never met McCormack, but of course I knew all about him. At the time, he was minority whip in the House of Representatives, having previously served as majority leader under Sam Rayburn. McCormack, who was the most likely candidate to succeed Rayburn as Speaker of the House, was easily the most powerful Democrat in New England, and anyone who wanted to do business in Washington had to go through him.

"You fellows put on a tremendous fight," he told me when I came in. He knew, of course, that we had really won the election, although he himself had nothing to do with the fraud. In any event, he quickly switched to other topics, and I must have spent three hours in his office as McCormack talked about everything under God's blue sky.

At long last he came to the point: "Have you ever given any thought to making the state house Democratic?" I certainly had not. It sounded like a ridiculous idea, but I listened politely as McCormack urged me to try to reverse the long history of Republican rule in Massachusetts.

When I returned to the statehouse, Tom Mullen, my legislative assistant, asked me how the meeting had gone. "What a windbag!" I said. "He told me he'd help us raise money if we wanted to try to make this place Democratic. Can you imagine that?"

But Tom, who was a real student of politics, didn't think McCormack's idea was so farfetched. A few days later, he brought me the charts from Maurice Tobin's successful campaign for the governorship in 1944. Tom had checked every district and every precinct, and he pointed out that Tobin, a Democrat, had carried 138 districts out of 240, including some where no Democrat had run for a state house seat in years. If Democratic candidates could somehow win the same districts as Tobin had—or even most of them—we could control the legislature.

Not that it would be easy. But when I considered the problem through Tom Mullen's eyes, McCormack's idea seemed to be worth a try. Within a couple of days, Tom and I pinpointed forty Republican districts across the state which might be vulnerable, and we set about the task of trying to make them Democratic.

We came up with about $26,000 for the project. John McCormack put his money where his mouth was and raised $7,000 for us. Jack Kennedy, who was a freshman in Congress, gave us another thousand. Paul Dever went out and raised $5,000, and even Jim Curley kicked in a grand. Overnight, we had ourselves a fair-sized war chest.

Now we needed people to run, so I put together a small team of men from the legislature to help me line up new Democratic candidates all across the state. One of them, an undertaker named Jerry Scalley, provided us with a limousine for our travels. It wasn't that we had any great need to arrive in style, but there were seven of us, and the Democratic party was so broke that we couldn't afford gas for two cars.

We began in the town of Athol, about an hour out of Boston, where the Republican representative had been in the state house for something like forty-six years. No Democrat had ever opposed him.

As soon as we arrived, I asked people for the name of the most popular man in town.

"That would be Sam Boudreau," they said. Sam Boudreau was an insurance agent and a former police officer and war hero. Shortly after he returned home from the army, he saved the lives of three little girls who were about to be run down by a truck. In the process, he suffered a broken back and spent a number of months in the hospital. When he finally recovered, he ran for school committee, and out of a thousand votes, he finished with something like 997.

I went right over to see him. "Sam," I said, "you're the most popular guy in town and people say you're a Democrat. I want you to consider running for the legislature."

"Oh, no," he said. "I could never afford to do that."

"Don't worry about the money," I said. "We'll take care of your campaign expenses."

Sam promised to talk it over with his wife, and we agreed that he would come to my office in the statehouse on Monday.

When he came in, he said, "I understand that the job pays two thousand dollars, and I'm seriously thinking of running. Now did I understand you correctly that the Democratic party would pick up my campaign expenses?"

I nodded.

"I don't know," said Sam. "We figured out what it would cost, and it's a lot of dough. If I'm not mistaken, it's going to cost you people at least a hundred and twenty-five dollars."

That's how much politics has changed since 1948. Today, that kind of money couldn't pay for a single billboard. And even then it was a ridiculously low figure.

Sam Boudreau may have been naïve about money, but in another respect he drove a hard bargain. He insisted on a pledge that if he lost the race but Dever became governor, we'd give Sam a job. It was a very tight election, but Sam won by something like four votes. In his second campaign, he won by eight, and then by twenty and eventually thirty—a real landslide for Sam Boudreau. At that point he got out and we found him a position on the state highway authority.

Now the interesting thing about Sam Boudreau is that on practically every vote that came up in the state house he sided with the Republicans. He always claimed that his constituents were so conservative that he had no choice but to follow their wishes. Given the political history of the district, we had no reason to doubt him. But the man who replaced Sam voted with us all the time, and *he* won by an even bigger margin.

What I arranged with Sam Boudreau we did all over the state. We'd go into an area and talk with a young lawyer. "You're just back from the war," we'd tell him, "and you're not allowed to advertise. Running for office is your golden opportunity to become known in the community. Get out there and ring the doorbells. Tell people you're an attorney and that you're running for the legislature. We'll do all we can to help you win, but win or lose, you'll be better off than you were. Look at it this way: meeting all those people can only help your career. How about it?"

Almost instinctively, we put together the most centralized state-wide campaign that Massachusetts had ever seen. Among other things, we printed up a standard leaflet for our candidates all over the state. The front page was left blank for a picture of the candidate and his family, and the back was reserved for his personal message. Inside, we outlined the program of the Democratic party. In addition to maintaining control over the various campaigns, we also saved a lot of money on printing costs.

We even created our own advertising agency, which allowed us to run political messages in local newspapers without having to pay the 15 percent agency commission. Everything was run from Boston. If we didn't like the way you were handling your campaign, we came to your town, took your mailing list down to Democratic headquarters, had the envelopes stuffed and addressed, put on the stamps, and then brought all the letters back to your town and mailed them ourselves. We were young, but when it came to running campaigns we had already learned the ropes. Above all, nothing was left to chance.

Another service we provided was to research the voting records of all the Republican incumbents, which we then supplied to our candidates. Things of that nature are taken for granted today, but back then, especially in a state house campaign, this represented a real innovation.

That isn't to say that everything we tried was successful. At one point, we sent out a fund-raising letter to the entire mailing list of the Democratic State Committee. The response, if I may dignify it with that word, was underwhelming. We received a total of one check—a contribution of fifty dollars from a fellow in the town of Greenfield. Years later, when he was interested in becoming a judge, we remembered his generosity.

On election night, Millie and I stayed up until two, following the results with a huge crowd outside the offices of one of the newspapers, which was a tradition in Boston. The results would be posted and updated on a big board, and a man with a megaphone would announce the latest figures. When it was clear that it would be several more hours before the final count would be known, we went home to Cambridge to get some sleep.

At around five in the morning we were awakened by the ringing of the telephone. It was my pal Mike Neville.

"Are you listening to the radio?" he asked.

"Hell, no," I said. "I'm trying to get some sleep!"

"Well you better get up, my friend, because I think we're actually going to win the legislature! And if it's a close vote, you know they'll try to steal it on us."

That was all I needed to hear. I had recently been victimized by the stolen election in the delegate fight, and believe me, one of those is enough to last you a lifetime. I jumped out of bed and called half a dozen fellows, and we all went down to the statehouse. Our intention was to bring in the police to guard the ballot boxes in case the Republicans tried any funny stuff.

Fortunately, this wasn't necessary. By the time we got downtown, the press was already there. I could hardly believe what they were saying—that we had carried the state!

When the votes were all counted, we had indeed won the house in a squeaker—122 seats to 118. John McCormack's crazy idea had borne sweet fruit. In the forty Republican districts where we had campaigned, our candidates were successful in all but two. And now, for the first time in more than a century, the state house was Democratic.

While I'm certainly proud of what I accomplished in that campaign, it wasn't only our hard work and sound organization that led to the victory. We were also lucky that in 1948 just about everything was going our way. A right-to-work referendum was on the ballot that year, so the labor unions turned out their people in full force. There was also a referendum on abortion, which prompted the Church to take an unusually active role in the campaign. Between the unions and the Catholics, the percentage of Democrats who voted in that election was unusually high—and every Democrat who ran for any public office that year was a beneficiary.

Finally, we were able to ride the long coattails of Harry Truman, who stunned Democrats and Republicans alike by winning the big one. A few weeks before the election, a group of us from the state house had gone out to Denver for a conference on taxation. We took the train, and on the way out we stopped overnight in Chicago. As long as I was there, I decided to conduct my own little poll. I asked a total of fifty-four people—porters, cab drivers, hotel clerks, elevator operators, waiters, and the like—whom they would be voting for in the election. Out of the fifty-four individuals in my not-so-scientific sample, fifty-three told me they were supporting Truman even though he had no chance.

The conventional wisdom at that time was that Harry Truman really *didn't* have a chance. Two years earlier, in the 1946 off-year congressional elections, the Democrats had been swept out of office. Now, in 1948, everyone expected that Dewey would win big. Poor Harry didn't even have much support from his own party. Nationally, the oddsmakers made him a twenty-to-one underdog.

When we arrived in Denver, I found time to visit the Colorado statehouse. Although the legislature wasn't in session that month, I was still interested in seeing the place. When I explained that I was the minority leader from Massachusetts, they opened up the house chamber for me.

"Why don't you come in and say hello to the governor?" somebody asked.

"Oh, no, I don't want to bother him," I said.

"No problem," he said. "I'm sure he'd love to see you."

Governor William L. Knous, a giant of a man, was sitting there in red suspenders, with his feet on the desk. He was drinking a cup of coffee, talking on the telephone, and reading a newspaper all at the same time.

He motioned for me to sit down. "Jesus," he said when he got off the phone. "That Harry Truman, what a licking he's going to get! I'm reading the polls and they're going to kick the crap out of him in the East."

"Not in Massachusetts," I said. "He's going to carry the state. I'm absolutely convinced of that."

"What are you talking about? The Gallup Poll shows it sixty-three to thirty-seven in your state."

"Well, Governor," I said, "I don't know about that. But I'm telling you he's going to carry Massachusetts."

"To be perfectly honest," said the governor, "he's going to carry Colorado, too."

Now it was my turn to be surprised. "That's not what the polls say. I read in the paper that it's Dewey by three to two in Colorado."

"Forget the polls!" he said. "Harry put through a great farm bill for the cattle guys. He gave us federal money and saved our ass. Remember, you don't shoot Santa Claus. Just watch. He'll carry Colorado by twenty thousand votes."

"Sounds like a close race," I said.

"Not out here, it ain't," said the governor. "In Colorado, twenty thousand is a lot of votes."

Now that we had each acknowledged that we were wiser than the "experts" when it came to Harry Truman's chances, I told him about the little poll I had conducted in Chicago. Then he told me about Louis Bean of the Department of Agriculture, the only pollster in America who predicted that Truman would win.

I had heard a similar prediction from Wilton Vaugh, the political editor of the Boston *Post*. Wilton had been on a whistle-stop trip with Truman, and he reported that the crowds were fantastic. Then he made a trip with Dewey, and the only people who turned out were schoolchildren. Apparently, the leading Republicans in the various towns had arranged to let the kids out of school to cheer on the candidate. But as everyone knows, schoolchildren don't vote.

Because of Vaugh, the Boston *Post* not only endorsed Truman but predicted that he would win. As far as I know, they were the only newspaper in America to make that prediction.

In Massachusetts, the oddsmakers made Dewey a six-to-one favorite in the state. I put twenty bucks on Truman and made myself a nice profit. John McCormack bet a thousand dollars that Truman would carry Massachusetts, and another thousand that he'd win the election. He did this publicly, and he also paid taxes on the winnings. I wish I had done the same, but who had a thousand dollars?

Truman, of course, won in the biggest upset in American political history. He carried Massachusetts by close to 300,000 votes, which was enough to make the difference in several state house races. And just as Governor Bradford had predicted, this good man, who had taken a chance and had been kind to Curley, lost his bid for reelection to my pal Paul Dever.

As the minority leader in the legislature and the engineer of the Democratic victory, I was the obvious candidate to become the next Speaker. The tradition in Massachusetts has always been to collect written pledges for that office. On the first Wednesday in December, the candidate with the most pledges from the victorious party presents them to the sergeant-at-arms.

After he counted and checked the pledges, Charlie Holt, the sergeant-at-arms, put on his tall silk hat and frock coat. Taking his staff and the ceremonial Bible, he asked me to follow him as he walked through the Hall of the Flags on the second floor of the statehouse and up the stairs to the Speaker's office.

As I was walking behind him, who should I run into but my good pal Eddie Boland. Eddie had served in the legislature with me and was currently registrar of deeds in Hampden County in the western part of the state.

"Tip, where are you going?" Eddie wanted to know.

"You'll see," I said. "Just come with me."

When we reached the Speaker's office, the sergeant-at-arms said, "I hearby turn this office over to you." And in the same breath, he added, "I resign." Charlie Holt had just conducted his last official act. He had served with the Republicans for twenty-seven years, but he'd be damned if he was going to stay around now that the Democrats were in.

Eddie and I walked inside and closed the door. Eddie had never been in the Speaker's office, for back when he had served in the legislature the place had been off-limits to Democrats. I had been there a couple of times, but only because Freddie Willis, the outgoing Republican Speaker, had liberalized the rules and had dared to allow Democrats inside the inner sanctum. Eddie gazed around in amazement at the most ornate and beautiful offices he had ever seen.

"Those bastards," he said. "Look, they've even got gold leaf in the ceiling. Can you believe they live in such splendor? No wonder they never let us in!"

I'm fairly sure that I am the only Speaker in the history of Massachusetts who took the streetcar to his own inauguration. Our family car had broken down several months earlier, and we were able to get along pretty well without one. On inauguration day, my father came by and picked up Millie and the kids—Rosemary, Tommy, and Susan, all of whom watched from the gallery. (Kip and Michael hadn't been born yet.) Just as I was being sworn in, Susan, who was two, yelled, "That's my daddy!"

Until the actual ceremony began, I was extremely anxious because it was snowing like hell that day and we had a majority of only four seats. If more than a couple of our guys didn't show up, the position of Speaker would go to a Republican. That would be a disaster, because the Speaker appointed the chairmen and the members of all committees from *both* parties, and had absolute control over legislation. Unless we had a Democratic Speaker, the majority we had worked so hard to achieve would be meaningless.

We were also worried about possible defections. There was a rumor floating around that a Democrat could make as much as $2,500—a very considerable sum of money in those days—by not showing up that morning and blaming it on the weather, and that he could earn twice as much if he was willing to vote with the other side. I can't vouch for the accuracy of these figures, but it was clear that some of our people had been approached. Paul Dever called in those members whose loyalty we weren't absolutely certain of, and laid it on the line to every one of them. Naturally, they all insisted that they were a hundred percent with us. Maybe they were, but funny things had been known to happen in the statehouse, so you couldn't be too careful.

Just in case it became necessary, Dever and I also called in half a dozen Republicans who were good friends of mine and who agreed to support me as Speaker, if necessary, in return for being made judges later on. Lindy Lindstrom, a rep from Cambridge and a close pal of mine, came to me and said, "If my side tries any shenanigans, I'll be with you." He was the last person to vote that day, but in the end we won without him.

Over the years, there's been a lot of talk about corruption in the Massachusetts legislature in the old days. Under the Republicans, there had been plenty of graft. It wasn't two-bit graft, either; these guys were big-leaguers. When the Democrats came into power, the Republicans and the Republican press liked to paint us as dishonest. I'm sure that a few of our people were getting gifts from lobbyists, but this was nickel-and-dime stuff compared with what had gone on under the Republicans.

During the eight terms I served in the statehouse, I frequently heard rumors about payoffs and things of that nature. But I can testify that nobody ever made an approach to me. I'm not saying that nothing shady ever happened, but I've always had the impression that there was a hell of a lot more talk on this topic than there was action. We certainly had our share of colorful characters, but I can't recall more than a very few really bad apples.

Until I became Speaker of the Massachusetts house, I never fully understood how much power the Republicans really had. After we passed the budget in 1949, I was furious that the state senate—which was still Republican—had cut out a project for my district. "That's all right," one of the senators told me when I complained. "We'll just put it back in."

"What are you talking about?" I said. "The budget's already been passed."

"Don't worry," he replied. "We stick in anything we want. After all, nobody knows what the figures were." I couldn't believe it, but that's the way things were done.

I can recall only one time when I had to lay down the law with regard to ethics. We were considering a bill that dealt with which materials could be used in mattresses, and it seemed clear to me that a fellow in our party was involved in some shady dealings with the mattress manufacturers. I called him up to the rostrum and said, "You see this gavel? If you ever louse up this house again while I'm Speaker, I'm going to break this thing right over your head." I know he appreciated my subtle approach because he never gave me any further trouble.

With only a four-vote majority, I became the strictest party leader that place had ever seen. I tried to be accommodating, and when Frank Oliveira, an undertaker and a Portuguese member from Fall River, asked for the chairmanship of the Committee on Health, I gave it to him. Before long, however, he started to vote with the Republicans. One day, he refused to get a certain bill out of committee and onto the floor.

I called him to my office. "The governor and I talked yesterday, and we want that bill on the floor next week."

"You won't get it," he said.

I said, "Listen, either it's reported out of your committee on Monday or there'll be a new chairman." On Monday, when the bill still wasn't out, I pounded the gavel and announced that the gentleman from Fall River had been removed from the chairmanship of the Committee on Health. I named a new chairman and moved Frank Oliveira to last place on the lowest-ranking committee. The new chairman brought out the bill the following day.

Oliveira had been humiliated and now he wanted revenge. He reacted to my move by charging that I was anti-Portuguese, which was too ridiculous to even discuss. He criticized my record and challenged me to a debate on his hometown radio station. That was more like it, but when I arrived at the studio, there was no sign of him. I went on the air anyway and said, "I have to tell you people the truth: you trusted this man and sent him to the house. This is a strong Democratic district, and the Democrats are working hard for the interests of this community. I'm sorry to say that Frank Oliveira isn't helping us." The next time around, Frank Oliveira got licked.

Because we needed every vote, I did everything possible to maintain our majority. I once chased Joe Leahy, a Democratic member, for a vote after I learned that he had made a commitment to an outside lobbyist to vote against us. I had locked the doors of the chamber, so the only places he could be were the reading room and the lavatory. When I couldn't find him in the reading room, I tried the other place.

I didn't see anybody there, but it occurred to me that he might be hiding in one of the stalls with his feet up on the toilet. "I know you're in there, Joe," I shouted, "so you better come out because we need you." My hunch was correct, and a red-faced Joe shuffled out and gave us his vote.

I was a tough disciplinarian. When I was Speaker, you couldn't read a newspaper on the floor of the house or put your feet up. You couldn't smoke unless it was after six in the evening. People have claimed that I used to shut off the microphones to stifle debate, but I never went that far. Besides, the mikes were controlled by the clerk of the house rather than the Speaker. But from time to time I did lock the doors to maintain a quorum—much as Christian Herter had done back when I was a newcomer.

I was often accused of being partisan, but I had just survived twelve years of Republican control so I knew what "partisan" meant. The Republicans, however, had trouble getting used to being the minority. They still felt that they ran the place.

Now it's true that I was tough, but I was never as unfair to the Republicans as they had been to us. The press, however, jumped on me immediately. They had long grown accustomed to Republican abuses, but when we asserted *our* will, there was hell to pay.

Most of my energy was devoted to legislation. Now that we finally had a majority, there were years of lost time to make up for.

During my first term as Speaker, we passed hundreds of bills, most of which were part of the "little New Deal," a series of social programs that did for Massachusetts what the New Deal had done for the nation. After my four years as Speaker of the state house, Massachusetts would never again be the same.

One of the most ambitious programs we put through had its origins one day after I came home from work. People used to come to my house constantly to ask for help, and on this particular evening one of my neighbors who worked for the gas company was waiting for me in our kitchen. He brought me over to his house, where I saw that he and his wife had two children with Down's syndrome, who were kept locked away, out of the neighbors' sight. I had known this man all my life, but I never had a clue that these kids existed.

Because the state facilities were antiquated and overcrowded, he and his wife were unable to get their kids into a mental institution. I hadn't known anything about mental health services, but as soon as my eyes were opened I went to Dever to tell him about this situation. He was as shocked as I was. In those days, Massachusetts was decades behind some of the other states in terms of services for the mentally ill.

Together with the governor, and Johnny Powers, the leader of the senate, I worked to put together a massive program to upgrade our mental health facilities. By the time we were through, Massachusetts had one of the best records in the nation. In my four years as Speaker, I probably did more for mental health than had been accomplished in the previous four decades. Of all I did for Massachusetts during my career, that's the accomplishment I'm most proud of.

I was equally committed to helping the working people of the state. The day I became Speaker, for example, was the last day that the financial institutions of Massachusetts were able to get rich on the backs of the poor. The state house controlled interest rates, and we immediately passed usury laws and cut the rates on small loans.

Until then, people were paying 2 percent a month on their loans. A fellow would borrow $300, and almost before he knew it he would owe twice that much. If he missed a couple of payments, there would be interest on the interest. It was our people who were out there being squeezed, and we soon put a stop to that sort of practice.

Many good laws, such as workmen's compensation, were already on the books when the Democrats came in. But because implementing them would have been so expensive, these laws existed only in theory. We changed all that. We also doubled the salaries of teachers and passed laws to benefit the veterans and the elderly. In addition, we passed antidiscrimination laws that made it illegal to bar anyone from employment because of color, creed, or age.

During my two terms as Speaker, I continued to be aware of Jim Curley, and from time to time I would run into him. We had long ago buried the hatchet following our big fight over the delegates, as conflicts of this nature were common in politics, and forgiveness was almost automatic. Curley knew he had stolen the election, and he appreciated that I took it like a sport.

Maybe that's why he was so helpful to me in improving my speaking skills. We had run into each other one evening at a banquet to honor a curbstone politician whom I didn't even know. I was exhausted that night, and I made a lousy speech. When I sat down, Curley came over to me and said, "You were really terrible because you weren't prepared. You're a young fellow with a great future in politics, but you've got a lot to learn about speaking. I'd like you to come to my house on Friday morning and I'll give you a few tips."

I was thrilled, because getting a lesson on public speaking from James Michael Curley was like taking batting practice with the great Ted Williams. When I arrived at Curley's mansion, he brought me into a sitting room and said, "I'm going to give you ten poems to memorize. Never again will you be in the position you were in the other night, because you can always recite one of these poems to fit the moment. Believe me, people love it when you quote poetry, especially when you do it off the top of your head. They might not remember anything else from your speech, but they'll remember that poem."

While I took notes, he went to the bookshelf, pulled out ten volumes with a great flourish, and gave me the appropriate citations. Then he played a recording of a speech he had given at Dartmouth College. Finally, he recited each of the ten selections. We were alone, but Curley was playing to a full house.

One of the passages was the famous advice of Polonius to his son, Laertes, in *Hamlet*, which includes the famous lines:

> *Neither a borrower nor a lender be;*
> *For loan oft loses both itself and friend,*
> *And borrowing dulls the edge of husbandry.*
> *This above all: to thine own self be true,*
> *And it must follow, as the night the day,*
> *Thou canst not then be false to any man.*

Another was "If," by Rudyard Kipling, and I can think of no better advice for a politician than the final stanza:

> *If you can talk with crowds and keep your virtue,*
> *Or walk with kings—nor lose the common touch;*
> *If neither foes nor loving friends can hurt you;*
> *If all men count with you, but none too much;*
> *If you can fill the unforgiving minute*
> *With sixty seconds' worth of distance run—*
> *Yours is the Earth and everything that's in it,*
> *And—which is more—you'll be a Man, my son!*

I've always had a special fondness for "Abou Ben Adhem" by Leigh Hunt. It fits all kinds of occasions, and it's short enough to quote here in its entirety:

> *Abou Ben Adhem (may his tribe increase!)*
> *Awoke one night from a deep dream of peace,*
> *And saw, within the moonlight in his room,*
> *Making it rich, and like a lily in bloom,*
> *An Angel writing in a book of gold:*
> *Exceeding peace had made Ben Adhem bold,*
> *And to the Presence in the room he said,*
> *"What writest thou?" The Vision raised its head,*
> *And with a look made of all sweet accord,*
> *Answered, "The names of those who love the Lord."*
> *"And is mine one?" said Abou. "Nay, not so,"*
> *Replied the Angel. Abou spoke more low,*

But cheerily still; and said, "I pray thee, then,
Write me as one that loves his fellow men."

The Angel wrote and vanished. The next night
It came again with a great wakening light,
And showed the names whom love of God had blessed,
And, lo! Ben Adhem's name led all the rest!

I no longer remember all the poems Curley gave me that morning, but every now and then, when I get a few pops in me, a few
of them come back. The one I have recited most often over the years
is "Around the Corner" by Charles Hanson Towne, a moving
tribute to friendship, and a vivid warning not to forget our old
comrades. Every year, at the Barry's Corner reunion in North Cambridge, I end the evening with these stirring words:

Around the corner I have a friend,
In this great city that has no end;
Yet days go by, and weeks rush on,
And before I know it a year is gone,
And I never see my old friend's face,
For Life is a swift and terrible race.
He knows I like him just as well
As in the days when I rang his bell
And he rang mine. We were younger then,
And now we are busy, tired men:
Tired with playing a foolish game,
Tired with trying to make a name.
"Tomorrow," I say, "I will call on Jim,
Just to show that I'm thinking of him."
But tomorrow comes—and tomorrow goes,
And the distance between us grows and grows.

Around the corner!—yet miles away. . . .
"Here's a telegram, sir. . . ."
                    "Jim died today."
And that's what we get, and deserve in the end:
Around the corner, a vanished friend.

Jim Curley did me a great favor that morning, but a couple of years later, without meaning to, he almost brought my political career to an end. A few years earlier, there had been a mayor in Boston by the name of Mal Nichols. Nichols had not been one of the greatest leaders of the city—he was a Republican whom the Democrats liked to refer to as "the night mayor"—but he was a good man who had done a decent job. Most people assumed he had money, but the truth was that he didn't have a quarter to his name. When I was Speaker, Nichols, who was then retired, wrote me to say that he had no government pension and didn't have enough money to live on. I felt sorry for him, and I put through a pension for him without any difficulty.

In 1952, during my fourth and last year as Speaker, Jim Curley came to see me. By this time he too was retired from public life. "Tip," he said, "you took care of Nichols. Now I'm broke too, and I'd appreciate it if you'd take care of my wife and me the same way." Curley had done a great deal for the city of Boston, and I thought he deserved a pension. But because he was so controversial, I cleared it first with the Republicans. I also made a point of clearing it with Norman MacDonald, head of the Massachusetts Taxpayers' Association.

"Norman," I said, "here's a piece of legislation that's meant for Curley. But if his name is on it, it won't have a chance. You remember how the Nichols bill went through. Will this one be all right with you?"

"No problem, Tip. I'm happy the old man is going to be taken care of."

Just before the House adjourned, I pushed through the bill for Curley's pension.

A month later, the papers carried a huge headline: CURLEY AWARDED PENSION BY STATE HOUSE. Old Norman had double-crossed me by talking to the press after giving me his word that he wouldn't. I was furious, and I gave him a piece of my mind.

"You're a no-good dirty bastard," I said.

"Politics is politics," he replied. "I don't stand on your side of the street."

In retrospect, I think I was too kind. During my fifty years in politics, I saw very few people break their word the way Norman MacDonald did that summer.

The press reaction to Curley's pension was so heated that I had no choice but to call the house back into session. Most people didn't really object to helping Curley, but they didn't like the fact that the bill had been passed quickly and without any debate. I had sneaked it through, although I had done so with the blessing of both parties. Naturally, I took the brunt of the criticism, which came, unfortunately, in the midst of the most difficult campaign of my life, the 1952 congressional primary. The damage was severe—almost bad enough for me to lose the race.

Curley lived on for another six years. When he died, his body lay in state at the statehouse, and tens of thousands of people came to pay their last respects. Some came to honor his memory. Others, no doubt, showed up to make damn sure he was dead.

Before he died, I had one more memorable encounter with Jim Curley, and it qualifies as my quintessential Curley story. It happened in 1954, while I was in Congress. I came home for a few days to campaign for reelection, and I ran into Curley on Beacon Street. He was, as people said in those days, "on his uppers," which meant that he didn't even have enough money to fix the heels on his shoes.

Still, he gave me a warm greeting. "How are you, Tip? You're going to win easy."

"I hope so, Governor, but I'm not taking any chances."

"That's smart of you, Tip, and I'd like to give you a hand. Do I have your permission to raise a few dollars for your campaign?"

I assured him that would be fine. The following Monday, he came to see me. "I raised five hundred dollars for you," he said as he handed me an envelope. I thanked him and put it in my pocket. But later, when I counted the money, I found that the envelope contained only $450.

The very same thing happened the following day, and the next. Curley didn't show up on Thursday, but on Friday he came in and said, "Here's a thousand bucks for you." By then I wasn't surprised to see that his 10 percent commission had already been removed. I didn't really mind, though, because he obviously needed the money. Besides, I didn't want to quarrel with my best fund-raiser.

"By the way, Governor," I said to him the following week, "I'd like the names of these people so I can send them a thank-you note."

"Oh, you're getting too smart. They've already been thanked." And that was the last time I saw Jim Curley.

Several months later, I was back home one weekend when a fellow came into my office to ask for help in straightening out a problem with one of the government agencies.

I had never seen the man before, so I asked if he lived in my district.

"No," he said, "I live in John McCormack's district."

"Then why don't you go and see Mr. McCormack?" I asked.

"Well, that's a fine way to treat a friend," he said, "after all I've done for you!"

"Excuse me," I said, "but what are you talking about?"

"Are you kidding? I gave you a big contribution during your last campaign."

We had a list of every contributor, so I excused myself and asked my secretary to look up this fellow's name. But there was no sign of him in our records. "You know," I told him when I got back to my desk, "I don't run this office on a quid pro quo basis. I do favors for people because they need my help, not because they contribute to my campaign. But the funny thing is that I don't even have your name in my book. Would you refresh my memory?"

"Sure," he said. "In your last election, I paid for your television ads on the final two nights of the campaign."

"You must be mistaken," I said. "You never paid for *my* television ads. I've never heard of you."

"What do you mean?" he said. "Jim Curley came to me and said he was raising money to put Tip O'Neill on television. And I'm the one who paid for your TV time the night you went on. Didn't he give you my name?"

So *that* was it! I told him the story of how Curley had asked me for permission to raise money, and how he had skimmed a little off the top. We both had a good laugh over that.

"Now I understand why you've never heard of me," he said. "But I remember how much money I gave to Curley to pay for those ads, and let me tell you something: Jim Curley made out just fine. I'm afraid *you* were the one who was working for ten percent!"

4

★★★★★

The Kennedys

THE first time I met Jack Kennedy, I couldn't believe this skinny, pasty-looking kid was a candidate for *anything*. It was just before St. Patrick's Day in 1946, and I was on Bowdoin Street, on my way to the Bellevue Hotel, a popular meeting place near the statehouse. Kennedy was living at the Bellevue, in the apartment of his grandfather John Fitzgerald, the legendary Honey Fitz, a former mayor of Boston and a longtime rival of Jim Curley. When I first saw him, he was talking with Chick Artesani and Peter Cloherty, two friends of mine from the legislature.

It was Chick who introduced us: "Tip, I'd like you to meet the next congressman from your district." I was sure he was joking. Although there was no incumbent in that race—Curley had been the representative, but had just been elected mayor for the fourth time—Jack Kennedy didn't seem vigorous enough to be campaigning for Congress. He was twenty-eight but looked younger, and he still hadn't fully recovered from his war injuries. He also looked as if he had come down with malaria. Certainly he was nothing like the hearty and extroverted types who dominated public life in Boston.

Besides, Chick knew damn well that I was with my pal Mike Neville, who looked like a lead-pipe cinch to win the Democratic nomination. Mike had worked his way up through the vineyards by serving in the Cambridge City Council, and he was a recognized leader in the legislature. In what was then the eleventh congressional district, the election of a Democrat was a foregone conclusion. People said that the Lord himself could not have won on the Republican ticket.

I wasn't the only one who had trouble imagining Jack Kennedy as a congressman. A few weeks later, when he formally entered the race, most of the local politicians were skeptical.

The few who took him seriously were also resentful. Here was a kid who had never run for anything in his life. He had done some newspaper work, but he had absolutely no political experience. Kennedy for Congress? It was hard not to see it as a lark. So young Jack Kennedy had thrown his diaper into the ring? He didn't stand a chance.

Actually, Jack Kennedy almost didn't run for Congress. At one point, it looked as if he would be running for lieutenant governor. Had he pursued that route, sharing the ticket with Maurice Tobin, he would have gone down to defeat in the great Republican sweep of 1946, and that might have been the end of Kennedy's political career.

Early in 1946, Governor Maurice Tobin had been looking forward to running for reelection with Paul Dever at his side as the candidate for lieutenant governor. But when the war ended and Dever came home from the war, his first priority was to make some money. Dever knew that Joe Kennedy was planning to put his son into politics, so he went to see the old man about having Jack take his own place on the ticket with Tobin.

From what I heard, Joe Kennedy was open to the idea. Then Dever went to Tobin to sell him on the plan: "I've got a young, able fellow for you with a great war record," he said. "And as you know, Joe Kennedy is loaded with dough." Tobin agreed to run with Kennedy instead of Dever, but in March, Joe Kennedy declared that his son would be a candidate for Congress. Mike Neville was already in the race, along with John Cotter from Charlestown, who had worked for Curley in Washington, and a group of lesser-known candidates.

Kennedy's candidacy for Congress was announced at a press conference at the Bellevue Hotel. I happened to be at the hotel for lunch, where I ran into Sonny McDonough, a local politician and a good friend of John McCormack's. Sonny had just come from the announcement, and he mentioned a couple of details about the meeting that surprised me. First, according to Sonny, Jack Kennedy wasn't even there when his father made it official. Second, Joe

Kennedy had declared that no contributions of less than a thousand dollars would be accepted, and that any money Jack received would come from friends of the family.

This type of self-imposed financial restriction was simply unheard-of. But everybody knew that Joseph Kennedy had a ton of money, and we assumed that he didn't want his son to build up any obligations or accept any contributions that might prove to be embarrassing.

At the time, I was running for my sixth term in the state house. Although I had no opposition in 1946, I still rang the doorbells in my neighborhood because, as I had already learned, people like to be asked.

This time, however, there was a new twist. I'd go to Mrs. Murphy's house and she'd say, "Tom, how are you? Come in and have a cup of tea."

"Well, I just came by to say hello. I'm running for reelection, you know, although this year I don't have any opposition."

"You don't? But isn't that young Kennedy boy running against you?"

"Oh, no," I'd explain. "He's running for the Congress down in Washington. I'm running for another term in the legislature on Beacon Hill."

"Well, thanks be to God. I was afraid he was running against *you.*"

Then it was on to Mrs. Sweeny's house. "Good Lord, Tom, we thought he was running against you. What a wonderful boy. We have all the literature, that beautiful story of the PT boat and how he got lost on the islands and all."

After visiting a few houses, I could see that Mike Neville was fighting a losing battle. He had been planning to mortgage his home to raise more money for the campaign, but I called to tell him the bad news. "I'm getting a Kennedy reading out there," I said. "We're in trouble, make no mistake about it. This young fellow has captivated everybody." If Jack Kennedy could get people excited in Cambridge, which was Neville's own backyard, there wasn't much hope for Mike in the rest of the district.

Things got progressively worse for Mike Neville. During the campaign, he hired a public relations manager named Eddie Martin for the tremendous sum of $800 a month. Eddie was a reporter for the Cambridge edition of the Boston *American*, a Hearst paper. But then word got out that he was called into the editor's office and given a choice—he could either work for Mike Neville, or he could continue writing for the paper.

Today, of course, holding these two jobs would represent a clear conflict of interest, but that wasn't why Eddie Martin had to quit working for Mike Neville. The real reason was that ten years earlier, when the Hearst empire was in deep financial trouble, Joseph Kennedy had come to the aid of his old friend William Randolph Hearst. And now, during the last sixty days of Mike Neville's campaign, neither Mike's name nor his picture was allowed to appear in the *American*. They wouldn't even accept his paid advertisements! Mike went in to complain, but it didn't help. That's how powerful the Kennedys were while Jack was running for Congress.

Jack Kennedy, of course, was a Democrat. But looking back on his congressional campaign, and on his later campaigns for the Senate and then for the presidency, I'd have to say that he was only nominally a Democrat. He was a Kennedy, which was more than a family affiliation. It quickly developed into an entire political party, with its own people, its own approach, and its own strategies.

As a party, the Kennedys began in 1946. They refined their operation in 1952 and again in 1958, during Jack's two campaigns for the Senate. By 1960, when their goal was to secure the nomination and then the election of Jack Kennedy as president, they had developed into one of the most successful political forces in American history.

Even in 1946, Jack's campaign was unlike anything that any of us had ever seen. To begin with, none of the faces were familiar. To work for Jack, the Kennedys recruited a group of energetic and talented volunteers, most of whom had never before worked in a political campaign. They were superbly organized, with each area in the district having its own Kennedy-for-Congress secretary and its own committee.

The mastermind behind the campaign was Joe Kane, a first cousin of Joe Kennedy and a brilliant political strategist who was known as the Connie Mack of Boston politics, after the legendary baseball manager. Kane, who operated out of Walton's Restaurant, a cafeteria near city hall, was a real charmer who liked to say that politics hadn't changed since the days of Julius Caesar. It was Joe Kane who had coined Governor Maurice Tobin's slogan, "The Dawn of a New Era," and for Jack Kennedy he came up with another winner: "The New Generation Offers a Leader."

It was also Kane's decision to stress Kennedy's war record, and together with Walter Cenarazzo, president of the Waltham (Massachusetts) Watchmakers Union, he convinced John Hersey to put together a major article on Jack's wartime adventures. Hersey had recently won the Pulitzer Prize for his novel *A Bell for Adano*, and he wrote about Kennedy and the PT boat for *Life* Magazine. When the story turned out to be too long for *Life,* it appeared in *The New Yorker* under the title "Survival." After it was published, Jack's old man arranged for the article to be reprinted in *Reader's Digest*.

During the campaign, the Kennedys flooded the district with copies of that article and sent reprints to every returning veteran. Using the mails to send out campaign literature was a new and expensive proposition. Normally, a volunteer would give it out on the street or hang a flyer on your door. Naturally, the Hersey article served as a good reminder that only one of the candidates had much of a war record.

The organization, the newcomers, the slogan, the war record, the reprints—all these played a part in the campaign. But what really made the difference was the money. It was said that Joe Kennedy spent $300,000 on that race, which was *six times* what I spent in a very tough congressional campaign in the same district six years later. Money didn't mean anything to Joe Kennedy, as there seemed to be no limit to his wealth.

A few weeks before the primary, the Kennedys approached a number of large families and promised them fifty dollars in cash to help out at the polls. They didn't really care if these people showed up to work. They were simply buying votes, a few at a time, and fifty bucks was a lot of money.

The Kennedys also put on dozens of cocktail parties and teas. If you agreed to invite a few friends to your house to meet Jack, they brought in a case of mixed booze, hired a caterer, and gave you a hundred dollars—which was supposed to pay for a cleaning woman to come to your house both before and after the party. If they could convince a large family with six or eight voters to host the event, so much the better.

The biggest event of all was a huge Sunday afternoon tea at the Hotel Commander in Harvard Square. Every woman in Cambridge was invited, and fifteen hundred showed up that day in their finest gowns. Jack spoke at the tea, and so did Rose, his mother. His sisters lined up on the stage and shook hands with everybody in the room. Even the old man was there, making his only public appearance in the campaign.

People said that some of the single girls showed up in the hope that lightning would strike, because Jack, after all, was still a bachelor—a bachelor who also happened to be the son of a millionaire. That was another innovative technique of the Kennedys—appealing directly to women. Women had been active in politics before, but nobody paid them as much attention as Jack did. He had what we called a warm hand, and the women would melt when he looked into their eyes. He certainly knew how to charm the ladies, and he always made a point of appealing to what he called, correctly, "womanpower, the untapped resource." Here, as in so many aspects of politics, Jack Kennedy was ahead of his time.

Jack was everywhere during that campaign, and he must have approached me seven or eight different times to ask me to be with him. Again and again I explained that Mike Neville was my pal, that Mike had served in the legislature with me, and that he deserved my support.

"But I'm going to win," Jack said.

"Maybe you will," I told him, "but I'm with Mike Neville if I'm with him alone. And I'm going to make damn sure we carry North Cambridge."

I was right about North Cambridge, but unfortunately for Mike, Jack was right about the election. He won with 22,183 votes. Mike Neville finished a distant second with 11,341.

The day after the election, Jack called me. "Tip," he said, "I can't tell you the number of politicians who announced they were with Neville, but were working *sub rosa* for me. I was a little disgusted with them, to be honest, because they had given Neville their word.

"I don't know how many times I came to see you to ask for your support, but you always said no, that you were Mike's friend, and that you would bust your ass for him. I was sure I could win you over, but I was wrong. Well, you're a man of your word, and I can see that when you're with a friend you're with him all the way. The next time I run for office, I want you on my side."

That, as they say in the movies, marked the beginning of a beautiful friendship.

Some years later, when Jack was president and I was a member of Congress, I was at the White House together with my pal Leo Diehl. It was a slow afternoon in Washington, and we were watching the World Series with Dick Maguire, Kenny O'Donnell, and Larry O'Brien from the president's staff. During the fourth inning, President Kennedy came into the room. He said hello to everybody, and then he turned to Leo. Leo was a little nervous because he was meeting Jack for the first time since he became president, even though they knew each other from Boston, where Leo had served in the state house with me.

"Hello there, Leo," said the president. "Do you still live on Magazine Street in that three-decker house off of Central Square? I remember the day I climbed all the way to the top to ask you to be with me for Congress. But you were with Mike Neville in that race, just like Tip. Now be honest with me, Leo. Did you ever imagine that I would end up as president, and that you and I would be here in the White House, watching the World Series together?"

"No, Mr. President," said Leo. "It never entered my mind."

"Of course not," I chimed in. "If Leo had figured on that, he never would have been with Mike Neville!"

We all had a good laugh, and then Kennedy said, "More power to you, Leo. You stayed with your friend, and that's where you should have been." Jack was perfectly sincere, for above everything else, he valued loyalty.

Unfortunately, some of Kennedy's people took the idea of loyalty a little *too* seriously. One day I arranged for the president to see Austin O'Connor, the head of a major construction company in Boston, who wanted to bid on a large job overseas. As the meeting ended, the president buzzed Kenny O'Donnell, his appointments secretary, and asked him to help out O'Connor.

As we walked out of the Oval Office, O'Donnell took me aside and said, "You have a hell of a nerve going over my head like this."

"Are you kidding?" I replied. "Those two have known each other since Jack was three years old. The president lived next door to Austy. He likes him. Not only that, but I brought Austy in three times during the campaign. The first time he gave twenty-five thousand dollars. The second time he gave twenty-five thousand dollars. The third time he gave fifteen thousand dollars. That's sixty-five thousand dollars he contributed."

"Sure," said O'Donnell, "but he wasn't with us until after West Virginia."

That's how the Kennedys operated. In 1960, they saw West Virginia, Jack's most difficult primary fight, as the line that separated their "true" friends and supporters from the Johnny-come-latelies.

The real force behind the Kennedys was old Joe, although he mostly stayed in the background. But he was still quite a power. Back in 1927, he had taken his family out of Brookline and moved to New York, where he hoped to find less anti-Irish prejudice than he had encountered among the Yankees of Massachusetts. But everyone in the state knew who he was, because he had accomplished so much, because of his wealth and his power, and especially because he had served as American ambassador to England in the late 1930s. This last appointment elevated Joe Kennedy to a rung of his own—about nine steps above the lace-curtain Irish.

He was an imposing man who looked more like a Yankee than any other Irishman I've ever seen. Like most of the Kennedy men, he was tall and handsome. He also had an impressive record of accomplishments. At the age of twenty-five, he had taken over the Columbia Trust, which made him the youngest bank president in the country. Later, in 1934, he served as the first chairman of the Securities and Exchange Commission, where he straightened out many of the abuses on Wall Street.

I met him once or twice before Jack's first campaign, and a few more times afterward. In 1945, a year before Jack ran for Congress, Joe Kennedy got himself appointed head of a commission to develop the postwar Massachusetts economy. At Joe's invitation, a group of us from the legislature went to New York for a couple of days, where he gave us a tour of the harbor and of Idlewild Airport (which was later, of course, renamed for Jack) so we could get a better idea of what was possible for Boston.

That day, Joe Kennedy took us to Toots Shor's for an early supper. After coffee and dessert, he said, "Well, boys, you have your choice of two Broadway plays. Tell me which one you'd like to see, and you'll have front-row seats."

I couldn't believe it. "Mr. Kennedy," I said, "it's seven-thirty. How are you going to get tickets at this hour?"

"Don't worry about that," he said. "I have tickets every night. I own both shows."

He also invested in politics, and at least two of those investments came back to haunt him. He once told me that in 1950 he had contributed $150,000 to Richard Nixon's Senate campaign against Helen Gahagan Douglas because he believed she was a Communist. Around the same time, he also gave $125,000 to George Smathers, who was running against Claude Pepper in Florida. Joe Kennedy was a reactionary, and he was afraid of Pepper, a liberal who was known in some circles as Red Pepper, and who was regarded as a possible candidate for the presidency.

Ten years after Joe gave all that money to Nixon, Nixon came within a hair of beating Jack in the presidential election. And at the convention in Los Angeles where Jack was nominated, George Smathers was a stalking-horse for Jack's main opponent, Lyndon Johnson. Claude Pepper, meanwhile, was doing everything he could to secure Kennedy's nomination.

Although he lived in New York, Joe Kennedy was an ongoing factor in Massachusetts politics. Every time a Democrat ran for governor, he would go down to see Joe, who would always send him home with a briefcase full of cash. The word was that if Joe Kennedy liked you, he'd give you fifty thousand dollars. If he *really* liked you, he'd give you a hundred thousand.

In 1960, Joe Ward was our nominee for governor. When he went down to see the old man, Kennedy had only one question: "If my son Jack wins the presidency and you become governor, who would you appoint to fill his seat in the Senate?"

"I'd give it to Jack's old friend Howard Fitzpatrick," said Joe Ward, who assumed this response would please his host. After all, Howard Fitzpatrick was the sheriff of Middlesex County. He was liked by everyone, and was one of Jack's main fund-raisers.

But this wasn't the answer old Joe was looking for, and the story has it that Joe Ward returned to Boston with an empty briefcase. If Jack had to give up his seat in the Senate, his father wanted it to go to Bobby or Teddy. At the time, Teddy was an assistant district attorney in Boston, but everyone knew he had political ambitions. The problem was that he was only twenty-eight, and you had to be thirty to be elected a senator.

When Jack became president, his Senate seat was kept warm by Ben Smith, Jack's old Harvard roommate and the mayor of Gloucester. In 1962, when Teddy turned thirty, he ran for that seat in a special election, and defeated Edward McCormack, John McCormack's nephew. Two years later, Bobby ran for the Senate from New York, defeating Kenneth Keating.

Joe Kennedy was a tough and meddling father, especially when it came to Jack. He had an arrangement with Grace Burke, a secretary in Jack's Boston congressional office, who used to report to him on everyone who came in and out. So did Frank Morrissey, the office manager. They kept a log of every visitor so Joe could be sure his son wouldn't be swayed by anybody with a bad reputation who showed up with a hard-luck story. The old man even had a maid in Jack's Washington house who reported to him. Joe Kennedy was determined that his son would go all the way to the White House, and he wasn't taking any chances.

I had my first encounter with Bobby in 1956 when, as a member of Congress, I was in charge of naming four delegates from my district to the Democratic National Convention. I selected three local politicians and kept the fourth spot for myself.

After I made the appointments, Jack called and asked me to name Bobby as a delegate. But the positions were already filled, and besides, Bobby didn't even live in my district.

"I'm sorry, Jack," I said, "but I've already notified the delegates." And I told him who I had picked.

But Jack would not be denied. "Tip," he said, "my brother Bob is the smartest politician I've ever known. He's absolutely brilliant. You know, lightning may strike at that convention, and I could end up on the ticket with Stevenson. I'd really like to have my brother on the floor as a delegate so he could work for me."

"If you feel that strongly about it," I said, "I'll make sure he gets there." So I took myself off the list and put Bobby on instead.

At the convention, Jack almost did become the vice presidential nominee, but in the end he lost to Estes Kefauver. It was a good thing, too, for if Kennedy had run with Stevenson, they would have gone down the drain together. As the Catholic on the ticket, Jack would have been blamed for the defeat, and he never could have won the presidential nomination four years later. As things turned out, Jack made a terrific impression on television during the 1956 convention, which helped set the stage for his national campaign four years later.

After the convention, Bobby showed no gratitude for the favor I had done. I once mentioned this to the old man, and I'll never forget what he said: "Tip, let me tell you something. Never expect any appreciation from my boys. These kids have had so much done for them by other people that they just assume it's coming to them."

On another occasion, Joe complained to me that Jack was too soft: "You can trample all over him," he said, "and the next day he's there for you with loving arms. But Bobby's my boy. When Bobby hates you, you stay hated."

I know what he meant. Of all the brothers, I knew Bobby the least. We weren't friendly, and to be blunt about it, I never really liked him. I'm sure the feeling was mutual. To me, he was a self-important upstart and a know-it-all. To him, I was simply a street-corner pol.

What soured me on Bobby Kennedy was not that he neglected to thank me for making him a delegate. That was a minor slip, and I've probably made the same mistake dozens of times. No, what disturbed me about Bobby was the way he treated Joe Healy. Healy was an old friend of mine and a real bookworm, and when we were younger we'd all kid him for being the one guy who went to the library even when it wasn't raining. There was nothing in the world that Joe Healy wouldn't do for Jack Kennedy. He had tutored Jack at Harvard, and had worked his butt off for him in the 1946 congressional campaign.

In 1957, Governor Foster Furcolo asked Joe to become commissioner of Taxes for Massachusetts. But Jack had never liked Furcolo, so Healy went to see his old friend in the Senate to make sure Jack had no objection. Jack just laughed. "I think you should take it," he said. "It's a good job. Besides, it's always nice to have a friend in the enemy camp."

Healy accepted the offer. Two years later, the old man called and asked Healy to sign on with Jack in his campaign to capture the Democratic nomination. When Healy said he'd be happy to help, Joe Kennedy told him to report to Bobby, who was running the show. Healy told me later that Bobby gave him the coldest look he ever saw. "We can't use you," he said.

"What do you mean?" said Healy.

"You were with Furcolo."

"But I cleared that with Jack."

"You can't serve two masters," said Bobby. "We'll get along without you." When people talk about Robert Kennedy's famous ruthlessness, that's the sort of thing they mean.

At one point, Bobby Kennedy almost ran against me for Congress—or so it appeared. There was a rumor that he had been thinking of running against Tom Dodd in Connecticut. When Dodd heard about it, he confronted Kennedy and asked if the story was true. "No," said Bobby, "but I am looking for a seat, and I may run up in Tip O'Neill's district."

I was in my second or third term when Dodd told me what Bobby had said. I was ripped, and I stormed into Jack's office in the Senate. "Listen," I said, "Tom Dodd says that Bobby may run against me. I've always been good friends with you and with your father. If Bobby runs, you'll never be able to outspend me. I can raise a quarter of a million dollars. And if you people spend more than that there'll be a backlash. And what about loyalty? I'm telling you, Jack, if Bobby runs against me it will be the dirtiest campaign you ever saw." I didn't specify exactly what I had in mind because I wanted to keep him off guard.

"I don't believe it," he said. "Let me check on it and I'll get back to you."

He called the next morning. "I talked to my old man," he said, "and these are his exact words: 'Bobby will not be a candidate in Tip O'Neill's district, and that's all there is to it. Tip is a friend of the family.'" I never heard another word about it, so I'll never know if Bobby had ever really intended to knock me off.

In 1968, a few weeks after Robert Kennedy was assassinated, I had a visit from John Lindsay, who used to cover Capitol Hill for *Newsweek*. John used to see me regularly, and I'd always tell him what was going on in the House and on the Rules Committee. "I've got to tell you a story," he said. "I was in the campaign plane with Bobby, and he asked me how I knew so much about the Congress. Where was I getting all my information? I told him that the sharpest guy on the Hill, the one person who always knew what the issues were and what was likely to happen, was Tip O'Neill.

" 'Is that so?' Kennedy said. 'Tip and I have never been friendly, but when I get back from this trip I'm going to look him up.' "

But he never did get back from that trip. A few days later, he was in Los Angeles for the California primary, where he was struck down by an assassin's bullet.

After the 1946 election, Jack Kennedy and I saw a lot of each other, and whenever he was in Boston he'd come over to visit. What I remember most from those days was how he just hated to be criticized. Jim Colbert, a political reporter with the Boston *Post*, used to knock Kennedy's ears in, which drove Jack crazy. Jim was a friend of mine, and every time he wrote a mean piece, Jack would come over to ask, "Why is he doing this to me?"

He had such a thin skin! If a group of politicians were talking and somebody said something mean about Jack and it got back to him, he'd be over to see me. "Why doesn't so-and-so like me?" he'd ask. "Why can't he and I sit down and straighten this thing out?"

Any other politician would have said, "Screw him, if that's the way he feels. You can't please everybody." But Jack was different. He hadn't grown up in the school of hard knocks. Politically he had lived an easy life and was used to people loving him.

There's no question that Jack played the game of politics by his own rules, which is why his fellow politicians were so slow to take him seriously. During his early years in public life he hated shaking hands, which was highly unusual in a city where some politicians had been known to shake hands with fire hydrants and wave to telephone poles. They say that a good Irish pol can carry on six conversations at once, but Jack was a different breed, a new breed. He hated crowds. When we went into a hall together, he'd immediately look for the back door. It was said that Jack Kennedy was the only pol in Boston who never went to a wake unless he had known the deceased personally.

He was very bashful in the early days, but that soon changed. In all my life, I never saw anybody grow the way Jack did; he turned into a great personality and a beautiful talker. But until he was in the Senate you just couldn't imagine that he was really going anywhere.

And yet I wasn't really surprised, because I always figured that the old man planned to make him president someday. Joe Kennedy had planned to make Joe junior the first Catholic president, but when he was killed in the war, old Joe decided to go with Jack. From the amount of money he spent in Jack's first campaign, you could tell he had his mind set on higher goals.

Jack used to talk about Bobby as a political genius, but Jack himself was very impressive. After his reelection to the Senate in 1958, when he had already made up his mind to try for the presidency, he came into my office and said, "I understand that Tommy Mullen knows more about our district than anyone else on earth." Tommy was my administrative assistant when I was in Congress, just as he had been at the statehouse. Together, the two of them, Mullen and Kennedy, went over the district precinct by precinct— where the Irish lived, where the Jews lived, and so on with every ethnic group.

Jack wanted to know how every group had voted because he intended to use that information to extrapolate about the national scene for the 1960 presidential campaign. I had never seen anybody study the voting patterns of ethnic and religious groups in a systematic way before, and I don't think that most people realized then or appreciate now that Jack Kennedy was a very sophisticated student of politics.

The intensity of his interest also had its funny side. There was one ward in my district with a large French Canadian population. "How did I do in that one?" Jack asked.

"You won a thousand and three votes to twelve," said Tommy Mullen.

"My God," said Kennedy. "I've never seen a vote like that. How did Tip do in that one?"

"Tip won by nine hundred and ninety-nine votes to sixteen. The Lefebvres were off us"—referring to a family that was apparently angry at me.

Now, Jack had a great memory for the details of politics. Two years later, after Jack was elected, I was at a White House reception on Shrove Tuesday, the day before Lent. "How are you, Tip?" said the president. "Say, I've been meaning to ask. What was the vote in that precinct where I won by a thousand and three to twelve?"

"I figured you'd ask," I said. "I checked the numbers yesterday. This time around, a thousand more people voted than in the Senate fight. And you got a thousand more votes than last time. This time it was two thousand three to twelve."

"And how did you do?" he asked.

"About the same," I replied. "I won by nineteen hundred and ninety-nine to sixteen."

Jack looked me in the eye and said, "Well, Tip, I guess the Lefebvres are still off you!"

Incidentally, when that story appeared in *Johnny, We Hardly Knew Ye*, a memoir about Jack by Kenneth O'Donnell and David Powers, I must have received close to forty letters from all the Lefebvres in Boston, who insisted that their family was never off me, and that Tommy Mullen had it wrong.

In the House of Representatives, Jack had been a fish out of water. He didn't get along with the leadership, and they resented his frequent absences and his political independence. Jack was never one to do his homework. He preferred to travel, and he was always being invited to speak around the state. Among other reasons, he never charged a dime for expenses.

He also liked the ladies, and he had more fancy young girls flying in from all over the country than anyone could count. In recent years there have been plenty of stories about Jack's fondness for women, both before and during the White House years, but I don't want to get into that. Let's just say that he enjoyed Washington a great deal. He flourished in the Senate, but the House just wasn't his cup of tea. In all my years in public life, I've never seen a congressman get so much press while doing so little work.

He didn't pay much attention to the public-service part of the job, either. When I was elected to Congress and Jack went to the Senate, our home offices were in the same building. In those days, if you wanted a part-time Christmas job with the post office you had to show up at the office of your congressman or senator and fill out an application. You could earn about a hundred dollars for a week or two of part-time work, which for working people was more than enough to make the difference between a nice Christmas and a shabby one.

In 1954, a total of twenty-two hundred people came into my office to apply for a Christmas job with the post office. But only seventy-eight came to Jack's office, even though he represented the entire state. In part, these figures reflected the standard difference between what was expected of a senator and a congressman. Whenever we appeared together at a political dinner, a hundred people would approach Jack for his autograph, while eight or ten would come up to me—and ask for a job.

Even so, Jack's reputation for public service was pretty low. Once, during the mid 1950s, the two of us got off a plane together in Boston. Joe Coan was driving me in those days, and he picked me up at the airport. Jack's driver was a fellow named Hart, who worked for the post office. Jack and I ended up speaking at the same meeting, although neither of us realized that the other would be there. I spoke first, and as I was leaving, Hart grabbed my arm. "Tip," he said, "I'd appreciate your help in getting a promotion at the post office."

"You're asking *me* for help?" I said.

"Sure," he replied. "I was with you in the Congress fight."

"That's not what I meant. You drive Kennedy. Why don't you ask him?"

"Oh, no," he said, "I'd never think of asking the senator." It was true: people just didn't think of Jack in that way.

In 1952, when I first ran for Congress, Jack was running for the Senate against Henry Cabot Lodge. (In 1960, of course, Lodge was on the Republican ticket as Richard Nixon's running mate.) I was busy with my own campaign, but one night I did Jack a favor which turned out so badly that I'm still embarrassed to think about it.

Just before the election, Kennedy and Lodge were both scheduled to make brief speeches on the radio. Jack had a conflicting engagement, and he asked me to speak in his place. I was scheduled to go on the air at seven o'clock, and Lodge would follow at seven-fifteen.

The Kennedy people had prepared a speech for me, but at five minutes to seven they still hadn't delivered it.

Lodge was a real gentleman. "Never mind," he said. "I'll take your turn and you can take mine. Maybe your speech will be here by then." At seven-thirteen, as Lodge was concluding his remarks, a messenger ran into the station and handed me the speech. Millie was with me that night, and during the commercial break just before I went on, Lodge said to her, "Why don't I sit out here with you and listen to what Tip has to say."

Well, that speech kicked the living hell out of Henry Cabot Lodge. I didn't have time to edit it or make any changes, and with Millie and Lodge looking right at me through the window as I read those remarks, I was humiliated. Lodge walked out in the middle, but before he left, he said to Millie, "You know, the Kennedys would never give a speech like that for him. And I would never say the things about Jack Kennedy that he's saying about me."

I felt terrible. Lodge had been so generous to let me take his turn that night, and look how I had treated him in return. Had I known what was in that speech, I would have thrown it away and spoken off-the-cuff. Instead of attacking Lodge, I would have told people why they should vote Democratic in the election. But I was so involved with my own congressional campaign that I would not have been able to speak that night without notes.

Kennedy won that election in a squeaker: 1,211,984 to 1,141,247—a margin of less than 71,000 votes. Lodge was the incumbent, but he had missed a number of important votes in the Senate because he was busy trying to get Eisenhower to run for president. This enabled Kennedy to focus on "Lodge's dodges," and to argue that his opponent was preoccupied with national issues and had lost touch with the people and the issues of Massachusetts.

Lodge ran out of luck that year. The night before the election, Eisenhower held a big campaign rally at the Boston Arena. Christian Herter was running for governor, and both he and Lodge were scheduled to appear on television with Ike. But Lodge had spent the day campaigning in New Bedford, and on the way to the rally he got caught in a Boston traffic jam that caused him to miss the televised portion of the rally. So instead of splitting his television time between Herter and Lodge, Eisenhower gave it all to Herter.

On election day, Eisenhower carried Massachusetts by 209,000 votes. Herter, riding Eisenhower's coattails, beat Dever by less than 15,000. So it could well have been that traffic jam that made the difference and elected Jack Kennedy to the Senate.

I knew Jack was serious about running for president back in 1954, when he mentioned that he intended to vote for the St. Lawrence Seaway project. The whole Northeast delegation was opposed to that bill, because once you opened the seaway you killed the port of Boston, which was the closest port to Europe. The Boston papers were against it, and so were the merchant marines and the long-shoremen. But Jack wanted to show that he wasn't parochial, and that he had a truly national perspective. Although he acknowledged that the seaway would hurt Boston, he supported it because the project would benefit the country as a whole.

In January 1960, following Eisenhower's State of the Union message, Jack came over to my office to let me know he was definitely a candidate for the presidency.

I said "I'm aware of that, Jack. How can I help?"

"Bobby will be running the campaign," he said, "but don't pay any attention to what he tells you. Here's what I want you to do. You feel at home with big-city politicians. You speak their language, while I blunder and stutter every time I'm in their company.

"Now I'm having trouble with two people—Bill Green, the Democratic leader in Philadelphia, and Dave Lawrence, the governor of Pennsylvania. They're both Catholics, and they're afraid that I, as a Catholic, will hurt them. They want to win Pennsylvania more than they want us to win the nation. I'd like you to go to work on them."

I didn't know Dave Lawrence, but I was friends with his pal Art Rooney, the owner and president of the Pittsburgh Steelers, who was close with my friend Tansy Norton. I knew Rooney because he was a frequent visitor at the Norton family's summer cottage at Priscilla Beach in Plymouth, which adjoined my family's cottage.

I called Art and said, "I need a favor. I've got to sit down with Lawrence. Kennedy wants him to be a delegate to the convention."

"I'm a Republican, myself," said Art. "But let me tell you who the real power is: a fellow named Joe Clark—no, not the senator, but a retired contractor with lots of money. He's the Democratic state treasurer. Joe Clark is the one who made Lawrence the governor and Green the boss, and they'll do anything he says. He's the man you want."

I thanked Art and called Jack to tell him about Joe Clark.

"Christ," said Jack, "I've been to Pennsylvania fourteen times, and I've never heard of the guy. Are you sure about that?"

"Absolutely," I said.

Two days later, Jack called me back. "Remember that fellow Clark you told me about? Where do you think he and his wife are tonight?"

I laughed. "How the hell should I know?"

"I told my father what you had said, and tonight Joe Clark and his wife are staying with my parents in their Fifth Avenue apartment in New York. I guess you had the right guy."

I never mentioned Joe Clark's name either to Bill Green or Dave Lawrence. But as the campaign progressed, I would call Green at regular intervals to tell him that the bus was pulling out and that he'd better climb on board before it left without him.

When I arrived at the Democratic National Convention in Los Angeles, one of the first people I saw was Bill Green. "Hey Tip," he said, "I'm not only *on* the bus, I'm *driving* it." I'll never know what Joe Kennedy said (or promised) to Joe Clark that night in New York, but evidently it was enough to swing the Pennsylvania delegation.

As the convention drew closer, the list of likely nominees was growing shorter. Jack was determined to win the prize, but many of the party regulars continued to underestimate him. The conventional wisdom was that Lyndon Johnson would head the ticket, with Jack as the likely nominee for vice president.

I asked Jack how he felt about accepting the vice presidency in case Johnson defeated him for the nomination.

"Forget it," he said. "I wouldn't take it in a million years. It's the worst of both worlds. You don't have any power, and the Secret Service is always on your tail." It's no secret that Jack always relished his privacy.

In the spring, the Kennedy team went to work in the primaries. They had many supporters in Boston, of course, including Eddie

Ford, a successful real estate man with a lot of dough. Eddie was a bachelor who lived at the old Statler Hotel, where he'd sit at his regular table in the coffee shop from noon, when he began his day, until eight or nine at night. If you wanted to see Eddie, you'd come to his table, which functioned like an office. And Eddie, of course, always picked up the check.

He loved Jack Kennedy, and a couple of weeks before the primary in West Virginia, he filled a suitcase with cash and drove through the state in a big Cadillac with Illinois plates. He'd pick out a sheriff who was powerful, and he'd say, "I'm a businessman from Chicago, and I'm on my way to Miami. I think this young Kennedy would be great for the country, and I'd like to give you three thousand dollars to see if you can help him. I'll be coming back this way, and I'll be happy to give you a bonus if you're able to carry the town."

These things happened, although Jack didn't always know about them. But the old man had made his own arrangements over and above the campaign staff. Although Jack certainly knew that his father was spending a lot of money, he wasn't always aware of the details. But during the campaign, he was able to defuse the criticism about all his father's money by repeating one of his famous jokes: "I have just received the following telegram from my generous father: 'Dear Jack: Don't buy a single vote more than is necessary. I'll help you win this election, but I'll be damned if I'm going to pay for a landslide!' "

At the convention in Los Angeles, I was responsible for lining up Kennedy delegates from Missouri. I was also asked to see if I could make any headway with the Arkansas delegation, but that was a hopeless cause.

On Sunday afternoon, together with Ted Reardon, who had been Jack's congressional secretary, I was asked to meet with the four delegates from the Virgin Islands. On the way over, we ran into Mike Kirwan, the congressman from Ohio and chairman of the Public Works Subcommittee of the House Appropriations Committee. I knew Mike from the Congress, and because all the public works bills from the Virgin Islands came under him, I asked him to join us.

At the meeting, I began by asking the Virgin Islands delegates which candidates they supported. The first one said he was for Kennedy. The other three supported Johnson, Adlai Stevenson, and Stuart Symington.

Then Mike Kirwan took over. "Do you know who I am?" he asked.

"You're Mr. Kirwan," said one of the delegates.

"And do you know what I do?"

"You're the chairman of the Subcommittee on Public Works."

"That's right," said Mike. "Now if I'm not mistaken, you could use a new school in St. Croix. And I've heard something about a new power plant. And wasn't there talk of a new sewage system?"

The delegates just nodded.

"Now I'm with Kennedy," said Mike, "and if Kennedy wins, I can get you these things. If Kennedy doesn't win, I can't. Now who did you say you were supporting?"

"Kennedy."

"Kennedy."

"Kennedy."

"Kennedy."

"Good," said Mike. "That's what I thought you said."

Before the convention was over, I played a very small part in helping Jack get Lyndon Johnson on the ticket. All of us on the Kennedy team would report every morning at seven o'clock to a daily meeting that was run by Bobby. At these sessions, virtually every delegate was discussed and accounted for so that no stone would be left unturned.

The day before the nominating vote on the convention floor, it became clear at our morning meeting that Jack would win on the first ballot. He already had more than the 761 votes he needed for the nomination, with Lyndon Johnson a distant second.

After the meeting, I went back up to the Massachusetts suite, where I found John McCormack, the House majority leader, together with old Sam Rayburn, the Speaker, and Texas congressman Wright Patman.

"Where do we stand?" McCormack asked me.

"It's all over," I said. "Kennedy has it wrapped up."

Although McCormack and Kennedy had never been friendly, McCormack supported Jack because Kennedy was a local boy, and John McCormack was the ultimate local politician. He turned to Sam Rayburn, who was Johnson's mentor, and said, "Sam, you heard him. Tom here says it's over, and with the accuracy the Kennedys have, I'm sure it is."

Now Sam Rayburn had already made it clear that he supported Johnson for president but was opposed to his taking the second spot on the ticket. But Wright Patman said, "Let me tell you something, Sam. If Kennedy wants Lyndon for the vice presidency, Lyndon can't turn it down. Never in the history of this country has the mantle of the vice presidency been put on a man's shoulders and he has refused it. Justice William Douglas claimed that he had said no to Roosevelt, but there was no truth to that."

Since that time, of course, the vice presidency was turned down by Ted Kennedy after the McGovern nomination in 1972, and presumably by other candidates as well.

To my surprise, Sam Rayburn agreed with Patman. "John," he said to McCormack, "if Kennedy wants Lyndon as his running mate, Lyndon has an obligation to this convention to accept it. You tell Kennedy that if he wants me to talk to Lyndon, I'll be happy to do it. Here's my private telephone number, which you can give to Jack Kennedy."

"I won't be seeing him," said McCormack, "but Tom will deliver the message."

The Speaker handed me the phone number. Then he repeated what he had said: "If Kennedy is interested in Lyndon being the vice presidential nominee, you have him call me and by golly, I'll insist on it."

I immediately called Bob Morey, Jack's driver, who told me that the best place to catch Jack was at Chasen's Restaurant that night, where the United Steelworkers Union was running a party for him. I arrived around eight, and when Jack was free, I told him I had a message from Sam Rayburn about putting Lyndon Johnson on the ticket.

"Tip," he said, "I want to hear the whole story. Would you mind going outside and waiting for me by the car?"

About forty-five minutes later, he came out and we stood talking on the sidewalk. The spotlights were on, and hundreds of people were standing in a circle around us. Trying to ignore the crowd, I told Jack what Sam Rayburn had said and handed him the Speaker's phone number.

He was delighted. "Of course I want Lyndon," he told me. "But I'd never want to offer it and have him turn me down. Lyndon's the natural choice, and with him on the ticket, there's no way we could lose. Tell Sam Rayburn I'll call after the session tonight."

When I returned to the convention, I walked over to the Texas delegation, where Sam Rayburn was sitting. "Mr. Speaker," I said, "I delivered your message. The gentleman has your phone number and he says he'll call you tonight."

On my first day back in Congress after the convention, I was sitting in the Speaker's lobby reading the Boston papers when Sam Rayburn came in. "Well, Tom," he said, "I guess we both played a part in Los Angeles that will never make it into the history books." That was all he said, but it was obvious that Kennedy had called him that night about Lyndon Johnson.

A great many Democrats were shocked and disappointed at Kennedy's choice of a running mate. Labor was furious because of Johnson's antilabor votes. The liberals preferred Humphrey, Stuart Symington, or Scoop Jackson, as they had no use for Johnson's poor record on civil rights.

But Kennedy made that decision himself. Bobby went crazy when he heard about it, but Jack was a pragmatist. If he had Lyndon, he had Texas, and if he had Texas, he could win several of the other southern states. Johnson was a national figure who had strong voter appeal in precisely those areas where Jack wasn't popular. Besides, he had run second to Kennedy in the balloting. Jack proved to be right. The Kennedy-Johnson ticket won in Texas—although by only 23,000 votes—as well as in Louisiana and the Carolinas. The election was extremely close, and without Lyndon on the ticket, the Democrats would have lost.

Directly after the convention, Jack called me. "We're bringing Lyndon to Boston," he said. "We've got to make his visit there a terrific success or people in Texas will be very unhappy."

Our biggest problem was how to fill the hall where Johnson would be speaking. After all, Johnson had been Kennedy's main opponent for the nomination, and Jack was incredibly popular in Boston as the favorite son and the new hope of the Irish and the Catholics.

We began by arranging for a divider which chopped the hall in half. Then we called every union in town and asked them to turn out a certain quota of members that night. We also called the high schools and colleges. And as quickly as possible, we put some spots on the radio to tell the whole city about the rally.

That afternoon, we set up a bandstand at the corner of Berkeley and Boylston streets in the Back Bay, and we brought Johnson over just as the crowds were pouring out of the office buildings. A mounted police officer was directing traffic, and he got off his horse so that Lyndon could climb on. Lyndon was wearing a ten-gallon hat, and when he made that horse rear up, the crowd absolutely went wild. I had known Johnson for years, and I had never seen him so happy.

The rally that night was so crowded that we took down the dividers, and still the hall was filled to capacity. This was a great relief, because if Johnson had been unhappy with his Boston trip there would have been hell to pay.

Because I was Jack's friend as well as an experienced politician, the Kennedys asked me to go out to Missouri as an advance man. Along with Bob O'Hayre and Charley Murphy, two old friends of mine from Boston College, I set up parades, lined up high school bands, arranged for police protection, made sure that supporters had signs, and attended to the hundreds of necessary details in the campaign. We also made a study of the local areas—the ethnic groups, the economy, and the unemployment rate—so that the candidate would appear to be informed about the people he was meeting and the communities he was visiting.

Advance men had been used before Jack Kennedy, of course, but in Jack's 1958 Senate campaign and in the presidential race of 1960 the Kennedys really made a science out of it. Their planning was so good that during the ten weeks between the convention and the election, Jack was able to appear in 44 states and 237 communities, traveling a total of 77,000 miles.

One of the Kennedy innovations was to send advance men who had the power to make their own decisions. Every state and city had its own local factions and conflicts, but the Kennedy people were outsiders who could quickly bypass all of that.

During the three weeks we spent in Missouri, it was up to us to settle any disputes among the politicians as to how the campaign would be run. When we couldn't get into Columbia the day of the Kansas State–Missouri State football game, we had to decide where to send the candidate instead. Kennedy was a hot item, and everybody wanted him in their part of the state.

We had a particular problem with the teamsters. Jack was coming in for a big rally at one of the hotels, and the teamsters were threatening to picket. Actually, their beef was with Bobby, who had investigated Jimmy Hoffa and other labor leaders while serving as counsel to the McClellan committee in the Senate, which was looking into the links between labor and organized crime.

When I heard that the teamsters were planning to demonstrate, I called the national treasurer, a fellow named Gibbons who operated out of St. Louis. "This is Congressman Tip O'Neill," I said. "I've always been a good labor man in Congress. When the Landrum-Griffin bill came up, I was one of the few who voted against it. I think you owe me one, and I'm asking you to pull out the pickets." And he did.

Twenty years later, I met him out in Palm Springs. "Tip O'-Neill?" he said. "My name is Gibbons, from the teamsters. I just want you to know that you owe me one."

The local party boss in St. Louis was a guy named Jack Dwyer. The Kennedys had sent out their own team to register the blacks, which upset the city bosses and threatened their power base. My assignment was to handle Dwyer, who had started to rebel against Kennedy. He was one of those Catholics who worried that a Catholic candidate would ruin everything. He was afraid that the Protestants would turn out in force and would vote Republican, and that his cronies would lose control of the city and the state.

As soon as I came to town, Dwyer called me up to his place. I can still see him sitting there: he had the gout, and his swollen leg was resting on a pillow in a chair. In his hand was a glass of bourbon.

He started right in on me: "Kennedy is an asshole for sending in all these jerks to register the niggers."

I just looked at him.

"But I called some people about you," he said, "and Lenor Sullivan and Mel Price from the Congress both tell me you're a hell of a guy—not like those jerks they're sending down here from Harvard and Princeton. They're looking right down their noses at me like I was a lump of crap. Boy, I could teach those babies a few lessons. Say, will you have a drink and a sandwich?

"Anyway, they say you're a good man and you're here to manage things. I understand you knew Curley. Is that so?"

Like so many politicians, Dwyer had read *The Last Hurrah* and wanted to know all about James Michael Curley, who had died two years earlier. We had a few pops and he kept asking me for more stories. Finally, at two in the morning, he called the chief of police and said, "I want the Kennedy people well taken care of. Anything they ask for, I want you fellows to do. And give them a couple of cars, too."

From then on, everything was beautiful in St. Louis. Jim Curley had departed from the scene, but that night he played a part in helping Jack Kennedy win thirteen electoral votes from the state of Missouri.

One of the most successful events we put together in Missouri was a fund-raising breakfast hosted by Augie Busch, who owned the brewery. Busch had invited thirty businessmen to meet with Jack Kennedy at a thousand dollars a head.

Twenty-nine of them showed up at the meeting. Augie Busch collected the money, and then he and I and Kennedy excused ourselves and stepped into the men's room.

"How did we do?" said Kennedy.

"We raised twenty-nine thousand," said Busch. "I've got seventeen thousand dollars in cash and twelve thousand dollars in checks."

"Great," said Jack. "Give me the cash and give Kenny O'Donnell the checks."

"Jeez," I said. "This business is no different if you're running for ward leader or president of the United States."

Over the years, I've received a lot of criticism for telling that story, but that's how things were done in those days. When I first ran for Congress in 1952, I raised $52,000, and I don't recall seeing a single check. It was just the custom to give cash.

. . .

Looking back, it's hard to believe how important Kennedy's religion was in that campaign. Some voters were genuinely worried that a Catholic president would be subservient to the pope, and that if Kennedy was elected the country would be run from the Vatican. Mixed in with these fears was a healthy dose of good old-fashioned bigotry.

Charley Brown, the congressman from Joplin, Missouri, had specifically asked me not to bring Kennedy into his district. "There's a religious war out here," he said. But as the campaign gathered momentum, the excitement over Jack Kennedy began to overcome the prejudice. Now, suddenly, he was begging me for a Kennedy appearance.

Just after we decided to bring Kennedy into Joplin after all, I received a call from Dick Maguire, who was coordinating the various campaign trips out of Washington. He called me at the Muehlebach Hotel in Kansas City, the very place where Truman had received word back in 1948 of his miraculous victory over Dewey. Apparently a wealthy physician from California was on his way to Missouri to put in a few days helping out in the campaign. He seemed to know his way around, so would I please give him a useful assignment?

Now that Jack was going to Joplin, we needed somebody there to drum up newspaper coverage in advance of his appearance. When the good doctor arrived, that's where I sent him.

A few days later, when we arrived in Joplin, a crowd of over twenty thousand people was waiting to greet Jack Kennedy.

I said to the doctor, "This is marvelous. How did you do it?"

"It wasn't easy," he replied. "When I got to town I was so nervous that I walked by the newspaper office five times in a row. I just didn't have the courage to go in. Finally, one of the editors came out and asked what was on my mind. I told him my name and said I was here as an advance man for Jack Kennedy.

" 'Come on in,' he said. 'Would you like to take out some ads in the paper?'

"That was the furthest thing from my mind," said the doctor. "It was free publicity that I wanted, but I decided it wouldn't hurt to take out an ad. So I asked what a thousand dollars would buy."

" 'I'll tell you what,' said the editor. 'Make it three thousand bucks for three ads, and I'll guarantee you a front-page story three days in a row.' I have a little money, so I took out three ads, he ran three front-page stories, and that's how we got all these people to come out."

From Joplin we went to Wichita, and then to Independence, where Harry Truman gave Jack a formal endorsement. When we returned to the hotel, the doctor said to me, "Can you do me a favor? I'd hate to go back home without meeting Jack Kennedy."

I went downstairs to Jack's suite and told his closest advisers how much this fellow had done for us. Jack was in the shower, but when he stepped out he wrapped himself in a towel and shook hands with his new benefactor.

When the doctor heard that Jack was flying on to California, he told me he would donate an additional ten thousand dollars to the campaign if he could fly in the *Caroline*, Jack's campaign plane, and get off in California, together with Kennedy. I told him I'd see what I could arrange.

But before I had a chance to make any inquiries, Jack turned to me and asked, "Tip, what's the story with that guy who wanted to shake hands with me when I was in the shower? I've never seen him before."

I explained who he was and told Jack about his latest offer. The last I saw of the doctor, he and Jack were climbing the steps of the *Caroline*. The two of them were deep in conversation, and Jack had his arm around him.

Jack Kennedy's election was one of the most thrilling nights of my life, and all of us on Kennedy's team had reason to rejoice. But for me, there was a little incident that took some of the pleasure out of Kennedy's great victory. On election day, Jack and Jacqueline went together to the polling station at the West End Library in Boston. But Jackie didn't vote that day. She was eight months pregnant, and just to be safe, she had already voted by absentee ballot. Hers was the only absentee ballot in the precinct, so when they checked it off everybody knew whom she had voted for. Naturally, she chose her husband for president. She also voted for Eddie McLaughlin for lieutenant governor. But she didn't vote for anyone else on the ticket—not even Tip O'Neill for Congress. I was crushed, and I couldn't understand how she could do that to me.

But time is a great healer, and I've always liked Jackie, who has never been anything but kind to the O'Neills.

A funny thing happened to me when Jack Kennedy was sworn in as president. It was a freezing winter's day, and it had snowed the night before, which is unusual in Washington. All over town, people abandoned their cars and walked home. The army was brought in to clear the streets for the inaugural parade, and they had to use flamethrowers to melt all the snow and ice around the inaugural stand in front of the Capitol.

Millie had come down with all five of our children. Jack had been to our house a number of times and he knew all the kids by name. It was a historic moment for us, for when would our family ever again be as close to a president as we were to Jack Kennedy?

I bundled up the children and took them to their seats. Then I went back to the hotel to fetch Millie.

"No, Tom," she said. "It's so cold today that I'll stay here and watch it on television."

I ran over to the Capitol, where the members of Congress were preparing to march over. Suddenly, I spotted a familiar-looking face standing at the door. It was Frank McDermott from Boston, and I had played basketball against him in high school.

"Tip O'Neill!" he called out. "What are you doing here?"

"I'm a member of Congress," I said. "What about you?"

"I'm with the Secret Service, and I'm in charge of this area. Where are you sitting?"

"About eighty-three rows back."

"Come on down with me," he said. "I'll put you right behind the family."

My older kids were big enough to take care of the younger ones, so I followed Frank up near the front, to a row with an empty seat one in from the aisle. On the aisle was George Kara, whom we used to call the ambassador because he came to Washington so often. George was an affluent businessman from Boston who was kind of a mystery man. He knew everyone and everyone knew him, but nobody could say exactly what he did for a living.

George Kara used to show up everywhere. If the governor was being sworn in, George was on hand. If the Yankees were in town to play the Red Sox, George would be sitting with the players' wives. If there was a championship fight, George had a ringside seat. Whenever there was a prominent event, George was there. There's a guy like George in every town.

"Push over, Ambassador," I said.

"Quiet, Tip, or they'll kick us the hell out." But he moved over to make room for me.

A moment later, Jack Kennedy was standing beside me, waiting to climb the steps to take the oath of office. "How are you, Tip?" he asked.

"Fine, Mr. President. Good luck and God be with you."

Then George Kara leaned over and said, "Mr. President, good luck and may God be with you."

Just then the band started playing "Hail to the Chief," and Kennedy marched down the aisle and up to the rostrum to be sworn in as president. As the music played, George leaned over to me and said, "Years from now, historians will wonder what was on the young man's mind as he strode to take his oath of office. I bet he's asking himself how George Kara got such a good seat."

I smiled. It was just like George to believe that at this great historic moment, Jack Kennedy was thinking about George Kara's seat.

That night, Millie and I were at the Mayflower Hotel for the inaugural ball when a Secret Service agent walked over to tell us that the president and the first lady wanted to say hello. We danced over and greeted them warmly. "Mr. President," I said to Jack, "I was so proud of you today. Your inaugural address will go down in the annals of American history as one of the great speeches of all time."

"Thank you, Tip," he said. "That's very kind. But there's something I've got to ask: Was that George Kara sitting beside you?"

"Yes," I replied. "And when the band played and you stepped forward to be sworn in, George told me that future historians would wonder what was on your mind at that moment."

"Tip," he said, "you'll never believe it. I had my left hand on the Bible and my right hand in the air, and I was about to take the oath of office, and I said to myself, *How the hell did Kara get that seat?*"

. . .

There's a postscript to this story. Four years later, in January 1965, I attended the inauguration of President Lyndon Johnson. I happened to be sitting with Bobby and Teddy Kennedy, and while we were waiting for the ceremony to begin, I told them about George Kara at Jack's inauguration in 1961. They both knew George, and they got a tremendous laugh out of the story.

A couple of minutes later, Bobby tapped me on the arm and pointed to a man in a dark coat. "Tip," he said, "is that where Kara was sitting?"

"Yes," I said, "that's just about the same location." Then I blinked hard and took another look, and wouldn't you know it—the man in the dark coat was George Kara! There he was, sitting in the very same seat for Johnson's inauguration as he had for Kennedy's. To this day, I still don't know how on earth he got there.

5

★★★★★

The Road to Congress

It was Jack Kennedy's fault that I ever ran for Congress. During my two terms as Speaker of the state house, my ultimate ambition was to become governor of Massachusetts. In those days, national politics didn't even interest me. Certainly I never imagined spending thirty-four years of my life in Washington.

My original plan was to begin my ascent to the governor's office by running for lieutenant governor in 1952. But when Jeff Sullivan decided to run for reelection on the ticket with Paul Dever, that option was no longer available. Instead, I decided to pursue the same goal through a rather more circuitous route—by way of Washington. If I could win a seat in the House of Representatives and could remain in Congress for six years, there would be plenty of time to broaden my base and become better known in Massachusetts. In 1958, Jack Kennedy would probably be running for reelection in the Senate. And if, as I expected, he would win in a landslide, this would be as good a time as any for me to run for governor.

I had been to the House of Representatives only once, while visiting a sick aunt in Washington in August 1941. At the time, Congress was absorbed in one of the most important debates in the nation's history. A year earlier, the Selective Service Act had established the nation's first peacetime draft. And now it was about to expire—unless Congress followed the president's wishes and voted an extension.

I watched as one member after another took the microphone and lamented the cost of the draft and its effect on the families of America. There were powerful isolationist forces in those days, together with the natural resistance of mothers to the draft, and the isolationists and the Republicans almost won the day. It was a tense and exciting session, but Sam Rayburn, the Speaker of the House, prevailed—although just barely. In the end, the draft extension passed by a single vote. And a good thing it was, for less than four months later the Japanese invaded Pearl Harbor.

Sitting in the visitors' gallery, I was mesmerized and enraptured by the quality and the excitement of the debate. What these men were discussing really *mattered*. For the first time, I imagined myself in the House of Representatives.

When I returned to Boston, I mentioned this fantasy to Paul Dever, but he quickly poured cold water on my dreams. "Forget it," he said. "If you're thinking about Tom Eliot's seat, Mike Neville is next in line." Mike was older and more experienced than I was, and it seemed fair that his turn should come first. I put Washington out of my mind.

In those days, the party organization was an all-powerful force, and decisions as to who would be a candidate for Congress were worked out well in advance. In 1941 we had no idea that Curley, who functioned as his own one-man organization, would jump into the race the following year. When he did, Mike Neville got out. Curley served two terms in the House, and when he left to run for another term in city hall, Mike ran for Congress against Jack Kennedy.

Eight and a half years later, in January 1951, I was having supper one night at the home of Joe Healy. There was a knock on the door, and who should come in but Jack Kennedy. He happened to be in the neighborhood, and Healy was doing some writing for him, so Jack stopped by to pick up the material. He joined us for coffee, and as always, we got to talking politics.

Jack did me a great favor that night. "Tip," he said, "I've decided not to run for a fourth term in the House. I don't know yet whether I'll run for the Senate or for governor, but you can be sure of one thing: my seat will be open. I won't be making any announcements for at least another year, so don't tell a soul. But in case you have any interest in running, I wanted to give you a head start."

I was definitely interested. The congressional district was far larger than the area I represented in the state house, so if I won, I would have a much broader base from which to begin my campaign for governor. I made up my mind to run for Congress with the hope and intention of spending six years in Washington before returning to Massachusetts.

In April of 1952, Kennedy announced that he would run against Henry Cabot Lodge for the Senate, and I announced for Jack's seat in the House. There were ten or twelve candidates in the race, but the only two with any real chance of winning were Michael LoPresti and myself. LoPresti, who was a few years older than me, was a member of the state senate from East Boston, and chairman of the Committee on Aviation, presumably because Logan Airport was part of his district. But poor Mike was afraid of flying, so every time the committee flew off to study airports in places like Miami, Pittsburgh, or Tulsa, Mike would have to drive or take the train.

Before his election to the Senate, LoPresti had served as the home office secretary of Tom Flaherty of Charlestown, one of Boston's most popular congressmen. Mike and I knew each other slightly, and we always got along well.

Because there were 240 legislators in the state house, and only 40 senators, LoPresti's political base was much larger than mine, which gave him a considerable advantage in our race for Congress. On the other hand, I was the Speaker of the house, so my name was already familiar to people outside Cambridge.

It was a tough and dirty fight. First, there was the problem of Curley's pension, which erupted during the final weeks of the campaign. But this wasn't my only problem. The previous December, a state rep named Eddie Donlan had filed a McCarthy-type bill to investigate communism in Massachusetts. Because the bill was filed late, it was automatically sent to the Rules Committee, which in the state house was chaired by the Speaker.

I thought Donlan's bill was a waste of time, and I ignored it. But on the final day of the session, Eddie Donlan suddenly demanded a hearing, whereupon Chester Dolan, president of the senate and a friend of LoPresti's, started accusing me of being soft on communism.

Between the Baby McCarthy bill, as it was called, and the Curley pension, I found myself on the defensive. To make matters worse, LoPresti's people also brought up the matter of the teachers' oath bill from fifteen years earlier. Fortunately, I had a fine record to run on, and I was able to point to such achievements as housing for the veterans and the elderly, facilities for the mentally ill, and play-grounds for children.

Early in the campaign, young volunteers for both candidates began ripping down each other's signs. One morning, a man with a gun showed up at the back door of our house. I was out, but he warned Millie that if my people kept tearing down LoPresti's signs, there would be problems. "People can get hurt," he said ominously. Millie was terrified and called the police, but by the time they arrived our visitor had vanished.

Given the way politics worked in those days, I guess it was inevitable that the race soon developed into an ethnic battle between the Italians and the Irish. The district was approximately 40 percent Irish and 35 percent Italian, with the rest made up of many different groups, including French Canadians, Lebanese, Armenians, Por-tuguese, Jews, and blacks.

Leo Diehl, my lifelong friend from the state house, took an active role in the campaign, and to help divide the Italian vote he brought in a candidate named Chris Carolina, who ran as a favor to us. LoPresti's people had already pulled the same trick on me with a fellow named Casey. Casey became a big problem, because this was the first state election in which voting machines were used in some of the precincts, and LoPresti's people somehow rigged it so that my name and Casey's were so close together on the ballot that unless you paid close attention, you could easily think you were voting for O'Neill but actually vote for Casey. In the precincts where ma-chines were used, Casey ran very strong. In the rest of the district, however, he wasn't a major factor.

Because LoPresti was my main opponent, I didn't pay much attention to the other candidates. One day I was walking down the street with Paul Feeney, a powerful and experienced member of the legislature. "See that fellow over there?" he said, pointing to a stranger on the other side of Beacon Street. "Believe it or not, his name is John F. Kennedy, and he's one of the guys running against you. Nobody knows him, but with a name like that he could cause you a lot of problems. Let's go over and say hello."

We crossed the street and Feeney introduced us. "You know, John," he said to Kennedy, "you really shouldn't be in that fight against Tip. After all, you've got no chance of winning, and all you're going to do is help LoPresti. You really ought to get out of the race right now. Now, I happen to have a withdrawal slip right here in my pocket. Would you be willing to sign it?"

Paul Feeney was a master politician who never missed an angle. He was prepared for any situation, and he kept all kinds of documents in his pocket. I was amazed that he happened to have a withdrawal slip with him. I was even more amazed that John Kennedy agreed to sign it. But somehow Feeney convinced him to get out of the race on the spot.

I was so impressed with what Paul Feeney had accomplished on my behalf that I, too, started carrying around a withdrawal slip. After all, maybe I would run into Casey and convince *him* to get out. I did meet Casey a few days later, but he made clear that he was serious about running against me. He was so upset at me for ignoring the Donlan bill and for pushing through the Curley pension that he genuinely wanted to defeat me. Casey had no chance of winning, but he ran so well in the machine precincts that he finished with a very respectable six thousand votes.

I could live with Casey in the race, but I realized later that if Paul Feeney hadn't pushed John Kennedy to get out, I would have lost that election. By 1952, after Jack Kennedy had served three terms in the House, the Kennedy name was so strong in our district that John Kennedy—who was not, of course, a "real" Kennedy—would have siphoned off many of my votes.

Another factor in the campaign that made me nervous was that there was no great excitement in our district about the race for state representative. John Toomey, a friend of mine, was running without opposition, which meant that many of the voters in Cambridge might not bother to go to the polls on election day. And if that happened, the margin I was counting on to compensate for LoPresti's inevitable sweep of the Italian areas might not materialize.

Over the years, I've heard people say that Tip O'Neill found a candidate to run against John Toomey just to turn out the votes. That's not exactly true. But when a kid named Jackie Reardon decided to run against Toomey, I encouraged him and helped him out with some money. Toomey and I were close, and everybody knew that Reardon had no chance of beating him. But if their race could develop into a real fight, it would turn out a greater number of Irish voters.

But I hadn't counted on the possibility that Jackie Reardon would run like hell. In the end, Toomey beat him—but only by a hair. There was a huge turnout, which was good for me. Toomey, however, was understandably furious, and my support of Reardon marked the end of our friendship. Toomey never forgave me, and he carried his anger to the grave.

The O'Neill-LoPresti race was the biggest and most difficult of my entire career, and I needed all the support I could muster from my friends and supporters who had put me in the state house. At one point, some of LoPresti's people came to my old pal Red O'Connell to try to convince him to be with their man. "You've gotta be kidding," he said. "I grew up with Tip and we're together until the day we die. I'd take off both my arms before I'd ever go against him."

"He'll never be able to outspend LoPresti," they said.

"I don't know about that," Red replied. "I can always go to the bank and borrow a hundred thousand dollars on my business. Tip doesn't have to worry. As long as I'm around, he'll always have plenty of money."

Red never had to go to the bank, but he did throw away a lot of dough on that campaign. He'd walk into a bar in East Boston and say, "Drinks on the house in honor of Tip O'Neill." He was so thrilled that his boyhood pal was Speaker of the legislature and was running for Congress that he just couldn't do enough for me. One night he went down to a couple of social clubs in East Cambridge and bought them some new furniture simply because it might bring me another couple of votes.

Red was a big, strong fellow who was known as the Moose. Even as a kid he had always been generous. At Barry's Corner, whenever we had trouble scraping together the rent, Red would come up with the cash. Later, at Frank's Steak House, his restaurant in North Cambridge, the local indigents knew they could always come around to the back and Red would feed them on the house.

He loved to gamble, and during the campaign he drove over to a crap game in Revere to try to win some money for me. "I almost brought you twelve thousand dollars," he told me the next day.

"What do you mean 'almost'?" I asked.

"I was ahead by that much and I wanted to leave," he said. "But then I took a good look at the gorilla I was playing with, and I figured I'd never make it out of there. So I kept playing, and as soon as we were even I walked out."

A few years later, Red called me in Washington and said, "Tip, I'm broke. I desperately need five hundred dollars." Now I'm the last guy in the world he should have been calling for that kind of money. But Red was my pal, so I went to the bank, borrowed the five hundred, and wired it to him.

Two days later, Red sent me a check for five hundred dollars.

"What was *that* all about?" I asked him.

"I'm sorry," he said. "But the other night I was with a couple of guys and I was bragging about how close I was to Tip O'Neill. They didn't believe me. So I told them that if I asked, you'd wire me five hundred dollars.

" 'Oh yeah?' they said. 'Prove it.' So I had to call you, old buddy. Otherwise they'd think I was lying."

How could I get angry at a guy like that?

Another time, Red inadvertently got me into trouble with Millie. I was home from Washington for the weekend, and Millie showed me a bill that had just arrived from the Waldorf-Astoria Hotel for three hundred dollars, for "Thomas O'Neill and friends."

"It must be a mistake," I said. "I haven't been to the Waldorf in years."

"A likely story," said Millie.

"Come on, honey," I said. "Look at the dates. The House was in session those days. What would I have been doing at the Waldorf?"

"That's what I'd like to know," she said.

I couldn't figure out who could possibly have signed my name. But there were two long-distance calls to Boston on the hotel bill, which gave me an idea. I had a friend who worked for the phone company, so I gave him the numbers and asked him to find out whatever he could.

He called back two days later. "The Brookline number is a private residence. I put a tap on the line, and the guy turns out to be a bookie. The Somerville number is a bar." He gave me the name of the place, and I called the owner and asked him who might have called his place from the Waldorf in New York.

"How would I know?" he said. "We have nutcakes calling here every night of the week."

I was going to have to solve this one in person. Millie and I had planned to drive to New York the following week to see the championship fight between Floyd Patterson and Ingemar Johansson. I decided that we'd stay at the Waldorf so I could straighten out the matter of the hotel bill.

As soon as I gave my name to the hotel clerk, the fellow pushed a buzzer and a woman stepped out from the back room.

"Can I help you?" she said. "My name is Mrs. Sullivan."

"Glad to meet you," I said. "I'm Congressman Tip O'Neill, and my wife and I would like to check in."

"Don't give me that," she said. "I know Congressman O'Neill. He's a big redheaded fellow. He was here two weeks ago, and he left me such a big tip that I'll never forget him."

It didn't take me long to figure out that Red O'Connell probably had something to do with this. And sure enough, when we got home, Red came by the house. "I was in New York with some friends," he said, "and we lost all our money at the races. I happened to read an item in the paper that the Waldorf-Astoria has a policy of never questioning diplomats or members of Congress. They take your word that you are who you claim to be, and you don't have to pay in advance. I was broke, so I signed in as Tip O'Neill. I've come by to see if the bill ever arrived, because I'd like to pay it."

Millie gave him a fishy look. "Did Tom put you up to this?" she said.

"Absolutely not," he said, which was the truth. Thirty years later, I'm still not sure Millie believes the story.

But aside from Red O'Connell, we didn't have too many laughs in my race against Mike LoPresti. Before the campaign there hadn't been much animosity between the Italians and the Irish, but now we were involved in a real war. One Sunday afternoon, I went to speak at the East Boston High School, never imagining that I would encounter a hostile crowd. But the crowd booed me and never let me get started. For the next three years I didn't set foot in East Boston.

For the Italians, LoPresti would have been the first of their own people to be elected in our district, and to some extent they looked on the Irish as we looked on the Yankees. Late in the campaign,

LoPresti's people put out circulars in Italian, saying "Vote for one of your own. LoPresti for Congress." These were sent to every Italian household in the district.

When Red O'Connell saw that leaflet, he had it translated into English and then dropped off copies in both languages in all the Irish bars in Cambridge. "Look what these people are doing," he said. "Are we gonna stand by and put up with this?"

The night before the election, we bought five minutes of time on television, and I went on the air to try to undo the damage that LoPresti's circulars had caused. I said: "I'm not going to ask for your vote because I'm Irish, or because I'm Catholic, or because my wife is part French and part German." (As long as we were in an ethnic struggle, there was no point in holding back.) "My opponent wants you to vote for him because he's Italian. I don't think that's the American way. And it's certainly not the way *I* want to run for public office."

I'll never know whether my TV appearance had any impact on the voters. Certainly it didn't affect the ethnic split. As everybody expected, LoPresti swamped me in the Italian areas while I murdered him in the Irish ones.

I could never have won that fight without the advice of Charlie McGlue, an old political adviser and an active force in the Democratic party. It was Charlie who pointed out to me that I had run unopposed for so long that many of the old Democratic voters in my district had stopped registering, which automatically turned them into independents. But most of them didn't realize that even as independents they could still vote in the Democratic primary. So we sent around a letter to all the independents in Cambridge, letting them know that they were welcome to vote and reminding them that this was their opportunity to send a local man to Congress.

That letter was a godsend, and as a result, I ended up with more votes in Cambridge than there were registered Democrats. LoPresti was convinced that we ran in repeaters and stole the election, but it was all those independents who made the difference.

On election day, we knew the race would be close. The machine precincts came in first, and by ten o'clock at night, when they were all counted, LoPresti was leading by eleven thousand votes. Then the paper ballots started coming in. We knew I'd win big in Cambridge, but that might not be enough. After all, eleven thousand votes was a huge margin to overcome.

Late in the evening, a group of us were on our way to my campaign headquarters in downtown Boston when we ran into LoPresti's victory parade. I was crushed. And I felt even worse when Bill Mullins, a reporter from the Boston *Herald*, called to say that his paper was preparing a story that LoPresti was the apparent winner. Leo Diehl picked up the phone and warned Mullins that it was too early to name a winner, and that our own precincts had yet to be counted. "Tip O'Neill is going to win," said Leo. "No question." I remember wishing that I shared his optimism.

The *Herald* didn't run the story, but the early edition of the Boston *American* ran a picture of LoPresti's parade and reported that he was the probable winner.

As expected, I beat LoPresti handily in Cambridge, 13,378 to 4,493. But even so, I was still trailing by several thousand votes. It all came down to Brighton, a largely Irish town with a scattering of Italians that was represented in the legislature by my friend Chick Artesani. Chick, a Boston College graduate who later became a judge, was a tremendous factor in that race. He would tell people at street-corner rallies, "I know both candidates, and Tip O'Neill is one of the finest men you'll ever see. If you're not going to vote for O'Neill, don't bother voting for me."

Chick Artesani's endorsement had a big impact. So did the fact that most of the Italians in the district assumed that Artesani was an Italian name. Chick happens to be Spanish, but we kept quiet about that and let people think whatever they wanted.

We won big in Brighton, which made all the difference. At three in the morning, when it was all over, I had won by 27,954 to 24,692.

Two years later LoPresti ran against me again. This time, he and I met in advance and agreed to go at it head to head, just the two of us. Anybody else who wanted to run could do so, of course, but this time neither of us would put in candidates simply to divide the other guy's support.

During my entire first term in Washington, I had been ostracized by the Italians, and was never invited into East Boston or the North End for any function or social event. They all knew that LoPresti was determined to run again to avenge the "stolen" election of 1952. This time, they were convinced, justice would prevail.

Still, when people in the North End or in East Boston had an immigration problem or needed any other kind of favor, they came to us and we did everything we could to help them out. The effect was dramatic. In 1952, I lost by a ten-to-one margin in the Italian districts, despite the fact that I had spent $10,000 in the North End and East Boston. Two years later, when I didn't spend a dime in those areas, the margin was only three to one.

I beat LoPresti pretty badly in the second race and ended up with about twice as many votes as he did. This time, he hired Harvard students to check all the polls to make sure we didn't use repeaters, which he was convinced we had done in the first campaign.

After that second election, Mike LoPresti came by to congratulate me on my victory. We resumed our friendship, which I appreciated; we hadn't spoken to each other after the first campaign. Unfortunately, some of our supporters didn't speak to each other for twenty years.

But it's always been a point of principle with me to remain friends with my political opponents. The first time I ran for the state house, back in 1936, there were eighteen candidates running for three seats. After the election, I went to see each of the fifteen defeated candidates to congratulate him on a good fight.

During my sixteen years in the legislature, I had over a hundred opponents. I'm proud to say that when I ran for Congress in 1952, every person who had ever run against me signed a slip saying he was with me. Nobody ever held a grudge, which shows the greatness of our democracy—that we can disagree in this country without being disagreeable.

After the 1954 election, LoPresti went back to the state senate, where his son serves to this day. For the next thirty-two years, until I retired in 1986, I would never again have a serious opponent.

In 1966, however, a candidate named Sam Cammarata decided to run against me at the last moment. I had never heard of him, but he showed up at my Boston office, introduced himself, and said he was opposing me for the Democratic nomination.

"That's fine," I said. "I'm glad to meet you."

"By the way," he said, "for five thousand dollars I'll get out of the fight."

"You've got to be kidding," I said.

"No," he said. "Otherwise, I'm going to raise a lot of money and make some problems for you."

"Let me tell you something, you son of a bitch. Nobody black-mails me. It might cost me *fifty* thousand dollars, but I'm going to take you before the Ballot Law Commission and check over all your signatures."

I filed a petition to get him off the ballot, and the press hit me like a ton of bricks. Who does Tip O'Neill think he is that he has the right to run unopposed? It's a free country, isn't it? Isn't this young fellow entitled to run against Tip O'Neill?

Sure he was. But the press didn't know the whole story.

We took Cammarata's signatures to the Ballot Law Commission and had a handwriting expert go over them. She found that four people had signed four times, eighty-one had signed three times, and twenty-six had signed twice; four other names were those of people who had died before the signatures were obtained. In addition, we found many other people listed on the petition who had never signed it.

My old friend Bob O'Hayre was the chairman of the commission—the same Bob O'Hayre who had worked with me as a Kennedy advance man in Missouri. I told him why I was so angry at Cammarata, and Bob told a reporter from the Boston *Globe* that Cammarata had tried to shake me down. Bob had said it in confidence—or so he thought. But it ended up in the paper, and Bob had to disqualify himself as a member of the commission.

Cammarata sued Bob for libel, and in court, Bob agreed to forfeit the case for a dollar. Otherwise, they would have had to drag me in as a witness and the incident would have ballooned out of all proportion to its importance.

The truly amazing thing is that after Cammarata filed the suit against Bob O'Hayre, and before the Ballot Law Commission had made its determination, he came to me again. "You have one more chance to get me off the ballot," he said. "But the price is now fifteen thousand dollars." I laughed him out of the office.

Two years later he entered the race again, and once more he came to my office. "This time my signatures are legitimate," he said. "If you want me out of the race, it'll cost you fifteen thousand dollars."

"This time you're staying in," I said. "I won't *let* you out. You're

going to run, and I'm going to teach you the lesson of your life."
He spent a lot of money in that campaign, but I murdered him all
over the district—including East Boston, where a few years earlier
I didn't stand a chance against an Italian candidate.

Several months after that election, I got a call from Dave Brick-
man, publisher of the *Malden Evening News* just outside Boston.

"What ever happened to Cammarata?" he asked.

"How should I know? You were the one who complained that
I wasn't letting him run."

"Well," said Dave, "he came to me with a great idea. He wanted
to go over to Vietnam, where he was going to interview all the
Malden and Medford boys for a special Christmas insert in our
paper. He asked for all kinds of tape equipment and cameras, and
I gave him whatever he wanted. He left my office with twelve
thousand dollars worth of equipment and I never heard from him
again!"

6

★★★★★

Giants of the House
McCormack and Rayburn

AFTER four years of running the Massachusetts legislature, it wasn't easy to start at the bottom again as a freshman in Congress. In those days, new members, like children, were expected to be seen and not heard. Our job was simple and basic: learn the ropes, follow the party line, and pay attention to what's going on around you.

As soon as I arrived in Washington, two members of the Massachusetts delegation offered me their advice. "You're going to hate it down here," said Foster Furcolo, who later became governor of Massachusetts. "You've never see anything like the Kennedys. Jack is a first-class snob. When you take your wife to an evening at the Congressional Club and the other women ask, 'How did you enjoy the Kennedy party?' and your wife says, 'We weren't invited,' you'll be humiliated. The Kennedys never invite anyone from Massachusetts to their parties. They think they're too good for us."

"Thanks for the warning," I said. "But first, my wife isn't coming down. And second, even if she does, we don't go where we're not wanted."

And third—although I didn't know this at the time—Jack always invited me to his parties.

The other piece of advice came from Jack himself. As I was moving into my office in room 317 in the Cannon Building, I noticed that Jack's office was right across the hall. As I was coming in, he was packing up and moving over to the Senate side of the Capitol. His door was open, so I stepped in to say hello. From the outer office I could hear him arguing with Mary Davis, his secretary.

"Mary, now don't be silly. You're coming to the Senate with me."

"No, Senator, I'm not. I'm going to be working with Congressman Lester Holtzman of New York."

"Now Mary, you *know* you're coming with me."

"I am *not*, Senator, and that's all there is to it."

They kept going back and forth like this. Finally, she said, "And the reason I'm not going with you is that Congressman Holtzman has offered me six thousand dollars."

When he heard this, Jack walked out, saw me there, and said, "Tip, can you believe this? I'm paying her four thousand dollars, and I've just offered her forty-eight hundred. That's a twenty percent raise. But this new guy wants to give her six grand the first day he's here!"

He invited me in and we chatted for a few minutes. "I'm glad you're down here, Tip," he said. "And I hope you won't mind if I give you some advice. Whatever you do, don't make the mistake I did. Be nice to John McCormack."

In political circles, it was well known that McCormack and Kennedy didn't get along. People said their feud had to do with McCormack's petition to pardon Jim Curley a few years earlier. Kennedy, who was a freshman at the time, was the only member of the New England delegation who refused to sign it.

But Jack assured me that the problem had nothing to do with Curley. The point was that Kennedy was a maverick who more or less ignored the leadership and didn't play by the rules. Unlike most young congressmen, he traveled a great deal and couldn't be counted on to show up for important votes.

Although he and McCormack were both Irish Catholics, they couldn't have been more different. McCormack was a South Boston man with parochial interests who was devoted to the Church and lived a very proper life. As for Jack, let's just say that during his years in the House he showed considerably more interest in his social life than in legislation.

As Jack described it, the real break between McCormack and Kennedy had come over the issue of patronage. Specifically, the Democratic members from Massachusetts were unhappy that McCormack was grabbing it all for himself. Kennedy in particular was so unsuccessful in the patronage game that people said he wouldn't know how to find a job for his own cousin. In their frustration, the delegation went to the White House to discuss the problem with President Truman. But it was Jack who actually made the appointment, as McCormack learned soon enough.

"But let me tell you what John McCormack did for me in my race for the Senate," Jack said. During the campaign, Henry Cabot Lodge had brought in Jacob Javits from New York to address a large Jewish gathering in Mattapan. In his talk, Javits stressed repeatedly that Jack was "the son of his father." He didn't have to be any more explicit, for every Jew in Boston knew that old Joe Kennedy was an anti-Semite. Javits also charged that Jack was anti-Israel, and that Kennedy had offered an amendment to cut aid to the fledgling Jewish state. When they heard that, the Jews all cheered for Lodge.

In reality, Jack had voted against an aid package for the entire Middle East, including Israel and several of the Arab states.

"When my father heard about Javits," said Jack, "he was tremendously upset. In his view, the only person who could put out the fire was John McCormack." I wasn't surprised. In Boston, McCormack was so solid with the Jews that he was sometimes known as Rabbi John.

Jack continued: "A few days later we held our own rally in the same theater. The place was filled to capacity. And John McCormack, whom I hadn't spoken to in years, and whom I always looked down on, got up on that stage and made a great speech. 'Let me tell you what *really* happened on aid to Israel,' he told the crowd. 'We had heard that the Republicans were going to defeat that bill and take out the money that was supposed to go to Israel. I walked up and down the aisle, looking for somebody who would put forward an amendment to soften the blow. And finally I found Jack Kennedy, and he agreed to offer an amendment that included only a token cut to Israel. *He* was the one who stood up there with guts and with courage. *He* was the one who saved the aid package to Israel.'

"The audience went wild," said Jack. "But the whole story was a figment of John McCormack's imagination. He made it up to save my ass, knowing damn well that I didn't deserve his help. So don't ever be rude or mean to him like I was, because in my hour of need he came through like a champion."

Jack may have been surprised by what McCormack had done, but I wasn't. Whatever sins Jack may have committed against the leadership of the party, he was still a Democrat, a *Boston* Democrat. And John McCormack understood loyalty.

Jack's advice turned out to be as unnecessary as Furcolo's. Not only was I prepared to be nice to McCormack, but I soon discovered that John McCormack, who was the minority whip when I came in, was eager to take me under his wing. I had known him since 1948, when he gave me the idea of trying to make the state house Democratic. I knew that he liked me, but I wasn't prepared for the great kindness and generosity that he extended to me from the time I came in until the day he retired in 1970 after serving nine years as Speaker.

McCormack was tall and lean, with yellowish-white hair, and he always wore a dark suit and a white shirt. He was a man of firmly fixed habits, especially around mealtimes. Every morning at exactly 8:25 he would arrive at his regular corner breakfast table in the House dining room, where they'd bring him a cup of coffee. (He had already eaten breakfast at home with his wife, Harriet.) He ordered the same lunch every day—a grilled cheese sandwich with a cup of tea and a dish of chocolate ice cream. He would ask for the dessert together with the sandwich, so that by the time he finished the sandwich, the ice cream would be melted, which was how he liked it. He ate supper with Harriet every night of their life.

As Jack Kennedy had discovered, John McCormack was always generous to his fellow man. Like so many Boston politicians, he had a steady stream of petitioners who came to see him, and whom he tried to help. He was equally generous to his colleagues. The meanest thing he was ever heard to say about a fellow legislator was "I hold him in minimal high regard."

McCormack had no children, and I became like a political son to him. As majority leader, and later as Speaker, he was invited to fund-raisers, parties, and receptions every evening. He would always make an appearance to lend the respect of his office to the event. But after a few minutes he would slip away to go home to Harriet. Usually, he'd bring me along to these various events, and during my early years in Washington I accompanied him to all kinds of gatherings, where I met congressmen, senators, generals, admirals, cabinet members, ambassadors, and other prominent people.

Before long, people started asking, "Who's the big Irishman with McCormack?" At first they thought I was his bodyguard! But soon people came to see me as McCormack's closest friend in Congress —or his protégé, which was closer to the truth. But although we knew each other for twenty-two years, he never called me Tip, because he disapproved of nicknames.

No matter where we went, he would always introduce me in the same way: "This is Tom O'Neill. Tom was the Speaker of the Massachusetts legislature. He's in Congress now, and I want you to keep your eye on him. Someday, he may become Speaker of the House." John McCormack was one of the most powerful men in Washington, and his introductions opened a lot of doors for me. Because of my association with McCormack, not to mention all the people he introduced me to, I was able to get things done a little easier than most of the other junior members of the House.

I was a regular at the McCormack breakfast table in the House dining room, where he would hold forth every morning between 8:30 and 9:55, when it was time for the committee meetings to begin. Often there were just a few of us, although on occasion there might be a couple of dozen. Listening to John was a real education. The talk was mostly business—politics, legislation—and gossip about members of the House. Most days there would also be a few minutes on sports, as McCormack was a passionate baseball fan.

In addition to being a great talker, he also knew how to listen— and how to pick a fellow's brain. Whenever a visitor came in from Boston, John would invite him to breakfast and ask him all about his business and how it fit into the economy. John was constantly learning, constantly preparing for the next debate.

Outside of politics, there wasn't much else in John McCormack's life. When he became Speaker, he made a point of never leaving the floor of the House when the House was in session. When the House wasn't in session, he was usually at home with Harriet.

Somebody once said that John McCormack was so conservative that he didn't even burn the candle at one end. He didn't like parties and never touched a drop of alcohol. His idea of a night on the town was to take Harriet out to Rockville, Maryland, for ice cream. He loved ice cream, and he'd always say, "You can't beat Howard Johnson's."

John had a younger brother who was his complete opposite. Knocko McCormack was a lovable and gregarious fellow who ran a saloon in Boston and weighed around three hundred pounds. He knew everybody in town, and some people said that it was Knocko's popularity that got John elected. Whenever Knocko wanted to get something done, he'd pick up the phone and imitate his brother's voice.

Every year they made Knocko Grand Marshal of the St. Patrick's Day parade in South Boston, which meant that he had to ride a horse. And every year people took pity on that poor animal. They'd find some skinny old dray horse, and as Knocko climbed aboard, the people would all laugh and cheer.

One time, as the horse was staggering down the street, a fellow called out, "Hey, Knocko, where are you going on that battleship?"

Knocko reached back, lifted up the animal's tail, and yelled, "Why don't you stick your head in the porthole and ask the admiral?"

John McCormack would sooner have died than have said anything like that.

But John was a great talker and the finest debater I ever heard. Charlie Halleck of Indiana was the Republican leader, and when the two of them faced each other on the floor of the House, the members would all be there and the galleries would be packed. McCormack and Halleck were political enemies, but they always maintained a good friendship.

McCormack also had a terrific memory. One afternoon in 1965 we were listening to a Republican member make a speech against Medicare. "You know," he told me, "that's the same speech that was given in 1934 by a Republican who was opposed to Social Security." He asked one of the pages to bring him the *Congressional Record* for 1934, and sure enough, he found that speech. He got up and said, "I must thank the gentleman for this nostalgic interlude. He has brought back the days of my youth." Then he read part of the speech from 1934.

John was a progressive and a great champion of the unfortunate, and I'm sure this attitude came from his own childhood. Somebody once asked him, "Why are you always fighting for minorities?"

His answer was simple and powerful: "No Irish Need Apply," he snapped. He knew what discrimination had meant to his own people, and he wasn't going to allow it for *anybody*.

I'll never forget the Poor People's March on Washington in 1968, when the Reverend Ralph Abernathy and about fifty marchers came into John's office. He invited in as many as the room would hold, and he listened intently as they talked. Suddenly he said, "You're talking down at me. Let me tell you, I was poor when poor was *poor.*" He told them what his young years had been like in Boston, when there was no public assistance and no medical care. When he was done, Abernathy said that John was right, that they really *had* been talking down at him.

John's wife, Harriet, was an invalid in her old age, and he spent a great deal of time and energy taking care of her. "Mr. Speaker," I said to him one day—as close as we were, I never called him John—"you're killing yourself. You're up most of the night taking care of your poor wife. You just can't go on like this. You've got to put Mrs. McCormack in a nursing home."

"Tom," he said, "don't you ever talk to me like that again. She's the woman I've been married to for fifty years, and I love her dearly."

But he did move Harriet into Providence Hospital. He moved into an adjoining room and had a door cut through to her room so they could be together. That way, at least he was able to sleep at night. There was an affection between the two of them that I've never seen again in my life.

McCormack lived modestly and didn't care for pomp and ceremony. When Jack Kennedy was killed and Lyndon Johnson assumed the presidency, John McCormack, as Speaker, was suddenly next in line. But John refused to have Secret Service protection. By a strange coincidence, Harriet suddenly became friendly with a succession of priests who lived in the next apartment. After a while, John started to wonder why there was a priest standing out in the hallway every time he came in. Finally it dawned on him that these weren't really priests at all. He was being given Secret Service protection whether he wanted it or not.

John was always prepared to help somebody in trouble, and always willing to grant one more favor. In 1956, when I gave up my own credentials so that Robert Kennedy could be a delegate to the Democratic National Convention, Ralph Granara, one of the great characters in Boston and a perennial hanger-on at City Hall, protested before the Ballot Law Commission that Bobby wasn't really a resident of the district. Kennedy's people made a deal with Ralph: Ralph would withdraw his complaint, and if Jack was ever elected president, he would give Ralph a job.

Not long after Kennedy was elected, the president and Jackie went to church one morning and found that Ralph Granara had slipped through the security guards. "Hello, Jack," he said. "I'm Ralph Granara. You promised me a job in 1956 if you got elected." Jack remembered him, and he wrote a note to Robert Weaver, head of the Housing and Home Loan Agency, asking him to give Ralph a job.

The next day, Weaver's man came to me and said, "Here's a letter my boss got from the president. Do you know this fellow Granara? The president said to give him a job, but Kenny O'Donnell said not to. What should I do?"

"If I were you," I said, "I'd do what the president wants. Never mind what Mr. O'Donnell says."

But O'Donnell prevailed and Ralph didn't get the job. Meanwhile, Ralph's wife was hurt in a bad car accident and had to spend a year in the hospital. He and I had never been that friendly, but he was hurting and he came to ask me if I could help him find work.

"I'm sorry," I said, "I don't have anything. But here's what you should do. Go over to see John McCormack. Be the last one in tonight, because he loves to talk and talk."

"Forget it," said Ralph. "McCormack would never help me. He's a Curley man, and I used to picket Curley." Years earlier, back in Boston, Curley had fired Granara, who had been commissioner of veterans' affairs for the city, after Ralph was indicted for election fraud. Although Granara was found not guilty, Curley refused to reappoint him to his former position. When he refused even to *see* Ralph, Ralph decided to picket City Hall with a sign that read, "Mayor Curley, you were convicted and served time, but you got your job back. I was found not guilty and you refuse to reappoint me."

The picketing attracted a huge crowd. Ralph was afraid that some of Curley's men might come after him, so he rounded up a contingent of fighters whom he knew from his own days as a boxer, and they surrounded him on the street. It was quite a scene.

Curley saw the commotion and relented. Somebody else had

already been appointed as commissioner of veterans' affairs, so the mayor made Ralph a contracting consultant on a subway project at a higher salary. Curley also gave him a thousand dollars in cash, allegedly to cover the expenses of the picket signs.

I reassured Ralph Granara that John McCormack was not likely to remember the picketing incident. "And even if he does," I said, "I don't think it means much to him. Just go in and tell him the truth about your problem."

As I had hoped, McCormack found a way to help Ralph Granara, and he hired him to make sure that visitors to the House gallery didn't bring in cameras. Ralph was so appreciative that he used to meet McCormack's car every morning at 8:20, and take the Speaker's hat, coat, and briefcase upstairs while McCormack walked to the House dining room. If it was raining, Ralph would be there with an umbrella. On Saturdays, he would offer to run errands.

Later, McCormack made Ralph an assistant doorkeeper, where he worked with Fishbait Miller. After that, he was put in charge of the chapel, which is located on the second floor of the Capitol toward the back, just off the Rotunda. Now Ralph Granara was just about the last guy in the world who should have been in charge of the chapel, but that was the way things worked out.

When McCormack retired, he had one request: take care of Ralph Granara. In 1971, when I became whip, I made Ralph my driver. He was quite a character, and we had a million laughs together.

One Thursday, when I was leaving to go back to Boston, Ralph asked me to do him a favor. He had a favorite horse who was going to be running in the Kentucky Derby, but he couldn't find a place in Washington that would accept his bet. Would I take his ten bucks and place the bet in Boston?

"Certainly," I said. I was happy to help him out—until Ralph told me the name of the horse, a thirty-to-one guaranteed loser. "You must be out of your mind," I said. "Maybe you caught too many left hooks to the head. That horse is going to run dead last."

"It's my money," he said, and I couldn't argue with that.

The following Monday I flew back to Washington with a wad of money for Ralph. That damn horse had won the race and paid $67.50. I was kicking myself for not tossing in a couple of bucks myself. On the other hand, I was extremely grateful that I hadn't succumbed to the temptation to keep Ralph's money in my pocket and give it back to him when the race was over. But that was Ralph Granara. The world might be falling apart, but he always landed on his feet.

But you didn't have to be a Boston Democrat to be the beneficiary of John McCormack's generosity. He was equally kind to Republicans—and southern Democrats. In 1964, when the civil rights bill came up, the two ranking Democrats on the Rules Committee, both southerners, stopped showing up at the meetings. The Republicans were against the bill, so we were left short of the quorum we needed to send the bill to the floor for a vote. John called Bill Colmer of Mississippi and said, "I need you for a quorum."

"Mr. Speaker," said Colmer, "I'm opposed to that bill and I'll do everything possible to defeat it."

I know your position," said John. "And of course I know you'll vote against it. But I promised the president I'd get a rule out. If you don't make a quorum, I'll break my word, which is something I've never done. I'm not asking you as the Speaker. I'm asking you as a friend."

Colmer loved McCormack too much to say no, and a vital part of the civil rights bill fell into place.

McCormack was a broad-minded man who was maligned and ridiculed because he believed in a bipartisan foreign policy. Near the end of his tenure, a group of younger members came along and criticized him. In 1968, they got Mo Udall to oppose McCormack, which was the biggest mistake Udall ever made. McCormack annihilated him, and later, when Mo ran for majority leader against Hale Boggs, McCormack got on the phone to remind people that Udall had once opposed him.

But that sort of thing is part of life in the House. There are always those who feel that they have the talent to be running things, and if they're not consulted by the leadership, they push for a change. I saw it happen under Sam Rayburn and John McCormack and Carl Albert, and when I became Speaker it happened under me.

Over the years, John McCormack brought me to a lot of places and introduced me to a lot of people. But perhaps the most important place he ever took me was Speaker Sam Rayburn's "Board of

Education," where I met some of the real powers in Washington.

The Board of Education was located downstairs on the first floor of the Capitol, behind the members' dining room. Throughout Rayburn's tenure, the Democratic leadership would meet there every afternoon around four-thirty or five. Most people are under the impression that the Board of Education originated with Rayburn, but it actually began a couple of decades earlier, when Speaker Nicholas Longworth would toss down a drink or two with his good friend John Nance Garner, who later served as vice president under Franklin Roosevelt. They referred to this as "striking a blow for liberty," and the phrase stuck.

The Board of Education got its name not because Longworth and Garner taught so much to the younger members who came by to see them but because of all they *learned* from their visitors. "You get a couple of drinks in a young congressman," Garner used to say, "and then you know what he knows and what he can do. We pay the tuition by supplying the liquor."

Garner continued the practice when he became Speaker, as Rayburn did when he took over in 1940. But Mr. Sam, as he was known, didn't care for the name Board of Education. As far as he was concerned, it was simply "downstairs." When he wanted one of the chairmen to meet him there, he'd say, "Come on down."

Under Rayburn, the Board of Education was more like a club, with admission by invitation only. John McCormack was a regular in those sessions, along with Carl Albert (who became Speaker after McCormack retired); Hale Boggs (who became majority leader under Albert); Homer Thornberry and Wright Patman from Texas; Lewis Deschler, the House parliamentarian; Richard Bolling from Missouri, and Lyndon Johnson from the Senate.

The room was unmarked, and a guard stood outside the door. The regulars would occasionally bring a guest, and from time to time I came in with McCormack.

The Speaker would always be sitting at his desk. Nearby, on a table, there would be a bottle of Virginia Gentleman bourbon, some water, and a bucket of ice. (McCormack, of course, never took a drink, and on my visits there I didn't either—not out of any principle, but because I hate the taste of bourbon.) The room was furnished with black leather chairs and a long black leather sofa with red pillows. According to legend, this was the sofa on which John Adams died after being stricken by a heart attack in Congress. And Vice President Harry Truman was sitting on that sofa on April 12, 1945, when Eleanor Roosevelt called and asked him to come to the White House. When he got there, he learned that the president was dead and that he, Harry Truman from Missouri, was now running the show.

In the Board of Education, the boys would have a few pops, and Mr. Sam would hold forth on legislation, the various committee chairmen, history, world politics, and sports. Occasionally, a couple of Republicans would be invited if it would help move along the legislation. Whenever I was a guest, Sam Rayburn would usually ask about my experiences in the Massachusetts legislature. He was especially interested in hearing all about how badly the Republicans had treated us.

Most of all, though, he wanted to know about James Michael Curley. Curley, of course, had served in the House a few years earlier, and apparently Rayburn had been well aware of his political talents and his great speaking ability. Rayburn also inquired about other Massachusetts politicians, including Maurice Tobin and Jack Kennedy. I wasn't the only one he quizzed; if somebody came in from Chicago, he'd want to hear all about Richard Daley. Through the various guests of the members, old Sam got a rundown on every major politician in the country.

By the time I got to Congress, Sam Rayburn had been a member for forty years. He had already been a legend for over a decade, and he had been a power in the House back in the days when one man could make an enormous difference.

McCormack used to tell a story about Sam Rayburn that absolutely thrilled me. In 1942, after America had entered the war, McCormack was at a meeting at the White House one night when President Roosevelt said to the group, "I want you all to meet me tomorrow morning at five-thirty. The Secret Service will pick you up and bring you to the meeting. Don't tell anybody where you'll be going." The next morning, they picked up McCormack and drove him all around the back streets of Washington. Finally, the car pulled up at the rear entrance of Blair House.

Sam Rayburn was already there, along with Joe Martin, the minority leader, and the rest of the leadership from the House and

Senate. The president was there, too, and with him was Albert Einstein. Einstein explained the theory of the atom bomb, and told the group that Hitler also had scientists working on it, and that the first nation to get the bomb would win the war and control the world.

Einstein estimated that the project would cost two billion dollars. Not surprisingly, the president was concerned about how to allocate that kind of money without alerting either the public or the press.

"Leave it to me," said Sam Rayburn.

The next day, Sam called all the committee and subcommittee chairmen and told them to put an extra hundred million dollars into their budgets.

"Yes, Mr. Rayburn," they all said. There were no questions asked and no meetings held. The Manhattan Project was one of the best-kept secrets in history. The money was allocated and nobody on the committees ever questioned why a chairman was setting aside a certain amount for reasons he didn't even know about.

But that's the way things worked in Sam's time. Today, of course, you'd have ninety-two guys wanting to know what was happening and where all the money was going.

Rayburn was a short, heavy-set, jowly man with a bald head that really shone. He was very sensitive about his head, which may explain why he often wore a black hat. He had once been married, but the marriage lasted only a few weeks, and he seemed to have lost interest in women. He was a man's man who loved to talk about sports and politics, and who really enjoyed the company of other men. For Sam Rayburn, "heaven" would mean spending eternity with a few of the boys in the Board of Education, talking politics and drinking bourbon.

He was a member of Congress for more than fifty years, and was Speaker for seventeen, which is by far the longest time anyone has held that office. Like John McCormack, he loved the House and thought about almost nothing else. He really knew the place, and people said he could take the *feel* of the House just by walking in. He once told the members that the House of Representatives was "the highest theater that anyone plays in upon this earth."

He was a loyal Democrat, but he never forgot that there was a higher allegiance. He used to say, "Number one, we're Americans first and Democrats second. And number two, we're builders, not obstructionists. Any jackass can kick down the barn door, but it takes a carpenter to build one."

In January 1953, along with the other freshmen Democrats, I attended an orientation luncheon in the Speaker's dining room, where Sam Rayburn gave us some good advice, including his most famous line, "If you want to get along, go along." This idea is no longer in fashion, as today's freshmen are more restless and independent. But when I first came to Congress, party discipline meant a great deal.

Another thing Rayburn told us was not to rush things. "Learn your job," he said. "Don't open your mouth until you know what you're talking about." He also reminded us to pay close attention to our districts: "Your first priority is to get yourself reelected."

He was famous for his adages, several of which were about the difficult art of not talking too much. "No one has a finer command of language than the person who keeps his mouth shut," he'd say. And "Always tell the truth. Then you'll never have to remember what you said the last time."

Rayburn didn't trust the press and refused to have a press secretary. He would probably have been horrified to know that during the 1980s, both the House and the Senate would bring in television cameras. When he did talk to reporters, he operated by his own rule—that everything was off the record unless he specifically said it could be used.

Once, when a group of reporters came to see him, he said, "You remember how things were yesterday?"

"Yes, Mr. Speaker," they all said.

"Well," said Sam, "they're the same today."

Although I was never personally close with Sam Rayburn, I knew him better than most of the other members because we used to see each other almost every morning in the Speaker's lobby. I was there before breakfast to get an early look at the Boston papers from the previous day. Most of the time, Rayburn was there too, reading the Texas papers.

At that hour, he and I were often the only two in the room. We didn't talk much, but whenever one of the younger fellows walked by he'd lean over and ask, "Tom, who is that fellow?"

It's hard to believe, but except for the committee chairmen, Sam didn't know twenty members of his own party. When he first became Speaker, he knew plenty of congressmen, but as the years went on, he became increasingly isolated in the party. By the time I came along, he was dealing almost exclusively with what the press called the College of Cardinals—the committee chairmen.

But in 1959, when Daniel Inouye of Hawaii came into the House, Rayburn knew him right away and always said hello. Inouye, who had lost an arm during World War II, was aware that this was unusual, and he once said to Rayburn, "Mr. Speaker, I'm very honored that you recognize me."

"Come on," said Rayburn, "how many one-armed Japs do we have around here?"

The following year, Sam Rayburn went up to Eddie Boland and said, "New member, son?" At the time, Eddie had been in the House for seven years and had served on the Appropriations Committee for five, but Sam had no idea who he was. He didn't care, either. As for Republicans, he probably didn't know more than three or four. If you wanted to see Sam Rayburn, you made an appointment two or three weeks in advance.

In 1977, when I became Speaker, I came into office with a very different approach. For one thing, I knew about 80 percent of the members. For another, if you wanted to see Tip O'Neill, all you had to do was show up in my office. I might have the biggest businessman in the world waiting for an appointment, but if a member of Congress wanted to talk, he always came in first.

In Sam's day, power was used more crudely than it is now. There was, for example, a fellow on the Ways and Means Committee who always did Sam's bidding. He was up for reelection one year, and it looked like a tough fight. This member told me later that Sam called him into the office, reached into the bottom drawer, and handed him $10,000 in cash. Sam's usual contribution was said to be $2,000, but this, apparently, was a special case. Nobody ever questioned where Sam got all the money, and I always assumed it came from lobbyists and from his rich oil friends in Texas. But the ethics of the Congress were very different in those days, and transactions of that sort were fairly common.

And yet his personal integrity was above reproach. Nobody could even buy him a meal. He took no trips—except once, to see the

Panama Canal, and he paid his own way. When he made a speech, he never accepted payment. He wouldn't even take expenses.

Sam had other ways to help a member get reelected. He'd call a committee chairman and say, "I want you to put in a dam for this guy." Or he'd call the Army Corps of Engineers and tell them, "Start that canal on Monday. I've got a member who needs it."

"But it isn't authorized, Mr. Speaker. And the money hasn't been appropriated."

"Don't worry about that," Rayburn would say. "You get started. I'll worry about the authorization and the money. We'll put it through next year, but we need this fellow back and this project will help him win." And they'd always do it for him.

My favorite example of Sam Rayburn's power goes back to the time that Representative Leo O'Brien came to see me in 1955. Leo was a Democrat from Albany who had his own radio show. He was such a popular announcer that the O'Connells, who controlled the Democratic party in Albany, approached him to run for Congress. Leo agreed—as long as he could continue doing his radio broadcasts.

He would go on the air right from his office in Congress: "This is the Leo O'Brien Show, brought to you by Tydol Gas." I was his guest on a number of occasions. It was a pretty good show, and everybody liked Leo. He had married a girl from North Cambridge, so I felt a special connection to him.

Leo's trouble began when the O'Connell brothers, who had been experiencing problems with the Internal Revenue Service, asked him to set up a meeting with Sam Rayburn. "Mr. Speaker," one of them said, "they've been holding our case up for years. My wife is in an institution, and this thing is driving us all nuts. We want them to make a decision: let them take it criminal or take it civil. We just want to know which way it will go so we can get this thing behind us and move on."

"Come back and see me at five o'clock," said Rayburn.

As soon as they left, Sam called the head of the IRS and asked him to come to the Capitol. (That alone is amazing to contemplate. When I was Speaker, I would never even think of calling the IRS on my *own* behalf.) When he arrived, Sam said, "I want to talk to you about the O'Connells from Albany."

"I've got that case sitting on my desk."

"From what I hear," said Sam, "it's been sitting there for three years. You're driving these people crazy. I want a decision by five o'clock tonight. Either take it criminal or take it civil. Personally, I think you should take it civil because these folks have suffered enough."

At four-thirty in the afternoon, the IRS called back and told the Speaker that the case was civil, with a fine of $42,000.

That was Sam Rayburn. He just assumed he had that power, and because he assumed it, people went along.

But there's a lot more to the story. When Leo O'Brien brought the O'Connells back at five o'clock, Sam told them the good news. "Mr. Speaker," they said, "we're eternally grateful for what you did. Anytime you need a vote, we can guarantee that our man Leo will be with you."

"Let me tell you something," said Sam Rayburn. "That's not how I operate. I've never done a quid pro quo in my life. I helped you because I thought the IRS was wrong in the way they treated you.

"But if you really want to help me out, there's an interesting bill coming up concerning off-shore oil. Most of the northern members want those revenues to go into a special fund for a national educational program. But there are many of us who think that money should go back to the states."

"No problem," said the O'Connells. "Leo will be delighted to vote with you on that one, won't you Leo?"

Leo just smiled.

It was about ten days later that Leo came to see me. "Tip," he said, "I'm in a hell of a mess, and I'm coming to you because you've had a lot of experience." Then he told me the whole story of how Sam had helped the O'Connells, and how they, in turn, had pledged his vote on the offshore oil bill.

"Here's my problem," he said, reaching into his pocket to show me a couple of clippings. Some things just can't be kept quiet, and now the Albany papers had run a story charging that Leo had pledged a vote to Sam Rayburn—a vote that his district opposed—in return for Rayburn's help on the O'Connells' tax case.

"You've got to help me," said Leo. "If I vote with the Speaker on this I'll be ruined for life. But if I vote against him, he'll never forgive me. What can I do?"

"Your word has been given?"

"Absolutely," he said. "I was right there with them and I agreed to their promise."

"Then you have no choice but to go to Sam with your hat in your hand. Show him these articles and say, 'Mr. Rayburn, I'm sorry, but look at the situation I'm in. I must ask you to release me from my promise.' It won't be easy, but you've got no choice."

Sam Rayburn was not pleased. He said, "I already told you that I've never done a quid pro quo. I didn't ask for your vote; they volunteered it. But you gave me your word and I expect you to keep it.

"However, I can certainly appreciate your situation, so here's what I'll do for you. On the day of the vote, I want to see you in the front row. Keep your eye on the doorkeeper. If I don't need your vote, Fishbait Miller will give you the sign and you'll be free to vote your district."

It was a close fight, but in the end Sam had enough votes to win without Leo O'Brien. The funny part of it was that when Leo took his seat in the front row, he looked around and saw *thirteen other guys* that Sam had in his pocket in case he needed them. It wasn't just Leo. The entire front row was sitting there and waiting for the nod from Fishbait Miller.

In January of 1955, when I returned to Congress for my second term, Fishbait Miller came into the House dining room one morning to say that the Speaker wanted to see me. Now the less said about Fishbait the better, because after everybody he knew had been nice to him, he went and wrote a gossipy book exposing their various weaknesses. As the doorkeeper, he was in charge of giving out tickets to special events, like the State of the Union address. But when he started saving them for his personal friends, the fellows got upset with him and voted him out.

When I got to the Speaker's office, Rayburn said, "I know all about you from John McCormack. And I know you understand party loyalty. So I'd like to make you a member of the Rules Committee."

The Rules Committee! Although I was ambitious, I had never dreamed of getting such a prestigious assignment—certainly not during my second term. Only once before had a second-term man gone on the Rules Committee, and that was Howard Smith, the new chairman. A sophomore member would normally be too inexperienced, but this is where my four years as Speaker of the Massachusetts legislature made such a difference.

During our conversation, the Speaker made it perfectly clear that he had chosen me for this singular honor for only one purpose: so that I could be counted on to vote with the party. In case I had any doubts about what he meant, he spelled it out for me: "Now I don't give a rat's ass whether or not you like the legislation. If it's a party issue, your obligation is to get it on the floor. Once it gets there, of course, you're on your own and you're free to vote your conscience—or your district. But on the Rules Committee, if we need your vote, you'll give it to us—even if you hate the bill, and even if it goes against the economy of your area."

What makes the Rules Committee so important is that it sets the agenda for the flow of legislation in the House and ensures that the place runs smoothly and doesn't get bogged down. Almost all congressional legislation goes to the Rules Committee, which decides when and whether to send a bill to the floor. The Rules Committee also decides on the rules that will apply to each bill: how much debate will be allowed, whether amendments will be permitted and, if so, what kinds of amendments.

On a major bill, the Rules Committee holds its own preliminary hearings around a large oval table in a cramped room and establishes rules that may apply only to that bill. If the committee or its chairman doesn't like a bill, they may choose to do nothing at all, in which case the bill never reaches the floor of the House.

As the group that sets the agenda, the Rules Committee holds a great deal of power, which is why Sam Rayburn was so careful to stress party loyalty. That's also the reason that the committee is sometimes referred to—only partly in jest—as the third branch of Congress, along with the House and the Senate.

In the House of Representatives, only two committees—Appropriations, and Ways and Means—have the right to send a bill directly to the floor of the House, where it can be decided by a simple majority. All other committees may, if they choose, bypass Rules and send a bill directly to the floor, but in that case the bill will require a two-thirds majority. Almost nobody wants to take a chance on a two-thirds vote, which is why just about every piece of legislation goes through Rules.

When Sam Rayburn put me on that committee, I was the junior man out of eight Democrats. Congress moved so slowly in those days that eighteen years later I had advanced only three notches.

During my first few terms on the Rules Committee I kept my ears open and my mouth shut. Back then, committee members spoke in order of seniority, so by the time they got to me, everybody wanted to get the hell out of there.

Of course I wasn't the only member of Congress in this situation. Bill Bates, a close friend of mine and a Republican from Massachusetts, was serving on the Armed Services Committee. Old Carl Vincent was the chairman, and Bill used to complain to me about how Vincent would monopolize two or three hours of the committee's time before he finally turned things over to the ranking Republican.

One day, when Bill finally got to ask a question, Vincent said to him, "Are you a new man on this committee?" Bill had been there for *twelve years*, but the old man conducted the hearings as he pleased. He wasn't even aware of the other members. It was situations like this that later prompted the House to institute a new system, allowing each committee member five minutes of questions on a rotating basis.

Looking back, I can see that serving on the Rules Committee was an important key to my future power in the House. Most of my fellow members of Congress were on committees that specialized in one particular area. But as a member of the Rules Committee, I had a general knowledge of every piece of legislation that came down the pike. I also came into contact with almost every member of the House, because no matter what kind of legislation was being considered, both its advocates and its opponents would come to us to make their arguments.

For this reason, the Rules Committee turned out to be an excellent spot from which to follow the various activities in Congress—as well as to observe many of my colleagues. I soon learned who was sharp, who had leadership ability, and who didn't bother to do his homework. For a lover of politics like me, being on the Rules Committee was like having a seat at the fifty-yard line.

I already had a knack for following legislation, and before long I had earned a reputation for knowing what was going on. Within a couple of years, my fellow members started calling me to ask what was coming up next week on the floor of the House. My reputation was enhanced when Tommy Dodd (the father of Senator Christopher Dodd of Connecticut) told people at the University Club that Tip O'Neill knew more about what was going on in Congress than any of the other junior members.

Once that got around, my phone was always ringing. "Tip, what's coming up next week? Will there be any roll calls? How will it affect my area? Is it a vote I can miss?" If a fellow missed an important vote, it would hurt him in the next election because his opponent was sure to bring it up. It didn't always matter *how* you voted, so long as you didn't miss the big ones. And I could spot the big ones a mile away.

Every Friday, I'd hear from members who wanted to know whether I thought they had to be back on Monday, or whether they could afford to stay home until Tuesday. Back then, we didn't yet have an effective whip organization to give out this kind of information, so I became a kind of informal whip to many of my colleagues.

There were twelve of us on the Rules Committee, but I guess I was more approachable than some of my fellow members. Dick Bolling of Missouri was a notch above me in seniority, but he and I were completely different types. I used to coach some of the witnesses, and I'd give people a break whenever I could, especially if my colleagues were being tough on them.

Dick, however, was often mean and impatient—as he'd be the first to admit. Whenever a witness couldn't answer one of his questions, Dick would go through the ceiling. He'd crush the guy and send him back to his own committee to study the bill further. In most cases, Dick had good reason to be disappointed. But in my view there was nothing to be gained by embarrassing people.

And yet Dick Bolling had more talent and brains than any other member I've ever served with. He was a real student of the House, and he very much wanted to be in the leadership. Eventually he became chairman of the Rules Committee, but he had always hoped to be Speaker. He had more than enough talent for that job, but he didn't relate well enough to other people and didn't show much patience for the "trivial" details of legislation. Dick Bolling was interested in depth, and nothing else mattered.

On paper, the Rules Committee consisted of eight Democrats and four Republicans. But Howard Smith, the chairman, and Bill Colmer, the number-two man, always voted with the Republicans. As a result, most votes would be tied at six apiece. When that happened, the Democratic-sponsored legislation wouldn't get out of committee. During the Eisenhower years, of course, that suited the administration just fine.

When he became chairman, Judge Howard Smith of Virginia had already served on the Rules Committee for twenty years. Smith was a taciturn man who used to wear rimless glasses and an old-fashioned wing collar. He was also an arrogant son of a bitch, and an ultraconservative who was no more a Democrat than the man in the moon.

As far as he was concerned, the Civil War was still going on. He even lived in the home where his mother had grown up in the 1860s. He had been educated in a military academy, and he came from the same district as Robert E. Lee. Smith had once been a supporter of FDR, but like many southerners, he abandoned the president when the New Deal came along.

Congress in those days was dominated by a handful of old, conservative committee chairmen from the South, and Judge Smith was the most powerful of them all. He did whatever he could to prevent the passage of liberal legislation. When it came to civil rights, which he especially hated, he once held something like sixty-seven days of hearings, which amounted to nothing more than a House version of a Senate filibuster.

There were times when he actually refused to schedule a hearing. Under the rules, if three members on the committee filed a petition, the chairman would be forced to schedule a hearing within ten days. On several occasions, Dick Bolling, Ray Madden, and I were forced to resort to this tactic. At other times, to get around Smith, the Democratic leadership would get its legislation passed first in the Senate before sending it on to the House. Thanks to Smith and Colmer, who always supported the interests of big business, a tremendous amount of progressive legislation simply never made it to the floor of the House.

Once in a while, to prevent the committee from meeting, Judge Smith would actually disappear. On more than one occasion he went back to Virginia, because, he said, it was time to milk the cows. He once left Washington after announcing that one of his barns had burned down. This prompted Sam Rayburn to say that while he knew that Judge Smith would do almost anything to block a civil rights bill, he had always assumed that the chairman would draw the line at arson.

Incidentally, Howard Smith was not the first chairman of the Rules Committee to exhibit such an attitude. In the 1920s, the chairman had been Philip Campbell of Kansas, who once told the House, "You can go to hell. It makes no difference what a majority of you decide. If it meets with my disapproval, it shall not be done. I am the committee. In me reposes absolute obstructive powers." I imagine that old Judge Smith found a lot to admire in those words.

Adolph Sabath, who served as chairman before Smith, had once faked a heart attack to prevent another member from diminishing *his* powers. I never knew Sabath, who died shortly before I came into the House. But I do know a marvelous story about the member who took his place.

When Al Sabath died, they held a special election in Chicago to replace him. Jim Bowler, who succeeded him, was eighty-six years old. When he came in, Eddie Boland went over and introduced himself. "Mr. Bowler," he said, "let me ask you something. Why did you want to come to Congress at the age of eighty-six?"

"I'll tell you," he said. "Fifty-two years ago, when I was just a young fellow, I served on the city council with Al Sabath. When a seat opened up in Congress, we took a vote to see which one of us would run. I received ten votes, and so did Al. We must have gone through twenty ballots, but it was still tied. Finally, we decided to flip a coin. The man who won would go to Congress, and the man who lost would take his place when he was done.

"Al Sabath won the toss. He came to Congress and stayed for fifty-two years. I've been on the city council all that time, and now that Al's dead, I figured it was my turn."

That was how the oldest freshman in the history of Congress ended up in the House of Representatives. It could only happen in Chicago.

7

★★★★★

Getting Along in Washington

"IF you want to get along, go along." As a newcomer on the Washington scene, I made sure to follow Sam Rayburn's excellent advice. During the 1950s and well into the sixties, I didn't even attempt to become a power in the House. Until 1958, as I've already explained, I still planned to return to Massachusetts. But even after I decided to remain in Washington, it was clear that in a system based on seniority, any interest I had in being part of the congressional leadership would have to be put on hold for a long time.

As a result, many of my recollections from the 1950s, in particular, have more to do with the personal side of life in Washington than with my role in national politics or legislation. Naturally, I continued to concentrate on public service, and my Boston office soon developed a reputation for being able to accomplish the impossible. For one thing, I had an excellent staff. For another, after my staff had completed the legwork, I would always pick up the phone to make the necessary follow-up calls. As a result, people from all over Massachusetts started appealing to my office for help.

During the first week of 1953, when I was sworn in as a member of the Eighty-third Congress, my family and many of my friends came down for the ceremony. My father hadn't been feeling well, but he wouldn't have missed this event for the world. We showed the older kids around town, and Jack Kennedy, now a newly elected senator, took them for a ride on the old Senate subway—an event they still remember.

Then, as now, the swearing-in of new members was conducted twice—once on the floor of the House, and later in the day in the

Speaker's office, where there is a mock swearing-in for the benefit of family, friends, and the media.

After the Republican sweep of 1952, the Speaker was Joe Martin. (Rayburn would become Speaker again in 1955, and would retain the position until his death in 1961.) So it was Martin who asked the new members to stand in the well of the House and to raise their right hand.

"Do you solemnly swear that you will support and defend the Constitution of the United States against all enemies, foreign and domestic; that you will bear true faith and allegiance to the same; that you take this obligation freely, without mental reservation or purpose of evasion, and that you will well and faithfully discharge the duties of the office on which you are about to enter, so help you God?"

"I do."

Millie and I had already decided that I would live in Washington and come back to Cambridge every weekend. Cambridge was our real home, and I didn't expect to be away for more than a few years. Every Saturday, I would walk the streets of my old neighborhood, stopping off at the deli, the supermarket, the barbershop, the shoe-maker's, and a dozen other places. Invariably, I'd come back to the house with a pocketful of messages and requests from all the people who had stopped me along the way.

Looking back on my career after fifty years in public life, there's not much I would do differently. But one mistake is all too clear. When I moved to Washington, I never should have left my family behind in Cambridge.

The saddest thing in my life is that I wasn't around for my children while they were growing up. When Kip fell out of a tree and broke his ankle, I was down in Washington. When Susan was in a car accident, I was five hundred miles away. When Rosemary and a group of her high school friends went to see Rock Hudson at a radio station in Brighton, and a car ran over her foot, I wasn't around. Almost every time there was a problem, I wasn't home to deal with it.

As a result, Millie had to play the role of both parents. It was she who brought up the kids and ran the household and made the decisions as to what we could and could not afford to buy. She has always been the Speaker in our house.

In my absence, Millie brought the kids up as good Democrats. We used to rent a summer cottage in Plymouth, on the beach. When my son Kip was four, he used to run down to the water yelling, "Last one in is a Republican!"

But I know it wasn't easy for Millie. When Tommy was young, one of the nuns at school asked him what he wanted to be when he grew up. "Do you want to be in politics like your father?" she asked.

"Yes," he replied. "But I'll have to wait until my mother dies."

"Whatever makes you say that?"

"Because whenever I tell Mommy that I want to run for Congress, she always says, 'Over my dead body!' "

But years later, when Tommy ran for lieutenant governor, Millie was just marvelous. She helped him so much, in fact, that I became jealous. "Honey," I said to her, "you go here and there and everywhere for that boy, but you wouldn't cross the street to make me president of the United States."

To which Millie replied, "Tom, after thirty-five years of living with you, why should I?"

Politics can be a very lonely life. I loved being in Congress, but during my first few months in Washington I was miserably unhappy. There's a terrible sadness when you walk away from your family, especially when the children are young and you're as close and as tight as we were. I was like a guy who goes into the Navy and is sent to boot camp, where he sits on his cot and begins to cry. That's what it was like for me. I was so goddamn lonesome it was unbelievable. On the weekends I just couldn't get home fast enough.

But it doesn't have to be that way. In 1977, when I became Speaker of the House, I used to meet with the freshman class at the start of each new Congress. In every case, I urged them to move their families to Washington as soon as possible.

"Don't make the mistake I did," I said. "After all, family is what America is all about. It's what *life* is all about. If you're separated from your family, a part of you will always be empty. And don't assume that you'll be able to make it up on weekends, because you won't. When you return to the district you'll have a thousand obligations in connection with your office—not to mention your reelection campaign."

It was good advice, and my only regret is that nobody gave me the same counsel when I came to Washington. On the other hand, I don't know what I could have done about it. When I was first elected to Congress, the salary was $12,500, with another $2,500 in travel expenses. With that kind of money, even in 1953, I couldn't possibly have afforded the payments on two homes.

I used to come back to Boston every Thursday night and return to Washington on Monday. Until 1978, when the kids were all grown and Millie moved down, I don't think I spent more than four straight nights in Washington in twenty-five years.

One night, when the train pulled in to Washington I was fast asleep. When I finally woke up, we were already in the switching yard. I stumbled out and ran into a watchman, who wanted to know what the hell I was doing there. When he noticed my suitcase, he just shook his head and pointed me in the right direction. It was a long, exhausting hike back to civilization.

But usually I would drive, together with Jimmy Burke, Harold Donohue, and Phil Philbin, all Democratic congressmen from the Boston area. We would go in Phil's Cadillac, or more often in Jimmy's little Lark, leaving around five, right after the Thursday session and arriving in Boston around three on Friday morning after ten hours of gabbing about politics and sports. Phil was a great talker who had served in the House for years. Later on, he was defeated by Father Robert Drinan because he didn't take a strong enough position against the Vietnam War.

Eventually, I started flying both ways. But in the 1950s there were still no nonstop flights between Boston and Washington, which meant that you had to fly to either Newark or La Guardia and sit around for an hour or two. One day in 1956 a fellow got on the plane in New York and sat beside me with a copy of *The Racing Form.* Neither of us said a word. I was engrossed in my mail and the *Congressional Record,* while he never looked up from his paper.

Later that day I was on the floor of the House, and who did I see but the same guy who had sat next to me on the flight. I went over to Jim Delaney from New York and asked him who it was.

"That's Charlie Buckley," he said. I knew the name because Buckley was chairman of the Public Works Committee. He was also known as a power in New York, and the last of the Tammany Hall crowd. According to Jim, he never came to Washington unless they needed him for an important vote. I learned later that Buckley owned several racehorses, which would explain his interest in *The Racing Form.*

I thought I knew every Democrat in the House, but I had never seen Buckley before. Otherwise, I knew just about every member on our side of the aisle, and many of the Republicans, too. My pal and roommate, Eddie Boland, made it a point to know *everybody* in the House, even though Eddie wasn't gregarious or a party-goer.

The other fellow who knew them all was Sparky Matsunaga from Hawaii, who later became a senator. One day I asked him how he did it.

"You know how all of us Japanese look alike to you?" he said. "I have the same problem with you people, so I always make sure to look for some distinguishing feature. You're easy, Tip, because of your gray hair and your bulbous nose. Eddie Boland's got the solid black hair. Somebody else has a mole on the side of his face. I pick out the special features, and that's how I tell them apart."

You can grow accustomed to just about anything, but I never really got used to the traveling. Every week was a struggle, as I had to decide whether to go back on Monday or stay over one more day. On a good week, I could have supper with my family four nights in a row.

In large measure, my schedule was determined by when we had a roll call. We rarely had any on Fridays, and in general we didn't have as many votes as they do now. In the old days, the members wouldn't have stood for it, because each roll call would waste at least half an hour of everybody's time. Today, of course, it's all done electronically.

But the family was always together during the annual Easter break, when we'd all go down to Daytona Beach, Florida, for the annual congressional baseball game between the Democrats and the Republicans. It was a long drive with the children, but you couldn't beat the price because the chamber of commerce paid all our expenses. Besides, the Democrats always won, so it was a special pleasure to drive down there.

In those days, nobody had ever heard of Daytona Beach, so the local merchants sponsored the congressional baseball game to get their town known around the country. They picked up the tab for everything—motels, meals, even gas for the cars. The only catch was that each family had to pose for a picture, which they would send to our local newspapers. It was a brilliant idea and a huge success.

The Cleveland Indians had their spring training camp in Daytona Beach, and we used to play our game on their field. Everyone in town would come to see us. I played first base, alternating with Eugene McCarthy, one of the stars of our team. Bill Natcher from Kentucky could really pound the ball, and he once won a watch for hitting one over the fence. Eddie Boland was our shortstop, and we had a pitcher named Fireball Wheeler from Georgia who used to mow them down.

The first time I met Fireball Wheeler was at a cocktail party the night before the game, when he came up to Millie and me and said, "I understand you folks are Catholics. You know, we don't have a single Catholic in my district. But I know a number of them in Congress and they seem like nice people."

"I'm sure they are," I muttered.

These days, the annual congressional baseball game is played in Washington. Sil Conte is the manager of the Republicans, and they've been winning every year. But enough about that. Let's move on to more pleasant topics—like Eddie Boland.

Now that I was a member of Congress, I needed a cheap place to live. I wasn't the only one with that problem, so I teamed up with Eddie Boland, my old state house pal, and we found ourselves an efficiency apartment at 1500 Massachusetts Avenue, Northwest. We slept on a couple of couches and paid a total of sixty-seven dollars a month in rent.

In housing, as in almost everything else, you get what you pay for. The place was ridiculously small, and a few months later we traded up to a one-bedroom apartment in the same building. The rent zoomed up to eighty-seven dollars, but this time our little palace included a living room and a kitchen. Eddie was a bachelor, and he brought down all the home furnishings he owned—a toaster and a coffee pot. Millie helped us out with linens and towels. She also brought us down some dishes and silverware, but I don't recall ever using them.

People used to say that Eddie and I were the original Odd Couple, and there's a lot of truth to that. Eddie was a natty dresser, whereas I've always been on the sloppy side. I'm outgoing and gregarious, while Eddie wouldn't cross the street to go to a party. Eddie is meticulous, neat as a pin; he'd always do the laundry and keep the place clean. I'd come home at night and throw my coat on the bed, and before I turned around Eddie would hang it in the closet. I'd return from a weekend in Cambridge and Eddie would have given the place a spring cleaning.

He would rise at six-thirty and run off to an early mass. An hour later he'd be back, hollering, "All right, big boy. Let's get going." While I was getting dressed, Eddie would make the coffee and pour the orange juice. Then we'd drive to the Capitol for a real breakfast in the House dining room.

As different as we were on the surface, we had a lot in common. We're the same age, we're both Irish Catholics, we had both served in the Massachusetts legislature, and we were both elected to Congress in 1952. We shared a passion for sports, and we spent a number of evenings going to basketball games at Georgetown University or watching the old Washington Senators in Griffith Stadium. We're also great friends, and in the twenty-five years that we lived together, I can't remember a single fight.

The O'Neill-Boland residence was a strange kind of home because we never once cooked a meal there. Even so, we had a lot of visitors, and whenever anyone from Barry's Corner came to town, I invited him to stay on our couch.

One time, while I was back in Boston, I let a fellow from Cambridge sleep in my bed for a week. When I came back, I found that Eddie had moved into the Drake Hotel because our visitor snored so loudly that he couldn't get any sleep. Fortunately, as a member of Congress, Eddie qualified for the special congressional rate of three dollars a night.

"Why didn't you ask him to leave?" I said.

But I already knew the answer. Eddie Boland just couldn't bring himself to inconvenience a guest.

Once, during the Christmas break, Eddie lent the apartment to a couple of ladies from his district in Springfield. When we came back in January we noticed a strange smell that we couldn't identify. We opened the windows, sprayed the place with Lysol, and checked the refrigerator—with no success. Finally, we opened the oven door and found a decomposing turkey that the ladies had left there several weeks earlier. Now, until this incident, we hadn't realized that we even *had* an oven. As for our refrigerator, that underused appliance was the butt of a lot of jokes among our friends because we never kept any food there. The only four items ever seen in that fridge were orange juice, diet soda, beer, and cigars.

Incidentally, I'm absolutely convinced that one of the secrets behind my eventual rise to power is that I ate in restaurants every night with my friends and colleagues from the House. My usual hangouts were Duke Zeibert's on Connecticut Avenue near the Mayflower Hotel, or Paul Young's, or Hunt's, a popular fish place.

Duke's was my favorite because it attracted a sports crowd and the ballplayers ate there. I got to know Vince Lombardi at Duke's, and Joe Cronin, president of the American League. When Joe Dimaggio was in town, he'd come by too.

Eddie and I stayed in that little apartment for ten years, until the day somebody broke one of our windows while we were away. When we got home, the landlord tried to charge us fifty bucks to repair it, which was an outrage. Eddie went down to see him. "We didn't break that window and we're not paying for it," he said.

"Then I'll take you to court," said the landlord.

Eddie replied, "If that's how you feel about it, we're moving out!"

Eddie didn't really mean it, and he certainly didn't say anything to me about moving. I got wind of it a few days later when I ran into Mike Macdonald, a friend of ours who for years had been wanting to move into our building.

"So you're finally leaving," he said.

"What are you talking about?" I asked.

"That's funny," he said. "They called me over to show me an apartment, and it turned out to be yours."

Eddie contacted the landlord, but by then it was too late. We moved into a place on 17th Street, but the neighborhood was so bad that in the few months we were there our apartment was broken into three times. Finally, we found a good building at 2601 Woodley Place and stayed there for fourteen years until 1978, when Millie and I moved into a condominium in Maryland.

For years, Eddie was one of the most eligible bachelors in town, and I just assumed that he would stay that way forever. But in June of 1973, I was at our summer house on Cape Cod when he called and asked to speak to Millie.

"You've always said there was a spot for me," he said. "Can I come down this weekend?"

"Sure," said Millie. "We'd love to have you." By that time, of course, Eddie had long been part of our family.

"If it's all right with you," he said, "I'd like to bring Mary Egan with me."

"That will be fine," said Millie.

When she got off the phone, Millie said, "Eddie is coming up for the weekend with Mary Egan. Who's Mary Egan?"

"I never heard of her," I said. "She must be somebody he's dating."

That Saturday night we had a big cookout on the patio. I took Eddie aside and said, "Listen, pal. Tomorrow the kids are going back to the city and the place will be quiet again. Why don't you and I take the rest of the week off, play a little golf, and do some fishing?"

"I can't," said Eddie. "We have to go back tomorrow afternoon." Then he got up and said, "Ladies and gentlemen, I'd like to make an announcement. Mary and I are leaving tomorrow afternoon to go back to Springfield. And Monday morning, on the Fourth of July, on the steps of city hall, I'm holding a press conference to tell the world that we're getting married during the second week of August. We wanted to come down here first because I didn't want my good friends Millie and Tip to read about it in the papers."

What a shock! I didn't even know Eddie had a girlfriend. He was sixty-one at the time, and today they have four wonderful children. Any day now, my pal will be the oldest third-base coach in Little League history.

There was a certain poetic justice to the fact that Eddie first announced his wedding on Cape Cod, because back in 1958, the two of us had filed legislation to create the Cape Cod National Seashore, which came into existence a few years later.

It all began one spring Monday when I returned from a weekend on the Cape and found that Eddie had just come back from the

dedication of the Cape Hatteras National Seashore in North Carolina, a seventy-mile seashore park. He couldn't stop telling me how
beautiful it was.

"It sounds marvelous," I said. "I wish I could say the same about
Cape Cod, but it's going honky-tonk. All I see are more hamburger
joints and motels." I wasn't yet a homeowner on the Cape, but I
loved the place and was upset by the direction in which it was
moving.

"You know," he said, "you and I ought to file a bill to do for Cape
Cod what they've done for Cape Hatteras." A few weeks later, we
introduced a bill to create a thirty-three-mile national park along the
outer beach of Cape Cod, from the middle of the Cape's arm in
Chatham, and up through Orleans, Eastham, Wellfleet, Truro, and
Provincetown.

Understandably, we ran into strong opposition from Cape Cod
residents who were afraid our plan would hurt the local economy
by removing taxable real estate. And property owners in the area
under discussion were not thrilled about the provisions in the bill
that would limit future building and development and would eventually allow the government to buy up their land.

Local feelings ran so strong against the plan that Eddie and I were
booed out of the town hall in Eastham and were hung in effigy in
Truro. We also ran into some heated opposition from Donald Nich-
olson, the congressman who represented the Cape. We had the
support of Senator Leverett Saltonstall, who filed a similar bill in the
Senate. But his colleague Jack Kennedy, deferring to the wishes of
the Cape residents, initially opposed it.

To anyone who would listen, we pointed out that our plan would
preserve the beauty of the Cape and would increase tourism. The
magnificent thirty-three miles of unbroken beach was one of the
great marvels of this country, and it would be criminal not to protect
it from commercial development. At that time, there were not more
than twenty-six miles of public beach in all of Massachusetts. And
although nobody talked much about ecology and the environment
in those days, we also pointed out that the area we wanted to save
included moors, marshes, forests, and freshwater ponds—home to
many species of birds, fish, animals, and plants.

Several years later, when Kennedy was president, he came out in favor of the project, and in 1964 the Cape Cod National Seashore was dedicated. Eddie and I went down for the ceremony and were seated in the front row. I'll never forget the woman who came up to us to thank us for all we had done. "You two were the original sponsors of this legislation," she said. "You ought to be up there on the platform. I remember the meeting in our town, where the vote was a hundred and seven to three against the plan. My parents and I were the only ones to vote for it, and nobody spoke to us for years. Today, everybody wants to share the honor."

I smiled. A few years earlier, I had heard a terrific piece of advice from Sam Rayburn, who said, "There's no limit to the amount of good you can accomplish if you're willing to let somebody else take the credit." That's much easier said than done, but I've always tried to keep it in mind. For example, during my thirty-four years in the House, I never issued a public statement or a press release taking credit for bringing government money into my district or into the city of Boston.

I can't leave the subject of Eddie Boland without mentioning the day we met J. Edgar Hoover. One afternoon in 1954, when the House was not in session, Eddie and I went to the track. We soon ran into Luke Quinn, a former air force colonel who was now in public relations, who invited us to sit up in his box. Between races, he introduced us to J. Edgar Hoover and Clyde Tolson, Hoover's top deputy. We had gone out by bus, and after the last race Hoover offered us a ride back to town. Hoover and Tolson rode in the front, and Eddie and I sat in back. Hoover drove straight to Harvey's Restaurant, where he ate every Tuesday and Thursday.

But when we arrived at Harvey's, Hoover realized that he had driven somebody else's car home from the races! This one was a late-model Buick, just like his own, and the keys had been left in the ignition. I always got a kick out of knowing that the head of the FBI was technically guilty of car theft.

I hadn't been in Washington very long before I met two presidents—Harry Truman and Dwight Eisenhower. When I first came to Congress, there was a three-week interval between the swearing-in of the new members and the inauguration of President Eisenhower. There weren't many freshman Democrats that year—the

Eisenhower sweep had taken care of that—but the sixteen or so of us who did make it to Washington were all invited to the White House for a special welcome breakfast with President Truman.

What I remember most about that morning was the intensity of Truman's dislike for his successor. At the same time, he felt very protective toward the new first lady. "Let me tell you something," he said. "Some of the newspapers are making snide remarks about Mrs. Eisenhower, saying she has a drinking problem. Now it wouldn't surprise me if she did, because look what that poor woman has had to put up with. She's married to a no-good son of a bitch.

"Don't forget," he continued, "this is the guy who in 1945 wrote a letter home to General George C. Marshall asking if it would hurt his military career if he divorced Mamie and married Kay Summersby." (Kay Summersby was Eisenhower's chauffeur in Europe.) "I've got no use for the man and I don't give a damn what you say about him."

(Twenty years after that breakfast, the story about Eisenhower's letter home surfaced in *Plain Speaking*, Merle Miller's oral history of Truman. But other than Truman's contention, there is no evidence that the letter ever existed.)

"But leave his family alone," the president continued, his voice rising. "If I ever hear that one of you attacked the wife or a family member of the president of the United States, I'll personally go into your district and campaign against you." Truman may have been a lame duck, but he was still fighting the good fight.

I've always followed Truman's advice, and the one time I slipped up there was hell to pay. It happened thirty years later, when I was Speaker, Reagan was president, and James Reston from the *Times* came in to interview me. When I started out in politics, nobody allowed reporters to tape them, and until recently that was always my policy. But Reston had arthritis in his hand and couldn't write easily, so for him I made an exception.

Early in our conversation, he asked me about Nancy Reagan. I didn't realize that his machine was running, and I made a facetious remark to the effect that when the Reagans were through—which I hoped would be in 1984—they could return to California, where Nancy could be the queen of Beverly Hills.

I didn't mean anything by it, and I certainly hadn't said it for attribution. The next day, when the quote appeared in Reston's column, I felt just terrible. I sent a letter of apology to Mrs. Reagan, but by then the damage had been done. To this day I feel bad about it.

Not long after our meeting with Truman, I met President Eisenhower and inadvertently caused a little trouble at the White House. Every couple of weeks, the administration would invite a group of first-term congressmen from both parties to a luncheon with the president. My invitation came in late February, for a Friday during Lent. A funny thing about that lunch was that we were told in advance not to ask any questions about the administration's policies. You could talk to the president about golf, about World War II, about almost anything. But legislation was off limits.

Now with every other president I've known, if you went to the White House for lunch, it was generally for the specific purpose of discussing upcoming legislation. Even if you were there on a social visit, you usually ended up talking politics. But with Eisenhower it was different.

We all sat around a big table, together with several of the president's aides. When lunch was served, a waiter brought me a filet mignon the size of my arm.

"I'm sorry," I told him, "but I'm Catholic and I don't eat meat on Fridays." Whereupon he took the steak away and replaced it with half a can of salmon.

While we ate, the president talked golf, which was fine with me because I've always loved the game. And whatever you think of his record as president, Dwight Eisenhower did more for the game of golf in this country than any other individual except Arnold Palmer and Jack Nicklaus.

He also enjoyed hunting and had recently killed some kind of rare animal. During the lunch, one of his aides claimed that they had to tie the animal to a tree so that Ike could shoot it. The president laughed and swore it wasn't true. After coffee and dessert we were taken on a tour of the White House and introduced to the first lady, who was very lovely and gracious.

A few days later I ran into Maxwell Rabb in the lobby of the Mayflower Hotel. Max had been a lobbyist in Boston and was now in Washington as secretary of the Cabinet. (He's currently our ambassador to Italy.)

"Tip," he said, "I noticed you had lunch with the president the other day. I wanted to come over and say hello, but I was too busy. How did everything go?"

I was in a jovial mood, so I started kidding with him. "Max, let me tell you, I was never so humiliated in my life. Here I am, Tip O'Neill, an Irish Catholic and everybody knows it, and they're serving me a steak on a Friday during Lent! Of course I had to send it back."

"I can't believe it," he said. "Did you tell anyone?"

"Well, I happened to run into Cardinal Cushing, but other than him I didn't tell a soul." I was only kidding about the cardinal, of course, but when the line occurred to me it was irresistible.

I didn't give the matter any further thought, but apparently Max Rabb did. The following day, I was on the floor of the House when one of the congressional pages came running down the aisle to find me. "Mr. O'Neill," he said breathlessly, "the White House is on the phone."

The White House! I was sitting with a group of other freshman members and they couldn't believe it. How did Tip O'Neill suddenly get to be important enough to be receiving a call from the White House?

On the line was General Homer Gunther from the White House staff. "Mr. O'Neill," he said, "the president has asked me to call you personally and apologize for having served you meat last Friday. He wants you to know that from now on, whenever there's a Friday lunch or dinner at the White House, the guests will be given their choice of meat or fish."

I suppose that means that Max Rabb and I can take credit for putting fish on the White House table eight years before the Kennedys came along.

I was soon at the White House yet again, when a group of congressmen, including Eddie and me, were invited to a confidential briefing on the Korean conflict. At that time, there were seven troop divisions at the front: one from the UN, two from the Republic of Korea, and four of our own. During the briefing, the president told us there wouldn't be peace in the region until he could withdraw the American forces and replace them with Korean divisions. I still remember how excited we were to be hearing this secret, inside report directly from the commander in chief.

The very next day, I came across a story in one of the Washington papers that included a word-by-word account of everything that was said at the briefing. I couldn't believe my eyes. I went over to Mike Kirwan, the veteran member from Ohio, and said, "How can this be? Yesterday I attended a confidential briefing and today the entire thing is in the newspaper."

"Let me tell you something," said Mike. "Don't ever go to a confidential briefing again, because whatever they tell you is always leaked. If you were there, you'll always be a suspect, and then you'll have the FBI on your tail."

Mike was a real operator in the House, and was chairman of the Subcommittee on Public Works of the House Appropriations Committee. He had so much power! At one point, during the building of the Cape Cod National Seashore, Mike cut three million dollars from our project, although he had promised me personally that he would leave it in. I called him on the telephone. "Mike, you knocked out three million for Cape Cod."

"You're damn right I did," he said. "It's a waste of money and we've got better things to do."

"Hold on, Mike. We were having dinner at Paul Young's and you gave me your word that you'd put that money back in."

"Well, you're a nice son of a bitch, taking advantage of me when I was half-stewed. But if that's really what I said, I'll put it back in." And he did.

Another reason Mike was powerful was that he served as head of the Democratic Congressional Campaign Committee, which meant that he traveled around the country raising money to elect Democrats to Congress—a position I took over after his death in 1970. Mike was out in California one day when he ran into Jimmy Roosevelt, a congressman from that area and the son of Franklin Delano Roosevelt.

Mike said, "Jim, we're having a fund-raiser here tomorrow night. I'm being honored for all the money I've raised in California, and I look forward to seeing you and some of your friends."

"I'm sorry," said Jimmy, "but I won't be in the district tomorrow. I have a commitment back in Washington."

"Gee, that's too bad," said Mike Kirwan. "By the way, will you still be appearing before my committee next week about that river you want dredged?"

"Oh, yes, I'll be there."

"Fine," said Mike. "Now where did you say you'd be tomorrow night?"

Jimmy was no fool. "Looks like I'll be at your party, Mike."

Years earlier, Mike had wanted to live at the University Club. But membership was restricted to college graduates, and Mike was a former coal miner without much education. One of his colleagues advised him to tell the applications committee that he was a graduate of the University of Heidelberg. This was deemed to be an excellent school to have graduated from, as all its records had been destroyed in the war.

Mike filed the application, the University Club wrote to Heidelberg, and lo and behold, all the records had been destroyed. Naturally, the committee had to accept Mike's word, because everyone knew that an applicant to the University Club would never tell a lie. And that's how Mike became a member. He always got a special kick out of being a "graduate" of Heidelberg because as an eight-year-old kid he had picked coal at the Heidelberg coal mines in Pennsylvania.

Mike was first elected to Congress during the Depression, when he was laid off his job at a steel mill. Until then his district had always been Republican, but the Depression had a profound effect on people. During the campaign, Mike's Republican opponent talked about how, if elected, he would go to Washington to tell the president what ought to be done.

Then Mike got up and said, "Like almost everybody else here, I'm out of a job. The reason I'm running for Congress is that I need the money. But I'm certainly not going down there to tell the president what to do. My opponent has a lot of nerve. I'm going down there to *help* the president on everything he asks for, because I know he cares about people like us." According to Mike Kirwan, that was enough to get him elected.

Mike used to love to tell the story of the time he was accused of election fraud by the Republicans in his district. He always swore it was a phony charge, but even so, the case went before a jury in Cleveland.

On a Friday, when the arguments were finished, Mike came home to Youngstown. The jury was due to render its decision the following week, and Mike had nothing left to do but wait for the verdict.

Finally, after hiding his face for weeks, he decided that he wasn't going to run from people anymore. That night, Mike Kirwan walked into the main dining room of the biggest hotel in town. As he sat down, he could see that everybody was looking at him. Evidently, people recognized his face from the newspapers.

I'll let Mike finish the story. "So the waiter comes over to me and he says, 'How you feeling, boss?'

" 'Not so good. You probably know my problems.'

" 'Boss,' says the waiter, 'you ain't *got* no problems.'

"I ate dinner, figuring that maybe the waiter didn't know who I was. But when he brought the check, he said again, 'Don't look so worried, boss. I told you, you ain't got no problems.'

" 'That's easy for you to say, but I'm in big trouble and the jury's still out.'

" 'Like I said, boss, you ain't got no problems. You know why? Cause I'm on that jury!' "

Mike used to tell that story at Paul Young's restaurant. "That waiter brought me the greatest news I ever had," said Mike. "I put him to work in my office and he stayed there until the day he died."

It was Mike Kirwan who introduced me to one of the sharpest men in Congress—not a member, but a doorkeeper. "See that tall fellow over there?" Mike said to me one day. "That's Jim Rowan. I go up to him every year and ask, 'How's the talent in the freshman class?' And he always tells me who looks good, and which ones won't be back. He's almost always right."

I made a point of getting to know Rowan myself, and a few months after the next election, I asked him how the new boys looked this year.

"Well," he said, "there are four fellows out there who won't be coming back."

"What makes you say that?" I asked.

"They're just down here and still wet behind the ears. They don't know what it's all about, but by God, they think they're experts on everything. Now the way I figure it, if they act this way in front of their fellow members who are the *real* experts, imagine what they must be like back home. They must be insufferable! Just about every time I see a young man come in here who thinks he knows more than his colleagues, he gets licked."

I had come to know Mike Kirwan because we were both part of a group that played poker every Wednesday night at the University Club. Those card games were a great way to meet some of my colleagues and to learn what was going on in their districts all over the country. On any given night, there would be two or three dozen congressmen, a handful of senators, and several former members eating together in a private room. After dinner, we told stories and played cards. As many as seventy-five men would play during the course of the year, and over the months I got to know them all, Democrats and Republicans alike. There were no parties and no factions in that room. There was only fellowship.

Politicians don't play cards much anymore, but in my time many successful pols were also good poker players. Maybe that's because poker and politics require some of the same skills. In each case, you need to understand the people you're playing with, as well as how to count and how to calculate the odds. Certainly, you need to know how to bluff. And it also helps enormously if you know when to bet, when to fold, and when to sit tight.

Now I don't want to stretch this analogy too far, however, because cards and politics don't always go together. Take Richard Nixon, for example. He had a very fine grasp of politics but was just miserable at poker.

Nixon had been part of the Wednesday night group for several years before I came in, and as vice president, he would sometimes join us. He thought of himself as a good poker player, but he talked too much and didn't follow the cards. Moreover, he used to take advantage of the fact that he was the highest-ranking person at the game by asking the other players how many cards they had drawn. That used to annoy me, and I would call him on it. "We're playing poker here," I'd say, "and we're playing for money. If you want to know how many cards I drew, pay attention to the game."

Nixon was a bright and gregarious person, but every time he lost a few bucks, which was often enough, he'd holler and complain. One night I said to him, "You know, I'm sick and tired of reading what a good poker player you are. As a matter of fact, you're one of the worst poker players I've ever seen."

"I was pretty good in the navy," he said. "But you fellows are tough."

"In the navy?" I replied. "Those were kids you were playing with. What did they know about poker?"

Years later, when Nixon became president, Millie and I attended several receptions at the White House. Invariably, the president would greet Millie with the line "Your husband is a terrific poker player."

Maybe so, I used to think, but any guy who hollers over a forty-dollar pot has no business being president.

On a Wednesday afternoon in 1959, Al Carter, a member from California, called me and said, "The vice president is coming to my place tonight, and we're having two tables. We're going to sit down at six-thirty, but he asked if you could show up a little earlier because he'd like to talk to you." I said that would be fine.

Everybody knew that Nixon wanted to run for president in 1960, and I wasn't surprised that the election was on his mind that evening. "Tip," he said, "they tell me you're quite a power in Massachusetts politics. I understand you were the first Democratic Speaker, and that you turned the state around. I figure that if you know Democratic politics, you probably know something about the Republicans, too. You see, I don't want to go to the Saltonstalls and the Adamses and the same old people. I'm looking for some new blood."

"You're wasting your time," I said. "Kennedy is going to carry Massachusetts."

"Come on," he said. "Kennedy doesn't have a chance. I'll be running against Lyndon Johnson and I'll have to go all-out to carry Massachusetts. My polls show me it should be a hell of a fight."

"You're wasting your time," I said, "but I'll be happy to give you a couple of names." I mentioned Brad Morse, the future congressman from Lowell, and one or two others. "Oh, yes," I added. "There's another guy you might look up. He's a lawyer in Boston, a sharp kid. His name is Chuck Colson."

Colson, of course, later went to jail after being convicted in the Watergate burglary. Nixon had never heard of him before that night, so I suppose I'm responsible for bringing those two together. But what stays with me is that Nixon—like so many other powerful people in Washington at that time—just couldn't imagine that Jack Kennedy would win the nomination.

Another regular at the University Club was Senator Joe McCarthy. He didn't play cards with us, but we often sat at the same table for dinner, so I got to know him a little.

McCarthy's heyday was in 1951 and 1952, before I came to town. But in 1954, as head of the Senate Subcommittee on Investigations, he was continuing to make his wild charges about the Communists who were allegedly all over Washington.

I said to him one night, "Joe, why are you doing this?"

"Jesus," he said, "I have all the evidence that these people are Communist sympathizers. They're lucky I'm not climbing over the fence after them. I'm a marine captain, you know."

I've always been opposed to witchhunts, and I hated what McCarthy was doing. Unfortunately, he had a huge following in my district—especially among the Irish. Around that time, a civic group in Charlestown asked him to speak at their annual Bunker Hill dinner, and when they didn't receive a reply, they asked me to intervene. Since I knew McCarthy, I couldn't really turn them down.

"What about that invitation from Charlestown?" I asked him.

"Oh, yes," he said. "They've got me at the Bunker Hill dinner and the parade the next day. My fee is eighteen hundred dollars. If I get the money, I'll be there. Otherwise, forget it."

I walked out of there thinking: I can't believe this guy! He's a mercenary! But I was also relieved, because I knew there was no way the people in Charlestown were going to raise eighteen hundred dollars—not even for Joe McCarthy.

In addition to the Wednesday-night card games at the University Club, there was also a regular Monday-night game in the office of John Bell Williams of Mississippi. John was a very intelligent man and a hell of a debater. He was also a war hero who had lost part of his left arm in combat. His office was up on the fifth floor of the Capitol, and because nobody else wanted to be that high up (although we did have elevators), John inherited a huge suite of rooms and a great deal of privacy.

On Monday nights, there might be two or three different games going on up in John's office, and sometimes you'd have your choice of poker or gin. For dinner we'd call over to Mike Palm's, a local restaurant, and they'd send up some steak sandwiches. The only drink that John Bell Williams ever served was bourbon and Coke, which I don't happen to care for. But then I rarely take a drink when I'm playing cards.

I really loved those Monday-night games, and I'd go up there whenever I was finished my work for the day. It was a great meeting place, even for guys who didn't play cards, because you could always just have a drink and kibitz. Your office staff always knew where you were, and if they really needed you they could just pick up the phone.

Politically, John Bell Williams and I couldn't have been further apart. I was a northern liberal, while he was a conservative Mississippi Democrat who did his best to block civil rights legislation in the House. But our political differences never caused any problems—at least, not until 1964. In that campaign, when the Republicans nominated Barry Goldwater to run against President Johnson, John Bell Williams deserted the party to support the Republican candidate.

The House Democrats retaliated by stripping Williams of his position as the number-two man on the Commerce Committee. It was a caucus vote, and although we liked John Bell Williams personally, all of the northerners voted against him. Naturally, he was bitter about it, and that was the end of the Monday-night games. Back home, however, the voters saw Williams as a hero, and they rewarded him by making him governor of Mississippi.

Compared with some of the goings on in Washington, the poker games I played in were small potatoes. But one time John McCormack invited Eddie and me over for supper at the Shoreham Hotel. This was followed by a poker game with McCormack and some of his high-rolling friends.

"I'm afraid this game is out of your league," said McCormack, who may have been the best poker player in the history of Washington. But Eddie and I already knew that any game that required five hundred dollars just to get in was well beyond our scope.

McCormack used to leave early to go home to his wife, which always resulted in an empty seat at the table. "Come on," Eddie said to me that night. "You play for both of us. We'll each put up two hundred and fifty dollars in checks."

The other players were more than happy to take our money, so

I joined them at the table. In the first hand I'm dealt two pair—aces and eights. Everybody kicks in five dollars to open. Then the first guy opens with a fifty-dollar bet and the second guy matches it. I raise him a hundred dollars. The betting continues and people start folding until only two of us are left. The other guy raises the bet by two hundred dollars and I match it. I draw one card. He stands pat.

"How much you got left?" he asks.

"A hundred and forty-five bucks."

"Throw it in," he says, and I immediately call.

Now it's time to see the cards. I turn mine over and show him two eights and two aces. He turns his over—and he's got nothing. He was bluffing! This fellow had a reputation for being tight with his money, so when he started raising the stakes, everybody else knew enough to get out. But I had never played with him before, and my ignorance saved me.

Suddenly I had over a thousand dollars in my pocket, which was a very new experience. I kept playing, and kept winning. Eddie left around one in the morning to get some sleep, and the game broke up an hour later. I drove home, and no sooner did I put the key in the door than Eddie was out of bed like a shot.

"How'd we do?" he asked.

"Let me put it this way," I said. "We've just paid our rent for the whole year."

"Terrific," he said. "So you'll go back next week?"

"Not me, pal," I said. "Not for those stakes. Do you want me to get ulcers? I love poker, but that game is a little too rich for my blood."

No description of my early years in Washington would be complete without a few words about my good friend John Harris. John worked for the Boston *Globe,* and for years he was their only full-time reporter in town. He was a great history buff, and when time allowed, we would get ourselves a couple of beers and go walking around the city, looking at the old buildings and checking out the many historical sights of Washington. Sometimes we'd trace Jefferson's route to and around Capitol Hill, or visit the spot in the old House chamber where John Quincy Adams was fatally stricken at his desk, or the place in the old Senate chamber where Daniel Webster stood as he delivered his great speeches.

One night in 1953, at around eleven o'clock, John knocked on the door. "Come on, you big bum," he said. "I know you're awake. I've got a real piece of history to show you."

"At this hour?" I said.

"Sorry," he replied, "but it might not be there tomorrow."

On the way out, John explained that he had been visiting the construction sight of the new AFL-CIO headquarters on 16th Street, where a huge steam shovel had smashed open a tunnel that ran from the old Madison Hotel, past St. John's Episcopal Church and under 16th Street to a building on the southwest corner of 16th and I.

I still didn't see what the fuss was about, but John had been talking to the night watchman at the site, who told him this was none other than Harding's Tunnel, a legendary but seldom-seen part of the city's history. Apparently, President Harding kept a mistress in a house at 16th and I, whom he used to visit on the sly. (The house was later owned by the Motion Picture Association, before they knocked it down and put up a new building.) Accompanied by his Secret Service escorts, the president would walk from the White House across Lafayette Park and into the old Madison Hotel. In those days, members of Congress used to stay at the Madison, and President Harding would tell his bodyguards to wait for him in the lobby while he went upstairs for a little poker with the boys.

But instead of going upstairs, he'd walk through the tunnel and into the home of his girlfriend.

"If I don't show you the tunnel," said John, "who's going to believe me when I write about it?"

"Fine," I said, "but can't it wait until the morning?"

"Absolutely not," said John. "Tomorrow they're building a new foundation and Harding's Tunnel will be closed off forever." We actually went down into the tunnel, which was damp and dusty, and I suppose we were the last two people to see it before it was demolished the next morning.

The following year, on March 1, 1954, John fully made up for that lost night's sleep by saving my life. He had come to the House to interview me during the debate on the St. Lawrence Seaway. He looked in, spotted me on the floor, and motioned for me to step out into the cloakroom.

As always, I was happy to give him my views. I told him that as far as I could see, the St. Lawrence Seaway would be a real disaster for New England. Right around the word "disaster," we heard several explosions on the floor of the House. "I can't believe it," I said. "Somebody's setting off firecrackers in there."

Just then Ben Jensen, a Republican from Iowa who played cards with us, stumbled through the door crying, "I've been shot!"

Without thinking, I started to run back into the House chamber. But I didn't get very far, as I ran right into a wave of members rushing to get out of there. A group of five Puerto Rican extremists in the House gallery had opened fire onto the floor.

Don Magnuson from Washington had been standing near us when the shooting began. He was on the phone to his press man back home when he looked out and said, "I think somebody's firing a gun at the Congress." Just then, a bullet passed through his sleeve. "So long," he said, "I'm getting out of here."

Although nobody was killed, several members were injured that day. Alvin Bentley, a Republican from Michigan, took a bullet in the chest. George Fallon, a Maryland Democrat, was hit, lightly, in his rear end. Kenneth Roberts, an Alabama Democrat, was shot in the leg and spent two years in a wheelchair.

The following day, when I went back inside the chamber, I noticed with horror that the seat I had been sitting in when John Harris called me out had a bullet hole through the back. If John hadn't come by that day, I might have caught a bullet right in the gut, which would have made Tip O'Neill a one-term congressman.

During my years in the House, I did a lot of favors for a lot of people. But none of them can compare with the favor John Harris did for me in 1954. I had no choice but to forgive him for dragging me down into a dusty old tunnel at an hour when sensible people were fast asleep.

8

★★★★★

President Kennedy

In 1960, when Jack Kennedy defeated Richard Nixon and won the presidency, the Democrats were ecstatic. More than a quarter of a century later, I can still feel the exhilaration and optimism that so many Americans felt when the Kennedys moved into the White House. Part of the excitement came from Jack's inaugural address, written by Ted Sorenson, which was the most stirring and eloquent political speech I had ever heard, and which thrilled us to the core:

"Let the word go forth from this time and place, to friend and foe alike, that the torch has been passed to a new generation of Americans—born in this century, tempered by war, disciplined by a hard and bitter peace. . . . Let every nation know, whether it wishes us well or ill, that we shall pay any price, bear any burden, meet any hardship, support any friend, oppose any foe, to assure the survival and success of liberty."

And then the famous lines "Let us never negotiate out of fear. But let us never fear to negotiate."

And finally, the president's direct appeal to all of us: "Ask not what your country can do for you—ask what you can do for your country."

At least part of the Kennedy vigor had to do with Jack's youth. At forty-three, he was the youngest elected president in our history. Jacqueline was even younger—thirty-one. Many of Kennedy's assistants were still in their thirties, and Robert Kennedy, the attorney general, was only thirty-five.

The administration's ideas were new, too. The Peace Corps was established during Jack's third month in office, despite the sarcastic sneers of the Republicans. There was also the Alliance for Progress, a plan to help Latin America in much the same way as the Marshall Plan had rebuilt Western Europe.

But the most visible changes had to do with style. When the Kennedys came to Washington, the whole town was aglitter. Suddenly, Democrats were wearing tuxedos. There was a new sophistication in Washington, which has never been the same since.

Jackie had a lot to do with this transformation, especially when she conducted a tour of the White House for television viewers. And it was Jackie who made the White House a cultural center—a place where Pablo Casals could perform, where ballet could be staged, where prominent writers were invited to dinner. The contrast with the Eisenhower years could not have been more striking.

And yet for all of the sparkle, and for all of Jack's tremendous personal popularity, he never had much success in getting his programs through Congress.

His legislative record might have been even weaker if Judge Howard Smith and his conservative allies on the Rules Committee had prevailed. During Eisenhower's presidency, Smith's power and the six-to-six stalemate on the Rules Committee had been frustrating for the Democratic Congress, but still bearable. With a Republican in the White House, not much progressive legislation was going to be initiated by the administration in any event.

But when Jack Kennedy came in, we suddenly had a whole new ball game. And it was clear to both Sam Rayburn and John McCormack that Kennedy's liberal legislation, which they fully supported, would never come to pass unless they could find some way to clear the road. As long as Judge Smith was tying up the Rules Committee, he was a kind of one-man veto, and only legislation that he supported reached the floor of the House. If Smith had his way, Kennedy's entire social agenda would be emasculated. Clearly, something had to be done.

But what? On the one hand, nobody likes to fool around with the rules of the Congress. On the other, it's the responsibility of the party in power to get the legislation onto the floor of the House, where it can be voted on by all the members. Unless the majority is able to rule, democracy isn't working.

To dilute the power of Howard Smith, Sam Rayburn came up

with a plan to add three new members to the Rules Committee—
two Democrats and a Republican. This way, instead of a six-to-six
stalemate, the Democrats would have an eight-to-seven advantage.
A similar tactic had been tried back in 1933, when the Democrats
expanded the Rules Committee to ensure that Roosevelt's New Deal
legislation would get out of committee and onto the floor of the
House. Ironically, the new member at that time was none other than
Judge Howard Smith of Virginia.

Despite the great power of Sam Rayburn, any move to change the
size of the Rules Committee would require the majority approval of
the entire House. On the surface, this should have been easy, as there
were 263 Democratic members and only 172 Republicans. But in 1961,
for the first time in the twentieth century, the party taking over the
White House had *lost* seats in the House—22, to be exact.

And of the 263 Democratic members, a good number were southerners or conservatives or both and would vote against the plan to
stack the Rules Committee. To compensate for this substantial loss,
the pro-Kennedy forces would need to line up 15 to 20 Republicans
who were sufficiently liberal and independent to support Rayburn's
plan.

Because everything else depended on it, the move to expand the
Rules Committee was the first vote of the new Kennedy administration. It was, of course, a fight that the president simply had to win
if he was to have any hope of passing his legislative program. The
struggle was equally important for Rayburn, for at issue was
whether the Speaker would prevail in Congress, or whether the
King of the Hill was going to be Judge Smith.

Rayburn went to work on some of the Democratic holdouts, and
we mainstream Democrats did our best to lobby our southern and
Republican colleagues. I remember working on Bill Bates, a moderate Republican with whom I was very close. What finally made the
difference in his case was a personal phone call from Kennedy, who
became directly involved in the lobbying effort. It's always difficult
to refuse the president of the United States, not only for psychologi-
cal reasons, but because everybody knows that somewhere down the
line he can do you a mighty big favor—or, if he chooses, can cause
you enormous problems.

The president had to walk a fine line on this one, for under the separation of powers, the executive branch has no right to interfere with the internal workings of Congress. But as an "interested citizen," Kennedy declared at a press conference that he hoped *all* the members of Congress, and not just the twelve of us who happened to serve on the Rules Committee, would have the opportunity to vote on the new administration's proposals.

It was looking like an extremely close fight, and Rayburn decided to delay the vote for six days in the hope that Kennedy's first State of the Union message might change a few minds. There was even a story making the rounds that the House leadership had sent a case of whiskey to a couple of the southern Democrats in the hope that they might be too drunk to show up for the vote.

The day of decision was January 31, 1961, with debate limited to one hour. Clarence Brown, the ranking Republican on the Rules Committee, argued that Rayburn's plan reminded him of FDR's misguided attempt to pack the Supreme Court. But Tom Curtis, a Republican from Missouri, rose to say what many of us believed: that there was "a basic proposition that whichever party obtains the responsibility to organize the Congress should have the necessary power to meet that responsibility."

It was close all the way, but the final count was 217 to 212, with 195 Democrats and 22 Republicans voting to enlarge the Rules Committee. The Republicans and the southerners who voted with us were not necessarily supporters of Kennedy's programs, but they shared our concern that something had to be done about the unbridled power of Judge Howard Smith. Still, as Kennedy was well aware, the administration had pulled out all the stops and still had won by only five votes. It wasn't a promising sign for the president's legislative program.

An ironic twist to the Rules Committee crisis is that one of the two new Democratic appointees was Bernie Sisk of California, who came in as a flaming liberal. Over time, however, Sisk turned into an archconservative who began causing us serious problems. After all that Sam Rayburn and John McCormack had gone through to put him on the Rules Committee, Bernie Sisk eventually started voting with the Republicans.

That same year, my ninth as a member of Congress, marked the first time I ever voted against my own party in the Rules Committee.

The issue was Kennedy's bill for federal aid to education, and the administration's slender new majority on the Rules Committee collapsed as Jim Delaney and I broke ranks with the liberals and voted with the conservative Democrats and the Republicans.

The White House wanted to extend the National Defense Education Act, a worthy piece of legislation that provided scholarship money, a program for teachers' salaries and the construction of classrooms, and a massive $2.8 billion program to establish academic facilities at universities and colleges. Delaney and I had no objection to the substance of the act, but we resented the fact that the administration opposed *any* benefits to parochial schools. As a Catholic, the president presumably felt he had to bend over backward to preserve the separation of church and state.

But for Delaney, an Irish-Catholic from Queens, and for me, this was going too far. We, too, believed in the separation of church and state, but along with many other Catholics, we also believed that Kennedy was carrying this principle to extremes. We were especially irritated about textbooks. In our view, when identical textbooks were used in both public and private schools, it was unfair for the government to subsidize the books in one school system and not in another.

Because Delaney and I were known as loyal Democrats, our opposition to the bill came as quite a shock to some of the members of our party. Ray Madden, our colleague on the Rules Committee and a Catholic Democrat from Indiana who sided with the administration on this one, was quoted as saying, "I never thought I'd see the day when Jim and Tip would join the coalition of Republicans and Dixiecrats. It's the strangest alliance I have witnessed in all my days in Congress."

Dick Donahue was the White House liaison man to Congress, and when he heard about my opposition to the bill, he came to my office for a little chat. "The president wants your vote," he said.

"Well, he's not going to get it," I replied. "You tell the president that I'm voting the same way that he would if he were representing our district and sitting on this committee."

Donahue reported back to Kennedy, who told him, "Tip's right." This particular version of the education bill never did make it out of the Rules Committee. Even so, the president and his staff understood our position, and I don't recall that there were any hard feelings at the White House.

Despite my close relationship with Jack, I did not have the access I expected to the Kennedy White House. While our personal friendship continued, I was frozen out of the White House by Kennedy's staff, including Kenny O'Donnell, Larry O'Brien, and Dick Donahue. This group constituted the so-called Irish Mafia in the White House, and I suspect that they didn't want yet another Boston Irishman around—especially a veteran of Massachusetts politics who might have represented a threat to their own turf. Another possibility is that I was kept away by O'Donnell at the specific request of Robert Kennedy, who saw me as a gruff, old-fashioned pol.

Whatever the case, whenever I did see the president, he'd always say, "Tip, why don't you ever stop by to say hello?"

"Because I can't get by Kenny O'Donnell and Larry O'Brien," I'd reply. Jack would always laugh, but I was serious. When I needed to speak to the president, I'd bypass O'Donnell and O'Brien by going through Evelyn Lincoln, Jack's personal secretary, or Dave Powers, his closest aide.

Every time I went over O'Donnell's head and approached the president directly, Kenny was furious. It happened the day I brought Austin O'Connor to see Jack, an incident I've already discussed. And it happened again with Speed Carroll.

Father James Carroll was an old friend of mine who was head of the New England division of the Catholic Youth Organization. His group was planning a national convention in New York, at the old Americana Hotel, and they wanted to award a medal to the president. They had reason to expect that Kennedy might show up, because that same day the president was scheduled to address an AFL-CIO convention directly across the street.

After trying, without success, to invite the president through the normal White House channels, Speed called me and asked if I could use my connections to help him out. When I called the White House, Evelyn Lincoln put me right through to the president.

"I'd love to come," he said. "Kenny will be in touch with you about the details."

O'Donnell was livid. "You went over my head!"

"Never mind that," I said. "The president wants to be there."

A few days later, the president himself called Speed Carroll. "I'll be happy to do it," he said, "but I want to be in and out. No meetings. Just take me to where I'm supposed to be, give me five minutes to freshen up, and then bring me out to meet the young people."

When the president arrived at the hotel, Speed was there to greet him. "I understand your wishes," he said. "But we have some bishops who are hoping to meet with you, and a group of nuns in the next room."

Kennedy didn't miss a beat. "The nuns I'll see," he said. "But not the bishops. They all vote Republican."

Jack always had good relations with the lower levels of the Church, but except for Cardinal Cushing in Boston, he wasn't close to the mostly conservative Catholic hierarchy. He did, however, have a special affection for nuns. I'll never forget the time in Missouri, in 1960, when Jack was being driven in a campaign parade. I was with him, and somebody mentioned that in the neighborhood we were driving through there was a good deal of concern over the Catholic issue. Then we passed a Catholic school, with all the nuns standing outside, holding their Kennedy signs. "Stop the car," said Jack. He got out and shook hands with all the sisters, and I loved him for it.

In 1961, Jack asked me to help him resolve a delicate political problem back in Massachusetts. His brother Teddy would be old enough to run for the Senate the following year, but Ted wasn't the only one with his eye on that seat. The other candidate was Eddie McCormack, the attorney general of Massachusetts—but far more important, John McCormack's nephew. Eddie, the son of McCormack's brother Knocko, was only thirty-eight but had a long list of qualifications and achievements, including three terms as attorney general. Whereas Ted Kennedy's best asset was his name.

Rayburn had died, and John McCormack was the new Speaker. The turns and twists of history are strange and unpredictable, for the man Jack had virtually ignored as a member of the House was now, suddenly, his most important ally in Congress. Whatever problems had existed between them in the past, it was clear that the president needed McCormack's full help and cooperation to get his legislation passed. But now, Jack's biggest fear was that a bitter Senate race in Massachusetts would reignite some of the old tensions between himself and the Speaker.

After Rayburn's death, the Kennedy people had toyed with the idea of running Dick Bolling against John McCormack for the position of Speaker. Although McCormack was the odds-on favorite, they thought he might be vulnerable on religious grounds, as the members might not appreciate serving under a Catholic Speaker during the administration of the first Catholic president. But when they conducted a poll among House Democrats, they found that McCormack could not be defeated.

At the request of the Kennedy people, I arranged a meeting between the administration's congressional liaison staff and the new Speaker. I was nervous because these young guys had just elected a president, and they looked on McCormack as an old-hat politician. (A similar situation prevailed in 1977, when the team that elected Jimmy Carter viewed another new Speaker, Tip O'Neill, in a similar light.)

We all met for lunch in the Board of Education. Kenny O'Donnell, Larry O'Brien, and Dick Donahue were there from the White House, and I was relieved to see how well they got along with John McCormack. They soon realized that the Speaker was no dinosaur, but a kind and canny veteran who really knew his way around, and whose political philosophy was very close to their own. From that time on there were good relations between the White House and the Speaker. And now, with his brother in the Senate race against McCormack's nephew, the last thing Jack Kennedy wanted to do was to risk upsetting that delicate balance.

That's where I came in. "I'm getting along well with McCormack," the president told me, "and I don't want this Senate race to come between us. Besides, with me in the White House and Bobby in the cabinet, I don't want to create a backlash by putting a third Kennedy into office.

"But you know my father. He's determined that my old seat belongs to Teddy, and that's all there is to it. But Teddy has a plan, and he'd like to run it by you and have you take it to McCormack.

You're close to both sides, and we hope you'll be willing to act as an intermediary."

I said I'd be happy to help. Ted came to see me in my Boston office on Washington's Birthday, and he spelled out his proposition: "Eddie McCormack and I will commission a poll. He can pick any pollster he wants, and we'll split the cost. Or if he prefers, I'll pay for the whole thing. If I beat him by more than five percent, he gets out of the fight and we'll support him for governor. If he beats me by more than five percent, I'll get out and support him."

"Wait a minute," I said. "Where the hell does that leave *me?* If McCormack wins the poll, what's to stop you from running against Tip O'Neill for Congress?"

Teddy looked me in the eye and said, "Never. My brother and my family have too much respect for you. I give you my word that I'll never run against you."

I took Ted's plan to John McCormack, who thought it sounded reasonable. But by then we both knew that the Kennedys had already commissioned a poll of their own, which showed Teddy beating Eddie by a margin of two to one.

McCormack took Ted's plan to his nephew, but Eddie wouldn't hear of it. "He may win in the polls," he said, "but I've got the delegates sewed up at the state convention."

But once the Kennedys got to work with their muscle and their money, the convention was theirs. Even so, Eddie McCormack wouldn't pull out.

Jack called me a second time and asked me to talk with Kenny O'Donnell about the problem in Massachusetts. I told him I'd rather not go through O'Donnell.

"You've got to, Tip. People are already getting the idea that I'm involved in this, and it doesn't look right. The papers will say I'm a Boston pol who can't stay out of a local fight."

I called O'Donnell, who got right to the point: "Teddy's going to beat him silly, and Eddie McCormack is going to be annihilated. Humiliated. But we don't want that to happen. We don't want any problems with the Speaker.

"So tell the Speaker that if Eddie drops out, we'll make him an ambassador to any country he wants. We also understand that he's in debt for a hundred thousand dollars. If he gets out now, old Joe will make sure that the debt is taken care of, and Eddie will be retained as a lawyer for some of the Kennedy ventures."

I went to John McCormack, and when he said he couldn't influence his nephew, I met with Eddie. He hated the idea of quitting, but he could also see the writing on the wall. He refused the Kennedy's offer to help with his debts, but as a graduate of the Naval Academy, he said he might be interested in being under secretary of the navy.

I took that back to O'Donnell, who said it was impossible, as the job had already been given to Red Fay, Jack's comrade in the PT boat during the war. "But anything else he wants, within reason, we'll try to give him."

Eddie thought that one over for a couple of days, but in the end he decided to stay in the race. I warned him against it: "Your uncle John has friends who are with you because they're loyal to him. But you're putting a lot of people in the middle. Do what you want to do, but I don't think you have a chance in the world of winning."

Eddie gave it everything he had, and it was a rough campaign. It was Eddie McCormack in 1962 who uttered that famous line "If your name was Edward Moore, instead of Edward Moore Kennedy, your candidacy would be a joke."

In a campaign debate, he tore into Ted Kennedy in a speech that had echoes of the Neville-Kennedy fight of 1946: "I ask my opponent, What are your qualifications? You graduated from law school three years ago. You never worked for a living. You have never run or held an elective office. You are not running on qualifications. You are running on a slogan: 'He Can Do More for Massachusetts.' . . . This is the most insulting slogan I have seen in Massachusetts politics, because this slogan means: Vote for this man because he has influence, he has connections, he has relations. And I say no. I say that we do not vote on influence or favoritism or connections. We vote for people who will *serve.*"

But when the votes were counted in the September primary it was Kennedy by a landslide, 560,000 to 257,000—better than two to one. In November, Ted Kennedy won handily against George Lodge, his Republican opponent and, appropriately enough, the son of Henry Cabot Lodge.

Fortunately, Jack Kennedy had worried for nothing. Although

both the president and the Speaker cared deeply about the outcome of that race, neither one blamed the other for anything that was said or done in the campaign.

One of my most vivid memories of President Kennedy involves his courageous handling of the Cuban missile crisis in October of 1962. The facts are too well known to need repeating here, but many readers will recall the deep anxiety and fear we all experienced when it suddenly seemed as if a nuclear war with the Soviet Union was a real possibility.

Congress was not in session at the time, so when the president asked to address the members by closed-circuit television, we were all flown to one of four locations: New York, New Orleans, San Francisco, and Chicago. The New England members flew from Boston to New York on an army plane, and I remember how quiet it was on that flight, despite the fact that it was filled with politicians. We had no inside information, and along with the rest of the country we thought that the president might decide to bomb Cuba to get rid of the missiles, an action that could have led to a war with the Soviets. In fact, many of us believed that the president was about to declare war.

When the plane landed we were all brought to the GSA Building in lower Manhattan, where we were given a briefing and shown photographs in which we could clearly see Russian ships unloading the missiles. Then the president described the blockade, and how he had already warned Khrushchev that we would challenge any Russian ships that tried to land in Cuba. Fortunately, this is one story without a punch line: the Russians took Kennedy's warning seriously, and the tension was soon defused.

It's funny how you often remember the small details from big events. One that stays with me from that day is that Percy Bass of New Hampshire was the only member of the New England delegation who didn't fly with us to New York. Among the members, Percy was affectionately called Small-Mouth Bass, to distinguish him from Congressman Ross Bass from Tennessee, a real yakker who was, naturally, known as Big-Mouth Bass. The reason that Small-Mouth Bass did not make the trip is that he stayed home to address a Rotary luncheon.

At the time, he was running for the Senate against a fellow named

Tom McIntyre. McIntyre had little chance of winning, but he kept hammering away at the fact that on the day when all the other congressmen from New England had flown to New York to hear the president's address on the Cuban situation, his opponent had chosen instead to make a campaign speech. McIntyre won that election. You never know for sure, but I would guess that Bass's decision to stay home that day was a major factor in his defeat.

Before we leave Jack Kennedy, there are a couple of myths about his administration that I'd like to clear up. The first misconception is that Jack had a first-rate congressional liaison team. Now it's true that Larry O'Brien knew everyone worth knowing on the Hill, and that he and Dick Donahue were friendly and popular, and that they were unusually adept at doing political favors for individual congressmen.

Unfortunately, they weren't nearly as effective at their job, which was to help get the president's legislation through Congress. Other than the Manpower bill, there wasn't much Kennedy legislation that actually passed during his shortened term in office. Eventually, most of his legislation did go through, but it took the political skills of Lyndon Johnson to make it happen.

But it would be unfair to judge Jack Kennedy only in terms of legislation. Despite his lack of success in dealing with Congress, his leadership set the stage for so many important changes in America. What would we have achieved in civil rights without Jack Kennedy? Or in space exploration? Or arms control?

When you consider the larger picture, it's clear that Jack Kennedy left a shining legacy. Perhaps his most important achievement was to draw a new generation of young Americans into politics and government. He brought government to the people, and, equally important, he brought talented people into government.

The other misunderstanding about Jack Kennedy is the misinformed notion that he was responsible for getting us into Vietnam. In my view, just the opposite was true. If Jack had lived to serve a second term—and there's no question that he would have creamed Goldwater—he would have pulled out all our troops within a year or two.

Certainly the Pentagon would never have exercised the kind of power over Kennedy that it had over Johnson. Lyndon Johnson revered West Point and the military leaders who came out of there, and he believed their judgment was infallible. Kennedy, on the other hand, was an Ivy Leaguer who was always skeptical of the military. There was no way he would ever allow them to call the shots.

Kenny O'Donnell used to say—and I believe him—that as president, Jack Kennedy agreed with Mike Mansfield on the need for a complete military withdrawal from Vietnam. But because the president knew that such a move might prove wildly unpopular with the voters, he intended to wait until 1965, the beginning of his second term, to put that plan into effect. Unfortunately, he never got the chance.

I vividly remember the last time I saw Jack Kennedy. I was flying in from Boston on a Monday afternoon in November, and when the plane touched down, Billie Smith, my secretary, was waiting for me. "The president wants to see you," she said.

When I got to the White House, Jack was already meeting with Dick Bolling and two or three of the other Democratic members of the Rules Committee. "The train is off the track," he said. "We can't get anything through Congress. I called you fellows over because you're my friends and your philosophy is the same as mine. I don't want the leadership to think I'm talking behind their backs, but what's going on here, and how we can we straighten things out?"

We explained to the president that the White House was taking too much for granted, and that his congressional liaison team hadn't been working closely enough with the members of the House. Jack was concerned, but he probably took our comments with a grain of salt. He was already looking ahead to November of 1964, and he simply relished the prospect of running against Goldwater, whom he regarded as a very weak opponent. After the anticipated Democratic landslide of 1964, which would bring a large group of new Democrats into Congress, he expected the House to pass all of his legislation without much difficulty.

When the meeting was over I left the White House through the back door, but Billie Smith had already driven off. I walked back inside to call my office, and I ran into the president.

"Tip, where are you headed?" he asked.

"I guess I'll walk to the University Club," I said. "My secretary drove off with the car."

"Come in and have a drink," said Jack. "Then I'll get you a ride."

We sat and talked for a while about the old days, and about what had happened to some of Jack's old friends, such as Billy Sutton, Mark Dalton, Joe Healy, Peter Cloherty, Jimmy Kelly, and Johnny Galvin, who was his press secretary when Jack was in Congress.

We also talked briefly about the president's upcoming trip to Dallas, where he hoped to straighten out the feud between two Texas Democrats, Governor John Connally and Senator Ralph Yarborough. Like so many of his friends and advisers, I didn't see the point of the trip, and I told him so. It just didn't make sense for the president of the United States to be spending his time and energy trying to patch up an internal Texas fight.

When it was time to leave, Jack walked outside with me and pointed to the back porch, where his father was sitting in a wheelchair, having suffered a serious stroke two years earlier. "Why don't you wave to my dad?" he said. "I'm sure he recognizes you."

"How is he doing?" I asked.

"He can't talk," said the president, "but he has a slate he can write on. His mind is as clear and as sharp as it ever was."

Who would have guessed on that day that this ailing old man was going to outlive his vigorous son?

I'd rather not dwell on Jack's death, because even now it's still too painful. I was in my Boston office when I heard the news. Cathy O'Brien, who had worked for me in Washington, came running in from Jimmy Burke's office, screaming and crying, "They shot the president, they shot the president. He's dead!"

I reached for the phone to call Bob Healy at the *Globe*. The receptionist recognized my voice.

"It's true, it's true," she said. Then she started to cry.

All of us in the office were absolutely stunned. We left and walked up the hill to the Arch Street Shrine. Hundreds of people were already there, and everybody was in tears.

Millie and I flew down to Washington for the funeral. We were standing in line to pay our last respects, and who do we see coming through but our son Tommy, who was a student at Boston College. We had no idea he was in town, but he said, "I just couldn't let Jack Kennedy go to rest without saying good-bye, so I hitched a ride down here."

It was such a sad day that it seemed like the whole world had come apart.

I was never one of those people who had doubts or suspicions about the Warren Commission's report on the president's death. But five years after Jack died, I was having dinner with Kenny O'Donnell and a few other people at Jimmy's Harborside Restaurant in Boston, and we got to talking about the assassination.

I was surprised to hear O'Donnell say that he was sure he had heard two shots that came from behind the fence.

"That's not what you told the Warren Commission," I said.

"You're right," he replied. "I told the FBI what I had heard, but they said it couldn't have happened that way and that I must have been imagining things. So I testified the way they wanted me to. I just didn't want to stir up any more pain and trouble for the family."

"I can't believe it," I said. "I wouldn't have done that in a million years. I would have told the truth."

"Tip, you have to understand. The family—everybody wanted this thing behind them."

Dave Powers was with us at dinner that night, and his recollection of the shots was the same as O'Donnell's. Kenny O'Donnell is no longer alive, but during the writing of this book I checked with Dave Powers. As they say in the news business, he stands by his story.

And so there will always be some skepticism in my mind about the cause of Jack's death. I used to think that the only people who doubted the conclusions of the Warren Commission were crackpots. Now, however, I'm not so sure.

But I'd rather focus on Jack's life. He really did have the charisma, the glamour, and the talent that has become part of his legend. He had a radiance that made people glow when they were in his company. He brought to all sectors of the American public a new feeling that they were wanted, that there was a place in America for them—regardless of religion or race. And perhaps most important, when Jack Kennedy was president, people had trust in their government. I look forward to the day when that will once again be true.

9

★ ★ ★ ★ ★

Lyndon Johnson

ONE reason Jack Kennedy was so successful as a politician was that he was one of the first to treat politics as a science. Lyndon Johnson was successful in a more traditional way—as a master of the *art* of politics. Kennedy was a cool and rational operator who could always tell you exactly what he was doing and why he was doing it; Johnson worked instinctively. If Kennedy's political style was in his head, Johnson's was in his blood.

During the 1950s, I knew Johnson slightly from Sam Rayburn's Board of Education, where, as the Speaker's protégé and fellow Texan, he was the only regular member of that group from the Senate. But my first close look at his political style came not on Capitol Hill but at Griffith Stadium in 1958. The Red Sox were in town to play the Washington Senators, and during the fifth inning, when the game was temporarily halted because of rain, I paid a visit to the visitors' dressing room. I knew many of the players personally, not only because I was a baseball nut, but also because Jack Burns, Boston's third-base coach, was a neighbor of mine back in Cambridge.

A few of us were sitting around and shooting the breeze when there was a knock on the door. Jack Burns got up to see who it was. "Tip," he called, "there's a fellow out here who wants to talk to the manager. Do you know a Senator Johnson?"

"Senator Johnson?" I said. "That must be Lyndon. You better get the manager because this guy may be president some day." A few years later, after Jack Kennedy's death, a couple of the veteran players reminded me of my prediction. But to anyone who lived in

Washington during those years, it didn't take any special vision to see that Lyndon Johnson, the senate majority leader, intended to go all the way.

That night, he strode into the locker room with his good friend Homer Thornberry, a member of Congress from Texas and one of my colleagues on the Rules Committee, and asked to see Pinky Higgins, the manager. I didn't know Higgins, and neither, it turned out, did Johnson. When Higgins appeared, Johnson introduced himself. "This is Pinky Higgins," he said to Homer, and to everyone else within earshot. "His brother Ox was the greatest athlete in the history of Texas. He's the fellow that originally put me in politics and elected me to Congress. I owe so much to Ox Higgins."

Now I would be very surprised if Lyndon Johnson had met Ox Higgins more than once or twice in his life. But by making such a fuss about him, he made Pinky Higgins look ten feet tall in front of his players. I smiled to myself, knowing I was in the presence of a real pro.

Johnson's political style was often overwhelming, and there was nothing subtle about it. One afternoon in 1959 I was in the House dining room with a visiting group from the Cambridge City Council when I saw Lyndon walking toward us. By then he was well known, and everybody at my table was dying to meet him. Apparently, the feeling was mutual. Lyndon knew instinctively that these were local politicians, and that they might be helpful to him as he lined up support for the 1960 presidential nomination.

This time, too, Johnson was with Homer Thornberry, and as he approached our table I could read his lips as he leaned over and whispered, "What's the name of the big Irishman from Boston who's friends with McCormack?"

"Tip O'Neill."

A moment later, Johnson greeted me like a long-lost pal. "Tip, how are you? Delighted to see you. Let me say hello to your friends."

He had the right idea, but he was crude about it. There was nothing wrong with asking Homer to help him remember my name, but he never should have let me catch him doing it. A Boston pol would have known enough to cover his lips by pretending to rub his nose while he asked a question like that.

Johnson needed no such coaching the following year, when he ran into me at Mike Kirwan's annual St. Patrick's Day party. "Tip," he said, "I'd like to see you tomorrow for a few minutes."

He came by the next afternoon. After some small talk, he asked if I would support him for the presidential nomination at the upcoming Democratic National Convention in Los Angeles.

"You and I have been good friends ever since the day you came down here," he said, stretching the truth just a little. "I'm told that you follow Massachusetts politics closer than any other member of Congress, and that you'll be a power at the convention. Now I realize you're pledged to the boy"—referring, of course, to Jack Kennedy. "But you and I both know he can't win. He's just a flash in the pan, and he's got no record of substance to run on. Will you be with me on the second ballot?"

During the entire conversation, he never once mentioned Jack Kennedy by name. It was always "the boy."

I said "Mr. Leader, let me tell you something. Jack Kennedy is going to be the nominee for president. He's going to win on the first ballot for several reasons—because of the innovative methods the Kennedys use, the untold wealth they have, their hard work, and the long arm of Joseph Kennedy. I promise you that the Kennedys are going to outwork, outspend, and outmaneuver everybody else along the line."

Johnson couldn't believe what he was hearing. "You're a professional," he said. "You *know* the boy can't win."

"He can and he will," I replied. "In 1952 I saw Kennedy run against Lodge, when people said he had no chance. But he won through sheer hard work and determination, as well as a great organization. When we get to that convention, there won't even *be* a second ballot."

I could see that Johnson thought I was nuts, so I continued: "You have to see it to believe it. You don't know the strength they have. You don't know how quickly they can move. And you have never seen money work the way the Kennedys know how to work it. They don't get into fights they can't win."

Johnson just shook his head. "Come on, Tip, you know better than that. That boy is going to die on the vine. I'm asking you for some aid and support in New England after he fails."

Johnson made the classic mistake of judging Jack Kennedy as a senator rather than a potential national candidate. In the Senate, Lyndon Johnson was far more impressive than his young rival, and if it had been up to his colleagues, Johnson would have won in a landslide.

But running for the presidential nomination is a very different matter, and requires a great deal of traveling. Johnson was so tied to the Senate that he wasn't free to move around the country, and he would soon discover that a position of leadership and responsibility can be a terrific obstacle when you're running for president. Being part of the Senate is certainly an advantage, but if you're the one who's obliged to run the place, there isn't much time or energy left to campaign.

When Kennedy was nominated, Lyndon must have received the shock of his life. The day he came to see me, he just couldn't imagine that Jack Kennedy was going to win the prize. But then, in March of 1960, not many people could.

The vice presidency is never an easy office to occupy, but it must have been especially difficult for Johnson. I'm sure it rankled him that this young, rich upstart was in the White House while he, who had come up the hard way, was the all-but-forgotten number-two man. Johnson had been in Washington since 1931, when he arrived in town as legislative secretary to Congressman Richard Kleberg, a Texas millionaire. Later, LBJ spent six terms in the House and another two in the Senate, where he served as both minority and majority leader. But he hated being vice president, and he used to complain that the job, in his endearing words, wasn't worth a pitcher of warm piss.

Although the president treated Johnson well, and invited him to attend staff meetings and cabinet meetings, Kennedy's staff looked down on the vice president and were continually rude to him. From what I heard, they were even mean to him on that terrible flight back from Dallas, after LBJ had been sworn in as the new president. They had a disdain for Johnson that they didn't even try to hide, and they relished talking about his crudeness and mocking the vulgarity of his language. They actually took pride in snubbing him.

After Kennedy's death, his staff people, who now worked for Johnson, would gather at Paul Young's restaurant for dinner and kick his brains in. They were embarrassed by Lyndon, who obviously didn't fit into their vision of Camelot. But even when Jack was alive there was so much tension between his staff and Lyndon's that Dick Maguire had to be appointed as the liaison between the two camps.

When Johnson became president, however, he was remarkably sensitive and restrained toward the Kennedy people, including Robert McNamara, whom he especially admired, as well as Robert Kennedy, Ted Sorensen, McGeorge Bundy, Lawrence O'Brien, and Kenny O'Donnell. Personally, I never could understand why he kept so many of them on after Jack's death; I would have fired them all. But Johnson respected these people, and he seemed to feel that this group would give him a connection to Kennedy's popularity, and to the intellectual community, which Lyndon admired.

And yet I can remember at least one incident where Johnson lashed out at the Kennedy people. Bob Griffin from Boston was a great pal of mine, with many friends in the Massachusetts congressional delegation. He was one of the top people in the General Services Administration, and in 1964, when the head of that agency resigned, a group of us went over to see the president about giving the job to Griffin.

When we arrived at the White House, Johnson came into the room and said, "Boys, I know what you're here for. You want this Kennedy man to get the GSA job, this guy who looks down his nose at me like I'm shit. Well, you can tell him that he's not going anywhere. He's damn lucky to be where he is. Every time I see that elongated son of a bitch with his PT-109 tie pin, flaunting it in my face, I almost go through the roof."

"Wait a minute—" somebody broke in.

"No, I will *not* wait a minute," the president replied. "No Kennedy man is going to get that job. I'm giving it to a Johnson man. Now let's go in and have a drink."

He cut us off at the knees. But once the Griffin matter was out of the way, we went into a side room and spent a very pleasant hour with the president.

But before we left we saw another side of Lyndon Johnson. "I've got to show you the polls," he said. "Wait until you see them. I'm going to *kill* Goldwater. Where's Jack Valenti?"

Valenti was Johnson's chief aide, but at that moment he wasn't around. Lyndon became enraged. *"Where's Jack Valenti?"* he screamed.

Valenti came in a moment later.

"Where the hell were you?" Lyndon roared.

"I was getting a cup of coffee," said Jack.

"You asshole!" said the president. "I told you never to leave my office!" And right there, in front of the Massachusetts delegation, Johnson proceeded to chastise Valenti and humiliate him. You would have thought that Jack had just committed some terrible crime.

I was stunned by the president's outburst and before we left, I took Jack aside. "How can you take it?" I asked. "I would have told him what he could do with the job."

"You just don't understand him," he replied. "Five minutes after it happened, it's all forgotten. By tonight, he won't even remember being mad at me."

After Kennedy's death, Johnson put through all of Kennedy's legislation and more, including the Economic Opportunity Act, the heart of Johnson's "war on poverty"; Medicare for people over sixty-five; Medicaid for the poor; the Civil Rights Act of 1964; the Voting Rights Act; aid for schools and colleges; aid for mass transit; highway beautification; increased social security; a higher minimum wage; and much more.

I believe that Lyndon Johnson was serious about wanting to eliminate poverty in America. He had seen poverty cut in half during his lifetime, from 50 percent in 1936 to around 25 percent in 1964. He was determined to finish the job, and he did succeed in cutting poverty by a further 50 percent.

I was delighted with Johnson's program, and I became an enthusiastic supporter of just about every bill he sent to Congress. Some of my fellow liberals found these bills hard to believe, because as a congressman and then a senator, Johnson had never been known for his progressive views. Besides, in recent years he had become a rich rancher who didn't seem to appreciate the problems of the poor.

But as president, his perspective changed. I believe he was deeply affected by the views of the Kennedy people, and that over time he came to believe in the need for increased social programs. He himself had come from a poor background, and he knew that America needed this legislation. He also understood that there was a place in history for him if he could bring it into being.

Unfortunately, the Economic Opportunity Act, which was his greatest accomplishment, was put together a little too quickly. I could only admire the purpose of the bill, which was to eliminate poverty, but the legislation tried to accomplish too much too soon. It was rushed through the House in the summer of 1964 because Johnson was preparing for the campaign against Goldwater, and he wanted to show that he was firmly in control. Technically, the bill was a mishmash, and many parts of it had to be corrected in later sessions.

Johnson's finest hour came on March 15, 1965, when he addressed a joint session of Congress to plead for passage of the Voting Rights Act. It was a spectacular performance, and a great moral statement against discrimination. Nobody who was there, or who saw the speech on television, can ever forget how, in the middle of his remarks, the president raised his arms and announced, "We *shall* overcome!"

The liberals and the liberal media were ecstatic over Johnson's address, but the House of Representatives was bitterly divided. Most of the southern Democrats voted against the bill, while the courageous few who stood up to segregation, including Carl Elliott of Alabama and Brooks Hays of Arkansas, were soon defeated by their constituents. It was the moderate Republicans from the Rockefeller wing of the party who made the difference, and we couldn't have passed the Voting Rights Act without them.

As a creature of Congress, Johnson was a master at working with the House. The congressional liaison people would meet every Friday, and the president would always be there. Shortly after Johnson moved into the White House, he met with his new team to discuss how to deal with the members. "Now each of you has done some favors for these people," he said, "so you ought to be able to work on these guys. If you find any of them who are hard to do business with, just let me know and I'll call them personally. Some of the big-city people, like Edna Kelly from New York, I'll handle myself. And Tip O'Neill—don't worry about him. He likes to deal with the head brass."

He was addicted to the telephone, and he'd call me frequently.

"Tip, how's it going on Rules?" The members of the House were like his constituents, and he liked to keep in touch. He always made you feel as though you were needed. And what a talker! That man could talk a bone away from a dog.

He understood that people like to be thanked, and he'd always be calling to express his appreciation for a vote. When he invited you to the White House, he invariably gave out gifts—especially cufflinks and pens. All presidents do this, but normally these items are handed out by his underlings. With Lyndon, however, it was always a personal gesture. By the end of his presidency I had a whole drawerful of these trinkets.

The Democratic members of Congress were often invited for photo opportunities, and there were probably more of these under Johnson than under all the previous presidents combined. You'd be told that between nine to ten during the next three days you could go to the White House and have your picture taken with the president. Several dozen members would be lined up, and as you were posing with the president he'd generally whisper something in your ear and ask you for help with some piece of legislation.

Most members were delighted to have these photographs, which could always be used in your campaign literature and sent to your hometown papers. As Johnson understood so well, no newspaper could turn down a picture of a local representative chatting with the president. When it came to politics, that man knew all the tricks.

But it wasn't just a matter of gimmicks. Lyndon Johnson worked more closely with the Congress and followed the details of legislation more carefully than any other president I've seen. He left nothing to chance. The Kennedy people had been excellent when it came to the details of campaigning, but they didn't follow through legislatively. Johnson was the opposite. He wasn't scientific about campaigning, but when it came to dealing with Congress, he was the best I've ever seen.

He got along beautifully with John McCormack, and was in constant touch with Homer Thornberry, his man on the Rules Committee. He also knew a great many congressmen on a first-name basis. He didn't have the charm and the charisma of Kennedy, but he sure had style, he sure had personality, and he sure had character.

During Johnson's years in the White House, I had a couple of memorable encounters with the president. At one point, Robert McNamara, the secretary of defense, came to Boston and wanted to close the Boston Navy Yard in Charlestown. McNamara hoped to shut down unneeded military bases, and in the case of the navy yard he complained about everything—the quality of the work, the morale, and the cost overruns.

For my district, closing down the navy yard would have been an economic disaster. Besides, it was an excellent yard for shipbuilding, and was right on the sea lanes to Europe. It was also the oldest shipyard in the navy.

To get the president's attention, I walked out of a meeting of the Rules Committee just before a vote on a bill to reduce federal regulation of rail rates for perishable commodities—a bill the administration cared about. A few days later, Johnson called in the Democratic members of the Rules Committee for one of his periodic meetings.

As we were leaving, he took me aside. "Christ," he said, "we had the chance to get that transportation bill out, and you left! What's going on?"

"Mr. President," I said, "I'm spending a lot of my time trying to save the Boston Navy Yard.

"What do you mean?"

"McNamara keeps threatening to close it."

"Don't you worry about that," said the president. "That navy yard will be around as long as I'm in the White House."

I kept quiet about our little understanding, because if word got out that the president was actively engaged in horse trading, everybody in the House would be doing it. A certain amount of this did go on, of course, but not on a regular basis. In Johnson's case, he would often do you a favor first so you'd owe him one.

During the summer of 1966, Lyndon Johnson performed a very kind and unexpected favor for me which made a considerable difference in my political career. Back home, for the first time since 1954, I was facing opposition in the Democratic primary. In retrospect, as I've explained, Sam Cammarata was not exactly a tough opponent. But I had seen a number of congressmen lose elections because of overconfidence, and I wasn't taking any chances. Besides, I wanted to make a good showing to protect my reputation among both my constituents and my colleagues. And if I could demonstrate that I was unbeatable, it would discourage future opponents from trying to knock me off.

To help raise money for the campaign, I held a fund-raising dinner at the Shoreham Hotel in Washington. In the days before political action committees, a group of lobbyists would form a committee and help you put on a fifty-dollar-a-plate dinner. Millie came down from Boston, along with Leo Diehl and a number of other friends and supporters.

It was a fine evening. Millie and I were celebrating our twenty-fifth wedding anniversary that week, which added a nice touch to the evening. We even had a little three-piece band playing in the background.

Suddenly, in the middle of the cocktail hour, my friend Peter Cloherty starts shouting to the band, "Play 'Hail to the Chief.'" Naturally, people look at Peter as if he's lost his marbles. But when he continues shouting, the band finally starts playing "Hail to the Chief." A moment later, who comes down the stairs but the president of the United States—dressed in slacks and a sports shirt.

I couldn't have been more shocked if Abraham Lincoln himself had walked in. Johnson was alone—the Secret Service was nowhere in sight—and people flocked to him. He stayed for about half an hour, working the crowd and allowing me to introduce him to all my friends.

The next day, the Boston papers featured the story with a picture on the front page: "President Honors Tip O'Neill." Suddenly, I was no longer a Massachusetts pol who was friends with Jack Kennedy. Now I had standing in Washington. As a result, I started receiving political contributions from a whole new group of people.

The day after the party, Carl Albert, the House majority leader, told me how the president ended up at my dinner. That evening, the Democratic leadership was at the White House for a meeting. First Hale Boggs, the whip, excused himself and came over to the Shoreham. Then John McCormack, the Speaker, said that he, too, had to leave early. Finally only Carl Albert was left.

"Let's have a drink," said the president.

"I'm sorry," said Carl, "but I've got to be at Tip O'Neill's fund-raiser."

"Tip's having a fund-raiser?" said the president. "He's my good friend. I'll go over there with you."

The president left the White House with Albert and hopped into Carl's car. The Secret Service went crazy, but before they could object, the president was gone.

I was a great supporter of Lyndon Johnson's domestic policies. But during the last two years of his term, I had a serious disagreement with the president over the war in Vietnam.

Of all the votes I cast during thirty-four years in the House of Representatives, the only one I really regret had to do with Vietnam, on August 6, 1964. A couple of days earlier, the *Maddox*, an American destroyer on intelligence patrol in the Gulf of Tonkin off the coast of North Vietnam, was allegedly attacked by enemy torpedo boats. Two days later, the *Maddox* and another ship were fired upon by North Vietnamese guns. Within a few hours, President Johnson ordered a reprisal raid over North Vietnam.

The following day, the president sent a joint resolution to Congress seeking our approval for him to take "all necessary measures" to halt Communist aggression in Southeast Asia. The resolution passed the House in under an hour, on a vote of 414 to 0. There was considerably more debate in the Senate, where the resolution passed 88 to 2, over the objections of Ernest Gruening of Alaska and Wayne Morse of Oregon, who insisted that the resolution was unconstitutional because only Congress can declare war.

Although I supported the president, the resolution troubled me. I couldn't prove it, but I had the feeling that the White House was using the Gulf of Tonkin incident as an excuse to open up a full-scale war. Later on it became clear that this was the case, when it was revealed that those enemy torpedo boats hadn't come within two miles of our ships.

On the morning of the vote, I was sitting as usual at John McCormack's breakfast table. The Speaker read us the text of the president's message to the House, and we discussed the resolution. During the course of the conversation, I mentioned that I was thinking of voting against it.

"Don't do it," said McCormack.

"I don't know," I replied. "It sounds to me like they were using a peasehooter to bring down a tank. They didn't even hit us. The president is using this as an excuse to get us in deeper over there."

"Tom," said the Speaker, "that's not the point. Nobody is going to shoot at an American vessel on the high seas."

After breakfast, he asked me to come to his office. "If you vote against this resolution," he said, "you'll be seen as a traitor to your country. It will be the worst vote you ever make. I urge you in the strongest possible terms not to do it."

I decided to go along with his advice. But I don't want to blame John McCormack, because I was free to vote my conscience. I just didn't have the courage.

That day, frenzy overtook the House. We'll show *them* who's in charge. Nobody is going to bully us and get away with it!

From what I remember, the only representative who raised any objections was Henry Reuss, a Wisconsin Democrat and the former general counsel of the Marshall Plan. Henry pointed out that it was a little late to pass a resolution approving a bombing that had already taken place. It reminded him, he said, of the bartender who calls the owner of the bar to ask, "Is Casey good for a drink?"

"Has he had it?" asks the owner.

"He has."

"Then he is."

But when it came time to vote, not even Henry Reuss opposed the president.

I made a big mistake that day by not voting my conscience. Politically, of course, McCormack may have been right. Had I been the only member in the House to vote against the resolution, I might have become highly unpopular among my colleagues. But that's no excuse for voting the wrong way. Since that time, I've often looked back and wondered what, if anything, would have happened differently if I had followed my instincts and opposed the president's request, which opened the door to our full-scale involvement in Vietnam.

But that's hindsight. Despite my questions about the Gulf of Tonkin Resolution, I remained loyal to Lyndon Johnson. Although I had some private doubts, I agreed with Sam Rayburn's famous saying that politics stops at the water's edge—that when it comes to foreign policy, you support your president. Besides, like most

Americans in 1964, I was convinced that Johnson's policy was essentially correct. After the resolution passed, my attitude was: if we're going to be in there, let's do it right.

Not long ago, I came across a faded newspaper clipping that accurately reported my views at the time: "I feel we're in the same position today as at the time of Hitler," I said. "Had we taken a stronger stand then, there would have been no World War II. I've been led to believe that the domino theory is true. If we lose in Vietnam, we'll lose Thailand, Laos and Cambodia. Then we'd lose face in the Philippines, and Pakistan, and with those who admired our stand in Berlin."

I remember going over to the White House in 1966 for a congressional briefing on Vietnam by the president and Dean Rusk, the secretary of state. Rusk was very impressive that day, and when he finished speaking I moved that all of us at the briefing should stand and give him a rousing vote of confidence for the way he was handling things. A few hours later, the president called me to express his appreciation.

I was aware, of course, that some people—especially college students—did not share my enthusiasm for the administration's foreign policy. In fact, I was highly aware of this because my district included twenty-two colleges, with more students and faculty members than any other congressional district in the country. Because of the war, I was continually invited to speak at the various campuses, including Harvard, M.I.T., Boston University, Boston College, Tufts, Simmons, Emerson, Leslie, and Northeastern. There was one stretch in 1967 when I spoke at eleven different colleges on eleven consecutive weekends.

Before each campus visit, I would be briefed by the White House, or Ambassador Lodge, or Dean Rusk, or even General Westmoreland. Often the State Department or the Pentagon would send over a team to go over everything I would tell the students. Many of my colleagues were also speaking at colleges, and based on points that students had raised with them, I would be given a list of likely questions and appropriate answers.

Most of the questions were hostile, but I could always handle them by saying, "You probably read that in the newspaper. But let me tell you the real story that I heard from the State Department yesterday." Whenever the questions grew tough, I would refer to a recent, confidential briefing. Because I was an insider, nobody could question the accuracy of what I was saying.

I had a harder time with my own kids and their crowd. The back door of our Cambridge house was never locked, and young people were always coming in and out. Every Sunday night, my kids and a group of their friends would gather on the floor of our living room and ask me questions—mostly about the war.

Without exception, they were opposed to our involvement in Vietnam. Some of Tommy's friends had even left the country to avoid the possibility of being sent to Vietnam. I thought that was shameful, and I told him so. "You'd be breaking my heart if you did that."

"No," he replied, "I wouldn't be breaking your heart. I'd be hurting you politically."

One Friday, I was invited to speak at Boston College, where Susan and Tommy were both undergraduates. I gave my usual talk on the war, which was followed, as usual, by a dialogue with the students. As always, they took issue with both my information and my views.

"You know," I told a young man who had challenged me, "I think I know more about this situation than you do. I've been briefed forty-three times. I've been briefed by Robert McNamara. I've been briefed by General Westmoreland. I've been briefed by the CIA. I've been briefed by Dean Rusk. And I've been briefed by the president of the United States."

"That's a lot of briefings," said the student, whose name was Pat McCarthy. "But how many times have you been briefed by the other side?"

The question came as a complete shock. Nobody had ever asked that one before.

That night, as I was lying in bed, thinking over the events of the day, I kept coming back to Pat McCarthy's question. And I had to acknowledge that I hadn't ever taken a good look at the other side of the issue. Before I fell asleep, I resolved to do just that.

I began my investigation of the Vietnam War during a poker game at the Army and Navy Club. One of the players was General David

Shoup, who had retired as commander of the Marine Corps because he couldn't go along with the administration's policy on the war.

"General," I said, "I'd like to sit down privately with you. This Vietnam business is beginning to disturb me."

When we met a few days later, Shoup described his opposition to the war. "It curdles my blood to think that we're sending our boys over there on a mission we're not out to win," he said. "But that's what's going on. The will to win just isn't there. The president is afraid that if he pushes too hard, he'll start the next world war."

Shoup wasn't the only one who felt this way. Over the next few months, I met a number of experts from the Defense Department and the CIA who supported the president publicly, but who were saying just the opposite over a few beers at night. After several such conversations, I received a phone call from John Walker, a State Department officer who invited me to a dinner with a group of top men from the CIA. When I arrived at his place on P Street in Georgetown, I recognized it as the same house where Jack Kennedy had lived when he was a member of Congress.

One of the guests at that dinner was Tom McCoy, a CIA official who had just returned from Vietnam. McCoy believed that the American public was simply not prepared to have our side do what was necessary to win the war—which was more or less to destroy North Vietnam. In his view, we ought to pull out and declare that we had already achieved our goal. A year later, McCoy left the CIA to work for Eugene McCarthy's presidential campaign.

Just about everyone I met during this period was opposed to the war—not because we had no right to be in Vietnam, but because the conflict was "unwinnable." These people were also aware of the tremendous opposition to the war from other governments, including most of our allies. But what really disturbed the CIA men who opposed the war was that they were having no success in conveying their views to the commander in chief. As they saw it, some of the president's top-level advisers, including Walter Rostow, John Roche, and McGeorge Bundy, were preventing their memos and reports from reaching the Oval Office.

And so they had a specific request for me: Would I be willing to tell Speaker McCormack that a high-ranking group within the CIA was opposed to the war, and that their views were not getting through to the president?

"You're asking me to talk to McCormack?" I said. "That would be like knocking my head against the wall. John McCormack is an avid hawk who supports the president completely. Why me?"

"It has to be you," they said. "Everyone knows you're the closest person to McCormack in all of Washington. They say you can talk to him like nobody else, and that he listens to you like a father to his son."

I was surprised to hear this, for although it was essentially correct, I had no idea that other people were so aware of our relationship. But then these guys were with the CIA, and they're supposed to know *everything*.

In June of 1967, Millie and I took a vacation to visit our daughter Rosemary, who was a foreign service staff officer over in Malta. By coincidence, Malta was one of the places where American troops stationed in Vietnam were brought for rest and relaxation. We were having lunch in a restaurant one day when a young man came over and introduced himself. "I understand you're Congressman O'Neill," he said. "I live in Buzzards Bay on Cape Cod, where my father owns a garage. When you get back, would you mind calling him to say I'm all right?"

I said I'd be happy to, and he wrote out his name and number. A few minutes later, a group of his friends came in. I ordered wine for everybody, and before long we were talking about Vietnam. These boys weren't opposed to our involvement over there, but they had a number of criticisms about how the war was being fought. We couldn't fire until fired upon. We couldn't mine their harbors. And many of our troops didn't understand why we were involved over there in the first place, in what appeared to be a civil war.

Before we left Malta, I also spoke with several admirals from the Sixth Fleet. What they told me was similar to the arguments I had heard in Washington: that we were involved in a struggle we couldn't win—that we weren't even *trying* to win—and that we could be stuck over there for *years*. The admirals spoke freely, as long as I agreed not to quote them by name.

By September, I had made up my mind that the Vietnam conflict was a civil war, and that our involvement there was wrong. But how should I make my views known? I was never one to run to the press, and even as late as 1967 I had never held a press conference. For one thing, my style has always been to operate behind the scenes. For another, every time my name was in the papers, we'd get another flood of new constituent requests. And we already had more of those than we could handle.

I decided that the most appropriate way to make my views known was in a newsletter to my constituents. With the able assistance of Joseph McLaughlin and Terry Segal, two interns in my Washington office who happened to be law students, I drafted a carefully worded letter in which I set forth my position. I explained that as a citizen, a congressman, and a father, I believed that by remaining in Vietnam we were paying too high a price in both human lives and money. At the time, twelve thousand Americans had already been killed. (Before it was all over, that number would soar to almost sixty thousand.) And for what? For an objective that most of our men weren't even sure of.

In the letter, I outlined three conclusions I had reached with regard to Vietnam: First, we had to stop further escalation and attempt to bring the conflict before the United Nations. Second, we had to stop the bombing of the North. Third, we had to promote an Asian solution to what was essentially an Asian problem. Part of that solution was to encourage democratic elections in South Vietnam.

For a mainstream Democratic congressman like myself, the newsletter represented a radical departure—not only from the views of my colleagues, but also from those of my constituents. For despite all the colleges in my district, the students who were old enough to vote did so in their home communities. Of my regular constituents, only 15 percent opposed the war. The day I sent out that letter, I told my son Tommy that I had just signed my political death warrant.

But I knew it was the right thing to do. I had been in a parallel situation thirty years earlier, when I opposed the teacher's oath bill during my first term in the state legislature. In the case of Vietnam, now that my decision was made, I had no choice but to follow my conscience. I knew that all hell might break loose, because I was not only going against my district, but also against President Johnson,

John McCormack, and most of the Democratic party. I would be squeezed from both sides, so I fastened my seat belt and held on tight.

Back home, the reaction to the newsletter was just as I expected. I remember one phone call from the wife of a state rep who said, "Tip, they're kicking your brains out over here. They can't believe that you've changed your mind on the war."

That didn't surprise me. But what I hadn't counted on was that the antiwar crowd would become increasingly active, and that before long, packs of students would start burning American flags and breaking windows in Harvard Square. After every such incident, people would say, "There go O'Neill's kids again." It infuriated me that I was being blamed for their actions. Of course, they were hurting not just me but the entire antiwar cause.

I was opposed to the war not because of those students but in spite of them. But some people refused to believe that. I still have a newspaper clipping from that period which says, "O'Neill has recently sprouted the wings of a dove, presumably in response to pressure from the academic community in his district."

Bullshit. Despite my progressive views, I never had much appeal among the Cambridge academics and intellectuals. I didn't need their support, and I never sought it. But I've always been ahead of them on the issues.

There were exceptions, of course. I always had excellent relations with John Kenneth Galbraith, whom I greatly admire. He used to tell me that his Harvard colleagues didn't appreciate me, even though I had an outstanding record on all the issues that the academic liberals cared about. "They don't understand you," he'd say. "They think you're another Curley."

"Ken," I'd say, "let's do each other a favor. I won't say anything bad about you, and you'll promise not to endorse me." Some things never change, and any endorsement of Tip O'Neill from a Harvard professor could only hurt me among my regular supporters.

When I first sent out my letter on Vietnam, nobody in Washington was even aware of it. But all that changed on the night of September 14, 1967, although, as things turned out, I was one of the last to find out.

That evening I was playing cards at the Metropolitan Club. I had never gone there before, and with good reason: it was a swank establishment that discriminated against blacks. But for one night only, the regular game at the University Club had been moved over there so we could avoid Ben Jensen, a member from Iowa who had been losing more money than he could afford. Poor Ben just couldn't bring himself to stop playing, so for a few weeks we played hide-and-seek with him, ending up in a variety of unlikely locations.

I got home late, around two in the morning. As soon as he heard me come in, my roommate, Eddie Boland, jumped out of bed. "How did you get in?" he asked.

"What do you mean? I parked the car and came in through the garage."

"The Secret Service has been waiting for you all night. They're down in the lobby, and the White House called four times. The president was looking for you. Where the hell have you been?"

"What's going on?"

"I guess you haven't seen the paper." Eddie brought out the front page of the early edition of the Washington *Star*, which included a story with the headline "O'Neill Splits with LBJ Over Vietnam Policy." I learned later that a reporter from the *Star* had come across my Vietnam statement while looking through various congressional newsletters at the congressional printing office in the Cannon Building. When he realized that nobody had reported my change on the war, he decided to write it up.

According to Eddie, I was supposed to contact the White House no matter what time I got home. When I called the switchboard, the operator informed me that the president had left word that I was to come and see him at nine o'clock in the morning.

There were just the two of us in the Oval Office, and it was the first time I had seen Johnson alone since the death of Jack Kennedy. He had read the story in the paper, and he was angry and hurt at what he saw as my betrayal. "Tip, what kind of a son of a bitch are you? You, of all people! You and I have been friendly since the day you came to Washington. We were at the Board of Education together."

He continued, his voice rising: "I expect something like this from those assholes like Bill Ryan"—Ryan was an ultraliberal member of the House from New York and an early opponent of the president's

Vietnam policy—"but you? You're one of my own. Tell me, do you think you know more about this war than I do? Do you think I don't lie in bed at night, tossing and turning over this war?"

"No, Mr. President," I replied. "But in my heart and in my conscience I believe your policy is wrong. I've talked to generals and admirals. I've talked to the CIA, and they say they can't even get their information to you. Everybody tells me you're wrong. You can't expect the country to stand behind you while you're fighting a war that can't be won."

The president calmed down. "Is that what you think?" he said. "I thought you did this for political reasons. I thought you took this position because of all the students in your area."

"No, Mr. President. The students in my area actually hurt me. My strength is not with them. It's with the back-street people. These days, my constituents cross the street when they see me coming. They don't agree with me; they agree with you. But I think this war is wrong."

"Come with me," said the president. "I want to show you something." Together, we walked over to the situation room. Johnson pointed to a huge map of Vietnam dotted with colored lights, indicating the position of our forces.

"I spend a lot of time in this room," he said, almost in a whisper. "I know where all the troops are. I really care about our boys over there."

"I know you do," I replied.

When we returned to the Oval Office, I tried once more to make my point. "Mr. President, I have talked with the people who advocate your views on television and on the campuses. But most of them have real doubts. You can't win this war if you're not mining the harbors and knocking out the bridges and the power plants."

The president shook his head. "I can't do those things," he said. "They're just too dangerous. I can't risk involving the Soviets or the Chinese."

"Then let's get out of there," I said. "If we really can't win, we shouldn't be there in the first place."

It was time to leave. We stood up, and the president put his arm around me. "Tip," he said, "we'll always be friends. I understand now that you're doing this because you really believe it. I'm very glad that you came in and explained yourself. As for those CIA reports you told me about, I'll make sure to see them every morning.

"Now, I want you to do me a favor. Give me time on this thing. Don't go running to the press or telling everybody your views on the war. You're the first member of the Democratic establishment to oppose me on this, and I don't want you to start the snowball rolling." He could see that the issue was ripe to explode.

I gave him my word, and we parted on good terms. In retrospect, I'm sorry I went along with his request. I wish I *had* talked to the press, and to my colleagues in the House. I can't say for sure that it would have made any difference, but it might have, which means it was worth trying.

Looking back, I see that Lyndon Johnson understood my power more than I did. After fourteen years in the House, I was only dimly aware that I had a following. Johnson, however, knew all about it. He watched the House very closely, and he had already marked me as a leader. He understood very well that if Tip O'Neill went public, it might set off a wholesale defection.

Within a few months, however, it no longer mattered. By early 1968, Eugene McCarthy was opposing the president in the New Hampshire primary, and the stampede had already begun.

But in 1967, I still had my district to contend with. Many of my constituents had sons or brothers in Vietnam, and they saw my statement as an act of betrayal. A woman on our street had a son over there, and my position on the war made her furious. She lit into Millie at the hairdresser's because she thought I was jeopardizing her boy's life. Millie tried to explain that I was trying to get her son and *all* the sons back home safely, but she didn't see it that way.

In Cambridge, the local chapter of the American Legion called a meeting to protest my views on the war, and seven hundred people turned out. But thank God for old friends. Red Fitzgerald from Barry's Corner got up and said, "Listen, we may be veterans, but Tip O'Neill knows a lot more about this war than we do. Besides, he's been taking care of us for years. There isn't a man in this hall who hasn't gone to him for help with one thing or another. When we were overseas during the war and there was a family problem, we wrote to Tip and he straightened things out. If your kid had problems, you wrote Tip and he always did what he could. I say that this meeting is all wrong." From what people told me, Red's comments turned the tide that night, and the meeting broke up a few minutes later.

In politics, I've always found that when you go out and explain your position, people will listen and respect you even if they don't agree with your point of view. Naturally, they're even more inclined to give you a fair hearing if you have a good reputation for public service.

In the fall of 1967, I must have appeared at every church in the district. I remember one speech in Brighton, at the Holy Name Society of St. Columbkille's Parish. There was a mass at seven-thirty, followed by breakfast, and nine hundred people showed up. Both Jack and Bobby Kennedy had spoken there, but I drew the biggest crowd they had ever seen.

The audience peppered me with questions, and at one o'clock, when it was finally over, they lined up to shake my hand. "I never looked at it that way," people said. "I came in here thinking you were wrong, but I've changed my mind."

Poor Millie was worried when I wasn't home by noon. We had both been nervous about my appearance, and she couldn't understand why it took me so long to come back. But that morning's program marked the turning point in terms of the district's response to my change of heart on the war.

While the conservatives were bitter about my new views, the leftists attacked me for not doing enough. In Cambridge, the antiwar crowd began to demonstrate outside my home, and one morning I had the honor of being picketed by Jane Fonda. I told them they were wasting their time, and that coming to me to talk about the war was like preaching to the choir.

Once my position became known back in Washington, all kinds of antiwar groups came to see me, including the Concerned Clergy, the Concerned Students, the Concerned Lawyers, the Concerned Everybody. One of the first groups to come in was a delegation of students from M.I.T., led by Jerome Weisner, the institute's president.

"Tip, what can we do?" he asked.

I explained that almost all of the New England members were opposed to the war, and that they should stop visiting people like me, who were already on their side of the issue. "But here's what you can do. Put together a group of volunteers, and have them call the parents of every student from outside of New England. Tell them you're concerned about the war, and that you hope they'll contact their congressman if they share your doubts about the president's policy."

Weisner took my advice, and his group contacted the families of just about every student at M.I.T. It was a terrific project.

By 1968, the tide had begun to turn, as a growing number of Americans were against the war. On March 12, Senator Eugene McCarthy stunned the nation by winning 42 percent of the votes and most of the delegates in the New Hampshire primary. Less than three weeks later, on March 31, Lyndon Johnson added a single sentence to the conclusion of his prepared speech to the nation: "I shall not seek and I will not accept the nomination of my party for another term as your President."

Suddenly, Gene McCarthy was a serious candidate for president. Back in November, when he had first entered the race to oppose Johnson's policy in Vietnam, the polls showed the president to be so strong that none of us in the House imagined that anything much would come of McCarthy's challenge.

I knew Gene from the House of Representatives, where he had served all through the 1950s before being elected to the Senate. When the bells rang for a roll call, a group of us who all had offices on the same corridor would walk over to the floor of the House. Jimmy Roosevelt would stop by my office with Gus Hawkins, and then we'd pick up Gene, who would join us if he wasn't writing poetry or reading a book. He was a whimsical fellow who would come over only if he happened to feel like it.

At the 1960 convention, where Kennedy was nominated, Gene had given an eloquent and memorable speech for Adlai Stevenson, which included the famous lines, "Do not leave this prophet without honor in his own party. Do not reject this man." But by then Stevenson's prospects were dead, and the only real purpose of Gene's remarks was to try to stop the Kennedy forces in favor of Lyndon Johnson. Eight years later, of course, it was Gene, as much as anyone else, who put Johnson out of business.

After McCarthy's speech for Stevenson, he came over to Eddie

Boland and me and said, "Actually, I'm the one who should be nominated. Any way you measure it, I'm a better man than John Kennedy. I'm smarter, I'm a better orator, and if they're looking for a Catholic, I'm a better Catholic. Of course, I don't have a rich father."

He said it with a smile on his face, but there was a meanness in his heart. Even then, as a first-term senator, he wanted to be president.

The voters in my district supported Gene overwhelmingly, and under the state law I was bound to support him on the first ballot. We had been friends for years, and I respected him, even though he was lazy and a bit of a dreamer. He was also a loner. For a guy who wanted to be president, he never really worked the streets by asking for help from organizational types like me. Instead, he made his move outside the regular party structure.

Robert Kennedy jumped into the race shortly after McCarthy's strong showing in New Hampshire, but at the time of the Massachusetts primary he was not yet a declared candidate. If the nomination vote went beyond one ballot at the convention, I expected to switch over to Kennedy. Despite the fact that we weren't friendly, and that I was a great admirer of Humphrey, Kennedy was the home candidate and the one I was expected to be with. And if he hadn't been assassinated in June of 1968, I believe he would have won the nomination.

As everyone knows, the 1968 Democratic National Convention was a disaster. Looking back, it's hard for me to separate that disaster from the McCarthy people. Gene had the support of all the way-out, flaky liberals in the country, and they were the ones who were causing all the problems in the streets of Chicago.

Although they were right about the war, the students and the activists behaved terribly in Chicago. They threw stink bombs into our hotel, and the smell stayed there all week. They didn't accomplish a thing by tactics like that. I'll never forget the sight of a protester taking a piece of human dung and smearing it across the face of a police officer. Did the police overreact? Sure they did. But who could have stood up to such provocation? When they were finally free to strike back, no force in the world could have restrained them.

Despite his public position on the war, I wanted Humphrey to win. There was plenty of speculation that Humphrey had private doubts about Johnson's policy, but I knew it for a fact, because Humphrey and I had talked. He was far closer to my position than to the president's, but the job of the vice president is to be loyal to his boss. Besides, if Humphrey had come out against the war during the campaign, Lyndon would have found a way to make him pay.

I idolized Hubert Humphrey. Throughout his life, he worked for the values that he and I shared. Together with Representative Lenor Sullivan of Missouri, he developed the idea of food stamps. Instead of having the government store surplus food in warehouses, they argued, why not distribute that food to the needy, taking advantage of the same distribution system the rest of us use—the supermarket? To give the bill a better chance in the Senate, Humphrey had it introduced by Robert Dole, a conservative, through the Senate Committee on Agriculture.

Humphrey once made a beautiful statement, and it used to hang on the wall of my office, because it spells out my own philosophy and values so clearly and succinctly: "The moral test of government is how it treats those who are in the dawn of life, the children; those who are in the twilight of life, the aged; and those who are in the shadows of life—the sick, the needy and the handicapped."

Hubert was a liberal who never changed his stripes. I remember the last conversation we had, shortly before he died, in 1978. Carter was president, and Humphrey was sadly disappointed that the progressive spirit of the Democratic party seemed to be vanishing. "You and I are the only ones left," he said to me that day. "The rest of them are folding up like Republicans. What happened? Do they feel guilty because this nation has been good to the senior citizens and to the poor? I won't be around much longer, but I know you'll be out there fighting for all the causes that you and I have supported."

Tears were rolling down my face, because we both knew he was dying.

What a great president he would have been! He almost made it, too, but was held back by two members of his own party—Lyndon Johnson and Eugene McCarthy. Even after Johnson took himself out of the race, he wouldn't allow Humphrey to oppose the war in Vietnam until the final days of the campaign, when it was too late.

As for McCarthy, after Humphrey defeated him on the first ballot, he should have thrown his support to Hubert. But he withheld it until just before the election, when it was too late. As the campaign drew to a close, Humphrey was gaining on Nixon, and if the vote had been two or three days later, Humphrey would have won.

In 1969, when Richard Nixon came into office, he showed no great interest in pulling out of Vietnam. In Congress, however, a growing number of legislators were opposed to the war. But because of a peculiar voting system in the House of Representatives, it was all too easy for members to sit on the fence. What constituents don't always realize is that the real action in the House is not necessarily on the bills, but on the amendments. And whereas votes on bills have always been a matter of public record, amendments, until fairly recently, have operated under a very different system.

Under the rules of the House, members voting on amendments would walk down one of two aisles of the House—depending on whether they were voting yea or nay. When they reached the front of the line, they were tapped on the shoulder by a teller—a fellow representative who was counting the votes. The final count would be recorded, but unless you were watching from the gallery and could recognize individual members from behind, it was almost impossible to know how—or even if—an individual member had voted.

Ever since I first came to Congress, I thought unrecorded teller voting, as the procedure was known, was a disgrace. Not only was it a tremendous waste of time, but it was also a cowardly system. It was embarrassingly easy for a member to duck a vote because he had made promises to both sides—and even to lie about it afterward, because there was no way anybody could check. But the whole point of having a Congress is that the representatives of the people are accountable to their constituents.

During the mid 1960s, when the Rules Committee was discussing ways to reorganize procedures in the House, I tried to put an end to unrecorded teller voting. Unfortunately, my proposal was defeated 8 to 7. But now, with Vietnam on the agenda, the issue came up again. With more and more members opposed to the war—not only doves, but also hawks, who were convinced that a half-hearted military effort made little sense—it was clear that if we had an on-the-record vote on Vietnam, the antiwar forces could demonstrate their real strength. That way, we'd show that we were a growing force, and we'd also know which colleagues we ought to be working on to try to change their minds.

Not surprisingly, I wasn't the only one who felt this way. The Coalition on National Priorities and Military Policy, a church-oriented lobbying group that supported arms control, had gone so far as to station several dozen volunteers in the House gallery. Each one was given the responsibility of recognizing the physical characteristics of four members of Congress, in order to monitor their votes on amendments. The coalition's action helped to dramatize the absurdity of the current system.

Meanwhile, Common Cause, the citizens' lobby, became involved in the issue, and they approached me for help. I was surprised to hear from them, because, as I've mentioned, I already had a couple of run-ins with these people. At one point, they had made a big stink about my ongoing insurance business back in Cambridge, which was earning me a grand total of seven thousand dollars a year. Common Cause claimed that it represented a conflict of interests, and I thought it best to give it up.

But Common Cause believed that a bill calling for an end to unrecorded teller voting, and sponsored jointly by Tip O'Neill and Charles Gubser, a California Republican, would sail through the house. Gubser was a very popular member; I was chosen not only because I had already raised the issue in the Rules Committee, but also because I was seen as a responsible, mature politician who could never be accused of being a wild-eyed radical. When Gubser and I agreed to become involved, Common Cause and the Democratic Study Group (a liberal coalition of House Democrats) promised to do the lobbying.

Before our amendment came to a vote, we had already lined up 182 cosponsors, and in August 1970, it was approved by the House. I spoke in favor of the bill, pointing out that the last three presidents—Nixon, Johnson, and Kennedy—had all served in the House of Representatives, and yet, if you were writing a history of their careers, you would be able to find no indication of how they had voted on the vital amendments of the day.

It was not, admittedly, the most pertinent argument against the old system, but the pertinent arguments were clear enough. Besides, unless I am mistaken, some of the members listening to my speech that day had no trouble imagining that at some future date, historians would be eager to learn more about *their* early years in the House of Representatives.

It wasn't until almost three years later that the antiwar forces finally triumphed on an amendment. On May 10, 1973, in a historic decision, the House voted 219 to 188 to stop the Defense Department from spending any more money on the war in Vietnam.

A few years later, the author of a book on the Vietnam War came to see me. "You know," he said, "I'll never understand why you haven't been appreciated by the liberal intelligentsia of this country. I've researched this thing from top to bottom, and more than any other person, you're responsible for bringing the war to an end. There was your break with Johnson, your educating of your Democratic colleagues, all those talks in your district, and your role in putting an end to unrecorded teller voting."

I thanked him for his kind words. He was exaggerating, of course, for I was far from the only politician to oppose our involvement in Vietnam. But it's nice to think that my actions back then may have helped save a few lives.

My last contact with Lyndon Johnson came during a televised football game. Lyndon was no longer in office, but when the New England Patriots were in Dallas to play the Cowboys, one of the announcers spotted the former president and conducted a brief interview. "I've got two great friends up in Boston," Johnson said. "I'm sure John McCormack and Tip O'Neill are watching this game, and I'd like to say a big hello to them both."

His greeting came as a complete surprise. But it meant a great deal to me, because it showed that although I had disappointed him on the war, he had found it in his heart to forgive me. A few months later, when he died, I felt I had lost a friend—a friend who made a tremendous difference for a lot of people in this country. If it hadn't been for Vietnam, Lyndon Johnson could have gone down in history as another Roosevelt.

10

★★★★★

Into the Leadership

As I look back on my career, I would love to be able to claim that my rise from humble member of Congress to Speaker of the House followed a natural and easy path, and that my political and legislative abilities were so self-evident that I was everybody's first choice by acclamation.

But politics doesn't work that way. If I was talented, so were a hundred other guys who served with me. Why, then, did I become Speaker whereas they didn't? The answer has to do with a combination of factors, including timing, fate, money, personality, and even tragedy—not to mention the usual list of human frailties, feuds, and jealousies.

Let's start with money, which is the lifeblood of politics. When Mike Kirwan, the veteran member from Ohio, died in 1970, I took over as chairman of the Democratic Congressional Campaign Committee, which raised and distributed campaign funds to Democratic candidates for the House. Mike's policy had been to give out $500 to every Democrat who was running, but I didn't care for that way of doing things.

Instead, my staff and I studied the various districts and commissioned polls, giving out money only to candidates who really needed it, and only if they also stood a good chance of winning. In addition, we started tracking the record of Republican members who seemed vulnerable, and in those districts we helped the Democratic challenger with his polling, phone calls, and fund-raising. I loved this work, which was a natural extension of what I had accomplished in Massachusetts in 1948, when, at John McCormack's urging, a few of us had worked feverishly to make the state house Democratic.

Another reason I was successful at the job was that I was willing to travel all over the country to help Democratic candidates. Mike Kirwan had pretty much stayed in Washington, and John McCormack hated to travel, but I went out to the districts and got to know many of the candidates and the party officials. I attended more cocktail parties than I care to remember, but I also did a lot of favors and became known as something of a power in the party.

As chairman of the DCCC, I was especially concerned about the 1972 congressional elections. When George McGovern was nominated in Miami, there was no question that he would lose big. The only thing left to determine was how badly he would hurt our candidates for the House and the Senate.

On the flight back from the convention in Miami, I shared my concern with Robert Strauss, the treasurer of the Democratic National Committee.

"If things are that bad," he said, "I'm going to raise a million dollars for the DCCC."

When you spend your life in politics, you hear a lot of grandiose promises, and I assumed that Strauss was talking through his hat. I smiled politely and said, "Fine. Let me know when you're ready to move."

Strauss called the next day. "I've been thinking about our conversation," he said. "I'd like to run cocktail parties in New York, Chicago, Dallas, and Los Angeles. But I'll need a guarantee that all the big names will be there, including Jackson, Mansfield, and Humphrey from the Senate, and Albert, Boggs, Wilbur Mills, and yourself from the House. If you can deliver these people, I can raise a million dollars in ten days."

For that kind of money, everybody was willing to sign on. And just as he promised, Strauss raised a million dollars, which we split among candidates for the House and the Senate. As a result, we were able to elect a good number of Democrats in spite of the Nixon landslide.

All of the parties were successful, but the ones in California were the best of all. I always enjoy fund-raising out there, because I've found that Californians give more freely than people in other regions of the country. If you have something to sell, that's the place to sell it.

In San Francisco, Walter Shorenstein was extremely helpful. In

Los Angeles, Gene and Roz Wyman were our chief people. There was a big party at the home of Gene Klein, the former owner of the San Diego Chargers, back when he was still a Democrat, and another run by Lew Wasserman, the movie mogul, for people in the film-and-entertainment business. Quite a few of them were famous, but their glamour was lost on me. I never go to the movies, so I didn't recognize a soul.

At one of the Los Angeles parties, our host got up and said, "Tonight we're going to try something a little different. Since we have such a marvelous group of entertainers who are here to help the politicians, we're going to ask the politicians to provide the entertainment."

Each of us had to get up and sing a song or tell a story. I told a couple of Irish tales about Uncle Denny, including one old chestnut in which Uncle Denny is walking down the street and meets the pastor.

"Good morning, Father."

"Good morning yourself," says the pastor. "Denny, you ought to be ashamed of yourself. Three weeks ago you came in and took the pledge and vowed that you'd never take another drink as long as you live. And now look at you—you're drunk!"

"I'm not drunk, Father," says Uncle Denny. "What makes you say a thing like that? I'm not drunk at all."

"Well if you're not drunk," says the pastor, "then why were you walking along with one foot on the curbstone and one foot in the gutter?"

"I was?"

"Indeed you were."

"Well, thanks be to God," says Uncle Denny. "I thought I was lame!"

The following year, when Bob Strauss wanted to become chairman of the Democratic National Committee, he called to ask for my support. I was happy to give it to him, although my endorsement annoyed some of my fellow liberals, who didn't trust Strauss because he was said to be no friend of labor. "What are you backing *him* for?" they all wanted to know.

"Because one hand washes the other," I said. "Because when we were stone broke, he's the guy who came through for us."

Bob turned out to be a hell of a chairman. He raised a ton of money to pay off the party's debts, and he was instrumental in helping us elect a Democratic president in 1976. Bob does have a tendency to brag, and it's always been a toss-up as to who had the biggest ego in Washington—Robert Strauss or Henry Kissinger. But there's no question that Strauss can really produce.

One reason I enjoyed my work for the DCCC is that I've always found it easier to raise money for other people than for myself. Fund-raising on your own behalf can make for some awkward moments, as I learned in 1971 when Davis Taylor, the publisher of the Boston *Globe*, came to me. At the time, I had some opposition in the primary, and Taylor said that he wanted to help me out with a donation. "I know how much you've done for the economy of our area," he said. "And whenever somebody at the *Globe* has a problem, you're the guy we call. I'd like to give you a contribution of five hundred dollars. But it wouldn't look right as a newspaper publisher to have my name listed, so could you put the money in some account where you don't have to make it public?"

This was easy to arrange, because in addition to my Boston account, I also had an account in Washington, where there was no law about disclosing the names of contributors. Maintaining a separate Washington account was a convenience used by a number of congressmen, because many contributors prefer to make their donations anonymously. It's not that they've got anything to hide, but they've learned from experience that if their contributions become public, they'll immediately start hearing from an endless stream of candidates, causes, and charities. So I put the Davis Taylor money in my Washington account, along with $11,500 in other contributions from my supporters in Boston.

A few days later, a reporter from the *Globe* who was writing a story on campaign finances came to me and said, "I'd like to know who gave you the twelve thousand dollars."

"I don't have to disclose that information," I said. "That money is in my Washington account."

"But it was transferred to your Boston account," he said, "and I want the names."

"Forget it," I said. "That money was given to me by people who don't want their names disclosed. They don't want to end up on everybody's hit list."

He persisted, but I refused to give him the names.

The next day, the *Globe* ran a story: "O'Neill 'Hid' Campaign Names in Legal D.C. List." Although the article made clear that I had done nothing illegal, there was certainly the suggestion that I had something to hide. The following day, the Associated Press picked up the story and sent out its own version to papers all over the country.

To put an end to the matter, I instructed John Linnehan, my campaign treasurer, to send the list to Davis Taylor. I attached a letter: "Dear Davis," I wrote. "In view of the fact that your paper insists on knowing who my contributors are, here is the complete list. You have my permission to use it—in full—or to give it to any other newspaper."

Then I wrote to Tom Winship, the editor of the *Globe:* "Dear Tom: I have just sent Davis Taylor a list of my contributors. Feel free to publish the names."

Not surprisingly, that was one story the *Globe* never followed up.

My rise to a more formal position in the Democratic leadership began in the spring of 1970, when John McCormack, the Speaker of the House, announced that he was retiring at the end of the year. Carl Albert was the majority leader, and most people expected he would be McCormack's successor. Certainly that's what McCormack had in mind. "Tom," he said to me, "I want you to get the signatures of the New England delegation for Carl Albert."

To be elected Speaker, a member of Congress needs the support of a majority of members from his own party. In point of fact, he doesn't require any signatures or pledges, but that was the custom in the Massachusetts state house, and McCormack thought it would be a nice gesture of support for Carl. At a meeting of the New England delegation, McCormack made a speech supporting Albert, and I got everybody to sign up for Carl.

Once New England was taken care of, Carl Albert went after the Illinois delegation. Here, however, he ran into problems. Mel Price was the titular head of the group, but the real power in that group was Dan Rostenkowski, who had his own ideas as to who should be Speaker. Rostenkowski was known as Mayor Daley's man in the Congress, which meant that he was the one who controlled the delegation.

Richard Daley's power and prestige were something to behold. Daley was the last of a dying breed of big-city bosses, and whenever he came to Washington, the entire Chicago delegation would drive out to the airport to greet him.

One afternoon in the late 1950s I was in the office of John Kluczynski when Daley telephoned. Klu was a big, strong, Polish guy from Chicago, and one of the most popular members in the House. I knew him well because he was also a great cardplayer.

"Johnny," said Daley, "I was talking to Sam Rayburn. There's going to be a Committee on Public Roads next year, and I want you on that committee."

"Mr. Mayor," said Klu, "don't do this to me. I've been on Banking and Currency for ten years. I have seniority. Next year I'll be a subcommittee chairman, and I'll have patronage. I'll have *jobs*, Mr. Mayor."

"I don't care how long you've been on that committee," said Daley. "I need you on the new one. The Calumet Bridge is costing us a fortune, and when you get on Public Roads I want you to transfer it over to the federal government."

Klu hung up the phone and reported the conversation to me, "Jesus," he said, "can you believe it? Ten years I'm on that committee and now I have to give it up."

"You've got to be kidding," I said. "If the mayor of Boston ever called and tried to tell me what committee to be on, I'd let him know where the hell he could stick it."

Klu just shook his head. "Tip," he said, "let me tell you something about Chicago. I'm loved in my district. I have the largest catering business in town, with eight hundred employees. But the mayor controls the election committee, and if the election committee doesn't support me, I'm out on my ass. I could spend a million bucks, but I'd never beat the Daley machine."

A year or two later, I had my own close-up look at the power of Richard Daley. Frip Flannigan, a dear friend of mine, was the Washington representative of the W. R. Grace Company. During my very first month in Congress, Frip had sought my help in straightening out a problem at the Dewey and Almy Chemical Company, a division of Grace and one of the largest employers in Cambridge. I took care of it, and Frip and I became great friends.

In 1959, Frip came to ask for my help again. "They've just opened the St. Lawrence Seaway," he said, "and the Grace Steamship Company has a passenger ship coming in from the port of Le Havre to Chicago. This is the first ship ever to cross the Atlantic and sail directly to Chicago, ánd we're very excited about it. We've got it in the locks, but two Dutch ships snuck in front of us and now it looks like they'll be the first ones in."

"What do you want me to do about it?" I said.

"We had hoped to receive a tremendous amount of publicity all over the world, and now we're about to lose it. Can you speak to some of your friends in Chicago?"

"I'll see what I can do," I said.

I took Frip with me to see old Tom O'Brien, the head of the Chicago delegation and the former sheriff of Cook County. (Rostenkowski was a freshman at the time.) Whenever Daley needed a vote, it was Tom who passed the word to the other members from Illinois. When Frip told him about the Grace ship, he put in a call to Mayor Daley. "Mr. Mayor," he said, "I've got Tip O'Neill here. Tip is one of the leaders of the New England group, and whenever you want something for Chicago, he always delivers New England for us. Maybe you could help him out."

"What the hell does he want?" growled Daley.

"Let me put him on," said Tom.

I explained the situation to Daley, and then I put Frip on the phone. Daley asked a couple of questions and told Frip he'd get back to us in twenty minutes.

When the mayor called back, he said to Frip, "The first Dutch ship is going to arrive tonight around ten o'clock. The second one will arrive around three in the morning, and your ship is due in around six. All three ships will be forced to stay out in the harbor while the health authorities run an inspection.

"At nine in the morning, your ship will be the first to come in. To celebrate this occasion, tomorrow will be a special holiday in Chicago. We'll have a big parade with high school bands and the whole works, and W. R. Grace will receive worldwide recognition for having the first ship to make the trip to Chicago without a stop."

That's the way they did things in Chicago. That's how powerful

Richard Daley was, and how well he could capitalize on opportunities.

All of which is to explain why Dan Rostenkowski, Daley's man in Congress, was so important. And neither he nor Richard Daley wanted Carl Albert to be Speaker. As far as they were concerned, the next Speaker was going to be Hale Boggs of Louisiana, who was the whip under John McCormack.

The bad feelings between Albert and the Daley people went back to the 1968 Democratic convention in Chicago. Humphrey won the nomination, of course, but that was almost secondary to the tremendous protests and demonstrations in the streets of Chicago. As chairman of the convention, Carl Albert did not have an easy time controlling the delegates. During one particularly chaotic moment, President Johnson, who was watching it all on television, phoned Daley and ordered him to get control of the crowd. Daley immediately sent Rosty to the podium to restore order. Rosty pulled the gavel away from Albert on national television, and Carl never forgave him for this humiliation.

Years earlier, McCormack had told me how both Carl Albert and Hale Boggs had become part of the leadership. Back in 1954, after the Democrats won the off-year election, Rayburn regained his position as Speaker, with McCormack as majority leader. McCormack informed Rayburn that he wanted Hale Boggs to be the whip. In theory, the majority leader chose his own whip, but in practice, that choice was always subject to the approval of the Speaker. (This all changed in 1986, when, for the first time, the whip was chosen by a vote of the Democratic caucus.)

When McCormack told Rayburn that he wanted Boggs, Rayburn replied by saying, "John, I'm going on a little errand and I want you to take a walk with me." Together, they went over to Carl Albert's office. In Albert's presence, Rayburn said, "John, as you know, Carl here comes from Oklahoma. But did you know that his district is right next to mine? Did you know that Carl was a champion orator in high school and in college? Did you know that he was a Rhodes Scholar? Did you know that nobody knows as much about legislation as he does?"

The word "whip" was never mentioned, but McCormack didn't need a road map to know that the Speaker was telling him to choose

Here I am at age five.

With my father, Thomas P. O'Neill; Millie; and Thomas III, Rosemary, and Susan.

Back row, family members Mary O'Neill Mulcahy, Sister Eunice Tolan, Rosemary O'Neill, Dorothy Miller Ryan; *center*, Millie and me; *front*, Susan with Michael, Christopher, Dorothy Ryan's daughter, and Tommy III.

From a 1952 campaign brochure: "WHERE GOOD CHEER AND HAPPINESS REIGN—The O'Neills make each day a new adventure and family fun places high on the list of daily musts. Here House Speaker Thomas P. O'Neill, Jr., and Mrs. O'Neill are shown with their five children (from left): Christopher, 2 1/2, on dad's knee; Thomas, 7; Rosemary, 9; Susan, 5; and Michael, 10 months, being held by mother." (Bradford Bachrach)

Our thirtieth wedding anniversary photo, 1971. (Bradford Bachrach)

With Kip and Stephanie's daughters Abby, six, *left,* and Catlin, eight, *center,* and daughter Susan's three-year-old, Michaela Daniel. (Leonard F. Rizzi, Photogroup Inc.)

With my father, *far right,* Flag Day, 1948. (Charles Flagg)

At the St. Patrick's Day parade, with some of my grandchildren, 1986.

The O'Neill for Congress headquarters, 1952.

"Class Opinion," Boston College class of 1936.

The Law Academy, Boston College law society, 1936.

class opinion

Class Adonis...........................Tom Brennan
Class Hero.............................Tim Ready
Class Artist...........................George Lovett
Class Crooner..........................Amby Flynn
Class Columnist........................Paul Power
Class Politician.......................Tip O'Neill
Class Actor............................Gerry Burke
Class Booster..........................Fred Roche
Class Philosopher......................Henry Beauregard
Class Scientist........................John Tosney
Class Punster..........................Paul Power
Class Editorialist.....................Paul Power
Class Dreamer..........................John Zuromskis
Class Caveman..........................Tip O'Neill
Class Handshaker.......................Marc Sullivan
Class Heartbreaker.....................George Goodwin
Class Satirist.........................Louis Mercier
Class Superman.........................Ted Galligan
Most Popular Senior....................Tim Ready
Most Versatile Senior..................Tim Ready
Most Promising Senior..................Lawrence Riley
Most Dignified Senior..................Lawrence Riley
Most Energetic Senior..................Henry Beauregard
Most Talkative Senior..................Maurice Fitzgerald
Most Ambitious Senior..................Henry Beauregard
Most Reserved Senior...................Tom Brennan
Most Suave Senior......................Bud St. Pierre
Most Chivalrous Senior.................George Goodwin
Most Helpful Senior....................Jim Keating

A 1938 campaign poster.

THOMAS P.

O'NEILL JR.

FIRST DEMOCRATIC SPEAKER IN HISTORY OF THE MASSACHUSETTS HOUSE OF REPRESENTATIVES

HE'S A LEADER!

HE'S A DOER!

HE FOLLOWS THRU!

HE'S YOUR MAN FOR

CONGRESS

From a 1952 campaign brochure. (Bradford Bachrach)

Eddie Boland and me outside the Capitol, 1956.

With Ralph Granara, political aide and practical joker.

Campaigning, Newbury Street Housing for the Elderly, Cambridge, Massachusetts, 1982.

With James M. Curley, governor of Massachusetts and legendary mayor of Boston.

Statue of Curley behind City Hall in Boston.

With Bobby Kennedy early in the 1968 campaign.

With Ted Kennedy after the 1962 elections.

With Jack Kennedy, as Dwight D. Eisenhower signs
legislation affecting New England.

Jack Kennedy meets the O'Neill clan on the old Senate
subway during my first week in Congress, 1953.

With Jack Kennedy at a
St. Patrick's Day party, 1959.

St. Patrick's Day with Speaker Sam Rayburn. *Left to right*, entertainer Phil Reagan, Congressman Mike Kirwan, Speaker Rayburn, me, Congressman Ed Boland.

At the Democratic convention, 1964, with Hubert Humphrey and John McCormack.

The Hubert Humphrey credo that I kept in my office.

The moral test of government is how it treats those who are in the dawn of life, the children; those who are in the twilight of life, the aged; and those who are in the shadows of life, the sick, the needy and the handicapped.

from the last speech of Hubert Humphrey
Washington, DC.
November 1, 1977

Being sworn in as Speaker for the first time, January 3, 1977. (*U.S. News & World Report*)

ABOVE RIGHT: Photo inscription: "To Speaker Tip O'Neill with my deep friendship and respect. John McCormack."

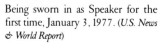

Reagan at State of the Union address, 1981. Inscription from George Bush reads: "Tip, OK for now, but please do not talk to me during the speech, OK? All best, George."

Democratic Club, St. Patrick's Day, 1982. (Stan Jennings)

With President Harry S. Truman, 1952.

President Eisenhower's luncheon for new members of Congress at the White House, 1953. Ed Boland is in the front row, second from the left; I am at far right. (U.S. Army photograph)

Leadership meeting on the Vietnam War, 1973.

With President Lyndon Johnson, 1966.

With Gerald Ford, 1973. (U.S. Senate photograph)

LEFT: On the golf course with Gerald Ford. (UPI Newspictures)

ABOVE: With Jimmy Carter, 1978. (U.S. Senate photograph)

With Nixon, Ford, and Carl Albert. (Official White House photograph)

To our great friends Tip & Millie

Jimmy Carter   Rosalynn Carter

Dinner with the Carters at the
White House, 1979. (Official
White House photograph)

Inscription from Ronald Reagan,
May 1981: "Dear Tip, Then the
one Irishman said to the other
Irishman—'Top of the mornin'
to ya.' Ron."

With Prime Minister Mena-
chem Begin, 1980.

With Prime Minister Anwar
Sadat, 1980. (Dev O'Neill, K.
Jewell)

(S. Kelly © 1986 San Diego Union,
Copley News Service.)

With Prime Minister Margaret
Thatcher, 1985.

With Soviet Premier Mikhail Gorbachev and, *from left*, Congressmen Silvio Conte, Bob Michel, and Dan Rostenkowski.

With Prime Minister Indira Gandhi, 1982.

On the green, 1982.

Saying farewell to Ireland after receiving the distinguished Freeman of Cork award in March 1985.

St. Patrick's Day, 1984. (*The New York Times*)

Carl Albert. McCormack selected Hale Boggs as deputy whip, and when Rayburn died in 1961, each of the three—McCormack, Albert, and Boggs—moved up one step on the ladder.

Now, in 1970, Carl Albert was the clear favorite to succeed McCormack, although Richard Daley and Dan Rostenkowski were determined to prevent that from happening. But Albert had very few enemies, and a handful of votes from Illinois was not enough to stop him. His only opponent for the job was John Conyers of Michigan, who received just 20 votes to 220 for Albert.

The real race was for majority leader, who, like the Speaker, is elected every two years by the majority party. Hale Boggs was the favorite, but there were four other announced candidates: B. F. Sisk of California, Jim O'Hara of Michigan, Wayne Hays of Ohio, and Morris Udall of Arizona.

Boggs was a hail and hearty fellow who was extremely popular among the members. But although he was already in the leadership, not everybody wanted to see him become the majority leader. As a southern moderate, Hale Boggs was squeezed from both sides: some of the liberals didn't accept him because he was a southerner, while some of the southerners thought he had become too liberal—especially on civil rights.

Boggs had another problem. He had recently made a speech on the floor of the House claiming the FBI was bugging his office. When his colleagues heard that, they said Hale was off his rocker, that he was paranoid, that he had been drinking too much. And what a charge! That the FBI was bugging the office of the whip? Everybody knew that the FBI didn't do things like that.

But I believed Boggs, and I still do. For one thing, I was convinced that the FBI *did* do things like that. For another, I knew from a mutual friend that Boggs had been informed of the tap by a fellow who worked for the phone company.

Boggs's leading opponent in the race for majority leader was Morris Udall, who was popular for two reasons. First, Udall was a true liberal in the days when liberals still represented the mainstream of the Democratic party. Second, Udall was responsible for a system of automatic pay raises in Congress. This endeared him to the members, because if there's one thing that congressmen really love, it's a pay raise. But if there's one thing they really hate, it's having to *vote* for a pay raise. Under Udall's plan, they would receive pay raises automatically—without having to cast a vote that would be unpopular at home.

The other three candidates were long shots. There are those who believe that Wayne Hays was a possibility, but I don't agree. Hays was an excellent orator and a smart and knowledgeable congressman, but he had a negative disposition. The man had a mean streak and was often abusive to people he didn't agree with. Even when he praised you he did it with a nasty twist. There was no way that someone with his personality would be elected majority leader. When Wayne Hays resigned from Congress, most of us were delighted to see him go.

It was Hays, of course, who hired Elizabeth Ray, a secretary who worked for the House Administration Committee and was paid $14,000 a year even though she couldn't type or file. In May of 1976, she got her boss in real trouble when she told two reporters from the *Washington Post* that her real job was to be his girl friend. I was majority leader at the time, and when the story broke, Carl Albert and I were on a plane to London to pick up the Magna Carta, which was being loaned to the United States for the Bicentennial. By the time we landed, the news was all over the world.

As soon as I returned to Washington, Hays came in to see me. "I've been to see the Speaker," he said, "and he says that we can forget about this thing, and that the leadership can let me off with a warning."

"No way," I replied. "You've disgraced the Congress and you've got to resign from your chairmanships."

"But Carl said it would be all right."

Carl's problem was that he said yes to everybody. "It may be all right with the Speaker," I told Hays, "but it's not all right with me. If you don't resign, I'm going to bring this business before the caucus, and we'll strip you of your chairmanships on the spot." Not surprisingly, Wayne Hays chose to resign.

Back in 1971, I, too, considered becoming a candidate for majority leader. I had been in Congress close to twenty years, and because of my outgoing personality, not to mention my position on the Rules Committee, I knew a lot of the members. My early opposition to the war in Vietnam had made me known as something of a leader, especially among the younger guys. And as chairman of the Democratic Congressional Campaign Committee, I had done a lot of favors for people. Perhaps this was the time to call them in.

While I was mulling over whether to enter the race, Eddie Boland started telling people that *he* was running for majority leader. That put an end to my plans, because there was no way I would run against my own roommate. Instead, I put my energy into running Eddie's campaign. I did a lot of work for him, and we could count on close to fifty votes.

In retrospect, I don't know how serious Eddie was about running, because he didn't do any work on his own behalf. Eventually, he withdrew from the race and announced he was supporting Udall. I suspect they had worked out a deal that if Udall won, Eddie would become the new whip. Perhaps this had been the plan all along.

As soon as Eddie withdrew, John McCormack called me from Boston. "Tom," he said, "I hope you're not supporting Udall." Mo Udall was a beautiful guy and a close friend, but he had made a big mistake a couple of years earlier when he had challenged McCormack for Speaker. There was no way he could have won, but even so, McCormack never forgave him. I liked Mo, but I was loyal to McCormack. Besides, I thought Hale Boggs was the better candidate.

With Boland out of the race, Boggs called to see whom I was supporting. When he seemed to be beating around the bush, I told him the story of how Mrs. O'Brien, who had lived across the street from us in Cambridge, had explained to me back in 1935 that people like to be asked.

Boggs laughed. "Okay," he said, "will you be with me for majority leader?"

"I'd be delighted," I said.

"And would you make some calls for me?"

"Certainly."

Later, Gary Hymel, Boggs's administrative assistant, told me that when Boggs hung up from that call, he said, "I've just been elected. Tip is good for twenty votes."

I don't know about twenty, but Boggs gave me a list of eighteen people to call. All of them had been pledged to Eddie Boland, and I was pleased that every one of them agreed to vote for Boggs.

A couple of days before the vote, I ran into Dan Rostenkowski in Paul Young's restaurant. At the time, Dan was chairman of the Democratic caucus, which was responsible for electing the Speaker and the majority leader.

"We gave you a screwing today," he said. "I met with the five announced candidates and we decided that if you haven't announced for majority leader, you can't run."

"I'm not running anyway," I said. "I'm with Boggs."

"Don't give me that," Rosty said. "We know you're trying to sneak in through the back door." Now it was true that Jimmy Burke and a couple of other guys had wanted me to run, but I could see that this wasn't my year. Besides, I had already pledged my support to Hale Boggs.

As things turned out, it was Danny who got the screwing. The next morning, there was a vote to select a chairman for the Democratic caucus. Rostenkowski was running for reelection, and he hadn't expected any opposition. But in a surprise move, the Texas delegation put up its own candidate, Olin Teague. Teague, who was known as Tiger, was a popular guy, a war hero, and chairman of the Veterans' Affairs Committee.

Teague had made it clear that he had no interest in the job, but that didn't stop his fellow Texans. So just before the vote, Tiger got up to let us know where he stood: "I'm not a candidate," he said. "My delegation is insisting on putting my name in nomination, but I myself am voting for Rostenkowski."

To everybody's astonishment, Teague defeated Rostenkowski. The liberals voted against Danny because of his ties to Daley, and some of Albert's friends voted against him because of their feud. And apparently Teague was even more popular than we knew.

The next task was to elect a majority leader. To win the caucus vote, a candidate needed 125 votes. If nobody received that many, there would be a second ballot, with the low man dropping out. The process would continue until we had a winner.

On the first ballot, Boggs led Udall 95 to 69. Sisk, Hays, and O'Hara trailed in that order, with Hays and O'Hara dropping out. On the second ballot, Boggs won easily, with 140 votes to 88 for Udall and 17 for Sisk.

Now it was time to choose the whip. While the majority leader helps set policy and carries out the duties assigned to him by the Speaker, the whip's job is to make sure that members of his party are present for important votes, and that they vote the way the leadership wants. The whip is the enforcer of party discipline, and the term comes from England, where "whipper-in" originally referred to the man who was assigned to keep the hounds from straying during a fox hunt.

Danny desperately wanted the job, but in view of the Chicago convention episode, and the fact that Rostenkowski had withheld his support from the new Speaker, there was no way on earth that Carl Albert was going to let that happen. And now he had the perfect excuse: Rostenkowski's own colleagues had rejected him as caucus chairman.

This put Boggs in an awkward position, as he had more or less promised Rostenkowski the job. But Albert held firm. "He insulted me and humiliated me at the convention," said Carl. "I won't have him."

Three times Boggs asked Albert to give the job to Rostenkowski, and three times Albert turned him down. Searching for a compromise candidate that the Speaker and the majority leader could both support, Boggs asked Gary Hymel to draw up a list of possibilities. Boggs took the list to Albert, who crossed off three names that he found unacceptable. That left five possible choices, including Hugh Carey of New York and Tip O'Neill of Massachusetts.

The following day the *New York Times* came out with a front-page story: "Whip Battle Between Carey and O'Neill." Hugh Carey and I were good friends. I had known from the papers that he was interested in the job, although neither of us had ever mentioned the topic to the other. That afternoon, I looked up at the House gallery and saw Carey's wife and all of their thirteen children sitting there. I figured it was all over.

Then Millie called. She had seen the story in the Boston paper, and she wanted to know if I was going to get the job.

"It's too late," I said. "It looks like Carey has already been notified.

"Tom," she said, "you haven't even asked for the position, have you? All your life you've been telling that Mrs. O'Brien story about how people like to be asked. Why don't you ask Boggs for the job?"

"It's too late," I repeated.

"You never know," said Millie.

I went to see Boggs and said, "Hale, remember that story I told you about Mrs. O'Brien? Well, I'm here to tell you I'm interested in the whip job. I'm a loyal Democrat every inch of the way, and I hope you'll consider me."

Hale thanked me for coming, and he said he'd consider my request. But he gave no hint one way or the other about his decision.

An hour later Carl Albert called me on the phone. "Tip, I'm sitting here with Hale Boggs, and he has something to tell you."

I assumed it was a courtesy call, and that Boggs wanted to let me know they had chosen Carey. But I was mistaken.

"Tip, how would you like to be whip?"

"I'd love it," I said.

"Then get right over here and I'll introduce you to the press."

I happened to be wearing a blue shirt and a red tie, and when I got to Boggs's office he teased me about my outfit. "You were expecting this, weren't you?" he said. "You came dressed for television."

But I had been certain that the whip job was going to Hugh Carey. Little did I know that John Rooney and Jim Delaney, two senior and powerful members of the New York delegation, had been in to see Albert. "Don't pick Carey," they told the Speaker. "He's a troublemaker and a publicity-seeker who takes credit for everything we've done. If you appoint him, don't ever expect any loyalty from us."

So now Carl Albert was vetoing Carey, just as he had already vetoed Rostenkowski. The one guy that both he and Boggs could agree on was Tip O'Neill.

Shortly after the appointment, John McFall from California stopped by to congratulate me. "Let's go over to the whip's office," he said.

"Fine," I said. "Where's that?"

I wasn't kidding. In all my years in the House, I had never been there. I never needed to, because I used to get all my information from the Rules Committee and from John McCormack's breakfast table.

During most of Hale Boggs's tenure, Lyndon Johnson had been

in the White House, and Lyndon more or less functioned as his own whip. Besides, Boggs was more interested in setting policy than in the behind-the-scenes legwork that the whip traditionally does.

For as long as I could remember, Torbert Macdonald had been the regional whip for New England, but except for the annual photograph of the regional whips, he never attended any meetings. Even after I became the whip, I couldn't get him to show up. Finally I confronted him: "Torbert, if you're never at the meetings, why do you want to keep the job?"

"To be honest with you," he replied, "I like it on my letterhead."

He wasn't the only one. In the past, the title of regional whip generally went to the member with the toughest fight in the area, in the hope that this extra honor might add to his stature and help get him reelected.

When I became whip, I was eager to tighten up the organization by giving it more prestige and more stability. I started by going to the Speaker and the majority leader and telling them, "Look, the only way this thing is going to work is if you'll show up at the meetings and report to the members." I did the same with the committee chairmen, who started coming in to explain the legislation they were dealing with. When the members saw that the party leaders were attending the Thursday morning whip meetings, nobody wanted to be left out. Suddenly, the meetings were jammed and we had ourselves a working organization.

I had functioned as a kind of unofficial whip ever since my early days on the Rules Committee, when members came to me to find out what was going on. Now, in my official capacity, I continued along the same lines. As I saw it, the whip office was a kind of service organization for the members. And the service we provided to our constituents was information.

Previously, the information had flowed in only one direction, as the leadership tried to learn how the members were leaning. I made sure that a constant stream of information was transmitted in the other direction, too, from the leaders to the members. Whenever the congressional leadership went to the White House for a meeting, I distributed notes to the members. I also made sure that the whip office sent out regular information packets to help the members become more knowledgeable about upcoming legislation. In the

Rayburn and McCormack eras, such tactics weren't really necessary. But during the 1970s, Congress was opening up and party
loyalty was on the decline, and the members needed to be told *why*
we wanted them to vote for or against a particular bill.

I loved this stuff—all the backstage maneuverings, the caucuses,
the back corridors and alleys of Congress. I made some big improvements in the whip organization, and my successor, John McFall,
built it up further. The next two whips, John Brademas of Indiana
and Tom Foley from Washington, continued to improve on the
efforts of their predecessors. As a result, the Democratic whip office
is now far more effective than ever before.

Brademas, by the way, was a great talent who could have gone
on to become Speaker if he hadn't been defeated in 1980, when
Reagan came in. John was a sharp young guy with a lot of courage,
and I always admired his style. I also admired the fact that he was
a shining liberal from a conservative district, although that's what
eventually did him in. Today, he's president of New York University, but it wouldn't surprise me to see him get back into politics.

After Brademas lost, Rostenkowski wanted to replace him as
whip. But Danny had just become chairman of Ways and Means,
and it wasn't right for one man to have both positions. I told him
he could choose one job or the other, and he elected to retain the
chairmanship of Ways and Means. No man has ever grown more
in the Congress, and in 1986, Rostenkowski's determined and able
leadership was responsible for the historic Tax Reform Act.

Danny wasn't the only member who approached me about
becoming whip. When Brademas was defeated back home, I must
have had about thirty requests, many of them from members I
couldn't imagine would be interested. Some of these guys hadn't
been active at all, and a few didn't even vote with the party. But
when it came to being part of the leadership, they were more than
willing to serve.

Throughout the 1970s and the first half of the 1980s, there was a
growing feeling in Congress that the whip, like the Speaker and the
majority leader, should be elected by the members. Although I'm
generally in favor of greater democracy, this is a move I've always
opposed. The whip's job is not to create policy but to determine
whether the votes are there for the policy that has already been

determined. Therefore, it's critical that the whip shares the basic philosophy of the majority leader and the Speaker, and that the three of them are able to work together on the same leadership team.

In 1977, when I became Speaker, I hung on to the old system as long as I was in office. But the younger guys saw things differently, and as soon as I retired from the House in 1986, the whip's job became an elected position, determined by a vote in the caucus. I hope it's the right decision, but I still think it's a mistake.

Now that I was the whip, I had to find a faithful, solid, and dependable person to run the operation. My kids all said, "Dad, Leo Diehl's been your closest political friend. Why don't you see if he'll come down?"

Leo and I have been pals since we were both seventeen, when he was the manager of the football team in another part of town. In 1936, we were elected to the state legislature together. I was the second-youngest member, and Leo was the youngest. Leo had stayed in Massachusetts, where he was commissioner of taxation.

I called Leo to offer him the job, and he gave me about eighteen reasons why he couldn't take it. "I don't know, Tom," he said, "this would be such a big change. I'm all set here in the tax department."

"I figured you'd say that," I said, "so I already called the governor to tell him you've resigned."

My first order to Leo was to clean out the hangers-on in the whip's office. McCormack's office had been swarming with lobbyists and visitors from Boston, a situation that led to problems and bad publicity in 1970 when one of his aides was charged with misusing the office of the Speaker and was sent to prison for perjury.

That was exactly the sort of thing I wanted to avoid, and Leo was the ideal man for the job. Until he came along, lobbyists used to sit around in the whip's office, where they would place phone calls and say, "Have him call me back at the whip's office," in order to make themselves sound more important. Leo cleared things up in a hurry by one simple act: he removed the telephone from the back room of the office. Leo was my gatekeeper, or, as Rosty liked to call him, my goaltender, and unless you were a member of Congress, you couldn't get in to see me unless you saw Leo first. Not a day went by that somebody didn't come to my office, claiming to be a great friend of so-and-so and wanting my help with something. Leo checked these people out and handled about 80 percent of their requests on his own. He stayed with me throughout my years as majority leader and Speaker, as my closest friend and trusted adviser.

Incidentally, Capitol Hill wasn't always swarming with lobbyists. When I first arrived in Congress, there were only a handful of organized lobbies, including labor, oil, coal, and the gun lobby. I remember how the insurance lobby got organized. One day in the late 1950s, Sam Rayburn called in the members of the Rules Committee to his office and introduced Wilbur Mills, chairman of the Ways and Means Committee. Mills told us that although the life insurance companies were the most flourishing industry in America, they paid no taxes. Then he outlined a plan to tax them by $400 million this year, $800 million next year, and $1.2 billion the year after that.

"But we can't have open hearings on this," he said. "If we do, there'll be ads in the newspapers all over the country with pictures of old people saying, 'Don't let Congress tax my savings.' If that happens, we'll never be able to get it through."

Quietly and quickly, Rayburn and Mills pushed the bill through the Rules Committee and got the members of the House to vote on it. The process took much longer in the Senate, where the dollar amounts were cut in half, but the whole episode certainly lit a fire under the big insurance companies. Never again would they be caught with their pants down.

Wilbur, by the way, was one of the two most able guys I've ever served with. (The other was Dick Bolling, whom I've already discussed.) The United States tax code is an incredibly complicated document, but Wilbur knew every comma in it. He was also a power, and had been chairman of Ways and Means since 1958. (When he became the chairman, he abolished all of the subcommittees, which made him even more powerful.) He made a brief run for president in 1972, which prompted Sam Gibbons of Florida to ask him, "Why would you want to do that, and give up your grip on the country?"

I was shocked when Wilbur got into trouble with Fanne Fox, a nightclub stripper, because although I was generally well-informed about my fellow members, I had no idea that Wilbur had a drinking problem. Later, some of the guys on his committee said that you could smell the liquor on his breath. Maybe so, but he always kept his mind clear. And to his great credit, Wilbur was able to overcome his drinking problem before he retired.

In October of 1972, about a month before the elections, Hale Boggs mentioned that he was leaving town to fly up to Alaska. He had made a promise to Nicholas Begich, a freshman member, that he would speak for him at a couple of dinners. But Boggs was exhausted, and he wondered whether I'd be willing to take his place.

"No thanks," I said. "This guy doesn't even have a fight. I don't see any point in either of us going."

Nick Begich had no opposition. He just wanted to impress his constituents by showing that he could deliver the majority leader. Perhaps, as the rumors had it, he was already making plans to run for the Senate.

On the night of October 16, the small plane carrying Boggs and Begich was reported lost in a rainstorm between Anchorage and Juneau. The rescue party involved close to a hundred planes, which searched the area for more than a month. The hunt for Boggs was said to be the most massive search for a human being in history, but no sign of the plane was ever found.

I hesitated for a long time before announcing that I was a candidate for majority leader. Certainly, this was the most delicate political problem I had ever encountered. As long as a legitimate hope existed that Hale Boggs was still alive, any announcement on my part would have been insensitive. But if I waited too long, somebody else might jump in.

Finally, at the suggestion of Gary Hymel, I called Lindy Boggs, Hale's wife. I told her that I was thinking of announcing, but that I would never do so without her permission. She replied that she knew Hale would want me to replace him, and that I should go ahead.

On election night, while I was watching the returns in my office, Gary Hymel and Hale's son, Tommy, came by to offer their support. I started making phone calls that night, and within a day or two I had lined up all the votes I needed. In January of 1973 I was elected without opposition.

If Hale Boggs hadn't made the trip to Alaska, he would have gone on to become Speaker after Carl Albert. But Hale's name lives on, in part through Lindy, a talented legislator who has represented Louisiana's second district since 1973, and also through their son, Tommy, a prominent Washington lawyer and lobbyist.

John McFall was our new whip, and John Brademas was deputy whip. John McCormack called me from Boston to ask me to add another deputy whip. "The party has always had a special Boston-Austin connection," he said. "There was Rayburn and myself. There was Kennedy and Johnson. Now that you're in the leadership, I'd like you to tell Carl Albert that I would appreciate it if he would keep the Boston-Austin axis going." McCormack had a candidate in mind for the job, a highly effective member of the House who had served in Congress almost as long as I had. His name was Jim Wright.

Until I became part of the leadership, I had always been a behind-the-scenes operator in Congress. A handful of journalists used to come to me for background information, but I was relatively unknown outside of Capitol Hill.

But now that I was majority leader, the media couldn't stay away. Unlike some of my colleagues, I have very few complaints against the press. I've had my share of criticism, but for the most part it has rolled off me like water off a duck.

Back in 1948, when I was minority leader in Massachusetts, I had a run-in with Bill Mullins, the political editor of the Boston *Herald*, a Republican paper. One Sunday he wrote a mean column about a disagreement I was having with Freddie Willis, the Speaker of the state house. That same day, a mutual friend had invited Mullins and myself to join him for a round of golf at his club.

I was so angry that I refused to say a word to Mullins. Finally, on the sixteenth hole, he turned to me and said, "What the hell's the matter with you? You and I have always been friendly, and today you're acting like I don't even exist."

"Are you kidding?" I replied. "You wrote another lousy article about me in the paper this morning."

"Come on, Tip," he said. "You know damn well that every time I write about you in a derisive way I make you a bigger man in the Democratic party."

"I don't know about that," I said. "All I know is that these columns are tough on my family and my friends."

"I'm sorry," he said. "I never intended to cause you any personal unhappiness. I'm going to promise you right now that I'll never even mention your name in my column again until the day I die. Let's shake hands on it."

He was true to his word. A few months later, of course, I went on to become Speaker of the legislature, and four years after that, I was elected to Congress. But Bill Mullins never referred to me again.

Every now and then, some friend of mine would shake his head and say, "Isn't that Mullins a son of a bitch, Tip. He never even mentions you!"

When I became majority leader in Washington, I was interviewed constantly. I was always happy to talk to the press, but I drew the line at the Sunday morning talk shows on television. After a full work week, consisting of long days and frequent late evenings, I insisted on keeping my weekends free for my family and friends.

In 1977, when I became Speaker, I started meeting with TV reporters each morning when I arrived at work. Later in the morning, I would hold a daily news conference before the House opened. I always told the truth, and almost never answered with "No comment." Ninety-nine percent of the time, if you're straight with the press, they'll be straight with you.

Once in a while, though, I was a little *too* straight. On one occasion, I was coming out of a meeting with President Reagan when Sam Donaldson came at me with a loaded question about our involvement in Lebanon. I just glared at him, but as I was walking away I heard Sam saying that Tip O'Neill didn't have the courage to answer his question.

I immediately spun around and called out to him, "Sam, you can kiss my Irish ass. Why don't you put *that* on the news!"

When I got back to the office and told my staff what had happened, they were worried sick. How would it look, they said, if Sam Donaldson called my bluff and put my remark on the air? That night, we all watched the ABC news in the office, but to our great relief, my name wasn't even mentioned.

Sam used to give me a hard time, but I could excuse him on two counts. For one thing, he gives *everybody* a hard time. For another, he does his homework and understands the issues.

My beef is not with Sam Donaldson, but with the young reporters around the country who try to emulate Sam's aggressive posture without really knowing the issues. These guys are just showing off, and they don't add anything to the public's understanding of the news.

In general, I have great respect for the press in our country. But there were two or three highly unpleasant incidents that still remain with me from my days as majority leader.

Shortly after I was elected to the position, the reporting team of Evans and Novak came to see me. I'm normally on good terms with journalists, but there's always been something about those two that I just don't trust. Apparently other people feel the same way, as they're known around Washington as Errors and Nofacts. They're also known for publishing negative stories about members of Congress, stories that are often leaked to them by people who don't have much knowledge and aren't much respected on Capitol Hill. Sometimes, a few days after one of these stories appears, I'll notice a line in their column saying that so-and-so is doing a good job on a committee. That's usually a tipoff as to the source of the earlier story.

When Evans and Novak came to my office, they had the gall to offer me a deal: if I kept them informed as to what was happening in Congress and the White House, they would see to it that I would receive great press notices, which would help smooth the way for me to be the next Speaker.

I was ashamed to be in their company, and I kicked them right out of my office. I'm a forgiving man, but I find it difficult to be charitable to these two.

My other gripe with the press was part of a larger problem that became known as Koreagate. Although I've made a few mistakes in my career, I've always prided myself on my reputation for honesty and integrity. But there's one undeserved blemish on my record, and I intend to take a moment to clear it up. I'm referring to my real and alleged connections to a man named Tongsun Park.

Tongsun Park was a wealthy rice-merchant—and, it later came

out, a suspected agent for the government of South Korea—who was a frequent visitor on Capitol Hill while I was majority leader. He was a friendly and outgoing fellow who seemed to know a lot of congressmen, and from time to time he would stick his head into the majority leader's office—mostly, I think, to impress the people he was with. I knew him casually, and I even recall meeting him a few years earlier, when he was a student at Georgetown University and John Brademas brought him to my office. "Keep an eye on this kid," John said. "He's an entrepreneur who's going to make a lot of dough." But I don't ever recall having a real conversation with Tongsun Park.

On December 10, 1973, at the invitation of Congressmen Richard Hanna and John Brademas, I attended a large dinner party at the Georgetown Club, which was cohosted by Tongsun Park. By this time, Park was known around town for giving good parties, and I assumed that he was just another political groupie who enjoyed rubbing shoulders with powerful people. Washington is filled with these people, and it never entered my mind that Park might be a lobbyist for the Korean government or anybody else.

I doubt if it entered anybody else's mind either, including all the congressmen who showed up at that party, as well as Vice President Gerald Ford, and Mike Mansfield, the Senate majority leader. Eddie Boland mentioned that I had just celebrated my sixty-first birthday, and the next thing I knew, Tongsun Park had sent one of the club's employees to buy me a gift—a pair of pewter hurricane lamps which sold for $263.55. (The lamps were later appraised and were said to be worth about thirty bucks apiece.)

Park must have made a note of my birthday, because the following December he threw a birthday party in my honor at the Madison Hotel. This time the invitation came through William Minshall and Richard Hanna, two members of Congress who were retiring to become lobbyists. They told me they were trying to attract clients and asked if I would agree to be honored. "Sure," I said, "as long as I get to invite half of the guests."

This time, too, nobody had any suspicions about Tongsun Park. Even President Ford had accepted an invitation to the second party. That afternoon, however, Jerry called me and said, "Listen, I'm really exhausted. Do I really have to show up tonight?"

"Of course not, Mr. President," I said. "I wish I didn't have to go myself."

Before the party, Park had collected ten dollars from each of the forty or so congressmen who showed up, which went to present me with a new set of golf clubs.

When I received the gift, I thanked all the guests. Then I turned to Tongsun Park and said, "This is some party you're running. I don't know what the hell you do for a living, but any guy who can get forty congressmen to kick in ten apiece for a set of golf clubs must be a pretty good operator."

I had no idea that Park was tape-recording my remarks, but later, when the FBI listened to the tape and heard me say outright that I didn't know what Park did for a living, I was glad that he had.

During the investigation into Tongsun Park's activities on Capitol Hill, the FBI asked me if I had ever received money from him.

"Absolutely not," I said.

"Then how do you explain this?" said one of the agents, showing me a check from Park made out to Tip O'Neill, which I had cashed.

Then I remembered. Earlier in the investigation, I had called in my entire staff to ask if they had ever seen Tongsun Park.

"He came in for the baseball tickets," said Dolores Snow, my secretary.

That year, just before the American League playoffs, Joe Cronin, president of the American League, had called me. "Listen," he said, "a lot of people in Congress will be going to the first game in Baltimore. Would it be all right if I sent you a hundred tickets, at face value, and they can pick them up from you?"

I agreed, and I found out later that Dick Hanna had ordered eight tickets for Tongsun Park. Park mailed in his check, but according to the FBI, he never went to the game. The tickets were found, unused, at his house.

"There's one thing I don't understand," said the FBI agent. "Isn't it strange for someone like you to be handling baseball tickets?"

"Not at all," I explained. "It's all part of building a power base in the House. How do you get tickets to the ball game? You go to Tip O'Neill."

When the story came out that Tongsun Park was a foreign agent who was trying to win influence on Capitol Hill, all hell broke loose.

In the wake of Watergate, every reporter in America saw himself as another Woodward or Bernstein. In August 1977, during a closed-door investigation of Park by the House Ethics Committee, the Los Angeles *Times* ran a front-page story that reported that a former aide to Carl Albert claimed that Tongsun Park had frequently operated out of my office.

That story came from a leak from the House Ethics Committee, where Suzi Park Thomson, a Korean-born woman who had worked in the Speaker's office, made this charge in secret testimony. Although there was no truth to her allegation, a number of papers printed it anyway. And, as always in these situations, people assumed that where there was smoke, there was fire.

A few weeks later, on October 7, another leak from the Ethics Committee made it into the press. This time, it was the Boston *Herald American*, which ran a banner headline on page one: WHO PAID TIP'S RENT?

Apparently, an anonymous source had contacted the committee with the "information" that Tongsun Park had been paying the rent on the apartment where Eddie Boland and I had been living. This charge too, of course, was completely without foundation, which Eddie and I proved easily enough when we brought our canceled checks to the Ethics Committee. But many people don't bother to read news stories; they just skim the headlines. A month later, when the charges were disproved, the *Herald* ran a brief story with a much smaller headline: "Ethics Group Clears Tip of Rent Charge."

I learned later that two newspapermen had concocted the whole story at Upstairs, Downstairs, a popular Washington bar. Knowing that the Ethics Committee would be investigating any and all tips, they convinced a friend of theirs to report that she had overheard two reporters saying that Tongsun Park had been paying the rent on Tip O'Neill's apartment. A couple of days later, the reporters called the realtors and confirmed that the rent checks had, indeed, been subpoenaed. And now, suddenly, they had a legitimate reason to run the story.

I know it sounds wild, but this sort of thing does, occasionally, happen in Washington. And although I've never been able to prove that this one happened just as I've described it, a number of people I trust have assured me that it did.

Now I don't blame the Ethics Committee for the decision to

subpoena the canceled checks. After all, it was their obligation to follow up every tip they received, no matter how crazy it sounded. But I do object when an anonymous source on a committee leaks information to the press before anybody has a chance to check it out. Almost invariably, the charges make the front page, whereas the denials are usually buried inside the paper. Which is how reputations are ruined.

During its investigation, the Ethics Committee looked into several other apparent links between Tongsun Park and myself. At one point, a document turned up that showed that both Park and my son Tommy, a stockbroker, were on the board of directors of a small company called McLaughlin Fisheries. At first glance, this looked a little suspicious, especially since I had already assured the committee that neither I nor any members of my family ever had any commercial dealings with Tongsun Park. In view of the document, the committee staff wanted to know whether McLaughlin Fisheries had been used as a conduit for funds from Park to Tommy.

The investigation soon revealed that the link between Park and Tommy existed only on paper. For one thing, the company's board of directors had never even met. For another, neither Tommy nor I was even aware that Park was on the board of McLaughlin Fisheries. When the investigators asked Tommy if he knew Tongsun Park, he answered in all candor, "Tongsun Park? I wouldn't know him from Fenway Park!"

But the wildest charge of all came out of the testimony of one Jack Kelly, Tongsun Park's financial adviser, who told investigators that in 1971 Tongsun Park had flown from Washington to New York with $20,000 in cash in a briefcase. According to Kelly, that money was a gift to me, and Park was en route to Nantucket to spend Thanksgiving at my house.

From the start, the story made no sense. For one thing, why would Tongsun Park fly from Washington to New York if he was actually heading for Massachusetts? For another, I don't have a house on Nantucket. But there was, it turned out, a grain of truth to Kelly's story. On November 23, 1971, two days before Thanksgiving, Park *did* hand over $20,000—not to Tip O'Neill, but to Cornelius Gallagher, a member of Congress from New Jersey. Gallagher was known to his friends as Neil, and Jack Kelly, the investigators concluded, must have thought that Park was referring to O'Neill.

When Jimmy Carter came into office, I said to him, "I want you to know that my name is going to come up in connection with Tongsun Park. But if he did anything wrong, I knew nothing about it and had no involvement in things of that nature."

"I've already checked into it," said the president, "and you've got nothing to worry about."

When the investigation was over, the congressional inquiry looking at my involvement with Tongsun Park came to the following conclusion:

"All allegations relating to Mr. O'Neill's relationship to Tongsun Park were investigated, even when the source was of questioned reliability. Having reviewed evidence thus gathered, the staff was unable to find any evidence that in his dealings with Tongsun Park Mr. O'Neill violated the Code of Official Conduct of the House of Representatives, or any law, rule, regulation or other standard of conduct applicable to his conduct as a Member and officer of the House of Representatives."

Washington is a tough town, and if somebody is out to get you, it's easy enough to get trapped. Morally and ethically, I did nothing wrong in the Tongsun Park affair. But some congressmen did take money from Park, and my name did appear in a number of stories about Koreagate. Unfortunately, the mere appearance of impropriety in the years following Watergate was enough to convince some people that Tip O'Neill was probably guilty of something.

But I know, and the record shows, that I have nothing to apologize for. In retrospect, of course, I wish I hadn't attended those two parties. But that's hindsight, which makes every man a genius.

11

★★★★★

Watergate

ALTHOUGH more than a decade has passed since the events of Watergate rocked the nation and toppled a president, I find to my astonishment that some people still believe that Watergate represented nothing more than politics as usual. According to this viewpoint, the only difference between the Nixon presidency and those of his predecessors is that Nixon was put out of business by the liberal media and a Democratic Congress, both of which were out to get him.

Nothing could be further from the truth.

Granted, Richard Nixon's immediate predecessors were hardly as pure as the driven snow. Jack Kennedy was no saint, and Lyndon Johnson was no angel, either. Both of them knew that power is never given—it is only taken. Both of them knew how to play tough. But I've been around politics for a long time, and I can say with assurance that what went on during the Nixon presidency was unlike anything I had ever seen, or even heard of. We're talking here about blackmail and corruption in the highest office in the land.

When it comes to politics, nobody has ever called me naïve. And until Watergate, I thought I knew all about political hardball. Hardball was ballot-stuffing in Illinois during the 1960 presidential election. Hardball was when you pressured somebody to make a donation on the basis of your friendship. Hardball was when organizations feuded and tried to destroy each other. Hardball was repeaters being run in and out of the polls in Boston.

As for dirty tricks, here, too, I thought I had seen it all. But compared with Watergate, the dirty tricks I had seen in Massachusetts were pretty tame: it sounds ridiculous, but if you really wanted to be nasty to your opponent, you'd pass out a phone number to his supporters in case they wanted a ride to the polls, and the number would belong to a pet cemetery or a mental institution.

Dirty politics? Once, back in the 1930s, Mike DeLuca ran against Charlie Cavanaugh for state senate in my own district. Mike had no chance of winning, but he was quite a talker. He'd get up on the platform and say, "Charlie, I see you're going around with the widow O'Grady. Is it true that she paid for your new car?" Everybody was aghast. Three days before the election, some of Charlie's friends kidnapped Mike DeLuca and held him for three days on a farm outside of the city. That was dirty politics in those days.

In 1972, I learned about a new kind of dirty politics in the Republican camp through an early warning from, of all people, George Steinbrenner, the owner of the New York Yankees. Once I was convinced that something was rotten in Washington, I became an active, behind-the-scenes player in the long, slow series of events that led from Richard Nixon's landslide victory in 1972 to his resignation less than two years later.

My contact with Steinbrenner began in 1969, shortly before I became chairman of the Democratic Congressional Campaign Committee. As one of the chief Democratic fund-raisers, I quickly got to know all of our party's big givers. (Given our financial condition, that didn't take very long.) And I still remember the day that Dick Maguire, the treasurer of the Democratic National Committee, first told me about George Steinbrenner.

"Tip," he said, "I met a young fellow from Lorain, Ohio, who's in the shipbuilding business. He invested in some plays in New York and he's made a lot of dough. In the past, he and his family have always been Republicans. But the family business was in the doldrums when he took it over, and he made a fortune under Kennedy and Johnson. He's been talking to some of his friends, and they all agree that they've done much better under the Democrats than they ever did under the Republicans. So now they're all asking, 'What the hell were we ever Republicans for?' "

A couple of weeks later, Dick brought Steinbrenner in to see me. George was a young, strong, good-looking, and gracious fellow, and we hit it off right away. Our friendship was enhanced by our mutual interest in sports, for not only was George a great fan, but he had also been a football coach at both Northwestern and Purdue.

At that time, the head coach of the Boston College Eagles was a fellow named Jim Miller, who had coached at Purdue with Steinbrenner. Jim had just gone through a losing season at B.C., but I've never been a fair-weather fan, and when he came to Washington for a coaches' convention, I ran a cocktail party in his honor. I remember that Steinbrenner was impressed by the fact that I honored his old friend even when things weren't going well for him. There's some irony in this, of course, because George Steinbrenner has not exactly become famous for the generosity and kindness he has shown his own coaching staff over the years.

At any rate, we used to have a big Democratic fund-raising dinner in Washington each year, and in 1969 I asked Steinbrenner to be the chairman.

"Fine," he said. "What's the most money this dinner has ever raised?"

"A couple of years ago we took in five hundred and ninety-five thousand dollars," I replied.

"Okay," said Steinbrenner. "This year we're going to raise three-quarters of a million."

That's when I knew we had a live one. As I expected, George turned out to be a terrific dinner chairman. Although we took in slightly less than six hundred thousand dollars, he went out and hustled the rest on his own. George Steinbrenner was a man of his word.

The following year, we asked him to chair the dinner again. This time, he broke his own record and raised a million bucks.

By now, George and I had become good friends. When he bought the New York Yankees, I'd visit him every year at Yankee Stadium—especially when the Red Sox were in town. Naturally, all of us in the Democratic party were thrilled to have a guy like Steinbrenner on our team.

In 1972, when I noticed that George hadn't made his regular contribution to the party, I picked up the phone and gave him a call. "What's the matter, old pal? Why don't I hear from you anymore?"

"Well," he said, "I've got a problem. And I'd like to come to your office and tell you what's going on."

When he came in, he said, "Tip, it's terrible. They're holding the lumber over my head."

"Who is?" I asked.

"Everybody. The government has been giving me problems ever since I became a Democrat. I've got the Labor Department investigating safety standards and working conditions. I've got the Justice Department looking at antitrust. I've got problems with a big cost-overrun on a government contract. I'm having all kinds of difficulties, and they're driving me nuts."

Steinbrenner soon learned that CREEP—the Committee to Re-Elect the President—wasn't too pleased that a wealthy businessman who used to support the Republicans had switched over to our side. Steinbrenner's company's lawyer, Thomas Evans, was a strong supporter of Nixon and was the deputy finance chairman of CREEP, and George was told that his problems with the government might disappear if he paid a visit to Maurice Stans, chairman of finance for the Committee to Re-Elect the President.

"We'd like you to head up a committee of Democrats for Nixon in Ohio," said Stans.

Steinbrenner replied that he wasn't interested.

"All right," said Stans, "maybe there are other ways you can be useful." He sent George to see Herb Kalmbach, a fund-raiser for CREEP who also happened to be the president's personal attorney.

"So you'll be helping us?" said Kalmbach.

"I'm a Democrat," replied Steinbrenner. "But I'll give you twenty-five thou."

"Twenty-five is not satisfactory," said Kalmbach. Then he took out a piece of paper and wrote some numbers on it: "33 @ 3; 1 @ 1." Steinbrenner got the message: Kalmbach wanted him to come up with a hundred thousand dollars. To get around the campaign-contribution laws, he was being asked to write thirty-three checks for three thousand dollars each, and one check for a thousand. At the time, three thousand was the maximum amount you could donate without having your name listed. Each check would be made out to a different committee that was eligible to receive contributions to help reelect President Nixon.

Steinbrenner came up with the money. Later, it came out that Steinbrenner had given bonuses to several of his employees, who had been asked to turn over the extra money to the Nixon campaign. While this wasn't an unusual way to funnel money to candidates, it was still against the law. On April 5, 1974, George Steinbrenner was indicted on five counts of violating campaign contribution laws.

On November 27, 1974, Bowie Kuhn, the commissioner of base-ball, suspended Steinbrenner for two years. I thought the punish-ment was a little excessive, so I called Kuhn and explained that what George had done was fairly common in corporate life, and that Steinbrenner hadn't realized he was doing anything wrong. But Kuhn wouldn't budge.

Later on, Edward Bennett Williams, the lawyer who represented Steinbrenner, asked the commissioner of baseball why he hadn't also suspended Cesar Cedeno of the Houston Astros, who was convicted of involuntary manslaughter.

"That was different," said Kuhn. "Cedeno did that in the off-season."

I found this wonderful story in *How the Good Guys Finally Won*, Jimmy Breslin's excellent book about Watergate. I first met Jimmy in the spring of 1973, when I gave him a ride from Cape Cod to Logan Airport in Boston. We talked about Watergate, and Jimmy said, "You know, I think I'll go to Washington and follow the Rodino committee. A lot of writers are doing books about the impeachment, but I think I'll write mine from the House point of view."

He interviewed me a couple of times, although I never saw him take a note. "You must have thought I had kidney problems," he told me later. "Didn't you notice that I ducked into the men's room to write down everything you said?" So *that* was his secret. I bumped into Jimmy the night Nixon resigned, and I said, "I'm sorry, Jim, but it looks like all your time and effort were in vain. He's not going to be impeached after all."

"Well," said Breslin, "I have a few pages written up, and I think I can put something together." He sure did. Not only was his book a best seller, but it was also remarkably accurate.

Around the time Steinbrenner came to see me, I noticed that I wasn't getting my phone calls returned by several other donors who normally gave money to the Democratic party. I knew this wasn't an accident—especially when I saw their names turning up in political advertisements as Democrats for Nixon. When I finally tracked them down, they told me that they, too, were running into problems on government contracts, or with the IRS. Like Steinbrenner, they had been led to understand that if they signed up with the Nixon campaign, everything would be taken care of. "They've got me, Tip," one of them said. "I have to look out for myself. Besides, McGovern doesn't have a chance of winning anyway."

In addition to my Democratic friends, I also had a source in the Republican camp—Tom Pappas, a very successful businessman in Boston and a big contributor to the Republican party. Tom and I were friends, and during the 1972 campaign he told me proudly that the Republicans were raising a lot of money from Democrats, that the minimum contribution was twenty-five *thousand* dollars, and that they were grabbing most people for a hundred thousand. Tom didn't reveal any dirty secrets, but he didn't have to. A twenty-five-thousand-dollar *minimum?* That was unheard-of.

These stories were more than enough to trigger my alarm. If I was picking up things like this without even looking for them, then we had a real problem on our hands. The conclusion was inescapable: what we had, plain and simple, was an old-fashioned shakedown. I thought I had seen it all, but never in my life had I seen outright blackmail.

At first I didn't quite believe it. I thought I knew how the game was played, but these were rules I had never heard of. Things like this weren't supposed to happen—certainly not in a democracy. This is too big, I said to myself. They'll never get away with this—not if I can help it.

What really scared me was that all of this funny business and intimidation was being carried out before an election that the Republicans couldn't lose even if they tried. If this was how these guys played the game in a campaign they had already won, what would they try if they ever found themselves in a really tough fight?

At this stage, I had no idea whether Nixon himself was involved. I hadn't seen him much since the card games back in the 1950s, when I had found him a gregarious and friendly guy. Although I didn't care for some of his views, I had to concede that no man was ever better prepared for the presidency. Nixon was a lawyer who had been a member of both the House and the Senate. He'd been a member of the select House committee that toured Europe in 1947 and developed the Marshall Plan. He'd served eight years as vice president under Eisenhower. Then, after losing to Kennedy in 1960, he'd spent another eight years traveling around the country and studying foreign affairs.

The irony about Nixon is that his pre-Watergate record is a lot better than most liberals realize. It was Nixon, after all, who opened the door to China and who eventually brought American troops home from Vietnam. On the domestic front, too, he was considerably more moderate than his image would suggest. For example, many of the poverty programs that had been passed under Johnson were actually implemented and funded under Nixon. And while Nixon did impound some of those funds, he could have brought these programs to a virtual halt if that had been his intention.

There was even a time, early in 1972, when President Nixon insisted on giving higher entitlement benefits than those favored by the Democratic congressional leadership. Wilbur Mills, who was then chairman of Ways and Means, had always opposed the indexing of Social Security benefits to the cost of living, but two weeks before the New Hampshire primary, where Wilbur was on the ballot, he changed his mind and suddenly favored automatic upward adjustments in Social Security.

But that wasn't enough to satisfy the president, who insisted on basing the increase on the inflation rate plus 1 percent. Years later, Caspar Weinberger, who had been Nixon's budget manager, told me that he had begged the president to maintain the cap on cost-of-living allowances for both Social Security and food stamps. But 1972 was an election year, and Nixon wasn't taking any chances.

At the weekly White House meetings with the congressional leadership, President Nixon came across as an extremely knowledgeable fellow who was always well briefed before we came in. No matter what the subject, he invariably knew what he was talking about. Of course he would sometimes overdo the talk, just as he used to gab too much during our poker games back when he was vice president.

After he became president, Richard Nixon seemed to change. He no longer played cards with our group, and I doubt that he played with anybody. Unlike Truman, Kennedy, and Johnson, Nixon didn't pal around much with his old friends. Instead, he became aloof and imperial.

Although Nixon was a brilliant guy, he had a quirk in his personality that made him suspicious of everybody—including members of his own cabinet. He installed one of his own people in every department, a special agent who was always checking on the top man and reporting back to Haldeman and Ehrlichman. Whenever possible, career people in the various agencies were encouraged to take early retirement so their jobs could be filled by political appointees. Nixon was a leery and nervous president who ran a closed shop.

The people around him were the same way, and he and his staff formed a close-knit, almost secretive group. His people were bright enough, and they did his bidding, but most of them didn't have much class or talent. Their philosophy was to win at any cost, and they truly believed that nice guys finished last. Merely winning the election wasn't enough for them; they wanted to see the Democratic party defeated so badly that it wouldn't mount a major challenge for another twenty years.

So that was the setting when, on June 17, 1972, agents of the Committee to Re-Elect the President broke into the headquarters of the Democratic National Committee in the Watergate complex. The Watergate, of course, is a fancy group of buildings, including a hotel, apartments, offices, and restaurants, on Virginia Avenue, overlooking the Potomac. When the Watergate buildings first went up, Clark Fisher from Texas tried to convince Eddie Boland and me to buy an apartment there. At the time, they were going for $25,000 and required only a small down payment. It would have been a great investment, but to us it seemed like a wild idea, and far too expensive for a couple of poorly paid congressmen to take advantage of.

Back in 1967, when the Democratic National Committee moved over to the Watergate, some of my colleagues objected because the new site was a little too fancy. There was a Democratic club downstairs, but it wasn't popular because it was difficult to park around there, and nobody wanted to spring for valet parking when all you wanted was a beer with your friends. The Watergate was centrally located, but it just wasn't our style.

At any rate, when the Watergate burglars were caught, nobody paid much attention. I thought the incident was stupid, and that a few dumb bunnies were trying to ingratiate themselves with the White House. But a few weeks later, when I put the break-in together with what Steinbrenner and Pappas had told me, I started to wonder. These guys weren't asking for contributions; they were *demanding* them. That disturbed me tremendously. I was going on political intuition, and I just knew something was fishy.

I don't remember exactly when I started using the word "impeachment," but it was very early in the game, and it upset my colleagues in the House. In January 1973, I went to see Carl Albert, the Speaker, to tell him what was on my mind. "We better start getting ready," I said. "This guy is going to be impeached before we're through."

Carl Albert was a good Speaker, but he wasn't the type who enjoyed controversy. Besides, as the head man in Congress, he had to remain neutral. He didn't say so directly, but it was clear that if the Democrats were going to make a serious response to Watergate, I, as majority leader, would be the one to do it.

The first time I approached Carl about Watergate, he thought I was talking nonsense. And he wasn't the only one. When I shared my suspicions with Peter Rodino, chairman of the House Judiciary Committee, Peter just shook his head. "You're not a lawyer," he said. "You're only going on intuition, and you can't prove a thing you're saying."

"Maybe not," I said. "I'm only telling you what I can hear and see, and what I know. But I'm picking up too many strange things, and it's got me worried." Besides, I couldn't help but wonder what else was going on in the Republican camp that I didn't even know about.

In retrospect, of course, we still wouldn't know very much if the president had followed his instincts and destroyed the tapes. In his memoirs, Nixon writes that he had considered doing so, but that Alexander Haig and H. R. Haldeman had convinced him that if he did destroy them, the public would definitely conclude that he was guilty. Maybe so, but given Nixon's character, I found his decision surprising.

The nation learned about the Nixon tapes on July 16, 1973, when

Alexander Butterfield told the Senate Watergate Committee that the president had installed secret recording equipment in the Oval Office and in certain other rooms of the White House. Those tapes are what undid Nixon. If he had destroyed them, he could have remained in office until the end of his second term.

To destroy the tapes, of course, would have been to compound the crime. But from Nixon's point of view, *not* to destroy them was irrational. I can only imagine how many times he must have said to himself, What a fool I was not to burn them!

I've always believed that he held on to them because he was greedy. He wanted to use them to write his memoirs, and he expected to make a fortune from them.

Let me explain. I had come to the conclusion that Nixon was taping conversations several months before Butterfield spilled the beans. On January 23, 1973, the president went on television to announce a cease-fire and a settlement with the North Vietnamese, which he said would bring the war to an end. Earlier that same evening, the congressional leadership had been invited to a dinner in the Executive Office Building.

I had never seen the president so exuberant. But Nixon was still Nixon, and once the dinner began we were locked in and couldn't leave the room. Even in his moment of triumph, the president was afraid that somebody might leak the news before he made his announcement. He didn't trust anybody.

Over coffee and dessert, the president asked Kissinger to brief us on the various developments that led to the Paris agreements. Among other things, Kissinger mentioned the decision to mine Haiphong harbor in April of 1972, in response to a massive North Vietnamese offensive, as well as the more recent bombing of Hanoi.

As Kissinger spoke, my mind flashed back to my confrontation with Lyndon Johnson on that September morning in 1967, when I told the president that I could no longer support the war. When Kissinger was finished, I asked him the following question: "In 1967, when I changed my mind about this war, I went to see Lyndon Johnson in the White House. I asked Johnson how he could justify fighting a war if we couldn't mine their harbors and knock out their power plants and hit their cities. And Johnson said, 'The reason we're not doing these things is that the risk is too great. I can't get any agreement from the Russians and the Chinese, and I don't want to bring on World War Three.'

"Therefore," I asked Kissinger, "can we assume that you had an agreement with the Russians and the Chinese?"

Kissinger cleared his throat, but before he could utter a word, Nixon broke in. "I'll answer that one, Henry," said the president. Then Nixon did something very strange: he paused, raised his voice, and looked up at the ceiling. I looked up, too, to see who he was talking to, but the only thing up there was the chandelier. "I want you all to know," he announced, "that as president of the United States, this was *my* decision. *I'm* the one who decided to mine the harbor last spring. It was a calculated risk, and I took it alone. There were no discussions with the Chinese. There were no discussions with the Soviets."

From the way the president moved his head, I realized that his real audience wasn't us at all, but rather a microphone that must have been hidden in the chandelier.

The truth about the Soviets and the Chinese came out a few months later, after Butterfield's shocking revelation. In October, Nixon convened the same group of congressional leaders in the Oval Office to discuss America's role in bringing an end to the 1973 Arab-Israeli war. By this time, of course, the White House taping system had been dismantled, which would explain why the president went on to contradict his earlier statement about all the risks he had taken for the sake of peace.

This time, Nixon was full of praise for the way the Russians had cooperated in making possible a peace settlement between the Israelis and the Egyptians. "We couldn't have done it without them," he said. "It was just like in Vietnam. We couldn't have made any deals with the North Vietnamese unless we had the cooperation of the Russians and the Chinese as we stepped up our offensive. Without their help, we could never have ended the war."

That was a more likely version. And this was when I realized that Nixon had probably intended to use the tapes to compose his own version of history—a version in which he would be the hero. He was going to put together a story that showed that he, Richard Nixon, was the greatest president in our history. And he planned to prove it all with his tapes.

. . .

Meanwhile, over on Capitol Hill, Congress was a little slow to respond to the growing evidence of crimes in high places. Although the job of the members is to represent their constituents, there are often brief moments when the partners in that relationship are not quite in step. Sometimes the Congress is slightly ahead of the people; at other times—and Watergate was one—the people are slightly ahead of Congress.

At first, most members in both parties were bitterly opposed to the idea of impeachment proceedings. For a long time, nobody even wanted to talk about it. Congress hadn't dealt with a situation like this for a century, and most of the members didn't want to touch it. Perhaps if they ignored it, the whole sordid business would just go away.

Thaddeus Dulksi, a congressman from Buffalo, spoke for many of his colleagues: "I'm a loyal Democrat," he told me in the summer of 1973, "but I couldn't vote to impeach *any* president. My father would roll over in his grave. Impeachment? It would be a sacrilege. We could never allow such a thing to happen."

Initially, Dan Rostenkowski was also in this camp. In addition to being the chief deputy whip, he also controlled a number of votes in the Illinois delegation. In April 1973, I turned Danny around by showing him a poll. As chairman of the Democratic Congressional Campaign Committee, I used to commission polls in various districts to see where we should spend our money to help Democratic candidates. My main pollster was William Hamilton, a prominent Democratic analyst and one of the pioneers in political polling.

Hamilton had showed me the results of a poll he had recently completed on behalf of AFSCME (the American Federation of State, County and Municipal Employees), which made a number of predictions about the 1974 congressional elections. Against the backdrop of Watergate, the poll measured the public's attitudes toward the president and analyzed how those attitudes would affect individual congressional races.

According to the study, 43 percent of the public would vote for a congressman who was in favor of impeachment, while 29 percent would oppose him. (The remaining 28 percent said the issue wouldn't affect their vote.) Hamilton's poll also showed that among

Democrats, only 7 percent would support a congressman who was opposed to impeachment.

I've never seen a poll make such a dramatic impact, but this one helped Danny and many other members change their minds. Instead of saying, "I'd hate to see that happen," they were forced to open their eyes and face the fact that the American people thought impeachment *should* happen.

The Republicans were even more rattled by Hamilton's poll, which showed that a lot of their people would be hurt as the nation searched for a way to purge itself after Watergate. In a presidential election year, that purge would have affected the White House race, but in an off-year vote it would be reflected at the congressional level.

According to the poll, 50 percent of Republican voters would vote against any member who opposed impeachment. I remember going up to Angelo Roncallo, a Republican kid from Long Island. "Angie, old pal," I said, "you really love it down here, don't you? I want you to know that my door is always open. And to show you how much I think of you, Angie, my door is still going to be open next year, when you're not going to be here because of the impeachment."

We both laughed. But poor Angie was in a difficult position, because no matter how he wanted to vote, the Republican machine in Long Island was one of the tightest political organizations in the country, and Angie would be forced to support the president no matter how guilty he was. Not surprisingly, Angelo Roncallo was not reelected.

When Angie's fellow Republicans realized how costly it was going to be for them to support the president, most of them came around. I know how to count, and I'm convinced that by the time it was all over, if the articles of impeachment had ever come down to a vote, Nixon wouldn't have had twenty supporters in the House.

The results of the Hamilton poll were confirmed when Teno Roncalio from Wyoming asked me to come out to speak at a fundraiser. Teno was nervous because while he intended to vote for impeachment, his district in Wyoming had supported Nixon by a ratio of three to one. Actually, his district *was* Wyoming, which is such a sparsely populated state that it has only one congressman. As far as I knew, my visit to Wyoming marked the first time that anyone from the Democratic leadership had ever been out there.

Wyoming may have been Nixon country in November of 1972, but the reception I received out there a year and a half later was unbelievable. Here was Tip O'Neill, a fairly well-known, pro-impeachment liberal Democrat, addressing an audience of Nixon supporters—and finding not an ounce of resentment. These people didn't like what was going on in the White House, and the mere fact that Richard Nixon happened to be president of the United States didn't mean he could get away with criminal behavior. They believed that he should be brought to justice, and that it was the responsibility of Congress to make sure he was.

As I spoke and answered questions, I could see that Richard Nixon didn't have a vote in the entire room. And if he didn't have a vote here, in Cheyenne, Wyoming, in the heart of the country, then he didn't have one anywhere.

Back in the House, Father Robert Drinan, a Democrat from Massachusetts, introduced a resolution on July 31, 1973, calling for the impeachment of Richard Nixon. Although Drinan was furious about Watergate, he was even more incensed that Nixon had ordered bombing raids on Cambodia without informing Congress—or anybody else, for that matter.

Morally, Drinan had a good case. Publicly, he's always been proud that he was the first member of Congress to file for impeachment. But politically, he damn near blew it. For if Drinan's resolution had come up for a vote at the time he filed it, it would have been overwhelmingly defeated—by something like 400 to 20. After that, with most of the members already on record as having voted once against impeachment, it would have been extremely difficult to get them to change their minds later on.

At Carl Albert's request, I went to Drinan and tried to talk him out of it. "The timing is wrong," I said. "It's premature. Let's wait a few months until the evidence is in and we can get the votes we need."

Drinan agreed not to press the issue, but by then the resolution had already been filed and could not be withdrawn. According to the rules of the House, any resolution on impeachment is, by definition, a privileged resolution, which means that any member, at any time, can call it up for an immediate vote. We could certainly see to it that no Democrat would bring it up, but who knew what the Republicans might try? If I had been in their shoes, I would have brought up Drinan's resolution immediately, because an early, overwhelming vote against impeachment would have been an excellent insurance policy against having to vote on a similar resolution at a later date. If it ever came up, the Republicans could legitimately say, "Why bother? We've already been through this."

To prevent this scenario from happening, three of us—John McFall (the whip), John Brademas (the deputy whip), and I—started watching the floor. In the event that any member of the House called for a vote on Drinan's motion, we would immediately move to table it. A motion to table is not debatable: the bells would ring and everybody would come running for the vote—which the Democrats, being the majority party, would win easily. We kept our plan among the three of us because we didn't want people to talk, and we certainly didn't want to give any ideas to our Republican friends. But for our strategy to work, one of us had to be on the floor every moment the House was in session, rather than in our offices or at committee meetings.

Finally, frustrated by all the time we were wasting, I went directly to Gerald Ford, the minority leader, and asked him straight out if the Republicans had any intention of bringing up Drinan's motion. By now Jerry and I had been working together for years, and I knew I could trust him.

"I took this up with the White House," Ford said, "and the feeling was that if we brought up this motion, people might think that where there was smoke, there was fire. Besides, they don't want to besmirch the presidency with a vote on something like this. They don't see impeachment down the road, and they think you guys are talking nonsense. So no, we have no intention of bringing it up." I knew that Jerry's word was good, and that on this issue, at least, we could afford to relax.

By not forcing an early vote on impeachment, Nixon's allies made a tremendous mistake. In addition to winning the vote, the Republicans could have turned impeachment into a party issue, which might have allowed Nixon to remain in office and blame the Democrats for harassing him. But in the summer of 1973, the White House just couldn't imagine that Watergate would end in the downfall of the president.

I, on the other hand, couldn't imagine anything else.

There's a nice irony to the fact that only three days after the Watergate burglary, Richard Nixon's downfall was almost guaranteed by a primary election in, of all places, Brooklyn. On June 20, 1972, Elizabeth Holtzman, a thirty-year-old attorney, upset Emanuel Celler for the Democratic nomination for Congress. At the time, Celler was the eighty-four-year-old incumbent; more to the point, he was also chairman of the House Judiciary Committee. Holtzman won by only 600 votes, but her victory had a profound effect on the country.

Elizabeth Holtzman became a member of the Judiciary Committee, but that's not why her election was so important. It was important because it knocked Manny Celler off that committee, and allowed the next-ranking Democrat, Peter Rodino, to take over. If Celler had remained as chairman, Nixon could have served out his entire second term.

Celler was no friend of the president, but he would have insisted either that the charges against Nixon were too weak to be taken seriously or that the whole issue was beyond the scope of his committee. Celler, who was a distinguished-looking old man and an eloquent speaker with the greatest vocabulary of any politician I've ever known, was very difficult to deal with. He had come to the House back in 1923, and he had seen it all. He was brilliant, but he was also arrogant and stubborn. Nobody could get him to move—not Sam Rayburn, not John McCormack, and certainly not Carl Albert. If the impeachment process had gone to the Judiciary Committee under Manny Celler, it would have died there.

Some members of the House did take the position that the Judiciary Committee was the wrong place to discuss impeachment. John Moss, a California Democrat who came to Congress the same year I did, wrote up a petition calling for a special impeachment committee. More often than not, the member who initiates a particular piece of legislation ends up as the chairman of the special committee appointed by the Speaker to deal with it, and that's probably what

John had in mind—a select committee on impeachment with himself as chairman.

Bob Eckhardt, a liberal from Texas and a real maverick, also pushed for a select committee, and wanted to see Richardson Preyer of North Carolina, a former federal judge, as its chairman. Eckhardt's reasoning was a little different from Moss's: it wasn't that he wanted anything for himself, but he just didn't think that Peter Rodino had the will and the toughness to do a good job. A number of members agreed with him that Rodino lacked the courage to investigate the president of the United States.

Not surprisingly, Moss and Eckhardt had plenty of allies on the Republican side. And there's certainly no question that the White House preferred a special impeachment committee as well. Not only could they control the appointment of the Republican members, but they also hoped to influence Carl Albert to appoint enough conservative Democrats to protect the president. With the Republicans already in the bag, it wouldn't have taken many.

Even before the Speaker decided which route to go, he began receiving phone calls from the oil interests back home in Oklahoma, urging him to consider certain Democrats who were friendly and beholden to the president to serve on the select committee. Carl made it clear to me that the White House was behind these calls, at least indirectly. Apparently, some of the callers were nominating congressmen they didn't even know. There's no question, said the Speaker, that these people had received instructions from Washington.

But Carl Albert didn't appreciate being pressured, and when the calls started coming, he realized he didn't want any part of a special impeachment committee. Instead, he ruled, the matter would be handled through the Judiciary Committee—which was, after all, empowered to deal with impeachments.

When I first came to Congress, every lawyer in the House wanted to serve on the Judiciary Committee, which was seen as a very prestigious assignment. In recent years, however, we've had trouble filling those seats. These days, Judiciary deals with such controversial issues as abortion, the death penalty, gun control, and prayer in the schools, and today's members feel there's nothing to be gained by becoming identified with such emotionally charged legislation.

"Why should I go on that committee?" they ask. "The bill may never get to the floor, but in committee I'll have to vote one way or the other." When you're faced with controversial issues, it's always easier not to have to vote at all.

But in 1973, the Judiciary Committee was still a plum assignment. Peter Rodino, the new chairman, had been my friend for years, partly because we were both Catholics and liberals from urban districts in the Northeast. Peter was a small man with a gravelly voice. He was active in Italian-American causes, and he and Frank Annunzio from Chicago were responsible for making Columbus Day into a national holiday. I had always felt sorry for Peter because he had been stuck behind Manny Celler for so many years that he never had many opportunities to shine. But after Celler was defeated, all of that changed.

Still, Peter was a cautious individual and a reluctant hero. He doesn't like to move until he knows where he's going, and he takes nothing for granted. At first he was scared to death of the enormous task that faced him. He sometimes needed prodding, and on more than one occasion I had to light a fire under his seat. We used to talk together in the front row of the House, right in front of everybody, and neither our fellow members nor the press ever guessed that we were discussing the Big Issue right in front of their noses.

"You've got to get ready," I would say. "This thing is going to hit us and you've got to be prepared for it. You also have to keep it from becoming political."

It was extremely important to keep the impeachment hearings from deteriorating into partisan warfare. For that reason, it was important for me, as majority leader, to keep my distance from the other members of Peter's committee. As for the hearings, I stayed home and watched them on television.

Naturally, there were those in the House and in the press who believed that the impeachment hearings represented partisan politics as usual. Nothing could be further from the truth. In fact, if the Democrats had really wanted to benefit from Watergate, we would have moved much more slowly. After all, the longer Richard Nixon remained in office, the more we would gain. Had the president stayed on through the 1974 congressional elections, we would have picked up even more seats than we did. And if Nixon had served out his full second term, the 1976 presidential election would have been a foregone conclusion.

Knowing Peter Rodino as I did, I wasn't surprised that he was moving ahead at a very slow pace. Besides, like any good politician, he knew that the ball could always bounce the other way, and he didn't want to be caught out on a limb. "You're not a lawyer, Tippy," he repeated. "You're working on intuition and hearsay. But hearsay isn't acceptable in the courts. You're collecting all these rumors, but you can't substantiate them." Who knows? If I had been in his position, I might have felt the same way.

The atmosphere in Washington heated up considerably after October 20, the date of the Saturday Night Massacre, when the president told Elliot Richardson, the attorney general, to fire Archibald Cox, the special prosecutor. Richardson resigned in protest, as did William Ruckelshaus, his deputy. For many members who had been willing to give the president the benefit of the doubt, this was the last straw.

I was on Cape Cod at the time and knew nothing about these events until the press called. But I remember saying to myself that the situation was now worse than I had realized. And I understood that we were in the midst of a historic process which, if it wasn't handled properly, could pose a fundamental threat to our nation's basic institutions.

Until now, I had stayed behind the scenes. But after the Saturday Night Massacre, I made a statement on the floor of the House in which I charged that no other president in our history had brought the highest office in the land into such low repute. "His conduct," I said, "must bring shame upon us all." I knew I was speaking for millions of Americans, because I had received an avalanche of angry telegrams. The Capitol required extra help on the switchboard, and the Western Union lines were jammed.

Of all the letters and telegrams I received from my constituents when Archibald Cox was fired, exactly two supported the president. The American people had agreed to go along with Nixon's pledge to follow the investigation of the special prosecutor wherever it would lead, and now they were furious at him for trying to change the rules in the middle of the game.

Naturally, they communicated their anger and frustration to their representatives in Congress. By now, many of the members were growing impatient, and they started complaining to me: "Tip, when is that committee going to move?" They'd come back from their districts after the weekend, and they'd feel a tremendous pressure to get on with the investigation. At the time, Carl Albert was busy with family problems, so as the majority leader, I had an obligation to keep the process moving.

But this time, when I tried to push Peter, he said, "Get the hell off my back, will you?"

"Wait a minute," I said. "You've got one guy on your back. But I've got two hundred and forty guys on *my* back."

Earlier in the month, Peter had bought a little time by putting out a 718-page book of historical documents on impeachment that was prepared by Jerome Zeifman, the chief counsel of the Judiciary Committee. When that book came out, it was like a godsend. It showed that the committee was really working, and that they had a specific goal in mind. I don't think anybody on Capitol Hill actually *read* the book, but it was the kind of concrete symbol that people were looking for. Each member of the House was given a copy, and my phone started ringing right away, as half of the law professors in my district wanted to see it. I sent mine to Father Monan, the president of Boston College, and was able to dig up another one for myself.

In the midst of all the shouting, I began to think about the lonely figure in the White House who was at the center of the storm. By this time, I was starting to have serious doubts about the president's mental stability. On October 10, 1973, with the Arab-Israeli war in its fifth day and with Vice President Agnew planning to resign that afternoon, the congressional leadership arrived at the White House for a briefing. Although the survival of Israel, one of our closest allies, was at stake, the president was in a jovial mood and kept interrupting Kissinger.

"We had a lot of trouble finding Henry," he said. "He was in bed with a broad."

Kissinger kept on talking.

"Which girl were you with?" said the president.

Kissinger ignored him and continued talking about the war.

"It's a terrible thing when you're with a girl and the Secret Service comes looking for you," said the president.

Nobody laughed.

Two weeks later, we were back at the White House for another briefing on the war. The meeting began promptly at eight-thirty in the morning. We were a little more rushed than usual, because the House was convening at ten o'clock and we all had to be there.

Kissinger had barely opened his mouth when the president interrupted him and started talking to us about the history of communism in the Soviet Union. He rambled on for almost half an hour about the czars and the revolution, about Marx and Lenin, and even the assassination of Trotsky in Mexico. Nobody could understand what, if anything, all of this had to do with the Middle East war.

Finally, the president stopped and said, "I'm sorry, Henry. I've taken some of your time. Please continue with the briefing."

Kissinger resumed speaking, but after a moment or two Nixon interrupted him again and went on for *another* twenty-five minutes about the Soviet Union.

As nine-thirty came and went, somebody said, "Mr. President, we have to go over to open the House." Kissinger never did get to brief us.

On the way back to Capitol Hill, I discussed the president's strange behavior with George Mahon, chairman of the Appropriations Committee, and Doc Morgan, chairman of the Foreign Affairs Committee, and a physician. George, sitting in the back seat, brought up the obvious question: "Don't you think the president acted a little strange this morning?"

"The man is paranoid," said Doc Morgan. "He's in real trouble. But I guess if we had his problems, we'd be the same way."

Doc's comment alarmed me, and I began to worry whether Nixon was now so unstable that the country might be in real danger. As soon as I got to my office, I called Mike Mansfield, the Senate majority leader. Mike and I had been allies on Vietnam, and I had great respect for him. "We're coming down the home stretch," I said. "The president isn't going to be around too much longer. But I'm worried about him. Is anybody over there watching to make sure he doesn't put his finger on the button?"

"Don't you worry about it," said Mike. "We've got Haig, and he's running the show right now." I had confidence in Alexander Haig, whom I knew from the weekly White House leadership meetings. Mansfield and Haig were apparently in close touch, which I found reassuring, as Mansfield was a man of great integrity and good judgment. I've never liked Haig's views on foreign policy, but I believe he deserves our gratitude for keeping his eye on things when Nixon was falling apart.

In retrospect, however, perhaps I had more confidence in Haig than he deserved. Several years later, on March 30, 1981, Haig's own character was called into question on the day of the assassination attempt against President Reagan. Haig, who was then secretary of state, stood at the podium in the White House press room in his blue pinstriped suit and pronounced those now-famous words "I am in control." But as everybody could hear by the tension in his voice, he was clearly *not* in control. This was Haig's Waterloo, and at the time it seemed to mark the end of his career in public life.

The Monday after Thanksgiving, the pressure from the members started all over again. I spent the entire morning hearing what I call "confessions," as the members came to me with their problems and their reports from home. I must have had sixty or seventy guys come up to condemn the Judiciary Committee for dragging its feet. They had spent the holiday talking to their constituents, and by now most people believed that the evidence was there against the president.

Jim Stanton from Cleveland came to me and said, "The whole country knows this guy is guilty. When are we going to get moving? My constituents aren't just disgusted with Nixon. They're starting to get on me, too. They don't think we're doing anything about it." It wasn't just Jim Stanton. By December we were all taking heat from our constituents. When they went back to their districts, the members were starting to look stupid because they didn't know what was going on in the Judiciary Committee.

Even the Republicans who still supported Nixon were angry at Rodino for moving so slowly. If there was enough evidence to impeach, they felt, let's get on with it. And if there wasn't, why didn't we leave the man alone?

"They think you're dragging your feet," I said to Peter.

"Well, they're wrong," he replied. "If there's any foot-dragging, it's by the president. He refuses to give us evidence. He refuses to give us the tapes. All he does is stall."

There's no question that I pushed Peter around, and that he resented it. To be fair, he and his committee had to prepare an ironclad case. This wasn't the time for a lynch mob. This was serious: we were talking about impeaching the president of the United States.

Still, he *was* moving too slowly and I kept up the pressure. When Peter took too long in naming a special impeachment lawyer, I gave him an order: pick your man before we go home for Christmas. Otherwise, the members would raise hell, and it would look as if the Democrats didn't have any guts.

I gave him some suggestions, but he objected that all the people I nominated were Americans for Democratic Action–style liberals who would be seen as overly partisan. Finally, on December 20, Peter named John Doar, a Brooklyn lawyer who had once headed the Civil Rights Division of the Justice Department. It was a brilliant choice, for among other things, John Doar was a Republican.

I gave Peter a hard time, but when the rest of us are all forgotten, he's the one who will be in the history books. People forget who worked behind the scenes, but they remember what the results were. They remember the hearings. And they remember that Peter Rodino performed his duties so carefully and so well.

By the summer, when the House Judiciary Committee finished its work, Peter's picture was all over the Via Veneto in Rome. And in the North End of Boston, and in other Italian sections of the country, Peter Rodino became a real hero, as he deserved to be. During the public hearings of the House Judiciary Committee, the image of Congress jumped about twenty points in the polls.

Peter is also a gentleman. One afternoon, when he was listening to the Nixon tapes, he heard the president talking to John Ehrlichman about the Italians. "They're not like us," said Nixon. "They smell different, they look different, they act different. The trouble is, you can't find one that's honest."

Peter got so mad that he called me in. "Listen to what these sons of bitches are saying!" he said.

To recall the way Nixon spoke about Italians is to be reminded of just how crude the man really was. For all his talent and ability, he desecrated the office of the presidency, and for that I will never forgive him.

Peter won't forgive him either, but he didn't want Nixon's remarks to prejudice the members of his committee, or the general public. "I'm not going to tell a soul," he said, referring to the president's views on Italians. "My people would be so upset." He kept it quiet, and he even arranged to have that section of the tape left out of the committee's version. He knew the Italians would go crazy, because they had been big supporters of Nixon. He knew this tape could finish the president. But he wanted the case to be decided on its own merits.

I certainly can't say the same for Nixon's people. As the investigation went forward, the Republicans were desperate to find a way to undermine Rodino's reputation. Their true nature came out in June 1974, when Jeb Magruder, the deputy campaign director of CREEP, was sentenced to Allenwood Prison. As soon as he arrived, he looked up Neil Gallagher, the former congressman and a lawyer from Bayonne, New Jersey. Gallagher was serving time for income-tax evasion. "If you give us a hand," Magruder told him, "we can get you out of here."

"What are you talking about?" said Gallagher.

"We've got the goods on Rodino," said Magruder. "If you could help us with information on him, we could get you out of this place a few months early. You could even get your license back."

Gallagher was outraged. He immediately called his friend John Murphy, the Democratic representative from Staten Island, New York, to tell him what Magruder was after. John Murphy called me, and I went straight to Rodino.

"Peter, there's nothing in the woodwork, is there?"

"Nothing at all," he said.

"Do you know why I'm asking?"

"Sure I do," he said. "They're going over me with a fine-toothed comb. But don't worry, because there's nothing there."

And there wasn't. Some people in the Nixon White House, however, seemed to believe that any Italian politician from New Jersey was automatically connected to the Mafia. Corruption is not exactly unknown in New Jersey, but anyone who was looking for dirt on Peter Rodino was looking at the wrong guy.

. . .

As if Richard Nixon didn't have enough problems in 1973, Spiro
Agnew, his vice president, resigned in October. Agnew had attacked the liberals so often that they had come to hate him, but in
Congress, many liberal Democrats had a soft spot for the guy. I
don't know how many of them will admit it, but when Agnew went
after the national media, claiming they were too liberal, a lot of us
in public office actually enjoyed seeing the press get its comeup-
pance. Reporters and editors are always doubting the sincerity of
people in public life, so Agnew's attacks on the news media were
not entirely unwelcome.

My own role in the Agnew affair began on September 25, 1973,
when the vice president appeared in Carl Albert's office. I was on
the floor of the House at the time, and a page came to say that the
Speaker wanted to see me immediately. A number of congressional
leaders were there as Agnew told us he was the victim of an ambitious and jealous young federal prosecutor, a Republican named
George Beall, whose father, James Glenn Beall, had been a United
States senator from Maryland when I first came to the House.
According to Agnew, Beall wanted to frame him, and rather than
continuing through the courts, the vice president asked to be investigated by the House Judiciary Committee.

Albert was inclined to go along with Agnew's request, but I
didn't like the idea. The vice president's case was already in the
courts, which is where it belonged. If it went to the House, the
whole investigation would slow down. I don't know whether
Agnew believed that the Congress would exonerate him, or whether
he merely wanted to delay the process. My own guess is that he was
trying to stall, hoping to remain in government long enough to
collect a pension. As things turned out, he missed out by only a
couple of weeks.

With Agnew gone, the administration was bound by the
Twenty-fifth Amendment, which Congress had ratified only six
years earlier, and which specified that "whenever there is a vacancy
in the office of the Vice President, the President shall nominate a
Vice President who shall take office upon confirmation by a majority vote of both houses of Congress." The amendment had become
necessary after Kennedy's death, when, with Johnson in the White

House, the country had been left without a vice president for more than a year. John McCormack, who was next in line for the presidency, was in his seventies, and Carl Hayden, the president pro tempore of the Senate, was in his eighties. Clearly, this was not an acceptable situation. Still, we never dreamed that the new law would be relevant so soon after it was written.

During the brief time between Agnew's resignation and Nixon's selection of a new vice president, the congressional leadership came to the White House for one of our regular meetings. On this particular morning, the president asked Carl Albert to show up early, and the two of them met privately before the rest of us arrived.

As our meeting was about to begin, Carl took me aside and said, "The president and I have been talking about vice presidential candidates, and what kind of man we could get through the House. I gave Jerry Ford a great plug, and I told the president he'd be confirmed without any problems. On your way out, why don't you tell him the same thing." I was happy to do it, not only because Jerry and I were good friends, but because I thought he'd make a fine vice president.

Still, those of us in the leadership didn't really expect that Ford would be the one. Some people thought the most likely candidate was John Connally, Nixon's secretary of the treasury, Kennedy's secretary of the navy, and the three-time governor of Texas. But Connally was a renegade, a former Democrat (he was riding with Kennedy at the moment of his death) who had achieved so much through our party, and had then switched over to the Republicans. He was a turncoat, and there was no way we would support him.

In his memoirs, Nixon revealed that he preferred Connally, but that it was clear that Connally would be opposed by most of the House Democrats, who, in Nixon's view, saw him as a potentially strong presidential candidate in 1976. Nixon also considered nominating Ronald Reagan but concluded that Reagan would split the party.

Another possibility was Nelson Rockefeller, who had great leadership qualities and who was one of the most charismatic politicians I've ever met. Although Rocky wasn't a great speaker, there was a sense of class about him that people really liked. When he walked the streets of New York, crowds of people would surround him. As one of a dying breed of liberal Republicans, Rockefeller was very popular among the Democrats. But as a member of the eastern wing of the party, he would have encountered a lot of opposition among the Republicans, many of whom still resented Rockefeller for his opposition to Goldwater in 1964.

That left Jerry Ford as the safe choice. Just about all of us liked Jerry and thought he'd do a fine job. True, he was too conservative for my taste, but what could you expect from a Republican? I agreed with Clarence Long, a member from Maryland, who said that while Ford voted wrong most of the time, at least he was decently wrong. Besides, Ford was a talented and forceful minority leader, and despite all the jokes about him that appeared later in the press, where he was depicted as clumsy and dumb, Jerry was a bright guy who had graduated from the University of Michigan and Yale Law School.

He was also beyond suspicion. After the Agnew affair, whoever Nixon nominated would be examined very closely. While none of us had ever made a special check into Jerry Ford's background, anybody who knew him could see that he was clean as a whistle.

Another reason we favored Jerry Ford was that we didn't think the Republicans should benefit from Agnew's resignation. While Jerry had been an excellent leader in the Congress, he didn't seem to have the desire, the personality, or the charisma to be elected president on his own. He had even said that in the event he was selected, he wouldn't seek the presidency in 1976. We found that reassuring, although nobody was prepared to hold him to that promise.

After Ford was selected, a handful of Democrats wanted to stall the confirmation procedure. With Agnew out of the picture, Carl Albert was suddenly the number-two-ranking official in the nation. If Nixon either was impeached or decided to resign, and no vice president had been confirmed, then Albert, a Democrat, would have become president.

This scenario made for some intriguing speculation in the press, but it was never something the Democratic leadership took seriously. And knowing Carl Albert as well as I did, I can say without hesitation that he wouldn't have stood for it. It was bad enough that he had to put up with Secret Service protection, which he hated, until Ford was finally confirmed. That was as close as Carl wanted to get to the White House.

On October 12, 1973, a large group from Congress was invited to the White House for the president's announcement of his new vice president. When I arrived, I was taken to a room upstairs together with Carl Albert, Jerry Ford, and Senators James Eastland of Mississippi and Hugh Scott of Pennsylvania, representing the Democrats and Republicans in the Senate. At ten minutes to nine, while waiting to be taken into the East Room, we talked among ourselves as to who it might be. Jerry admitted that he was under consideration, but maintained that he didn't know whom the president had selected.

Then General Haig came in and announced the order in which we would be walking into the East Room for the televised announcement. "The president will name Jerry Ford," he said, "but don't give it away." We all congratulated Jerry, who seemed genuinely surprised. A couple of days later, however, he told me that Nixon had called him at home the night before to give him the news, but had asked him not to tell anyone.

Following the announcement there was a champagne reception for Jerry at the White House. Given the fact that Spiro Agnew had just resigned for taking bribes in his office, some of us felt that this wasn't an appropriate time to celebrate. But that was a decision for the Republicans to make.

At the reception, James Lynn, secretary of housing and urban development, a tough, two-fisted Republican whom I liked, came over and said to me, "Tip, what do you think of this? History is being made tonight. The Twenty-fifth Amendment is being enacted for the first time. I bet we'll never see another night like this one."

"No," I said, "not for another eight months."

He was visibly shocked when I said that. James Lynn is now a lawyer, and every time he sees me he mentions what I said to him that evening. "When I went home that night," he told me years later, "I felt sick. I told the people around me, and they said, 'Tip must know something that we don't.' Then I called some other people, but they told me not to pay attention to Tip O'Neill, because he's so partisan that he says all kinds of things."

As soon as Jerry was confirmed on December 6, the members of the House gave him a hell of a present. For years, I used to drive past the Naval Observatory, a huge home on Massachusetts Avenue where the head admiral of the navy was living, and I'd shake my head. Why the hell was *he* living there when that home would be much more appropriate for the vice president?

When Jerry Ford was confirmed, we turned the Observatory into the official residence of the vice president. But although we rushed the bill through the House especially for our good friend, the wheels of government turn slowly. By the time the new vice president's home was ready for the Fords to move in, they had found something even better over on Pennsylvania Avenue.

Nelson Rockefeller had the opportunity to live in the vice president's house, but this guy needed another mansion like a hole in the head, and he used it only for ceremonial occasions. The first person to actually live there was Walter Mondale.

Most members of the House find that their careers in politics inch ahead very slowly. But for Jerry Ford, it all happened at the speed of light. Only a few weeks before Agnew resigned, when Jerry was still minority leader in the House, he and I were playing golf together at Andrews Air Force Base in the annual Democrat-Republican tournament. As we were riding together in the cart, he said, "Tip, I'm getting out. I promised Betty I'd quit after one more term, and that's all I want. I've got it figured that my pension's worth about twenty-six thousand dollars a year. But you've got to get us a pay raise. You're the majority leader, and you're the only one who can do it. Naturally, I'll do what I can to help you."

"What do you have in mind?" I asked.

"Well," he said, "I'd like to get my pension up to thirty thousand. Then I can go back to Grand Rapids. I want to practice law three days a week and play golf the other four. I figure I can make around twenty-five thousand in my practice, and together with the pension I'll have a good living. Betty and I will take a vacation in the winter, and I'll be living the life of a gentleman."

Little did he realize that within a few weeks he would be confirmed as vice president, and that within a year and a half he'd be living in the White House. But then, as I've always said, it couldn't have happened to a nicer guy.

Jerry and I both love to play golf, and some of our most memorable moments together have taken place on or around the golf course. One scene that remains vivid in my mind is the morning of July 29, 1974, when Jerry and I and a few congressional leaders flew up to play in the Pleasant Valley Classic in Worcester, Massachusetts.

We were traveling in the vice president's plane. Jerry was late, and while we were sitting in the plane, waiting for him to arrive, I got into a conversation about the president with Les Arends, the Republican whip. To my surprise, he didn't seem to realize that it was all over but the shouting.

"Nixon is dead in the House," I said.

"No, he isn't," Arends replied. "You're just playing politics."

"Les," I said, "believe me, I don't like to see this happening any more than you do. This is not a partisan issue. You've got to face facts, and there aren't forty members in the House who will support the president at this point. And if it goes to the Senate, I don't think you can count on twenty-four votes."

"You don't know what you're talking about," he said.

"I've always known how to count."

"Well, those aren't the numbers we're getting," said Arends.

"My numbers come from counting the members," I said. "Where do yours come from?"

"The White House," he said.

"You've got to be kidding," I said.

Just then Jerry's press secretary came on the plane. "Gentlemen," he said, "Mr. Ford is here and we'll be taking off momentarily. But the vice president doesn't want any talk about impeachment or about the president, because when we land, the press is going to ask what you talked about."

When Jerry came aboard, I said, "Where the hell have you been?" Even when Jerry became president, I could always talk to him as a friend.

"I'm sorry to keep you all waiting," he said, "but Betty had the interior decorators over at the new vice president's house on Massachusetts Avenue, and she wanted me to look at the drapes."

"What are you bothering with that for?" I said. "You're never going to live in that house. You're going to be living on Pennsylvania Avenue."

"Oh, don't talk like that," said Jerry.

As soon as we were in the air, Jerry and Arends went off to Jerry's office in a small compartment at the back of the plane. I wasn't trying to listen in, but the "office" was marked off by a thin panel, and I couldn't help but overhear most of their conversation.

"Jesus, Jerry," said Arends, "do you have any idea how serious this thing is?"

"What do you mean?"

"You could be the new president very soon."

"Don't be ridiculous," said Jerry.

"Listen, according to Tip—"

"Oh, Tip doesn't know what he's talking about."

"Come on, Jerry, there's nobody who can count better than Tip. He knows damn well what he's talking about. He says we're dead in the House and that we won't get twenty-four votes in the Senate. Let's face it—he's probably right."

It's hard to believe, looking back, but until the end, some of the Republican leaders really believed that things were under control, and that impeachment was merely a Democratic fantasy.

When Jerry came back out, he looked upset. When he sat down beside me, I said, "Jerry, let me tell you a story. Before long this country is going to need a new vice president, and you're going to have to nominate somebody. I'm sure that Elliot Richardson will be on your mind, so let me tell you a little about him. That way, you won't be caught by surprise if this story comes up during Elliot's confirmation hearings."

Whereupon I proceeded to tell Jerry Ford the story of Elliot Richardson and Bill Callahan.

When Elliot Richardson was a U.S. attorney in Massachusetts, he absolutely hated Bill Callahan, who was the commissioner of the Massachusetts Turnpike Authority. There were those who thought Callahan was a rogue in the Curley tradition, but he put a lot of people to work and did a great deal of good for the city. Still, many Bostonians thought he was a crook, and Elliot Richardson was determined to indict him. Nobody really understood why, but Richardson continued going after Callahan even after Callahan's death.

In 1964, after the old man died, they brought Helen Healy, his secretary, before the grand jury.

"Is it true that you were the only person who knew the combination to Mr. Callahan's safe?"

"Yes," she said.

"And is it true that you were the one who emptied the safe?"

"Yes," she said.

"Now would you please tell the court what you found in the safe?"

"Oh, no," said Helen Healy. "I couldn't do that."

Then Helen Healy was excused so she could consult with her lawyer. He told her to go back in and reveal what was in the safe.

"I'm asking you once more," said the prosecutor, "what did you find in that safe?"

"I found fifty copies of the Master Highway Plan for the Commonwealth of Massachusetts."

"Was there anything else?" said the prosecutor.

"Yes there was," said Helen Healy. "I also found five thousand copies of Elliot Richardson's drunk-driving record from 1939."

Elliot Richardson was only eighteen at the time of his conviction. But Callahan hated him so much that each month he used to mail copies of his driving record to groups of prominent businessmen in Boston. Eventually, these mailings were traced back to Callahan. And Elliot Richardson was determined to get back at him if it was the last thing he ever did.

Jerry got a great kick out of that story. He also got a great kick out of all the people who were there to greet him with welcome signs when the plane landed. He was just like a kid, he was so excited. On the way to the country club, a few houses had signs in front saying, "Worcester Welcomes Gerald Ford." It was all so new that Jerry was absolutely thrilled.

When we got to the golf course, Jerry and I posed for a few pictures and walked with our arms around each other for the benefit of the photographers. The next day, one of the New York papers ran that picture with a nasty caption: "Looks like it's all over."

A week later, when Nixon made a few more tapes available, I knew it really *was* all over. These tapes revealed that he had known about the Watergate break-in almost from the start, and that he had deceived the country ever since.

At the last moment, John Rhodes, who had taken Jerry's place as minority leader, came to see me. "Can't we work something out?"

he said. "Nobody wants to see the president impeached. Couldn't we just censure him?"

"I'm afraid it's too late," I said. "Unless he resigns, he'll be impeached in the House and found guilty in the Senate, and he'll have to go to jail."

On the night of August 7, John Rhodes called to tell me in confidence that he had just come from the White House, and that the president was going to resign on August 9.

I immediately called Millie on the Cape. "The president is going to resign within forty-eight hours," I said. "I think you should be here for Jerry Ford's swearing in."

"I'm not coming," she said. "I don't have a dress with me to wear to the White House."

I asked my daughter Rosemary to convince her mother that she had to come down. Rosemary did a good job. "Mother," she said, "you're really expected to be at Dad's side at a time like this." So Millie drove to Cambridge, packed her dress, and flew down to Washington.

On August 8, at two forty-five in the afternoon, Jerry Ford called. We talked about the golf tournament and joked about the picture of the two of us that had just appeared in *Newsweek*, which seemed to show him with his hand in my pocket. Then Ford told me that at ten the next morning, the president was submitting his letter of resignation to Henry Kissinger. Jerry would be sworn in at noon, and he wanted me to be there.

"Are wives invited?" I asked. "I've already told Millie to pack her things and get down here."

"Actually, wives were not invited," he said. "But they are now."

I had already prepared a statement, and I read it to Jerry on the phone.

"That's just fine," he said. "I'll be counting on your advice and assistance."

"Well, Jerry, the first piece of advice I'll give you is not to choose a Democrat for vice president. There's been some talk about a bipartisan ticket. It's a nice sentiment, but we both know this country doesn't work that way."

There was a moment of silence, as neither of us wanted to hang up. Then I said, "Jerry, isn't this a wonderful country? Here we can talk like this and we can be friends, and eighteen months from now I'll be going around the country kicking your ass in."

I made good on that promise. When it came to politics, I was as partisan as ever. At the same time, my friendship with Jerry Ford and our previous working relationship made life easier for both of us. During the Nixon years, when the Democratic congressional leadership met with the president and his staff, it was all business. Under President Ford, however, the atmosphere was much more congenial and relaxed. The president would tell us what legislation he was sending over, and if I didn't think it had a chance, I'd say, "Jerry, that's not going anywhere. We're going to knock your jock off on this one. But send it over anyway if that's what you want."

The night before Nixon resigned, he met one last time with the congressional leadership. This time, I was not invited. As Nixon describes the scene in his memoirs, Carl Albert was the first one to arrive. Before Nixon could say a word, Carl blurted out, "I hope you know, Mr. President, that I have nothing to do with this whole resignation business."

"I understand, Carl," said the president.

That night, I watched Nixon's resignation speech together with Leo Diehl in the majority leader's office. I had a touch of sadness in my heart, because nothing like this had ever happened before. My sadness was not for Nixon, but for the nation. Nixon would do all right. By resigning when he did, the president was able to retain his pension, free office space, and various other perks. And I had to smile when Nixon said that he had lost his political base in Congress. That was an understatement. On August 20, when the House voted to accept the impeachment report of the Judiciary Committee, only three members voted against it.

One of the most important decisions that Jerry Ford ever made was to pardon Richard Nixon. As I made clear to Jerry at the time, I thought it was a terrible mistake. I learned about the pardon when the phone rang at my Cambridge house on September 8, 1974, a Sunday morning, shortly after Jerry had become president. I had just come back from mass at St. John's, and I was about to leave for a round of golf with my old pal Pat Casey.

"Hello, Tip? This is Jerry."

"Jerry?"

"Jerry Ford."

I've received many phone calls from the White House over the years, but this was the first time a president had ever called me directly, without going through his secretary.

"What gives, Mr. President? You're making your own phone calls?"

"Yes," he said, "I just got off the phone with Carl Albert and Mike Mansfield, and now I'm calling you. I just came back from church, and I've made up my mind to pardon Nixon. I'm doing it because I think it's right for the country, and because it feels right in my heart. The man is so depressed, and I don't want to see the president go to jail."

"You're crazy," I said. "I'm telling you right now, this will cost you the election. I hope it's not part of any deal."

"No, there's no deal."

"Then why the hell are you doing it?"

"Tip," he said, "Nixon is a sick man. You can tell a lot by a man's attire, and he's become unkempt and seedy."

I told Jerry about Nixon's strange behavior at the two White House meetings the previous October.

"I'm not surprised," he said. "He was sick then and he's sick now. And Julie has been calling me every day because her father is so depressed."

"Look," I said, "I know you're not calling for my advice, but I think it's too soon. The press is going to beat you over the head with it. Just yesterday I spoke to an audience of Yankee aristocrats, and a number of them came up to me and said that Nixon should not be let off."

"Some people will holler," he said, "but I don't think the American people are vindictive. Nixon has suffered enough. Besides, I can't run this office while this business drags on day after day. There are a lot more important things to be spending my time on."

Although I thought the pardon was wrong, I didn't want to send Nixon to jail either. Like Jerry, I believed that he had suffered enough. After all, it's not where a man lands that marks his punishment. It's how far he falls.

. . .

In 1977, I was sworn in as Speaker three weeks before Jimmy Carter took over from Gerald Ford. A few days before the transition, Jerry called me and asked me to help him with one last favor.

"Sure, Mr. President," I said. "What's on your mind?"

"Next week, when I leave office, I'll be flying back on Air Force One. I'd like to take a helicopter from the grounds of the Capitol, but the Capitol police don't want to let me do it."

"What the hell are you calling me for?"

"Because the chief of the Capitol police is under the Capitol Building Authority, and as the Speaker, the Capitol Building Authority is under your command."

"Really?" I said. "That's news to me, but I'll see what I can do."

I called the chief of police, who explained that with the inauguration going on, if President Ford took off from the Capitol, they'd need to put on another thirty-five men for security reasons, which would be too expensive.

"Do it anyway," I said. "It's the president's last wish."

On the morning of the inauguration, Millie and I went over to Blair House, which houses official guests of the government, and where the president-elect traditionally stays before he moves into the White House. As Speaker of the House, it was my duty to escort Jimmy Carter, the president-elect, across the street to his new residence, while Millie did the same for Mrs. Carter.

Betty and Jerry Ford were waiting for us, and we all shook hands. Then the three wives got into one limousine, and I climbed into the other with the president and the president-elect.

There wasn't much conversation in the car. Carter was in a quiet mood, and during the ride to the Capitol he spent the whole time looking out the window and waving to the people. Every now and then he'd say, "Great crowd."

Then Jerry turned to me and said, "By the way, Tip, thanks for helping me out with the helicopter."

"No problem," I said. "But I've been meaning to ask you. Why don't you just leave from the White House?"

"For two reasons," he said. "First, I don't want to go back there. I've already said my good-byes to everybody, and I'd hate to go through all that again. The other reason is that I'm in a hurry to get

to the airport because I want to get out to California in time for the
Bing Crosby Golf Tournament."

So that's what was on the mind of my pal Jerry Ford during his
final hour in office. I guess golfers are all alike.

Jerry and I were good friends before he became president, and we're
still good friends today. A couple of years after he left office, I was
out in Palm Springs for the Bob Hope Tournament, when Susan
Ford, the president's daughter, came up to me. "Mr. Speaker," she
said, "I want to ask you a favor. A lot of people are asking my father
if he'll run for president in 1980. But nobody in the family wants him
to. My mother's doing beautifully. She's got her life back under
control, and now she's helping other people with alcohol and drug
problems. My father serves on a few boards, he does some speaking,
and he's feeling great. Everything's going so well and the family has
never been happier.

"The people who want him to run for president don't really care
about my father. They just want to feather their own nests. Would
you be willing to speak to him to try to get him not to run? I think
he'd listen. He likes you and he has a lot of faith in you, and he
knows you've always been straight with him."

"I'm flattered that you'd ask me," I said. "But it just wouldn't be
right for a Democrat like me to advise a Republican on whether he
should run for president. Your father and I are close friends, but
when it comes to party politics we've always gone our separate
ways."

A year went by and Jerry and I found ourselves playing in the
Hope Tournament again. "I'm thinking of entering the race," he
said. "But I don't know yet whether or not I'm going to be a
candidate. Reagan has a strong organization, and the only other guy
out there with an organization is me. I don't think Bush can put one
together. If Reagan goes into Iowa or New Hampshire and falls flat
on his face, I'm going to be ready."

I said, "Jerry, it's really none of my business, and I don't know
whether I should tell you this or not. But since you brought it up,
let me tell you about a conversation I had with your Susan last year."

When I finished, he said, "I'm glad you told me that, Tip. I asked
my family how they felt about my running for president, and they

said, 'Anything you want, Dad.' But I'm glad to know how they really feel."

Reagan made a strong showing in the New Hampshire primary, so Jerry's decision was made for him. But if he had entered the race, I know his family would have been there at his side. It wasn't what they wanted, but they would have gone along with whatever he chose.

God has been good to America, especially during difficult times. At the time of the Civil War, he gave us Abraham Lincoln. And at the time of Watergate, he gave us Gerald Ford—the right man at the right time who was able to put our nation back together again. Nothing like Watergate had ever happened before in our history, but we came out of it strong and free, and the transition from Nixon's administration to Ford's was a thing of awe and dignity.

I've never been a Nixon-hater, and I felt no pleasure when he resigned. But if it had to be, I'm glad it happened the way it did. A president fell and a new president took over, and yet there was no scuffling, no guns, no harsh bickering, no crowds in the streets— not so much as a fistfight. The whole world was watching, and other nations couldn't help but be impressed. After all, when leaders fall, their governments usually collapse as well. But our transition was orderly and by the book, and this period, as much as anything in our history, showed the strength of our great democracy.

From now on, Watergate will serve as a vivid reminder about the dangers of abusing presidential power. Fortunately, we came out of Watergate without suffering any permanent damage. But we will have to stay vigilant to make sure that such excesses never happen again. In the memorable words of James Mann, a Democrat from South Carolina and a member of the House Judiciary Committee, "The next time there may be no watchman in the night."

12

★★★★★

Speaker of the House

SOME politicians have a yearning to be president, but from the time I first came to Washington in 1953, my private ambition was to become Speaker of the House. I had done the job successfully in the Massachusetts legislature, and I was confident that I could do just as well in the House of Representatives. Once I gave up the idea of running for governor of Massachusetts, my friends back home started saying that if I stayed in Washington long enough, I might end up as Speaker. In my heart I agreed with them, although this wasn't a topic I ever discussed out loud.

During my years as majority leader, Carl Albert had assured me half a dozen times that I'd take over as Speaker when he stepped down. But in June 1976, when Carl announced that he wasn't going to run for another term in the House, I was caught by surprise. I was out in California, helping to raise funds for the congressional campaigns of Charles Wilson and Norman Mineta. A group of us were sitting around the pool at the hotel when Norm came over and said, "Tip, I just heard on the radio that Carl Albert is retiring. Let me be the first one to support you for Speaker."

I started rounding up commitments, but it soon became clear that I had no opposition.

The Constitution mandates that "the House of Representatives shall choose their Speaker," but it doesn't say anything about his duties and powers. In fact, the Constitution doesn't even specify that the Speaker has to be a member of the House, although in practice he always has been.

Many nations have a Speaker in their system of government, but in our case the position is a substantial and complicated one involving several dimensions of power. First, the local level: although the Speaker of the House holds the highest legislative position in the land, he can't serve in Congress unless he is elected by his home district. So in addition to all his other duties, the Speaker must continue to represent his own constituents.

On the next level, he represents the majority party in Congress. In this capacity, he is the guiding force behind both the development of legislation and the process of winning enough votes to get it passed.

But his most important power is to set the agenda, and if he doesn't want a certain bill to come up, it usually doesn't. The Speaker also has the power of recognition, whereby he determines which members will speak from the floor. And he picks the members of his party who will serve on the various select committees, as well as on the powerful Rules Committee.

In addition to his more partisan duties, the Speaker is also the presiding officer of the House, and in that capacity he must protect the rights of the minority members, too. He is also the chief administrative officer of the House side of the Capitol, and oversees all the House office buildings and grounds.

As the highest-ranking officer of the Congress, the Speaker also represents the legislative branch on ceremonial occasions. Finally, he is third in the line of succession to the presidency. For that reason, his office is expected to keep the White House informed of his whereabouts at all times.

On January 3, 1977, when I was sworn in as Speaker at the start of the Ninety-fifth Congress, I was as excited as a starting pitcher in his first World Series. Over two hundred friends from my district came to Washington for the ceremony, and there were so many visitors that we ran out of room in the House gallery and had to set up folding chairs in Statuary Hall, where our guests could watch the ceremony on closed-circuit TV. Millie and the kids were with me, of course, as well as many of my old pals from Barry's Corner. We even had a few relatives from Ireland who flew over to join us.

The Republicans nominated John Rhodes, and when he lost

the vote, which was merely a formality, he announced that "Tip O'Neill is going to be the greatest one-term Speaker that the House has ever had."

It was a good line, but I got right back at him. "I understand John has his eye on the Speaker's seat," I said. "I assure him that's *all* he's going to have on it."

Now that I was Speaker, and the children were grown, it finally made sense for Millie to move down from Cambridge. It wasn't easy to buy a place in the Washington area, where housing prices were shockingly high. But with the help of our friend Corinne Conte, a real estate agent (and Silvio's wife), Millie found us a two-bedroom condominium in Bethesda.

Millie soon became popular with the congressional wives—not through the usual social route of parties and receptions, because we didn't go in for that, but for a much more practical reason. When John McCormack and Carl Albert were running the place, these women never knew what time their husbands would be home for dinner—if at all. But Millie laid down the law: "Listen," she told me, "you're always urging the new members to bring their families to Washington, so I don't want you keeping them in the House until eight or nine at night."

And that, more or less, marked the end of evening sessions in the House.

Each Speaker sets his own agenda, and mine was to have the House pass a tough, new code of ethics. Although Watergate had involved wrongdoing in the White House rather than in Congress, and although the image of Congress had risen considerably during the Watergate hearings, the fallout from that period was so widespread that aspersions were cast on *all* elected officials in Washington. Besides, the House had recently earned its own share of bad publicity. Not long before I became Speaker, Wilbur Mills and Wayne Hays had both undergone public humiliations as a result of their fondness for wine and women. Several other members had found themselves in trouble for various offenses, including campaign law violations, ties to organized crime, and even bribery.

There was also the Tongsun Park affair, which raised a cloud of suspicion over several members, including me. As Speaker, however, I was able to convince Leon Jaworski, the former Watergate special prosecutor, to return to Washington to head up the inquiry on Tongsun Park. In the end, two former congressmen, Richard Hanna of California and Otto Passman of Louisiana, were indicted as a result of the investigation by the Ethics Committee, although Passman was later acquitted.

In order to put together the kind of tough ethics package I was looking for, I decided to appoint a special commission consisting of five Democrats, three Republicans, and seven members from the public who represented business, education, and labor. I put David Obey of Wisconsin in charge of the group, because a year earlier he had raised the issue of a revised ethics code. "Davey," I told him, "if you're going to write one, go all the way. I want a damn good code, one we can all be proud of. You produce it, and I'll back you up."

Although the members of Congress certainly appreciated the need for a strong ethics bill, we had some bitter fights over the guidelines. Most members could understand the need for complete financial disclosure, and for a law against using campaign funds to pay off personal debts. But there was a major controversy over whether we should set limits on outside income.

I argued strongly that we had no choice but to set a firm limit of 15 percent on the amount of money that a member could earn outside of Congress. This was a very unpopular idea, as members of Congress have traditionally held outside jobs, most often in law firms back home. Although there was really nothing wrong with this practice, in the current climate it just didn't seem right. For one thing, there was always the possibility of a conflict of interest, or at least the appearance of one. For another, there was a growing belief in the country that being a member of Congress ought to be a full-time job.

Some of the loudest protests to a limit on outside income came from members of the Rules Committee, several of whom earned more money from their second jobs than they did as legislators. Morgan Murphy of Illinois had a large law practice. Claude Pepper was a successful lawyer in Miami. Bernie Sisk was in real estate.

Many members maintained, with some justification, that if their outside income was reduced to 15 percent of their congressional salary of $44,600, they couldn't afford to continue in the House. "If you're really serious about this," said John Anderson of Illinois, "I'll have to leave this place. I don't want to try to educate five college-age children on fifty-one thousand a year."

On February 24, 1977, during my second month as Speaker, I invited the Democrats on the Rules Committee to a breakfast meeting, where I laid it on the line, much as Sam Rayburn had done in 1955 when he had appointed me to that same committee. "Look," I said, "I've committed myself as the leader of the party to the strongest ethics bill in the history of this country. You're my handpicked people, and you all serve on this committee at my behest. I need you on this one. Believe me, I realize that for some of you the fifteen percent limit will mean a major sacrifice. When this bill gets to the floor you can vote your own conscience, but I need your support now to get it out of Rules."

It was a hard speech to give, because if I had still been on the Rules Committee, I, too, might have objected to this proposal. Not only would it cause major financial problems for many members and their families, but it also discriminated in favor of legislators who were wealthy. After all, nobody was proposing to set any limits on unearned outside income, such as investment dividends and trust funds.

We were able to work out a compromise. The Rules Committee reluctantly went along with my request to bring the ethics bill to the floor of the House, while I agreed to allow a separate vote on the issue of limiting outside income.

But the members had no choice but to bite the bullet. They could see that if some of us held outside jobs, it would mean that no matter how strict a system we set up for financial disclosure, we were still creating the appearance of wrongdoing in the public mind. "The issue before us," I said during the House debate, "is not unofficial office accounts, honorariums, or outside income, earned or unearned. The issue is credibility—restoring public confidence in this House as an institution, restoring confidence in its membership."

I called in all my chips that day, and the vote to limit outside income was overwhelming—344 to 79.

Because many were being asked to make a major sacrifice, I had promised that if the House passed the new ethics bill, I would do my best to put through a significant pay raise that would bring congressional salaries up to $57,500—a 29 percent increase over the current figure. Congressional pay raises are almost always controversial, but this time every leading newspaper in the country agreed that a pay hike for the members was long overdue. Even with our 29 percent increase, we were still below our peers in most other professions.

I've always believed that congressional salaries were too low, and I'll never forget what John Rhodes once told me. "You know," he said, "I go around the country trying to line up new candidates for our party. I'll have lunch with a dynamic young lawyer, and I'll ask him straight out if he's interested in running for Congress. But sooner or later the subject of money comes up, and when I tell him what the members earn, he just shakes his head. He's usually making two or three times that much in his current job, and on the money we pay he just can't afford to move to Washington with his wife and kids. And so the Republicans end up with a lot of people who are wealthy and want to be in Congress for the prestige."

I didn't agree with John Rhodes very often, but he certainly made a lot of sense on this point.

As I write these words early in 1987, members of Congress receive $89,500 a year. That may sound high, but for well-educated and knowledgeable executives who work with a trillion-dollar budget, it's still too low. If it were up to me, I'd raise congressional salaries all the way up to $150,000. Given the work load and the responsibility that members have, they deserve that much.

I realize that the folks back home don't always see it that way. But most people just don't understand all the financial obligations that a member with two homes has to carry—assuming, of course, that he can afford two homes. Not long ago, the *New York Times* ran a story about Daniel Lungren, a Republican from Long Beach, California. In 1978, when he was first elected, Lungren, who is a lawyer, moved his family to Virginia. But to afford their new house, they had to sell the house back home. In the summers, when the family returned to California, they would either stay with his parents or house-sit for people on vacation.

Housing is the worst of it, but there are other special expenses for members of Congress. Every time you go out with a crowd, they expect you to pick up the tab. For years, people from home would drop by my office at eleven forty-five in the morning with the expectation that I would invite them to lunch. And then there are wedding gifts and flowers for funerals, and the expectation that you will support every charitable event that comes along. Unless we raise the salaries for members of Congress, we could end up with a House of Representatives that represents only the rich.

Even with the anticipated pay raise, the ethics bill was highly unpopular, and on a secret ballot it would have been defeated overwhelmingly. Although Dave Obey did a terrific job, that bill made him so many enemies that a couple of years later he was narrowly defeated in the caucus for chairman of the Budget Committee, a vote he should have won easily. Obey is a great legislator, but my confidence in him may have inadvertently thwarted his rise to a position of elected leadership.

But whatever their private reservations, only a handful of members were willing to go against the mood of the country by opposing the new ethics bill. In addition to limiting outside income, the bill also set tough limits on how much members could earn from speeches, and made it illegal for a lame-duck member to travel at government expense. Until 1977, any money in a member's office account that wasn't spent by the end of the year used to go to him personally. Now, at long last, this practice was ruled illegal. On the other side of the ledger, the Obey commission made it possible for members to travel back and forth to their districts at public expense and without any limits.

The bill was adopted by the House on March 2, 1977, by an overwhelming vote of 402 to 22. The following day, the *Washington Star* ran a front-page headline: HOUSE VOTES ETHICS CODE AND A NEW HILL STRONGMAN IS BORN. While this was an overstatement, it was true that I had put the prestige of my office on the line and had won my first major test.

The ethics issue flared up again a couple of years later with the ABSCAM affair, when the FBI arrested seven members of the House and one from the Senate for taking bribes from undercover agents posing as wealthy Arabs.

As far as I'm concerned, ABSCAM was a rotten business from

start to finish. Entrapment is un-American and has no place in law enforcement. But what I didn't know at the time was that I, too, had been targeted by the FBI.

In 1979, my daughter Susan was a union organizer for the International Brotherhood of Police Officers. Out of the blue, a member of the vice squad in Fort Lauderdale phoned Susan's boss with a warning that on my forthcoming trip to Florida to help a local member of Congress raise money for his campaign, I was going to be set up. It wasn't clear exactly what was supposed to happen, but it sounded as if I might be offered a bribe.

Susan and her brother Kip passed this information along to Kirk O'Donnell, my general counsel, who immediately called Bill Nickerson in the Treasury Department, which oversees the Secret Service, to see if he could arrange for some protection during my trip. Bill said this was a job for the FBI, and he brought Kirk over to see Francis Mullins, the deputy head of the Bureau, who agreed to check out the rumors. A couple of days later, Mullins assured us that we had nothing to worry about. But just in case, Kirk agreed to accompany me to Florida.

While we were there, I was far more cautious than usual. We allowed no pictures, for example, because somebody might have been trying to photograph me with a gangster. That night, Kirk and I went to a nightclub owned by the Loconto Brothers, a singing group from my old neighborhood who used to be known as the Lane Brothers. For old times' sake, I even got up on stage and joined them in a couple of songs.

When we returned to the hotel, which was right on the water, we ran into a friendly bunch of partiers who invited us to come with them for a drink on their boat. But the hour was late, and besides, after that warning, I wasn't about to go anywhere with people I didn't know.

Several months after the ABSCAM affair became public, I was walking out of a meeting on Connecticut Avenue when a fellow came up to me and introduced himself as an FBI employee. "Remember when you were down in Florida," he said, "and some people in your hotel invited you to go on a boat? That was a setup. They were going to offer you a bribe, and a fellow was being paid fifty thousand dollars to see if he could get you to bite. They were also going after Ted Kennedy, and the reward for getting him was a hundred thousand."

The agent who told me this added that he had recently left the FBI in disgust because of ABSCAM and was planning to write a book about it. Assuming he was telling the truth (and I believe he was), the FBI, which refused to give me protection in Florida, was actually trying to do me in.

Later, using his own sources, Jack Anderson reported in one of his columns that both Peter Rodino and I had been on the FBI hit list. I was angry, of course, but the most insidious result of AB-SCAM, in my view, was that a member from Pennsylvania who was targeted by the FBI but who never even *met* with the agents was defeated in the next election. ABSCAM may not have been intended as a smear campaign, but that was certainly one of its results.

At the time, there were questions raised in the press as to whether President Carter had any advance knowledge of ABSCAM. I'm sure he didn't, but I have my doubts about Griffin Bell, the attorney general. And I find it difficult to believe that William Webster, the head of the FBI, had nothing better to do than to arrange for the entrapment of members of Congress.

ABSCAM, of course, brings to mind the larger issue of corruption and bribery in politics. As I was working on this book, a number of people asked whether I would "come clean" about this topic. Because corruption among public officials is of such great interest to the public, I have searched my memory for incidents where I, personally, was approached for unsavory purposes. It may be hard to believe, but I can recall only one time when somebody tried to bribe me—and it wasn't exactly a case of organized crime, either.

It happened during one of my regular weekend trips back to Cambridge, when I used to make the rounds of my neighborhood, stopping in to visit the supermarket, Frank the barber, John the shoemaker, and the local Chinese laundry where I took my shirts. I was friendly with them all and had once helped the laundryman get his brother over here from China. He had another brother who was still there, and I was planning to help him out, too.

At Christmas, the laundryman handed me a couple of cigars wrapped up in tinfoil. I thanked him, and was pleased to see that he had broken his usual pattern of giving me a wash-and-wear shirt that was invariably a couple of sizes too small. I stuck the cigars in my coat pocket, and when I got home I put them on a shelf.

A few days later, my daughter Susan was going out to dinner with a young man she was dating. When he came by to pick her up, I asked him if he ever smoked cigars. He nodded, so I said, "Try these," and tossed him the two cigars from the laundryman, which I still hadn't bothered to unwrap.

Later that night, Susan came back to the house in tears. After dinner, her date had unwrapped the cigars to find five one-hundred-dollar bills wrapped around them. Susan, of course, was humiliated and enraged. "Daddy," she said to me, "is this what politics is all about? Is this how it really works?"

I told her the truth—that I was shocked—and prayed that she believed me.

The next morning, I took the money back to the laundry. "Is this the way you think our country works?" I shouted. "Don't you ever ask me for anything again. I ought to have both you and your brother sent back to China!"

The poor fellow started to cry like a baby. Later, after I calmed down, I realized that somebody must have told him that this was how things were done in this country. How was he to know?

Contrary to the popular view, politics today may be one of the cleanest professions rather than the dirtiest. I'm not saying that politicians are inherently better people than their counterparts in other careers, but in our case there are two special considerations.

First, we operate in a fishbowl. These days, almost everything we say or do is reported in the press, whether we like it or not. Second, the plain truth is that most politicians don't really have the power or the clout to get things done on their own. In the great majority of cases, anyone who tries to bribe a politician is throwing his money away.

As Speaker, I continued my practice of staying in close touch with the members—to the point where I probably knew more Republicans than Sam Rayburn knew Democrats. Most of my time and energy, however, went to members of my own party. My door was always open, and not a day went by when a member didn't come to see me for advice, either in my usual spot in the front row of the House, or in my office, which was just down the hall.

Typically, one of the younger members would come by to say that although he had promised the people at home that he would vote a certain way, he had changed his mind and wanted to get out of that commitment. What should he do?

"Tell them the truth," I would reply. "Come clean about it, and do it quickly. Issue a statement saying that you were convinced by one set of arguments, but now that you've had a chance to hear the other side, you believe your earlier position was mistaken." Occasionally, I would describe my own reversal on the Vietnam War, and how I patiently explained my new position to the people in my district, some of whom were convinced I was a traitor.

It wasn't only members who came to the Speaker's office, and not all the problems I listened to had to do with legislation. Some congressmen showed up to discuss personal matters, and over the years a number of their wives came by to ask if I would speak to their husbands and help straighten out their marital problems.

One story I'll never forget came to my attention back when I was Speaker of the Massachusetts legislature. One afternoon, the wife of a member came in to complain that her husband was always running around and that he never came home. He didn't give her any money, either, so there was nothing to eat in the house. The poor woman was so broke that she actually had to hitch a ride to my office in Boston.

I was outraged by what she told me, and I ordered her husband's paycheck from the legislature to be mailed directly to his wife at home. When the fellow learned what I had done, he came to my office and wanted to fight me. But it turned out that this guy was married to two women at the same time—one in his district, and the other in Boston! Still, that didn't stop him from becoming a major power in the state.

It would be hard to imagine a situation like that today—not because people are different than they used to be, but because members of Congress have changed so dramatically. One effect of Watergate was that it brought in a whole new breed of legislators, including a huge group of 118 Democrats who were elected for the first time in 1974 and 1976, just before I became Speaker. The class of 1974, which came in less than three months after Nixon resigned, included no less than 71 new Democrats, including Norman Mineta and Henry Waxman (California), Tim Wirth (Colorado), Mary Russo (Illinois), and Thomas Downey and Stephen Solarz (New York). The class of 1976 was also substantial, although not as large, and included such new faces as Leon Panetta (California), Barbara Mikulski (Maryland), Ed Markey (Massachusetts), Ted Weiss (New York), and an impressive young man from Missouri named Richard Gephardt.

These so-called Watergate Babies were a highly sophisticated and talented group. They were also independent, and they didn't hesitate to remind you that they were elected on their own, often without any help from the Democratic party. In some cases they had managed to tip over the regular Democrats in their districts. In others, they had defeated the entrenched Republican machine. A few, like Jerry Patterson from Orange County in California, were elected from districts that were six-to-one Republican.

These new members, then, were outsiders, even more so than Jimmy Carter, who was elected in 1976. They hadn't come up through the state legislatures. Some of them had never run for city council or county office. Close to half had never campaigned for *any* elective office before running for Congress.

Many of the new members had never rung doorbells, or driven people to the polls, or stayed late stuffing envelopes at campaign headquarters. A good number were activists who had run for office because of Vietnam, or Watergate, or the environment. As I got to know these people, I was struck by how many told me they had no interest in politics until Robert Kennedy's presidential campaign in 1968. Kennedy was their hero, and he was the one who had turned them on to the possibility of running for office.

With such a large group of outspoken new members, Congress became more difficult to control than ever before. Party discipline went out the window. These people were impatient, and they wanted to be part of the action right away. New members once were seen and not heard, but now it seemed that even the lowliest freshman could be a power in the House. Almost before we knew it, there were 154 committees and subcommittees, each with its own chairman. Mo Udall used to say that if you didn't know a member's name, you were on pretty safe ground if you addressed him simply as "Mr. Chairman."

As soon as the class of '74 came in, they asked several of the committee chairmen to meet with them. Edward Hebert, chairman of the Armed Services Committee, a real power in the House who referred to himself as the Grand Titan, and a veteran who had served in Congress all through the Rayburn years, gave a Rayburn-like speech about how freshmen should be content to sit quietly and learn the ropes for a few years. The new members were furious that Eddie, in their view, was talking down to them. The following month, their votes in the caucus were enough to overthrow him, as well as W. R. Poage of Agriculture and Wright Patman of Banking and Currency.

I was shocked when this happened. I knew there was some discontent with several of the older chairmen, but I never dreamed that the younger members, together with some of the liberals like Jonathan Bingham and Frank Thompson, would put together enough votes to overthrow three of the entrenched powers. In all my years in the House, this was one of the few times when I was genuinely caught by surprise.

Despite their lack of political experience, the new members were mostly well educated and well informed on the issues. And unlike my own generation, they were also media-oriented. In years past, most of us had been reluctant to appear on the national Sunday-morning talk shows like *Meet the Press* and *Face the Nation*. These forums were the exclusive prerogative of the senior members, and anyone who violated this unwritten rule was seen as an upstart who needed his wings clipped.

But the new members of the mid-1970s had no such reservations. Their attitude was "I know more about what they're going to ask me than *they* know, so what is there to be afraid of?" And because they were perfectly willing to criticize their own committee chairmen, or even the President, some of them became very popular with the news media, which like nothing better than to feature politicians blasting each other.

To many of the new members, of course, Tip O'Neill was an old fogey, a symbol of the established system they were so eager to bypass. At the same time, I had their respect: they knew I had taken a strong stand against the Vietnam War, and that Tip O'Neill had been an active backstage player in the Watergate drama. Besides, I've always been able to get along with people, even when we don't agree on everything.

There were some terrific individuals in the class of 1974, but what really annoyed me about this group is that as late as 1979 they still had their own caucus. I could go along with the need for a freshman caucus, but I naturally assumed that after their first term was over, the new members would join the mainstream. But almost overnight, Congress was crowded with all kinds of caucuses: the freshman caucus, the sophomore caucus, the junior caucus, the black caucus, the Hispanic caucus, the steel caucus, the women's caucus—not to mention the various regional caucuses. As Speaker, I used to meet with them all.

Although the new members came in with a million grievances, the longer they remained in Congress, the more they began to appreciate the ways and customs of the House—including the seniority system. There were times, however, when they had to be reminded that their lack of experience was a real drawback. I recall one meeting when some of the younger members complained that I didn't include them in the decision-making.

"Do I take you seriously?" I told them. "Of course I do. But when a storm comes along, I don't want to grab on to a young sapling that sways in the wind. In difficult times, I prefer to go with the sturdy old oak."

Within a few months of becoming Speaker, I could already see some positive changes in the House—and so did the press. I especially liked what Joseph Kraft wrote in his syndicated column—that "in O'Neill, the House has found not only a leader, but also a champion. He has arrested the demoralization of the past few years. He gives the members a feeling of pride, a little touch of class."

I certainly tried to make the House a more open and effective place, and I believe I succeeded. In my daily news conferences, I tried to give the press something real to write about, and I never had any inclination to hide my legislative priorities. I also tried to be more open in the exercise of power. When Carl Albert was Speaker, he and I used to make all the decisions. But when I took over, I relied on a whole group of talented people, including Jim Wright, the majority leader; John Brademas (and later, Tom Foley), the whip; Dan Rostenkowski, the chief deputy whip and chairman of Ways and Means; and Bill Alexander, the chief deputy whip after Dan. The whip organization was now far more sophisticated than when I first took it over, and I relied on it extensively in making decisions about upcoming legislation.

I managed to keep the lines of communication open to all Democrats, including the growing number of conservative members, with whom I differed on matters of policy. Some of them, especially the southerners, would occasionally ask me to say hello to a delegation from their districts. "These people don't exactly *like* you," I would be told, "but heck, they're just dying to meet you."

Whenever possible, I would try to accommodate the member by inviting his constituents to come by the office. In these situations, I'd always say something like this: "Your congressman is a terrific guy. We're close personal friends, although we don't agree on the issues. He never gives me a vote, but I like him anyway."

As a party man, I always urged the Democratic members to use me to their best advantage: "If you want to praise me, that's fine. But if it will be more useful back home for you to throw darts at Tip O'Neill, that's fine, too."

Now that I was running the show, I was continually being asked to visit the districts of Democratic members to give a boost to their campaigns. In addition to the prestige of having the Speaker of the House at your side, there's a more practical concern: the experts estimate that a political fund-raising event will bring in twice as much money if you can get the Speaker to show up.

I said yes to these requests whenever I could, especially if it was possible to get back to Washington the same night. That's usually not practical with commercial flights, but with a private plane you can often manage it. Naturally, it's the responsibility of the candidate to provide the plane.

Most of these trips were fairly routine, but two or three still stand out in my mind, such as the time I inadvertently agreed to attend a fund-raiser for the John Fogarty Hospital in Rhode Island. The dinner was being held at the Pleasant Valley Golf Club near Worcester, Massachusetts, the same night I was scheduled to be at a fund-raiser of my own on Cape Cod.

"I just can't make it," I told the chairman of the hospital event. "My neighbors are throwing a party for me."

"But you've *got* to come," he said. "We're using your name and all the tickets have been sold. We've got a thousand people coming. I'll even send down a helicopter so you can go to both parties."

What could I say?

I met the helicopter at the Hyannis airport. As I got in, the pilot tossed a road map in my lap.

"What's this for?" I asked.

"Didn't they tell you?" he said. "This chopper is brand-new. There's no radio in here yet, so we'll use the map. I'm going to follow the ocean until Plymouth, and then we'll take Route 44 to Taunton and on into Worcester."

"You've got to be kidding," I said, but by then we were already in the air.

When we reached the Cape Cod Canal, the pilot decided to turn left and proceed to Middleborough. But then he turned left where he should have turned right, and I found myself shouting, "Wait a minute, that's the *ocean* down there!"

"You're right," he said. "We better ask directions." He turned around and kept going until we were over a farm, where he landed in the middle of a field. The farmer rushed out, followed by about a dozen kids.

"How do we get to Worcester?" asked the pilot, as if it were the most natural question in the world.

The farmer directed us to the nearest major highway. By now, though, it was growing dark, and a few minutes later we hit a fog bank. "Watch out!" I yelled. "I can feel the tops of the trees."

"It's not the trees that worry me," he replied. "The only thing I'm afraid of is hitting a live wire. As soon as I find an opening, I'll see if we can land."

Somehow we made it safely to the ground. As we got out, we could hear people shouting, "Hello there! Are you all right?"

We hollered back so they could trace our voices. Somebody called the state police, who came to pick us up. In the car, we heard a report over the radio that an unidentified member of Congress had gone down in a helicopter. By now it was too late to go to Worcester, but the police were kind enough to drive me back to Cape Cod.

When I awoke the next morning I was shaking all over. Our little adventure hadn't affected me all that much at the time, but the next day I was a real mess.

Another time I flew down to New Mexico to help Bill Richardson, who was friendly with my son Kip. I didn't think Bill had much of a chance, but he told me that if I showed up at his dinner, he could raise $150,000 for the Democratic party. How could I turn down a request like that?

When I arrived in Albuquerque, Bill said, "Tip, it's my practice to knock on a few doors and ask people for their support. Would you join me? I'll work one side of the street and you can take the other."

That sounded fine to me, and I agreed at once. Bill's people had arranged for the press to be there, and his plan turned out to be one of the greatest political gimmicks I've ever seen. I rang the bell at the first house, and the lady opened the door, looked at me, and just about fainted. "It *can't* be," she said. "No, it *can't* be. Honey, come down and see who's at the door. I can't believe it!" Even if we didn't win her vote, it made for some great television coverage for the candidate.

I was used to being recognized in my own district, but now, as Speaker, my face was known all over the country. I was out in Sun Valley, Idaho, a couple of years ago, and as I was leaving church after Sunday morning mass, a tourist with California license plates on his car came over to me and said, "Did anybody ever tell you that you look a lot like Tip O'Neill?"

"Oh, yes," I said, "people tell me that all the time."

"I can't get over it," he said. "You're the spitting image of Tip O'Neill."

I smiled. "Listen, pal," I said. "Suppose I tell you that I *am* Tip O'Neill?"

"If you told me that," he said, "I'd know you were a damned liar. Tip O'Neill happens to be a good friend of mine!"

As he went back to his car, I could hear him telling his friends, "See that guy over there? He tried to tell me he was Tip O'Neill. Now, I *know* Tip O'Neill, so he can't fool me."

One reason my face was so familiar was that in 1979, during my third year as Speaker, I agreed to permit live, televised coverage of the House of Representatives—which turned out to be one of the best decisions I ever made.

People get used to new situations very quickly, but when television first came into the House, many of the members were skeptical. In the past, even committee hearings were off-limits to radio and television. Sam Rayburn used to say that microphones and cameras would detract from the dignity of the House, and long after his death that view continued to prevail.

Another reason most members were wary of allowing TV cameras into the House was that we were disgusted with how the major networks covered the Republican and Democratic national conventions. If a guy was reading a newspaper, they'd always show a close-up of him. If a delegate was picking his nose or scratching his ass, that's what you'd see. If somebody had a bald head, you could be sure of getting a close-up view of the shiny spot. No wonder so many of us were skittish. After all, why should the greatest legislative body in the world allow itself to be demeaned and humiliated before millions of people?

But what if we allowed TV cameras on the floor of the House that were controlled by us instead of the networks? And what if those cameras showed only the person who was actually at the microphone and nobody else? That struck me as a reasonable compromise, and that's exactly what we did in setting up the cable network known as C-Span.

Today, of course, it's hard to imagine Congress without it, and the results of our broadcasting experiment have exceeded my wildest hopes. One benefit is that Americans who watch C-Span are much better informed on the issues. Another is that in a nation where an embarrassingly high percentage of voters just don't bother to go to the polls, it's heartening to know that over 90 percent of C-Span viewers voted in the 1984 elections.

Television has also led to a tremendous improvement in the image of the House. Before we allowed the cameras in, 90 percent of the press stories about Congress had to do with the Senate. That, of course, has been a problem ever since our system of government started. With only a hundred members to keep track of, the Senate has always been easier for the media to cover and for the public to follow. After all, most people can name their two senators, but how many can run down the list of their state's members of Congress? For this reason alone, the Senate has always seemed more glamorous than the House.

But is it really more important? It's the House, not the Senate, that controls taxes and appropriations. And it's in the House where most of the work in Congress actually gets done. I've always been partial to the old saying that the difference between the two bodies is that the congressmen are the workhorses while the senators are the showhorses.

Thanks to television, the House of Representatives is now recognized as the dominant branch of Congress,. In 1986, the Senate brought in TV cameras as well. But the senators ramble on for hours, whereas our members can speak for only five minutes, apart from "special orders" at the end of the day, and a few other exceptions. Unlike the rules of the House, those of the Senate allow for unlimited debate and unrestricted amendments. Now that the Senate is on television, the prestige of the House should continue to increase.

But even with all my appearances on C-Span, not to mention the network news, every now and then I would run into somebody who apparently didn't watch TV. I once promised Margaret Heckler that I'd say a few words at a Washington meeting of the National Organization for Women. I was driving Millie's Chrysler, and, as instructed, I pulled into a parking space marked "Reserved for the Speaker."

The security guard, an elderly man, came over and knocked on the window. "Get that car out of here," he hollered. "This space is reserved for the Speaker."

I got out of the car and said, "I *am* the Speaker."

"Mr. Rayburn," he said. "I didn't recognize you!"

Sam Rayburn had been dead for twenty years, but his legend lives on in Washington.

Another time, at a charity golf tournament, I was teamed up with Sam Snead, one of the greatest golfers of all time. We had a marvelous afternoon, and at the end of the day he turned to me and said, "O'Brien, you're a hell of a guy. What do you do for a living?"

I guess he could tell I wasn't a golfer.

In all fairness, though, I have no right talking about people who don't know who I am, because I'm terrible at recognizing other celebrities. Millie and my two daughters still don't believe this story, but a few years ago, when I was passing through Stapleton Airport in Denver, a good-looking fellow came up and said, "Hello, Tip, how are you?"

I didn't know the guy, so I said, "Isn't this a beautiful city. Those mountains are twenty miles away, but you can almost reach out and touch them."

"You don't know me, do you?" he said.

"Listen," I said. "You recognize me because I'm on television every day and I'm in politics. I have white hair, a big bulbous nose, and cabbage ears. Everybody knows this face. So what's your name, anyway?"

"Robert Redford," he said.

It gets worse. The following week, when I told this story at a political dinner, I messed up the punch line so that my new friend's name came out as Richard Roquefort.

At least I wasn't the only member of Congress who made these mistakes. In 1979, when Dan Rostenkowski and I were out in Palm Springs to play in the Bob Hope Golf Tournament, we were invited to a party with a number of Hollywood people. Mary Martin was there, and Danny couldn't wait to meet her.

"You know," he told her, "when I came back from Korea, I must have seen *South Pacific* a dozen times. To me, you've always been a great star."

"Thank you," she said. "But I'm not a star any longer. These days it's my son who's the real star. You know, J.R., from *Dallas.*"

"No," says Danny, "I've never been to Dallas so I never met the guy." Then he turned to me and said, "But you've been there, Tip. Do you know Mary's son?"

Danny must have been embarrassed when he realized his mistake, because ever since that party he's been telling that same story—about me! I didn't watch *Dallas*, either, but at least I had *heard* of it.

While fame leads to some funny moments, it has a dark side as well. Next to the president and Ted Kennedy, nobody in Washington received as many death threats as I did. There were plenty of times when I came out of my apartment in the morning and noticed the Capitol police sitting in the lobby, just to be sure that everything was all right. And I would know that yet another threat had come in overnight.

One evening, when I flew back to Boston to attend to some work in my district office, an airline representative came on board and asked me to wait until all the other passengers had left the aircraft. When the plane was empty, a state trooper came aboard with an FBI agent. They had received a serious death threat and had sent a police car to pick me up on the runway and drive me back to Cambridge, where they intended to guard my house.

"That's very thoughtful of you," I said, "but my wife is on Cape Cod and the house is empty, so I'm in no hurry to get home. Besides, I haven't eaten. Jim Rowan from my Boston office is here to pick me up, and we're going over to Joe Tecce's restaurant in the North End for some dinner."

That was fine, they said, as long as they could stay near me through the evening.

The police drove me to Joe Tecce's, and told Jim Rowan to meet me there. As soon as I walked in, Joe Tecce said, "What the hell are you doing, Tip, bringing four cops into my place?"

"Don't worry about it," I said. "There's a threat on my life. Give them a table and take good care of them. Jim and I will sit in the corner and take care of some business."

"A threat on your life?" said Joe. "You're in the safest place in town. Tip, you ain't getting shot in *my* place. No sir. I ain't gonna lose *my* license!"

Despite a few tense moments, I loved almost every minute of my ten years as Speaker. And no other activity during that time was as interesting—or as enjoyable—as the congressional trips I led to other countries.

The press, in its cynical way, loves to portray just about every congressional trip as a junket—an elaborate foreign vacation by a group of members at public expense. I think that's ridiculous. With such a large piece of our federal budget going to military expenditures and foreign aid, it's important for members of Congress to stay informed about the rest of the world. And when you consider that we routinely invest hundreds of millions of dollars overseas, it only stands to reason that our representatives should be visiting some of these places. Besides, we Americans live sheltered and insulated lives, and it's only through foreign travel that most of us become aware of the problems—and solutions—that affect other nations, including our own allies.

Congressional trips are equally important for the countries that invite us. The Congress of the United States is the greatest and freest legislative body in the world, and our visits are always seen as a great honor. A few years ago, when I took a delegation to Australia, Prime Minister Malcolm Fraser told me I was the highest-ranking American ever to visit his country, even though the Australians had fought alongside us in both world wars. I'll never forget what he said—that the Mediterranean was the sea of the past, the Atlantic, the sea of the present, and the Pacific the sea of tomorrow.

"We know everything about your country," he continued, "and you know so little about ours. But if there's ever a war in this part of the world, you're going to run out of matériel, and we're the ones who are going to help you out. You may be needing us in a few years, so it's about time you dropped by to say hello."

When I first started traveling overseas, I found that the people we were meeting with were far better informed than our own delegations. When I became Speaker, I put an end to this discrepancy. I made sure to bring along members with real knowledge and expertise in a variety of fields, and they've always held their own in the discussions we've had with experts from the countries we visit.

In 1985, when I led a congressional delegation to the Soviet Union, I called everybody in to my office two months before the trip and we divided up the topics: trade, human rights, arms control, dissidents, Soviet Jews, and several others. I made damn sure that our people were fully briefed by every possible agency, and when we got to Russia we knocked them dead. We had four separate meetings with the Russian leadership, and our people were so well prepared that when we finally saw Mikhail Gorbachev, he spent the first two hours going over reports of the previous meetings, saying, "You said this and our answer was that, but let me tell you what we *meant* to say."

When I was first introduced to Gorbachev, who had just come to power, he said, "Your friend Anderson tells me you're a good fellow."

"Anderson?" I replied. "You must mean Dwayne Andreas, the soybean king." Dwayne is the chairman of Archer-Daniels-Mid-land, the world's largest processor of farm commodities. He and Gorbachev had known each other because of Gorbachev's earlier role as the Central Committee secretary in charge of agriculture.

"I played golf with him a couple of months ago," I told Gorbachev, "and he told me you were going to be the new leader of the Soviet Union. But I had never heard of you."

"Well," Gorbachev replied with a smile, "Russia is a big country, with many places to hide. But Anderson told me about you, too. He said you were the leader of the opposition. I don't understand what that means. As far as I can see, the Democrats and the Republicans are both opposed to us."

Gorbachev was speaking English and showed a much better command of the language than we had been led to expect. But as soon as we started meeting officially, he spoke only Russian. Even so, he interrupted the interpreter on several occasions when he didn't think the translation was conveying exactly what he had said.

Gorbachev struck me as sharp, talented, and charming, with a great sense of style. He's a very appealing guy, which is what makes him so dangerous. The Russian leadership may have affected a new and more sophisticated style, but the Soviet bear remains as aggressive and unpredictable as ever. Even so, it's critical that we keep the lines of communication open between our two countries.

"We'll never have any problems with the United States," Gorbachev told me, "as long as you don't try to interfere with our economic system. We believe that our system is right and that yours is wrong, just as you think yours is right and ours is wrong. We won't try to change yours, and you shouldn't try to change ours."

He continued: "But I don't like the way you demean us. You look upon us as though we're from the Stone Age and we live in caves. Your experts are always saying that our economy is falling apart. But tell me, which one of us is a debtor nation?"

He may have been right on that score, but it was hard to be impressed by what I saw of the Soviet Union's economic development. I'll never forget the ride into Moscow from the airport: the countryside seemed unbelievably dismal. We stayed in a government-owned hotel where the beds were so small that I had to put two of them together—and it still wasn't big enough. Inside the

Kremlin walls, however, the buildings were fantastic. And although the Russians are officially atheists, I've never seen so many carefully preserved paintings of the saints.

Gorbachev also made a point of objecting to President Reagan's famous characterization of the Soviet Union as an "evil empire." As I told the president upon our return, this seemed to upset him more than anything else.

At the end of our four-and-a-half-hour meeting, I handed Gorbachev an envelope containing a list of dissidents and refuseniks—Soviet Jews who wanted to leave the country, but who had been denied exit visas. To my relief, he accepted the envelope. But when he started to open it, one of his aides stopped him.

Despite his charming manner, Gorbachev left no doubt that he resented this "intrusion" into internal Soviet affairs. How did we know, he asked, that these people hadn't broken the law? And what gave us the right to raise this issue when the Soviet Union did not try to interfere in *our* internal problems, such as the homeless, the poor, and the native Americans?

Still, I left the Soviet Union more convinced than ever that in Russia, as everywhere else, the squeaky wheel gets the grease. When it comes to helping Russian dissidents and Soviet Jews, I believe that public protest is more effective than silent diplomacy. But there's no reason in the world that we can't do both.

Over the years, I've led congressional trips to China, Egypt, Israel, Greece, and several other places, and in each case we've returned with a far greater understanding of these nations and the problems they face. And because we're members of Congress, rather than diplomats, we can—and do—ask direct and candid questions. In return, we usually hear forthright answers. When you're in a country for only three days, there's a special incentive to get right to the point. Diplomacy has its place, of course, but it's always useful to both sides to open up a more direct dialogue as well, with one pol talking straight to another.

But the most important aspects of these trips is so simple that it's easy to overlook—good will. We take our own country so much for granted that we don't always stop to realize how important the United States is to the other nations of the world as a symbol of freedom and democracy.

Americans are outgoing and gregarious people, and when we travel, we tend to mix with the crowds. Through our conversation, our curiosity, and our confidence, we're constantly exuding the fact that we're a free nation. And that alone makes these trips worthwhile.

13

★★★★★

The Carter Years

When it came to understanding the issues of the day, Jimmy Carter was the smartest public official I've ever known. The range and extent of his knowledge were astounding; he could speak with authority about energy, the nuclear issue, space travel, the Middle East, Latin America, human rights, American history, and just about any other topic that came up. Time after time, and without using notes, he would tick off the arguments on both sides of a question. His mind was exceptionally well developed, and it was open, too. He was always willing to listen and to learn.

With one exception. When it came to the politics of Washington, D.C., he never really understood how the system worked. And although this was out of character for Jimmy Carter, he didn't want to learn about it, either.

While Carter was not very popular by the end of his term in office, his image is already improving. Undoubtedly, future generations will look upon him more kindly than his contemporaries do. They will see that it was Jimmy Carter who forced us to respond to the energy crisis, and who raised a powerful voice on behalf of human rights around the world. They will remember that it was Jimmy Carter who arranged the Panama Canal Treaty, who established diplomatic relations with China, and who negotiated the historic Camp David accords between Egypt and Israel. And although the Iran hostage crisis was ultimately his undoing, Americans are already starting to appreciate that he eventually brought the hostages home alive, without breaking any laws and without selling arms to the ayatollah.

It was also President Carter who responded to the Soviet invasion of Afghanistan by stopping the exporting of our grain and high technology, and by refusing to send our athletes to the 1980 Olympics. People criticized him for that decision, arguing that sports should not be confused with politics, but Carter knew that to the Soviets, the two were already deeply entangled. Our withdrawal from the Moscow games signified the true extent of our anger and came as a resounding thud to Soviet prestige.

But despite these and other accomplishments, Jimmy Carter was a victim of bad luck and bad timing. It wasn't his fault that oil prices tripled and wrecked our economy, or that a band of Iranians seized our hostages and held them for over a year. The critics howled, but nobody came up with a better plan than his—other than bombing Tehran, which would have killed them all. Eventually, thanks to Carter's patience and persistence, the hostages made it home alive. But by then, Ronald Reagan was already being sworn in.

The first time I can remember hearing Jimmy Carter's name was in 1972, on my way back from the Democratic National Convention in Miami. To my great disappointment, our party had just nominated George McGovern. I had gone down there as a big supporter of Senator Ed Muskie, but by then poor Ed didn't stand a chance. Personally, I thought McGovern's nomination was a disaster. I tried not to show it, but when the press asked me what had happened to Muskie, I couldn't resist saying, "We got beat by the cast of *Hair*."

I had known McGovern a little during his two terms in the House in the late 1950s, before he was elected to the Senate. As a member of Congress, he used to stand in the back of the House chamber, and he didn't participate much. Frankly, I never expected him to go any further in politics, and I was absolutely shocked when the young people picked him as their champion. While I respected his strong position against the Vietnam War, I didn't think he had much of a record to run on.

And, Lord knows, he certainly didn't have the polish or the charisma of a Kennedy—or even a Muskie, for that matter. In 1970, when the Beacon Club in Boston asked me to recommend an affordable guest speaker from the Senate, I gave them McGovern's name because people said he would appear anywhere for two hundred dollars plus expenses.

"McGovern?" said the man from the Beacon Club. "We wouldn't take him for *nothing.*"

Flying back from the 1972 convention, I had a long talk with Bob Strauss, the treasurer and future chairman of the Democratic National Committee, and Senator Henry Jackson of Washington. All of us were bitter at what we had just witnessed. The convention was filled with first-time delegates, mostly women and minorities who spent the bulk of their time fighting over the various planks of the party platform. Because they were new to the system, these people failed to understand that the real purpose of a platform is to express a general philosophy, and to be as inclusive as possible. Instead, they seemed eager to come up with a document that would be taken literally. For once, I agreed with those critics who speak of occasional suicidal tendencies among the Democrats.

As for the candidate himself, you didn't have to be a pollster like Lou Harris to see that McGovern was going to get creamed. In 1972, in the eyes of many Americans, George McGovern and the Democrats were so far to the left as to be off the map. McGovern was regarded as an extremist and a loser—much like Barry Goldwater in 1964.

It was obvious that McGovern's coattails weren't going to be very long. Therefore, our only chance to maintain a Democratic Congress was if voters split the ticket, choosing Democratic candidates for the House and Senate even as they reelected Richard Nixon as president. Fortunately for us, this was exactly what happened.

In the plane, Jackson, Strauss, and I discussed some of the upcoming congressional races, as well as the Democratic Congressional Campaign Committee, of which I was still chairman. Then Strauss turned to me. "I've been meaning to ask you," he said. "Do you have anybody out there who can be the top man in our speakers' bureau?"

"Not really," I replied. "I usually go out myself to speak for our candidates."

"Well, I've got a guy who'll go *anywhere,*" said Strauss. "His name is Jimmy Carter and he's the governor of Georgia. He wants to be president, and he's willing to speak wherever you need him."

That sounded fine to me, so I signed up Carter, who delivered just as Strauss promised. Over the next couple of years, Jimmy Carter did a great deal of speaking for the party—much of it in remote areas for candidates who didn't have a prayer. Along the way, however, he got to meet thousands of Democratic activists, especially in small cities and rural towns.

Carter knew exactly what he was doing. When a governor arrives in a small community to speak on behalf of a local candidate, that candidate is suddenly seen as a very important person. In 1976, he and his friends would certainly remember the great favor that Jimmy Carter had done for them merely by showing up.

It wasn't until January 10, 1975, when I was majority leader, that I finally met Jimmy Carter. I was in a conference with my staff when Eleanor Kelley, my personal secretary, stuck her head in and said, "There's a gentleman in with Leo who'd like to meet you. He says he's running for president."

"That's nice," I said. "What's his name?"

"Jimmy Carter."

It took me a moment to remember who that was. I knew, of course, that Carter hadn't done all that speaking for Democrats around the country merely out of the goodness of his heart. Still, the idea that this Georgia peanut farmer, a complete unknown, saw himself as a serious candidate for the highest office in the world struck me as pretty farfetched.

I was still smiling when Jimmy Carter strode into my office, full of confidence and vigor. I began by thanking him for all the trips he had made on behalf of Democratic candidates, and for hiking into the hinterlands to help the party. Carter listened graciously as I spoke.

Then he got to the point, which was that he was dead serious about becoming the nominee for president at the 1976 Democratic convention in New York. "At the moment," he acknowledged, "I'm only one-half of one percent in the polls. But by the time we get to Madison Square Garden, I'll have this thing wrapped up. I know you're boosting Ted Kennedy, but Kennedy won't be running because of Chappaquiddick. Neither will Humphrey. He's got his own problems, and he's still in debt from 1968. Scoop Jackson has the support of the Jews because of his positions on Israel and Soviet emigration, but his political base isn't broad enough, and he'll drop out after three or four primaries. Udall may run, but he doesn't have a chance. As I look at it, there's only one man who can beat me, and that's Walter Mondale. But he's not running."

Mondale had originally planned to be a candidate in 1976 but had recently decided that he just wasn't prepared to go through the tremendous ordeal of a campaign. As he put it, he didn't want the job badly enough to spend a whole year traveling around the country and sleeping in Holiday Inns. Two campaigns later, of course, he would change his mind.

After dismissing just about all his potential opponents in less than a minute, Carter made an astonishing prediction: "Mr. Majority Leader," he said, "I'm telling you right now that I'm going to be nominated on the first ballot, and that in November of next year I'll be elected president of the United States."

I thought that was impossible, but Jimmy Carter hit it right on the nose. He ran a great campaign, which was made easier by the fact that in 1976 there were no other strong Democratic candidates. I was supporting Udall, who came in second in New Hampshire, ahead of Birch Bayh, Fred Harris, Sargent Shriver, Hubert Humphrey, Henry Jackson, and George Wallace—but behind Jimmy Carter, who finished with 28.4 percent of the Democratic vote, well ahead of Udall's 22.7 percent. After Carter continued winning primaries—including Illinois, Wisconsin, Pennsylvania, Indiana, Michigan, and Ohio—he soon became the uncontested front-runner. The turning point was Florida, where the other Democrats cleared out of the race, allowing Carter to defeat George Wallace.

But luck was only part of Carter's winning formula, and luck alone can't explain his success. He won because he did everything right in pursuing the nomination. That's what impressed me so deeply about him—that he set himself so high a goal and didn't stop working until he reached it. Although I barely knew him, I was terribly excited when Jimmy Carter was elected. Here, I thought, was a guy who knew how to get things done.

What I hadn't realized, and what almost nobody in Washington knew at the time, was that Carter's greatest political achievement was already behind him. He got himself elected as an outsider, but once he got to Washington, he had to deal with other national politicians.

That's why Carter's choice of Walter Mondale for vice president was so important, for only a veteran of Capitol Hill could compensate for Carter's lack of experience in Washington. During the summer of 1976, when Carter was in the process of selecting a running-mate, I had insisted that he at least consider a man from the House. Until then, the only candidates on his list were senators, including Muskie, John Glenn, Mondale, Frank Church, Adlai Stevenson, and Henry Jackson. But I thought the House should also be represented, so I called Carter and asked that he consider Morris Udall or Peter Rodino.

But I certainly wasn't disappointed when he chose Mondale, an outstanding liberal senator in the Humphrey tradition. I wasn't surprised, either. Ever since my first meeting with Carter, when he told me that the only Democrat who could beat him was Mondale, I expected that Mondale would be his choice. Later, I was pleased to see that Carter gave Fritz an office in the White House, and involved him deeply in legislative affairs. But not even Mondale could help Carter with the political savvy he would need.

After he won the election, but before he took office, Jimmy Carter came to see me again. This time we met in the Speaker's office. Our meeting was scheduled as a routine and largely ceremonial affair, in which the president-elect paid a courtesy call to the new Speaker. On such an occasion, I thought it would be fitting to tell my visitor a little about how the legislative process worked. In view of Carter's remarks during the campaign, when he ran against Washington, I wanted to make sure he fully understood the difference between rhetoric and reality. But when I tried to explain how important it was for the president to work closely with Congress, he didn't seem to understand. As governor of Georgia, he had run into certain problems with the state legislature, and he assured me that if he didn't get his way with Congress, he wouldn't hesitate to do what he had done back home—which was to go over the heads of the representatives by appealing directly to the voters.

"Hell, Mr. President," I said, "you're making a big mistake. You don't mean to tell me that you're comparing the House and the Senate with the Georgia legislature? The Congress of the United States includes some of the most talented and knowledgeable lawmakers in the world. Some of them have been here for years, because the people at home have such faith in them.

"As for the younger members, you better watch out. Many of them got here by running against the Washington establishment, just like you did. A lot of the Democrats ran ahead of you in the election, and believe me, next time they won't hesitate to run *against* you."

From Carter's questions, I could see he had been paying close attention to recent developments and changes in the Congress. Despite his lack of national experience, he was a great student of government. What he didn't know, he was eager to learn, and he retained virtually everything. Unlike the other presidents I have known, most of whom were good talkers, Jimmy Carter was also a good listener.

Before the president-elect left my office that day, he leaned forward to ask me one final question: "I've heard a lot of talk about the strength of the Israel lobby," he said. "Tell me, is it as powerful as they say?"

I replied that it was certainly a strong group, in part because there are so many more Jews in this country than Arabs. The Turks, by the way, have a similar problem with regard to the Cyprus controversy. Americans of Turkish descent used to ask me why the Greeks always got a hearing for their side, while the Turks couldn't get anywhere. "That's because nobody knows a Turk," I'd tell them. "But everybody knows the people who run all those restaurants."

It's the same with the Arab-Israeli conflict. The experts can come up with a dozen reasons to explain why America supports Israel— that Israel is the only true democracy in the Middle East, or that the Soviet Union provides huge arms shipments to Israel's enemies. All of that is true enough, but to the average American it often boils down to something more basic—the fact that some of his friends and neighbors happen to be Jewish. Again, all politics is local.

Another reason the Israel lobby is powerful is that the Jewish people are so active in public life. At one point my district included Brookline, a heavily Jewish area, and I was amazed that my constituents there used to write me letters even when they *agreed* with me. Beyond that, Jews are also generous givers to political campaigns on both sides of the aisle. Finally, every now and then a war breaks out and threatens Israel's survival, and you realize that there *is* a real danger, and that the Jews haven't merely been crying wolf.

So yes, I told Carter, the Israel lobby is certainly powerful. "But make no mistake," I told him. "If it ever comes down to a conflict between Israel and the United States, the Jews are Americans first."

Carter's final question about the Jewish lobby sticks in my mind so vividly because four years later, after Ronald Reagan was elected president, he too came to see the Speaker of the House on a ritual visit. And just like his predecessor, he had one urgent and sensitive question before he left.

"Tell me about the Israel lobby," he said. Naturally, I gave him the same answer I had given Carter.

I've always said that power is when people think you have power, and by that standard the Israel lobby is as effective an operation as there is in Washington.

My next meeting with Carter was at Blair House, where we discussed the president-elect's ideas regarding his cabinet. After I mentioned a few of my favorites from the Hill, Carter asked me if I knew Joe Califano, a former aide and speechwriter in the Johnson White House, and now a Washington lawyer. I had a special affection for Joe, in part because he was a graduate of Holy Cross, and we Jesuit college men took pride in each other. I had known him since the Johnson days, and more recently I had followed his growing reputation as a lawyer.

"I have him in mind for secretary of HEW," said Carter.

"That's the toughest job in town," I replied. "Joe is an excellent choice, and I'm sure he can handle it. But I doubt he'd be interested. Why, just the other day I read in the paper that he's making half a million dollars a year. I can't imagine he'd give that up to work for the government."

Over the years, I've seen a lot of small and seemingly trivial social encounters among politicians turn out to be significant. Joe Califano may have been appointed to Carter's cabinet simply because I ran into him that night at Duke's. I told him about my meeting with Carter, and how I had told the president-elect that Califano probably wouldn't be interested in a cabinet appointment.

"Are you kidding?" said Joe. "Do you realize what an honor this would be for my family? My parents were both born in Italy, and they came to this country as immigrants. Can you imagine the son of an immigrant as a member of the cabinet? I'd be thrilled to accept it."

The following morning, I called Carter to tell him I was wrong about Joe. He got the job.

. . .

Although Carter and I came from vastly different backgrounds, we grew to appreciate each other. This took time, however, and required some adjustments on both sides. When Carter's people came north to Washington, they just didn't understand Irish or Jewish politicians, or the nuances of city politics. The southerner is a different breed from the other pols I've known: he's a sweet talker who can skin you alive with his charm. In the North, politics is far more blunt and rambunctious. Whereas the northerner enjoys conflicts and will actually seek them out, the southerner does his best to avoid political quarrels and skirmishes.

This might explain why it took me so long to understand Carter's manner—to realize, for example, that his silence on a particular topic didn't necessarily mean acquiescence. I would tell him what I thought, and he'd look at me and nod. But he wouldn't always offer a comment or ask a question, and often I wouldn't know exactly where he stood.

Or I'd give him my views, and he'd say, "I understand, I appreciate that," and I'd leave the White House under the mistaken impression that we were in agreement. A few days later, however, he would say something that made me realize that his views and mine were actually very different. Jimmy Carter was so polite and gracious that he was often reluctant to express open disagreement. This took some getting used to, as I was accustomed to dealing with politicians who told you straight out when they thought you were wrong.

Culturally, urban Boston and rural Georgia are a million miles apart, and so another difference between Carter and me was that we didn't always speak the same language. Leaving the White House one day, I called to the president, "Keep your left hand high." That's a boxing term, meaning that you shouldn't forget to defend yourself with your left hand while you're punching with your right. But Carter didn't know what I was talking about. This minor lack of communication may sound insignificant, but these expressions are part of the chemistry that helps people work together effectively.

But despite these surface differences, there was a genuine affection between us. And Millie and I spent several warm evenings in the private living quarters of the White House, enjoying dinner and conversation with the president and first lady.

Although we relished these intimate social occasions, we preferred to stay away from the larger gatherings. When the president and the Speaker come from the same party, it's customary to invite the Speaker to every state dinner that comes along. But I declined them all, and explained to the president that these events just weren't our style. For one thing, Millie and I have always been homebodies. For another, I used to hear enough speeches during working hours. At night I preferred to play cards, watch a ball game, or socialize with my family or friends.

In January 1979, however, the president himself called me at the office to ask us to attend an upcoming state dinner for Deng Xiaoping, who was then the vice chairman in China. "Deng represents the biggest nation in the world," said the president. "I want everybody to be there. I'm even inviting Nixon and Ford."

"You know how we feel about those big dinners," I said. "If it's that important, you'd better clear it with Millie."

Ten minutes later, the president was on the line again. "I'll see you at the dinner," he said. "Millie said it's okay."

When the president called her, Millie, who speaks her mind as much as I do, said, "Tom and I will be happy to come, but please don't put us at Nixon's table." Somebody in the White House leaked her remark to the papers, and we were both embarrassed. But inviting Nixon to that dinner was the right thing to do, because if it hadn't been for his initiatives, Carter would never have been able to establish diplomatic relations with the Chinese.

Husbands and wives are generally seated separately at these dinners, and I was at the president's table along with Deng, his translator, and the actress Shirley MacLaine, who was among the first Americans to visit China after the thaw. While the president talked with Deng, I told Shirley a story about her brother, Warren Beatty. I had been out in Kansas City for an off-year Democratic convention, and was eating breakfast with Joe Moakley, a member from Massachusetts. Warren Beatty was there too, and Joe invited him to join us.

Not being a moviegoer, I had never heard of Warren Beatty. At one point, I turned to him and said, "You know, Warren, you're handsome enough to be in the movies."

Later, when Beatty had left, Moakley said, "You've got to be kidding. Don't you know that was Warren Beatty?"

"Who's Warren Beatty?"

"You know, the movie star."

"You mean the animal trainer?"

"Come on, Tip, you're thinking of Clyde Beatty. That was thirty years ago."

Shirley roared when I told her the story. "You sure took him down a peg," she said. "And he could use it, too. I love my brother, but he's one of the most conceited men you'll ever meet."

A couple of years later, I met Deng again, this time in Beijing. "You know," I said, "you and I have a lot in common. You're a revolutionary, fighting for a better life for your people. I know what you want: better health care, better education, and a higher standard of living. There's only one thing I don't understand. Why are you always talking about Taiwan? Here's a little island of less than twenty million people. The way I figure it, Taiwan should mean nothing to you. Surely you have more important things to worry about."

"You're absolutely right," said Deng. "But just between us, it's something our people love to hear about, and that's why I keep harping on it."

Deng once spent a day on Capitol Hill, where he paid a visit to my office. He listened with great interest as I explained our system of checks and balances, and how our president is not all-powerful. I'm sure he already knew the fundamental principles of our system, but he seemed awfully eager to hear about it directly from me. It's been my experience that foreign leaders often have trouble understanding that their American counterparts have specific limits on their power, and they're both fascinated and amused by our system of government. In any case, I must have made a good impression on Deng Xiaoping, because every time a group from China came over, they always asked to meet with the Speaker of the House.

The first time Millie and I visited the Carters in the White House, we had barely sat down to dinner when the president wanted to hear all about James Michael Curley. Then he asked about some of the other political leaders I have known. I told a few stories, including one about a frank exchange between President Jack Kennedy and Speaker Sam Rayburn. Kennedy had wanted to know the terrible things that members of Congress were saying about him, and Mr.

Sam dutifully went down the list, starting with the complaint that Kennedy had forgotten his early supporters.

"They won't say that about me," said Jimmy Carter with a grin. "I've brought all of mine up here with me."

That was true enough, but it was nothing to laugh about. After eight years of Republican rule, Jimmy Carter rode into town like a knight on a white horse. But while the gentleman leading the charge was capable, too many of the troops he brought with him were amateurs. They didn't know much about Washington, but that didn't prevent them from being arrogant.

Too many of Carter's people—especially Hamilton Jordan, the president's top aide—came to Washington with a chip on their shoulder and never changed. They failed to understand that the presidency didn't operate in a vacuum, that Congress was fundamentally different from the Georgia legislature, and that we intended to be full partners in the legislative process.

Like some of Jack Kennedy's staff in 1961, Carter's people assumed that because they had succeeded in capturing the White House, they had Washington all figured out. I had my share of complaints about Kennedy's people, but at least they looked after the Democratic members of Congress. Their attitude was: we want you to be reelected and we're working to help you.

But during the Carter years, congressional Democrats often had the feeling that the White House was actually working against us. Once, when the city of Boston applied for a government grant for some new roads, I called the Carter people to try to speed it along. Instead of assisting me, however, they did everything possible to block my way. When it came to helping out my district, I actually received more cooperation from Reagan's staff than from Carter's.

If that's how they treated the Speaker, you can imagine what it was like for the other members of Congress. John Brademas, the Democratic whip, couldn't believe that he actually had to spell his name whenever he called the White House.

Maybe he shouldn't have bothered, because our people didn't get their calls returned in any event. Frank Moore, a former public relations man from Georgia, was the congressional liaison, but he didn't know beans about Congress. On the other hand, you don't have to be a legislative genius to figure out that Pennsylvania Ave-

nue is a two-way street, and that members of Congress are entitled
to certain basic courtesies. As Speaker, I didn't always have time to
return my phone calls, either. But at least I made sure that somebody
on my staff got back to the callers.

I must have told Carter about his inadequate staff a dozen times
or more, but he never acted on my complaints. In his position,
though, I might have done the same. When people have criticized
my staff from time to time, my attitude has always been: they must
be doing something right—look at the success I'm having.

Carter probably felt the same way. After all, these were the people
who got him elected. They had proven abilities, and he was loyal
to them. What he failed to understand is that their one great talent
was to get him to the White House. Unfortunately, they lacked the
other skills he needed to be effective once he got there.

It was the greatest frustration of my career: we had a chance to
accomplish so much, but the White House people simply wouldn't
cooperate. We had members who busted their butts campaigning
for Jimmy Carter, but nobody they knew was appointed to anything. They'd call up a federal agency to discuss a program in their
district, and they'd find themselves talking to the very same bureau-
crats they had dealt with under Nixon and Ford. The Democrats
had won the election, but you'd never know it.

Many of the Carter appointees who came into the federal agencies
acted as though they were hired strictly on merit, and didn't owe
anything to anybody. They refused to see themselves as team players. I wasn't the only one who had problems with them; not even
Frank Moore could accomplish much with these people, who simply refused to follow his directives.

One member of the White House staff whom I did respect was
Stuart Eizenstat, who was responsible for preparing domestic legislative proposals and for keeping an eye on the various bills being
considered by Congress. I had great admiration for Stu's abilities,
and the members of Congress certainly appreciated him. But we
always had the feeling that he wasn't fully accepted into Carter's
inner circle.

From what I could see, the biggest influences on Carter were
Griffin Bell, his attorney general; Charles Kirbo, a lawyer from
Atlanta and the president's best friend; and Bert Lance, director of

the Office of Management and Budget. Bell was a southern conservative who was out of step with the northern liberals who controlled
the Congress, and who probably would have been more at home in
the Reagan administration. Kirbo was another Georgia conservative
who acted as a restraining force on Carter's liberal instincts.

With any luck at all, Bert Lance, who was highly regarded by his
fellow politicians, could have made a big difference. But we'll never
know, because his banking problems back home caught up with him
in Washington and he was forced to resign. I used to call him often,
because Lance really knew the score. The president was devastated
when he left, and history may show that his departure was a major
step on Jimmy Carter's road to defeat in 1980.

From Carter's own perspective, his key staff member was Hamilton Jordan. In an ideal world, the president's top aide and the
Speaker of the House work hand in hand to carry out the legislative
goals of the administration. But in the real world of the Carter
administration, we barely spoke to each other.

Unfortunately—but symbolically, it turns out—my problems
with Jordan began even before the new administration took over.
The night before the president was sworn in, there was an inaugural
gala at the new Kennedy Center. Because I was now the Speaker,
Millie and I were seated with Jimmy and Rosalynn in the presidential box. Members of Congress had the right to buy seats for twenty-
five dollars each, and I asked for a dozen—a pair for Eddie Boland
and his wife, and the rest for members of my family. When I called
to order the tickets, I was assured that my guests would be seated
down in front, in the special section reserved for members of Congress.

During the course of the evening I kept scanning the audience,
trying to spot Eddie and my kids. I had invited them to visit us
during intermission for a buffet supper, but they didn't show up.
When the program was over, they told me they had been seated in
the last row of the second balcony.

I was furious. These things don't happen by accident, and by
insulting the Speaker, Carter's people were already showing their
contempt for Congress.

The next morning I called Hamilton Jordan and said, "Listen,
you son of a bitch. When a guy is Speaker of the House and his

family gets the worst seats in the room, he figures there's a reason behind it. I have to believe you did that deliberately."

"If that's the way you feel about it," he replied, "we'll give you back the three hundred bucks."

"Don't be a wise guy," I said. "I'll ream your ass before I'm through."

Ten minutes after that phone call, Bob Strauss was on the line to say he was bringing Jordan over to my office. Jordan apologized and swore that the seats were an accident, but I found that hard to believe—and still do. As far as Jordan was concerned, a House Speaker was something you bought on sale at Radio Shack. I could see that this was the just the beginning of my problems with these guys. And I didn't see Hamilton Jordan again until at least a year later, when Barbara Walters gave a dinner for the Egyptian and Israeli ambassadors.

From then on, I started referring to the White House chief of staff as Hannibal Jerken. He was supposed to be the president's top man, but I remember seeing him only about three times in four years. To this day, I can't understand why the closest man to Jimmy Carter, the key staff guy at the White House, didn't even join us at the White House breakfast meetings where we discussed upcoming legislation with the president. This was unprecedented. People used to say that Jordan was the most brilliant guy around, but you couldn't prove it by me.

I wasn't the only one in Congress who felt that something was wrong. Halfway through the Carter administration, Dan Rostenkowski came to me and said, "The problem between the White House staff and ourselves is getting out of hand. We ought to have a party where we can all get to know each other better."

It was a terrific idea, and my old friend Silvio Conte volunteered to help. "Danny," he said, "if you can get us some of those great steaks from Chicago, we'll have a barbecue in my backyard."

Sil is a great cook, and we had ourselves a hell of a party with steaks, corn on the cob, and plenty of beer. We invited committee chairmen and leading members from both parties, as well as everyone who counted from the White House staff. Hamilton Jordan showed up, and he seemed to be having a wonderful time. But he still didn't know enough to stay in touch with us on a regular basis.

Later, Lud Ashley, the Ohio Democrat, told me about a revealing comment that Jordan made to him that night. Early in the evening, a group of us were sitting around and swapping jokes. Lud came in and took a seat next to Jordan, just as I began telling one of my favorite stories, about an old Jewish guy named Jakie Bloom.

Jakie Bloom was a good man, a poor but generous shopkeeper who allowed all his customers to buy on credit during the Depression. But now Jakie is in his seventies, and he's despondent because his dear wife has passed away. His friends take up a collection to help him out, and Jakie Bloom is gradually able to put his life back together. Over the next few months he becomes a new man. First he gets a hair transplant. Then he loses some weight and buys some fancy clothes.

Next, Jakie grows a beard, starts working out every day, and moves down to Miami. Soon he takes up with a beautiful lady half his age.

They walk along the beach, he with his new look and she in her red bikini. Suddenly there's a tremendous storm, and Jakie is struck by lightning. A moment later he finds himself in heaven, where he demands to speak to the Boss.

"This isn't fair," he cries. "All I ever did was good, and now, in the twilight of my life, I'm finally having a little fun. How could you do this to me?"

"Jakie? Jakie Bloom?" says the Lord. "Is that really you? I didn't recognize you!"

I always get a big laugh with that one, and everybody at the barbecue roared. According to Lud Ashley, Hamilton Jordan roared too. Then he gave Lud a nudge and said, "Can't he tell a story!"

"The poor bastard," Lud said to me later in disbelief. "Imagine, this is his third year in Washington, he's the right-hand man to a Democratic president, and he doesn't even know that the Speaker of the House is a great storyteller. No wonder we're having problems!"

To Jordan and his pals on the White House staff, Tip O'Neill represented the old way of doing things, which was precisely what their candidate had run against. I could live with that, because I took it for granted that their anti-Washington talk was merely campaign rhetoric that would fade away after the election. But I was wrong. They really believed these things.

A few years later, during my final session as Speaker, Hamilton Jordan sought to have Congress pay for the legal expenses he incurred when a special prosecutor investigated him on a phony drug charge back in 1980. Although the prosecutor found no evidence of wrongdoing, Jordan had been faced with $60,000 in legal fees.

Following this investigation, Congress passed a bill to provide for reimbursement of legal expenses for any senior government official who was investigated but not indicted. President Reagan's pal Ed Meese, for example, received a substantial reimbursement after he was investigated by an independent counsel following his nomination as attorney general. So I was sympathetic to Jordan's problems when Dan Glickman from Kansas brought a bill on Jordan's behalf to the floor of the House in the summer of 1986. We moved quickly, and the House approved an appropriation of $60,000 to indemnify Hamilton Jordan for his legal fees.

The bill then went to the Senate. But much to everyone's surprise—especially Dan Glickman's—Jordan announced that he was running for the Democratic Senate nomination against Wyche Fowler, a popular House member from Atlanta. Moreover, Jordan never even gave Dan Glickman the courtesy of a telephone call to tell him of his plans or to thank him for his efforts.

One of the themes of Hamilton Jordan's campaign for Senate was that he was "not another Tip O'Neill." I don't know what, exactly, he hoped to gain by that slogan, but he lost the primary in any case, so maybe there's justice in the world after all.

All things considered, I expected a more liberal President Carter than we got. He was progressive on foreign affairs and human rights, but on economic issues he was still a lot more conservative than I was. It was Reagan who promised to get government off our backs, but it was actually the Carter administration that initiated deregulation in banking, railroads, trucking, airlines, and oil.

And it was Carter who alerted the country to the problems of the federal deficit, back when it was only a fraction of what it grew to be under Reagan. While I shared his concern, I winced as he cut down on some of our social programs, including public works jobs and more aid to the cities. Reagan, of course, would go much further, and where Carter had used a steak knife, his successor wielded a cleaver. And yet Carter was able to cut the deficit from $79 billion in 1976 to $27 billion in 1979. By the standards of the Reagan era, when the Pentagon went unchecked, this was practically a balanced budget.

Jimmy Carter was no hypocrite: if there was going to be restraint in the federal budget, it would have to start in the White House. He believed—correctly, in my view—that the modern presidency has become overly imperial. Carter's moral zeal was admirable, but morality and intelligence are not enough in politics. You also need a third ingredient—political style—and this, as I say, is what Carter lacked in Washington.

With the best of intentions, Carter went too far in his attempt to portray himself and the administration as "just plain folks." To drive home the importance of conserving energy, he eliminated chauffeurs and limousines from the White House staff. To make the presidency appear more accessible, he banned the playing of "Hail to the Chief" by the Marine Corps Band. To save energy, he ordered the White House thermostat to be set at sixty-five degrees.

I'm a pretty down-to-earth guy, but it used to irritate me to see the president of the United States carrying his own luggage. One morning, when we were leaving Blair House together a few days before the inauguration, Carter picked up his garment bag and a valise. I grabbed the bag away from him, but he snatched it back.

"People love to see you carrying your own bags," he said.

"Not if you're the president, they don't," I replied. "And what about the bellhops? They vote too, you know."

What Carter failed to understand is that the American people love kings and queens and royal families. They *want* a magisterial air in the White House, which explains why the Kennedys and the Reagans were far more popular than the four first families who came in between. The fact is that most people prefer a little pomp in their presidents.

Of Carter's various misguided attempts to cut down on "frills," the worst move of all was his decision to get rid of the *Sequoia*, the presidential yacht. Eisenhower used to have congressmen and senators down for a drink on that boat, and so did Johnson and

Kennedy. More than any of the other trappings of power, the *Sequoia* provided a unique opportunity for the president to spend a relaxed couple of hours socializing and talking business with small groups of legislators in a serene and friendly environment. In such a setting, Jimmy Carter could have been enormously persuasive. He and Rosalynn were charming and gracious hosts, and if somebody had only arranged a few evenings on that yacht with the right people, the president could have accomplished far more on Capitol Hill than he actually did.

Jimmy Carter's preoccupation with saving money even carried over to the Tuesday morning White House breakfast meetings with the congressional leadership. At the first of these meetings, I couldn't help but notice that the entire "breakfast" consisted of coffee, orange juice, and a roll. I let it go once, but the following week I spoke up: "Mr. President," I said, "if you're getting me out at eight in the morning, you're getting me out for breakfast. Hell, *Nixon* served us better than this!"

I explained that the usual White House procedure was that if a morning meeting began before nine o'clock, you served a complete meal. After nine, you could get away with coffee and rolls.

From then on we received a full breakfast, including eggs, toast, sausages and bacon. We were also served grits, a dish I had never really cared for. But Carter used to kid me about those grits until I finally tried them. I have to admit they tasted pretty good, and one morning, when they gave us hot cakes instead, I hollered in good-natured protest.

At the start of these breakfasts, we would all hold hands and bow our heads, and the president would call on one of us to say grace. After the prayer was said, a few of us would privately grade it on a scale of one to ten.

One morning, after we returned to Capitol Hill, Dan Rostenkowski said to me, "Do you notice that he never asks any of the Catholics to say the prayer?"

"Come on, Danny," I said. "You know those Protestants are professionals. They pray so beautifully."

Sitting with us in my office was Henry Hubbard from *Newsweek*, who went back and filed a little item for the "Periscope" section of the magazine, saying that the Catholic members of the congressional leadership were upset that the president never called on them to say grace.

The next day, Hubbard told me that a *Newsweek* editor had called the White House to verify the story. Apparently the president went off the beam when he heard about it, and the magazine agreed to delete the item.

The following Monday, Millie and I went to dinner at Paul Young's, where we ran into Rosty. "Danny," I said, "tomorrow morning you'll be called upon to say grace."

"Don't be silly," he said. "We've been through all that, remember? He only calls on the Protestants."

"You never know," I replied, saying nothing about the *Newsweek* incident.

When we went in for breakfast the following morning, we all held hands as usual. Then the president said, "Danny, you'll say the prayer today."

I grinned and waited to see how Danny would handle it.

To my utter surprise, Danny came up with the most eloquent prayer we had ever heard, asking the Lord to give us the strength he had given the Founding Fathers, and so on and so forth. Everybody was highly impressed, and we all agreed that Danny's prayer was definitely a ten. The president even made a special point of complimenting Danny for his inspiring words.

Later, when we were back on the Hill, I said, "Danny, that was just marvelous. How did you do it?"

"It wasn't easy," he said. "Last night, when you said the president would call on me, I was sure you were kidding. But at five in the morning I woke up and started worrying. I said to myself, that big Irish son of a buck always knows what's going on. So I went into the other room and sat down and wrote out a prayer. I couldn't get back to sleep, so I had plenty of time to get it right."

As I frequently told the president, my main complaint about these breakfast meetings was that Carter got wrapped up in foreign policy instead of the more pressing domestic issues. Unemployment was rising, inflation was soaring, and interest rates were going crazy, but the president preferred to discuss Angola, Rhodesia, the Middle East, and just about every other place under the sun.

To be fair, Carter wasn't the only president with this problem.

Nixon was the same way, and even Jerry Ford, my old and dear friend, who could hardly have cared less where the hell Rhodesia *was*, became enamored with foreign policy as soon as he moved into the White House. But in all my years, I have yet to meet a politician who was elected to anything on the basis of his foreign policy.

I don't mean to ignore Carter's very real achievements in foreign affairs. Certainly I'll never forget the warmth and excitement we all felt when the president reported to Congress on the peace agreement he had negotiated at Camp David between Israel and Egypt. It had been an immensely difficult week, but Carter had shown great patience, restraint, and fortitude. Prime Minister Begin and President Sadat were looking on from the House gallery that night, and it was one of those moments when you couldn't help but feel a sense of history in the making.

At the time, however, what I felt most was the heat. Whenever Sadat or Begin was around, the Secret Service insisted that I wear a bulletproof vest. Although the vest was remarkably light, wearing it, especially under the lights, was like being in a sweatbox. But it was a small price to pay for safety, as I was reminded on that terrible day in October 1981, when President Sadat was gunned down in Cairo. Thanks in part to his good friend Jimmy Carter, Sadat's greatest achievement lives on.

I have another memory of Camp David, which is a much less positive one. In July 1979, the president retreated there and convened a series of meetings at which White House aides and high government officials came together to discuss the many problems affecting the administration and the nation. But the effect of these meetings was to identify Carter with the national lethargy he spoke about, at Camp David and later to the public—which made him look like part of the problem rather than the solution.

I attended several of these sessions, and I recall being angry that Carter had invited three Republican senators to join us. What the hell were *they* there for? Later, I learned that the president hadn't even consulted with Howard Baker, the Republican Senate leader, before inviting his people to Camp David. This was exactly the sort of thing that got Carter in trouble on Capitol Hill.

On July 15, President Carter addressed the nation about the Camp

David meetings. Although he never actually used the word, the president's remarks have become known as the "malaise" speech. I remember being shocked by what he had to say. There was little to be gained by telling people how bad things were, as they already knew the effects of Watergate and were well aware of the energy crisis and our various other problems. The responsibility of leadership isn't to dwell on the negative, but to offer a positive way out of the morass. That speech was one of the biggest blunders Jimmy Carter ever made.

A day or two later he blundered again when he purged his cabinet instead of his staff. Specifically, he promoted Hamilton Jordan from chief staff aide to chief of staff; until then, Carter had left that position vacant. At the same time, the president clumsily fired several members of his cabinet, including Joe Califano (HEW), James Schlesinger (Energy), and Michael Blumenthal (Treasury). Now the president has every right to fire cabinet members, although it grieved me that he chose to dump his best people. But the way he went about it was inexcusable. Instead of asking these men to step down, Carter asked the entire cabinet to resign and then accepted the resignations of only those people he wanted to get rid of.

To make matters worse, he engineered the entire arrangement without even informing the Speaker. I learned about the firings from the wire services, and only later was I notified by the White House.

Ultimately, a president is judged by the legislation he initiates, and this is where Carter's political problems came home to roost. The first legislative item on his agenda—and by far the most important—was energy. But if the president's energy program was going to be passed by the House, it would be up to me to make it happen.

Over the years, there have always been those who said that Tip O'Neill wasn't much of a legislator. I guess it depends on how you define that term. There have been countless brilliant lawmakers in Congress, but the details of legislation have never been my strong suit, which is why I've always left them to other people.

My own skills had more to do with powers of persuasion and with getting things done. While other members drew up the laws, I was like a shepherd who knew how to move legislation forward and get it passed. While I couldn't always cite chapter and verse, I always knew what a bill meant, what it stood for, and which members were most likely to support it.

The energy problem had been with us since 1973, when the oil embargo following the Arab-Israeli war threw us into a panic. Four years later, we had done nothing to solve this problem, which was steadily growing worse. At the time of the embargo, for example, we were importing one-third of our oil. In 1977, when Carter came in, we were importing *half* our oil—approximately nine million barrels a day. It was amazing, but we were the only developed nation without an energy policy.

It was clear to the president that our available supplies of gas and oil would not last forever. It was also clear that it was dangerous for us to be so reliant on foreign sources of energy—as we learned all too well during the subsequent crisis with Iran. Fortunately, the solution was equally clear: we had to find ways to conserve more energy, generate more domestic production, and discover alternative sources of new energy.

The extent of our problem was driven home to me by, of all people, the shah of Iran. He was a cocky little guy who marched into my office in 1977 wearing all his medals. Right away, he started chastising me—and the entire country: "What right do you people have to be so selfish? You're only six percent of the world's population, but you use thirty-five percent of the world's energy. You're the ones who are driving up the price of oil. Right now, my country exports four million barrels a day. But next year I'm going to cut it to three million, and then down to two, and then to one. You'll have to learn to get along with less."

He never got the chance, of course, as he was overthrown by his own people. But as much as I disliked the guy, he was right about energy: we *were* being wasteful and irresponsible. The president was well aware of this, and he took extraordinary measures to rally the nation behind him.

On February 2, 1977, less than a month after he was inaugurated, Jimmy Carter gave his first speech about energy. To drive the message home, he wore a cardigan sweater and spoke from the White House library, in front of a fireplace. (I'll always remember the scene: there was only one log burning in that fireplace, which to a New Englander is a preposterous sight.)

That night, the president spoke about the importance of energy conservation. The words of his speech were terrific, but Jimmy Carter was never very effective as a communicator. People were amused by the sight of their president in a sweater, but it wasn't enough to get them to change their behavior. If Ronald Reagan in his prime had given that same speech, thermostats all over the country would have been turned down on the spot.

The president tried again in his address to the nation on April 18, when he referred to the energy crisis as "the moral equivalent of war," and "the greatest challenge our country will face in our lifetime."

After the speech, I went up to congratulate him. "That was a fine address, Mr. President," I said. "Now here's a list of members you should call to keep the pressure on, because we'll need their votes."

"No," he replied, "I described the problem to the American people in a rational way. I'm sure they'll realize that I'm right."

I could have slugged him. Did he still think he was dealing with the Georgia legislature?

"Look," I said, trying to control my frustration. "This is politics we're talking about here, not physics. We need you to push this bill through."

"It's *not* politics," he replied. "Not to me. It's simply the right thing, the rational thing. It's what needs to be done."

He was right in theory but wrong in practice. It was true that his energy plan was a rational response to a real crisis. But the president just didn't understand how to motivate Congress. The textbooks all say that Congress reflects the will of the people, and, over time, that's true. But it doesn't happen overnight. Sometimes the people are slow to catch on, and Congress has to take the lead.

The way the president goes to Congress is not always by going to the people. It's also by communicating directly with the members.

The energy package that was sent over by the Carter White House was so enormous and complex that I took one look at it and groaned. What the president and his staff failed to understand was that their legislation would be taken up by as many as *seventeen* different committees and subcommittees of the House, and that each of these committees included members who opposed certain parts of the package. I shuddered to think what would be left of the bill when it was all over—assuming we managed to get any of it through.

Forget it, I thought, as I leafed through the five volumes of legislation, each one the size of a telephone directory. This bill was going to pit one region of the country against another. A representative from Maine or New Hampshire would certainly see things very differently than his colleagues from Texas, Oklahoma, or Louisiana would.

And that was just the tip of the iceberg. The automakers would resist any efforts to force them to turn out more fuel-efficient cars, although consumer groups were insisting on it. The environmentalists wanted strict controls on pollution, while the coal producers and the utilities were screaming that we had already gone too far in that direction. The conservatives would hate the prospect of increased regulation and new taxes on energy, while the liberals would be angry that the bill didn't go further.

Everyone knows the old saying that politics is the art of the possible, but this one looked hopeless to me. And under the existing structure of congressional committees, there really *was* no way.

Unless, of course, we changed the existing structure.

When it was all over, the press and many of my colleagues called it a master stroke. To me, it was survival. I *had* to get that bill through—and quickly, so that Congress could move ahead on other fronts.

The only way to score on this play was to make an end run around the existing committees of jurisdiction, and the only way to do *that* was to create a whole new committee just for this bill. I checked with Bill Brown, the House parliamentarian, who said that although it was a little unorthodox, there was no reason it couldn't be done.

I went to John Rhodes, the Republican leader in the House, and told him I wanted to set up an ad hoc Committee on Energy. He understood perfectly that we couldn't proceed in the usual way, with the legislation going to different committees and being reported as individual bills. Not only would it take forever, but it would be nitpicked to death.

On the other hand, the relevant House committees and their

chairmen would be furious if we simply ignored them. So we worked out a compromise—that the new committee would not be empowered to initiate legislation. Instead, we took the bill, divided it up, and sent it to the respective committees of jurisdiction, including Interstate and Foreign Commerce, Ways and Means, and the Subcommittee on Energy and Power. The package would then come back to the ad hoc committee, which had the right to suggest amendments.

Just about every member in the House wanted to be on the new Energy Committee, and no wonder. Here was a chance to protect the economy of your area and to be a hero back home. Besides, in 1977 energy was a hot issue and people were eager to jump on the bandwagon.

But who should be appointed? Naturally, I included the chairmen and a few key members from the standing committees which dealt with energy. But, as always, there were other considerations as well. Walter Flowers from Alabama came to me and asked to be on the committee. "I'm from a conservative area," he reminded me, "but I give you a vote whenever I can. Don't I deserve to be part of this?" He did. I also included several of the more talented younger members, who had no intention of waiting ten or twenty years before becoming involved in major issues.

We also needed the good will of members who were not on the committee, but who would be voting on the package if and when it reached the floor. I was especially concerned about Joe Waggonner of Louisiana. He was one of the leading conservative Democrats in the House, and I knew he'd be a tough adversary. But if I put him on the committee, he'd have to play ball. I did—and so did he.

To chair the new Committee on Energy, I chose Lud Ashley of Ohio, who had been in the House almost as long as I had. Lud had been an occasional participant at John McCormack's breakfast table, where I was always impressed by his intelligence. He was one of many members whose abilities were often overlooked because he didn't happen to sit on one of the major committees. As a result, he never had the chance to show his stuff.

But Lud had an excellent reputation among his colleagues. And because he knew nothing about energy, and didn't owe any favors, he could come in as an impartial outsider. His talent was like a light hidden under a bushel, and when it came to the surface, it shone brilliantly. Lud Ashley did a great job.

In addition to organizing the entire operation with the able assistance of Ari Weiss, my brilliant young legislative aide, Lud served as the liaison among the various committees that dealt with energy matters. But his most important achievement was that he avoided creating any dislike of him as an individual. There are always institutional jealousies in the Congress, and if I had given Lud's job to one of the other chairmen, or even to a member of one of the committees that were involved, the whole thing might have dissolved in an ocean of rancor and bitterness. Lud was able to create a real team, united toward a common goal and remarkably free of bickering.

As soon as I named the team, I called in all the Democrats. "You've got to move fast," I told them, "and I'll be biting your ass to make sure you keep going. Remember, I selected you people from over a hundred and fifty applicants. My reputation, our party's reputation, and the reputation of the Congress are all tied up with this legislation. You've got to get it out.

"Now I realize that each of you is opposed to some part of this bill. And I appreciate how much you're concerned about its effect on your own region. Believe me, nobody understands that better than I do. But this is an emergency, and you've got to think in terms of the national interest."

As the package moved forward, President Carter kept coming up with new ideas. We'd get part of the bill taken care of, and then he'd issue another recommendation. Carter was a great idea man, but he didn't always appreciate the difficult process of moving a bill through the House. Even with the new structure, it was a mighty struggle.

The final vote came on August 5, 1977, less than four months after the process had begun, when the president's energy package passed the House by a vote of 244 to 177. The bill succeeded for a number of reasons, but one key element was that I had managed to put the right people together to work it all out.

Unfortunately, the energy bill ran into big problems in the Senate, where two of the most influential Democrats, Russell Long of Louisiana and Henry Jackson of Washington, had strong differences of opinion, not only with the White House, but also with each other. It took more than a year before it was finally passed by the Senate, where it was watered down considerably, thanks to aggressive lobbying on the part of the auto and oil industries. The president wasn't too pleased about the bill he finally got, but as I told him more than once, he was damn lucky to have one at all.

The energy crisis affected many segments of American life, but none so much as the automobile industry. In 1979, I heard from my old pal George Steinbrenner, who asked if I would meet with his friend Lee Iacocca, the new chairman of Chrysler. At the time, Chrysler was in deep trouble, and the company was about to appeal to the government for loan guarantees. I had never met Iacocca, but I told George I'd be happy to see him.

When Iacocca came into my office to tell me about Chrysler's problems, he brought along an entire entourage, including members of his board, lawyers, and lobbyists. As soon as everyone was assembled, Iacocca held forth on the various pressures affecting Chrysler and outlined his plan to bring the company back to life. When he finished, I thanked him for coming in and explaining the situation.

The following day, Steinbrenner called again. "Tip, what went wrong?"

"What do you mean?"

"Lee called me and said you were the coldest bastard he ever met."

"What did he expect?" I said. "He came in with a whole damn army. Do you think I'm going to tell him how to get the job done in front of all those lawyers and lobbyists? They'll just take credit for my ideas. Tell Iacocca to come back and see me, just the two of us, head on head, and I'll tell him what to do." Although I had never been a great friend of big business, I wanted to help Chrysler survive because their crisis boiled down to the loss of jobs, a problem that has always been foremost on my agenda.

When Iacocca returned, I said, "Tell me, how many people in my district work for Chrysler or one of its suppliers?"

"I have no idea," he replied.

"Find out," I told him. "That's the key to this thing. And do the same for every district in the country. Make up a list, and have your employees and dealers in each district call and write letters to their own member of Congress. You've heard my famous phrase that all politics is local. A lot of jobs will be lost if Chrysler goes under, and believe me, no member wants to see something like that happen in his district."

Iacocca and his people did a terrific job. By appealing to the local economy of each area, Chrysler was able to put together enough votes to get their loan guarantees.

At one point during the battle to save Chrysler, Representative Jim Blanchard from Michigan and Senator Paul Tsongas from Massachusetts asked me to host a meeting of the chairmen and the leadership from both houses. The conference was held in my office, and I opened it with a strong plea for support of Chrysler, whose bankruptcy, I felt, would lead to severe repercussions on an already unstable economy.

As soon as I finished speaking, a senator whom I had never seen before spoke up in a very forceful tone: "You are *wrong*, Mr. Speaker," he said, and then proceeded to argue that the Chrysler crisis could be handled through the courts and through the usual bankruptcy procedures.

Now Speakers don't normally get disagreed with so bluntly—especially by a colleague they don't even know. In response to the gentleman's comments, I repeated my views even more forcefully than before. When the meeting was over, I asked Tom Foley, "Who was that guy who said I was wrong?"

"Are you kidding?" said Foley. "That was Bill Proxmire. Didn't you recognize him with his new hair transplant?"

I had known Proxmire for years, and I've always prided myself on recognizing people. But this was the first time I had ever seen him with hair, and I was completely fooled.

Just before the vote, I made a speech on the floor of the House and described how, during the Depression, I used to hand out snow buttons on winter mornings to the unemployed men in my neighborhood. I reminded my colleagues that I had always fought hard to save even a hundred jobs. Wasn't it crazy, I asked, for us to sit here and argue when the economic prospects of half a million families were at stake?

When the votes were counted, Chrysler won its case by a two-to-one margin.

Today, of course, Iacocca is looked upon as a hero. And yes, I think he'd make a hell of a president. His only weaknesses that I know of are that he's impatient, and that he tends to pop off whenever he's criticized. But from what I can see, he's not interested in running.

By the fall of 1979, the president was starting to think seriously about his prospects for reelection. In October, he invited me to the seventh game of the Pittsburgh-Baltimore World Series, where he asked me to be chairman of the 1980 Democratic National Convention, and I accepted. Everybody knew that Ted Kennedy was going to be Carter's main opponent for the nomination, and the president must have known that because of my friendship with Ted, I might end up supporting Kennedy. Unless, of course, I was the chairman, who had to remain neutral.

Ted had already come to see me about the race. "I'm going to win," he said. "I've got him beat two to one in the polls."

"Forget the polls," I said. "You can't beat an incumbent president. Remember, he's got a hundred billion dollars at his disposal to distribute back to local governments, and he can send that money anywhere he wants. Everybody from Alabama to Alaska files for projects, and the administration decides which ones to approve. In an election year, they go where the votes are.

"Besides," I added, "you've got the morality issue."

"I don't know about that," he said. "My pollsters say it's a factor for only five percent of the voters."

"Come on, Ted," I said, "you can't measure morality. What's thoughtless for one person is immoral for another." As much as I love Ted, the events of Chappaquiddick are a millstone around his neck that just won't go away.

He remained in the race, but Carter whipped his ass—just as he had promised. Ted, of course, never should have run. From what he told me, some of his Democratic colleagues in the Senate had prevailed on him to jump in because they were afraid that with Carter heading the ticket in 1980, their own seats wouldn't be secure. They were right about that, as the Republicans took over the Senate.

Although I was neutral in the Carter-Kennedy fight, members of my family were active on both sides. My sons Tommy and Kip supported Kennedy, while my daughter Susan and Kip's wife, Stephanie, were working for Carter. One of the papers ran a story about the split in our family, and a friend of mine in Chicago sent me the clipping with a note saying, "Looks to me like the only time the O'Neills stand together is during the Gospel."

In November of 1983, Ted Kennedy came by for another chat about his political plans. "Are you sure you want my advice?" I said. "I gave it to you last time and you didn't follow it."

He laughed. "Well," he said, "you were so right four years ago that I wanted to ask you again."

"Who are you kidding?" I replied. "You've already made up your mind."

Over lunch, he told me that he was going to be a candidate for president in 1984.

"Ted," I said, thinking of Chappaquiddick, "I'm still not sure you can go all the way, but you can certainly beat any Democrat for the nomination. I'll do everything I can. I was in a box last time because I was part of the president's team. This time I can really work for you."

A couple of weeks later, on the Sunday of Thanksgiving weekend, the phone rang at our house on Cape Cod. It was Teddy.

He said, "Tip, I just want you to know that my children and I have just enjoyed some of the most glorious days of our lives. It was a beautiful time. I told them I was going to run for president, and they asked me not to. I'm going to acquiesce to their wishes, and on Tuesday I'm taking myself out of the race."

I don't want to close the door on Ted, but he's got a tough problem. Maybe time will heal it. I hope so, because I really love the guy, and I think he'd make a great president. And in the year 2000, Ted Kennedy will still be younger than Ronald Reagan was when *he* was elected.

Jimmy Carter spent the final year of his administration wrestling with the problem of our hostages in Iran. The president was perfectly willing to keep them on the front page, even though the nation's anger at their continued imprisonment was directed at him. Because of Iran, Jimmy Carter really aged in office. He came in young and vigorous, but he left a tired man.

People were frustrated at Carter's lack of action, but what could he do? I certainly didn't have any better ideas, and neither did anyone else. Once or twice, at the Tuesday morning leadership meetings, we talked briefly about a possible rescue mission, something along the lines of what the Israelis had accomplished in 1976 when their people were held at the Entebbe Airport in Uganda. But our hostages were in the heart of Tehran, which made a rescue seem impossible. When the failed mission took place on April 24, 1980, I was as surprised as anyone. The disappointment of that day only deepened the sense that Jimmy Carter's presidency was a time of American failure both at home and abroad, which is the real reason he lost the election.

I've already described how my first run-in with Carter's White House staff took place the day before the president was inaugurated. So I suppose it's fitting that our last feud came on election day, 1980, as Jimmy Carter was being defeated by Ronald Reagan. Here, too, the problem concerned the White House's lack of regard for Congress—only this time it was not merely symbolic.

On November 4, by seven-thirty in the evening, the television networks were projecting a Reagan victory. A few minutes later, Frank Moore called to ask me to join the president as he made his concession speech.

"Don't let him concede *now*," I said. "It could cost us some seats."

My mind was on the western states, where the polls would remain open for another two hours. Back in 1959, a freshman in the House had come up to me. "Tip O'Neill?" he said. "I'd like to thank you for electing me to Congress."

"What are you talking about?" I said.

"I'm from California," he replied. "And on election day, when you were managing the gubernatorial campaign for Foster Furcolo in Massachusetts, we saw you interviewed on national television. You said there was a Democratic tidal wave sweeping the country. It was just after eight o'clock in Boston, and you were reporting on your own state and on Connecticut, where the polls had closed at seven.

"But it was only five o'clock in California, and we still had three hours to go. We had given up, and were sitting in my headquarters with our tails between our legs. But after hearing what you said about a landslide, we ran out and worked like hell. It was a miracle."

Because the western states still had three hours left to vote, I begged Frank Moore not to let the president concede so early. A few minutes later, he called back to tell me the decision had already been made. I was livid. The President had nothing to gain by giving up now, while some of our guys were still involved in tough fights. As it turned out, James Corman from Van Nuys, California, lost his seat by only a few hundred votes; if the president hadn't conceded early, Jim would have won.

Because our nation includes several different time zones, the only fair solution is to arrange staggered voting hours so all polls close at the same time. But to this day I'm angry at the Carter people for allowing the president to make an early concession. I really lost my temper that night. "You guys came in like a bunch of jerks," I told Frank Moore, although I used a more colorful expression, "and I see you're going out the same way."

In his memoirs, Carter acknowledged that his early concession may have been a mistake. But he didn't want to come off as a bad loser, as Reagan's victory was already painfully clear. Looking back, it's hard to blame him, for how often in our history has an incumbent president been defeated so decisively?

I miss Jimmy Carter. With his intelligence and energy, and his tremendous moral strength, he could have been a great leader. But talent isn't enough, and raw power won't do it either. As Carter found out the hard way, even the president of the United States needs all the help he can get.

14

★★★★★

Ronald Reagan

ALTHOUGH I've enjoyed more than my share of good fortune over the years, there's one aspect of my career for which no future Speaker of the House will envy me.

During my ten years on the job, I served with two presidents, one from each party. My fellow Democrat was certainly capable, but as we've already seen, he came to town with a weak staff and was never able to garner much popular support. The Republican who followed him, however, quickly became as beloved a leader as this nation has ever seen.

If only this pattern had been reversed! If Jimmy Carter had come to town with Ronald Reagan's luster and some of Reagan's staff, who knows how much we could have accomplished?

At least on the surface, President Reagan and I have a lot in common. We're roughly the same age (he's two years older). We're both of Irish ancestry. We're both sports buffs. We're both sociable and outgoing. We both come from modest backgrounds and had FDR as our hero as we came of age in the 1930s.

We also both had a parent who was especially benevolent to our less fortunate neighbors and friends: my father was a one-man service institution in North Cambridge, and Reagan's mother used to visit hospital patients and prisoners in Dixon, Illinois. In view of the many parallels in our lives, I've often wondered how we came to have such different visions of America.

Maybe it all boils down to the fact that one of us lost track of his roots while the other guy didn't. I'm always amazed when I think that during the campaign of 1948, Ronald Reagan worked hard for

Democrats like Truman and Humphrey. He attacked reductions in Social Security. He condemned cuts in school lunches. He called for the tough enforcement of civil rights laws, and for low-cost public housing. He was, in other words, the quintessential New Deal Democrat.

But somewhere along the line, Reagan forgot where he came from and started picking up a different set of values. In my view, this change had to do with the company he keeps. For years he's been surrounded by wealthy friends, to the point where he no longer knows any working people—not to mention anyone who's actually poor. He's been out of touch with how regular Americans live and the problems they face. His whole world is Hollywood.

As a man of wealth, he doesn't really understand the past thirty years. God gave him a handsome face and a beautiful voice, but he wasn't that generous to everyone. With Ronald Reagan in the White House, somebody had to look out for those who were not so fortunate.

That's where I came in.

People think that old-time politicians have all known each other since birth. But the fact is that I had never met Ronald Reagan until two weeks after he was elected president, when he came to my office on a courtesy visit to the Speaker of the House. I knew *of* him, of course, and I remembered him as the congenial television host of *General Electric Theater*, which Millie and I used to watch on Sunday nights at nine o'clock during the 1950s. I had also seen Reagan's political debut on television during the 1964 campaign, when he gave a tremendously effective speech for Barry Goldwater a week before the election.

In 1966, he ran for governor of California and won by a million votes, which certainly grabbed my attention. After all, any Republican who could do that in a Democratic state the size of California was capable of going all the way. Besides, the benchmark of any campaign is money, and this guy was the greatest fund-raiser ever.

When President-elect Reagan came to my office in November of 1980, we two Irish-American pols got right down to business by swapping stories about the Notre Dame football team. I told Reagan how much I had enjoyed his Knute Rockne movie, and he graciously pointed out that his friend Pat O'Brien was the real star of that film.

Then he told me how, back in 1948, he and O'Brien had been part of Harry Truman's campaign train. O'Brien used to warm up the audiences, and Reagan would introduce the president. He took great delight in that story. I would have loved to hear how he came to sign on with the Republicans in 1962, but this didn't seem like the right time to bring that up.

My own guess is that Reagan's political shift had to do with taxes. When he hit it big as a movie actor after a brief career as a radio announcer, he must have been astounded at how much of his paycheck went straight to the government. What a shock it must have been for this young man from a poor family who suddenly found himself in the 90 percent bracket.

Our meeting that day had the same purpose as Jimmy Carter's visit to my office four years earlier, when *he* was elected. But whereas Carter had come to learn about the Congress, my strongest recollection of the Reagan visit is that while it was good-humored and amiable, it was also perfunctory. It was clear that he was there only out of obligation.

Even so, I tried to explain the essentials about how the system really worked. I explained how the powers of Congress had eroded during the years between Roosevelt and Nixon, and how, more recently, we had regained those powers. But I could see that my guest wasn't really paying attention. Reagan's people had obviously told him that it was appropriate for the president-elect to call on the Speaker of the House, but he didn't come seeking any knowledge or any ideas. I could have been speaking Latin for all he seemed to care.

When I was done, Reagan told me that he expected to get along with Congress because he had been on good terms with the California legislature. But where Jimmy Carter had expressed disdain for the state representatives of Georgia, Reagan was proud that he, a Republican, had worked harmoniously with the Democratic state assembly.

"That was the minor leagues," I said. "You're in the big leagues now."

He seemed genuinely surprised to hear that. Maybe he thought that Washington was just an extension of Sacramento.

Before Reagan left my office that day, I let him know that although we came from different parties, I looked forward to working with him. I reminded him that I had always been on good terms with the Republican leadership, and that despite our various disagreements in the House, we were always friends after six o'clock and on weekends.

The president-elect seemed to like that formulation, and over the next six years he would often begin our telephone discussions by saying, "Hello, Tip, is it after six o'clock?"

"Absolutely, Mr. President," I would respond. Our watches must have been in sync, because even with our many intense political battles, we managed to maintain a pretty good friendship.

The second time I met Reagan was the day he was inaugurated, when he came to my office to change clothes after being sworn in. This time, we had a little chat about my desk.

It was hard to miss that desk, which seemed to take up half the room, and which deserves a word of explanation. Back in 1977, when I was first elected Speaker, the Speaker's office was completely unfurnished. That's because when a Speaker retires, he is allowed to move everything in his office to a site of his choosing, where the reconstructed office stands as a national keepsake. Carl Albert had moved his to the University of Oklahoma (just as I later moved mine to Boston College in 1987), so when I became Speaker in 1977, we had to furnish the place from scratch.

The Speaker is one of three public officials in the nation (along with the vice president and the chief justice of the Supreme Court) with the right to borrow historic artifacts from the government. At the Smithsonian Institution, Eleanor Kelley, my personal secretary, found a huge oak desk that had belonged to President Grover Cleveland almost a hundred years ago, and we arranged to have it assembled and reconditioned. During my years as Speaker, that desk dominated my office and was a terrific conversation piece.

After I told President Reagan about the desk, he said, "That's very interesting. You know, I once played Grover Cleveland in the movies."

"No, Mr. President," I said. "You're thinking of Grover Cleveland Alexander, the ball player." Coincidentally, I had just seen *The Winning Team,* an old Ronald Reagan movie, on late-night television.

I made a point of not mentioning this anecdote to the press, but Reagan's gaffe quickly got around among the House Democrats. Barney Frank, who took over Father Drinan's seat, quipped that perhaps the president was under the impression that Grover Cleveland had pitched a few seasons for the old Washington Senators during the four-year interlude between his two terms in office.

Not long after the inauguration, the Reagans invited Millie and me to dine with them at the White House. Reagan, of course, asked me about James Michael Curley, although he was about the only politician I ever met who hadn't actually read *The Last Hurrah*. But he had seen the movie, which was made in 1958 and featured Spencer Tracy as Curley. It was a pretty good film, and I've watched it myself half a dozen times.

While Mrs. Reagan took Millie around the White House and told her about some of the decorating changes she was planning, the president and I sat around and swapped Irish tales. I told him the one about the time Uncle Denny is in church, and old Monsignor Ryan is giving the sermon. Sometimes the monsignor would get his sentences mixed up, and that Sunday he quotes incorrectly from Scripture, saying, "And the good Lord fed five men with five thousand loaves of bread and two thousand fishes."

"Big deal," mutters Uncle Denny. "I could do that myself."

When the mass is over, the old monsignor says to the curate, "I see that Uncle Denny was in the second row, talking while I was giving the sermon."

"Yes, Monsignor," says the curate. "I'm sure you meant to say that the good Lord took five loaves and two fishes and fed five *thousand* men."

The following week the monsignor gets up and says, "I have a correction to make in last week's sermon. As you all know, the good Lord fed five thousand men with five loaves and two fishes."

Whereupon he looks down at Uncle Denny and says, "Well, Denny, could you do that?"

"Indeed I could," says Uncle Denny.

"How?" says the monsignor.

"It's very easy," replies Uncle Denny. "I'd give them what was left over from last week!"

The president and I went on like this for an hour or so, and that night I learned what so many people had already discovered—that Ronald Reagan is an exceptionally congenial and charming man. He's a terrific storyteller, he's witty, and he's got an excellent sense of humor.

But unlike the other presidents I have known, Ronald Reagan always seemed distant from the details of public policy and legislation. Given the choice, he invariably preferred to talk about sports and the movies. "Tip," he'd say, "let me tell you the latest," and he'd come up with yet another story about the World Series, or football, or show business.

I once attended a dinner party at the White House where a group of us were discussing political affairs while the president just sat there in silence. There was an awkward feeling in the room, so to bring him into the conversation I asked him a question about his old Hollywood days. The transformation was amazing, as though I had switched on a light. He suddenly became animated and entertained us with great stories for the rest of the evening.

And for a fellow his age, I've never met a man in better physical condition. I touched his arm one day and it was like iron. "Is this from chopping wood on your ranch?" I asked.

He nodded, and with real enthusiasm he described the special double-edged ax he liked to use. A few weeks later, when my daughter Rosemary asked me what I wanted for Christmas, I told her about the president's ax, and said I just might go out and chop a little wood for our fireplace on Cape Cod. She bought me the ax, and on the first mild day after Christmas I went out back and started swinging. I survived about fifteen minutes before I had to come inside, tired and sore.

The next time I saw the president, I asked, "By the way, when you chop wood, how long do you keep it up?"

"Oh," he said, "I'm usually at it for a couple of hours."

They say that when Reagan was younger, he could hit a golf ball a mile. I'll say this: the Democrats were damn lucky that he and I never had to settle our disagreements with boxing gloves.

I'm convinced that the president's hardy constitution is what kept him alive after the attempt on his life on March 30, 1981, during the third month of his presidency. I learned about the shooting from a television bulletin. (The set in my office was always tuned to

C-Span, with its live coverage of the House of Representatives.) A few minutes later, my office received a call from FEMA, the Federal Emergency Management Agency. Because the Speaker is third in the line of succession (after the vice president), it was FEMA's responsibility to make sure they knew where I was and what my immediate plans were.

I wanted to visit the president in the hospital, and I checked with the White House to make sure it was appropriate. Yes, I was told, come at two o'clock tomorrow, but please don't comment on the state of his health.

As a get-well gift, I brought the president a book of Irish humor. But I was shocked by his condition, which seemed much more serious than what had been announced. This was three days after the shooting, and he was clearly exhausted and in pain. I stayed only a moment, as he obviously was in no shape to receive visitors. I suspect that in the first day or two after the shooting he was probably closer to death than most of us realized. If he hadn't been so strong and hardy, it could have been all over.

Now, before I go into the details of my political battles with Reagan, there's something I want to get straight. Despite what many people believe, and what the Republicans want us to think, Reagan's victory in 1980 did *not* represent a revolution in American values. And despite what the media claimed, Reagan was not elected because people were fed up with the huge federal deficit and were clamoring for budget cuts. As far as I'm concerned, that's looking at history through a rear-view mirror. I didn't buy the idea of a Reagan mandate then, and I certainly don't buy it now.

Ronald Reagan didn't win the 1980 election as much as Jimmy Carter lost it. Despite my affection and respect for Carter, the fact is that by election day a great many Americans couldn't wait to get rid of him. Reagan's people like to claim that their man's victory symbolized some kind of grand New Beginning, but the real reason he won is that the country wanted to dump Carter. Against a strong Democratic opponent in a healthy economy, Ronald Reagan would have had no more chance of being elected president of the United States than the man on the moon.

It's hard to believe, looking back, but as the 1980 campaign got under way, Ronald Reagan was not especially popular. Like many Democrats, I had actually been hoping that he would win the Republican nomination because I was sure he would make an easy target. Only two years earlier, Reagan had gone on record as favoring a voluntary approach to Social Security, which would, of course, destroy the entire system. If he revived that idea, Carter's reelection would be assured. Or so we thought.

The Democrats were also delighted that Reagan's campaign promises were so clearly preposterous. We were convinced that the voters would reject his opposition to the Camp David peace accords, and to SALT, not to mention his desire to cut Social Security and other entitlement programs. And surely everybody could see that you couldn't balance the budget, cut taxes, and increase defense spending all at the same time. Moreover, Reagan loved to downgrade the poor of America, and while this attitude may have been music to the ears of the rich, we felt certain that it wouldn't play in Peoria. Wrong again.

The turning point in the campaign came only a week before the election, when Reagan and Carter met for their debate in Cleveland. Looking back, I can think of three political debates that changed the direction of our history. The first was the series of televised meetings between Kennedy and Nixon in 1960, where Jack appeared so much livelier and more secure than his opponent. The second was the debate between Carter and Ford in 1976, where Jerry didn't seem to be aware that Poland was under Soviet domination. The third was the Carter-Reagan debate on October 28, 1980, when Reagan was running only slightly ahead of President Carter in the polls.

During the debate, Carter talked about how his daughter, Amy, was worried about the prospects of a nuclear war. His point was that if this was what a twelve-year-old was thinking about, it showed the extent to which the fear of nuclear war had seeped into the national consciousness. But Carter didn't explain himself very well, and both Reagan and the news media ridiculed him for bringing Amy into the discussion. His remarks on Amy were about five years ahead of their time.

Although most people agreed that President Carter won the debate, it was a hollow success—much like Lyndon Johnson's "victory" against Eugene McCarthy in the 1968 New Hampshire

primary. Feelings against Carter were running so high that when
Reagan appeared as his usual charming self, the election was as good
as over.

The day after the debate, my friend Lou Harris, the pollster,
called to warn me that Reagan would win with very long coattails.
And, as he predicted, election night was one of the worst experiences of my life. I sat in my office at the Capitol as the calls started
coming in about some of the finest Democrats in the House: Ull-
man, Ashley, Johnson, Corman, Brademas—all defeated, along with
twenty-one of their colleagues.

It was a stunning loss for the Democrats on Capitol Hill, and
when it was over, the Republicans controlled the Senate for the first
time since the Eisenhower administration. In the House, the generous margin of 143 Democrat seats when I was elected Speaker back
in 1977 was now reduced to 49. The reality was even worse than the
numbers suggested, as the election was especially tough on the
senior members of the House, including several of the chairmen and
other leaders.

The message to the surviving Democrats was clear: if the members of the leadership, with their considerable campaign funds and
impressive power, could not protect themselves when they were
targeted by the National Republican Committee, how could the
Speaker protect the younger members who might well be targeted
in 1982?

Suddenly, we were playing in a new ball game. Not so long ago,
when Jerry Ford was president, the Republican party was so broke
that they actually offered to sell their Capitol Hill club to the Democrats. But now, only five years later, they had hundreds of millions
of dollars to spend on campaigns, not to mention an impressive
party organization. In addition, right-wing outfits like the National
Conservative Political Action Committee were spending millions of
dollars in negative political advertising—which had been remarkably successful.

Following the election, the Democrats were demoralized, dis-
credited and broke. The next election was only two years away, and
if the Republicans did as well in the House as they had in 1980, they
would soon control both branches of Congress. The GOP was
obviously relishing the prospect of a grand realignment, but I was

determined not to let that happen. Tip O'Neill was not about to become the last Democratic Speaker of the House in the twentieth century.

To me the scenario looked vaguely familiar, as the successful "vote for a change" Republican slogan of 1980 was reminiscent of the "had enough" Republican slogan of 1946. That had been a great year for the Republicans, but only two years later, Harry Truman won a tremendous upset victory—in part because the Eightieth Congress had tried to repeal the New Deal. I wondered whether my Republican colleagues in the House were about to make the same mistake. You might even say I was counting on it.

But what about Ronald Reagan? In terms of electoral votes, he won in a landslide. Out of fifty states, he carried forty-four, including my own. As a result, the public was left with the logical conclusion that an overwhelming majority of Americans had voted for the new president.

But the popular vote did not bear this out. First, Reagan received slightly less than 51 percent of the total. (Carter ended up with 41 percent, with 6.6 percent going to John Anderson.) Second, only 54 percent of the eligible voters actually went to the polls—the lowest participation since 1948. When you did the arithmetic, it turned out that Ronald Reagan was elected by less than 28 percent of the eligible voters. He won fair and square, and he won big. But was it really a landslide?

It certainly seemed that way to most of the press, which changed its attitude toward the presidency in the blink of an eye. Almost overnight, many in the news media, who had been cynical and jaded ever since the death of Jack Kennedy, dropped their negative posture and embraced the new hero. They had seen Johnson as crude, Nixon as a liar, Ford as a bumbler, and Carter as incompetent. But they were certainly rooting for this guy.

Reagan himself, of course, had a lot to do with this shift. Unlike Carter, who used to stick to the issues, Reagan invariably projected his hale-and-hearty personality. To a remarkable degree, he succeeded in turning the presidency into one long photo opportunity. He is brilliant at avoiding tough questions with a smile, a handshake, or a wave, and you almost never see him get angry.

He learned reporters' names, and would always come up with a quotable quip. They liked him as an individual, and instead of the hard questions they should have been asking, they tended to throw creampuffs. (Sam Donaldson, of course, was an outstanding exception.) In addition, the White House staff showed a superb ability to politely deny access to reporters whose questions might be hostile or embarrassing.

In 1980, the media's love affair with the new president was so intense that the press soon began offering a retroactive interpretation of the election. The votes had barely been counted before the press took Reagan's triumph one step further by telling the public that the New Deal era was finally over, and that the American people were now demanding a massive cutback in social programs.

I honestly don't believe that this idea was uppermost in Reagan's mind, and I certainly don't think that the average American was worried about the federal deficit until the press announced that this was the Big Issue. But once the bandwagon started to roll, the president's staff was quick to seize on it and to move his program more quickly and more firmly in the direction of cutting the budget.

Or so they claimed. In fact, the Reagan years have been one long Christmas party for the Pentagon and the wealthy, while the federal deficit has continued to grow to record proportions.

Despite his rhetoric, I wasn't prepared for the size and the extent of Reagan's cuts in domestic spending. According to my friends in the California legislature, Governor Reagan had been all bark and no bite. Despite his conservative pose, he turned out to be a moderate. And despite his threats to cut social programs, he actually raised taxes and increased spending. During the 1976 primaries, President Ford's campaign literature called Reagan the biggest taxer and spender in California's history. It was true: during Reagan's eight years as governor, the annual state expenditure soared from $4.6 billion to $10.2 billion, although, to be fair, much of that rise was due to inflation.

With a Republican in the White House, and the House still controlled by the Democrats, I now assumed a new role—leader of the opposition. And with Jimmy Carter back in Georgia, and Ted Kennedy submerged in a Republican-controlled Senate, I also became the chief spokesman for the Democrats. In February 1981, during the new president's first address to the joint session of Congress, I sat behind him in the Speaker's chair, just as I had done under Carter.

This time, however, sitting next to me was George Bush, the new vice president. As the president spelled out his new economic program, I couldn't resist the opportunity to tease Bush by whispering in his ear during the interruptions for applause, "Voodoo economics, George. You understand that, don't you?" (Only a year earlier, in the New Hampshire primary, Bush had been using that same taunt to attack Reagan.)

"Quiet, Tip," he kept saying.

"Quiet?" I replied. "You've got to be kidding. You don't actually believe this bullshit, do you?"

During the entire speech, we both kept a smile on our faces. A few days later, George began to get letters: "Why are you so friendly with that nasty-looking son of a bitch?"

In 1981, Ronald Reagan enjoyed a truly remarkable rookie year. He pushed through the greatest increase in defense spending in American history, together with the greatest cutbacks in domestic programs and the largest tax cuts this country had ever seen.

Reagan's success didn't happen by accident. As soon as he came into the White House, his staff imposed strict party discipline in Congress. In the past, there were two or three dozen Republicans, mostly from the Northeast, whom we could always count on. But after 1980 we lost them—along with the southern Democrats. As a result, the huge majority we had enjoyed during the Carter years disappeared, a situation that wasn't helped by the loss of thirty-three seats in the 1980 elections. (We did so badly in that campaign that only three Republican incumbents were defeated in the House.)

The new president jumped in with both feet. Some House members said they saw more of him during his first four months in office than they saw of Jimmy Carter during his entire four years. Despite the attitude he displayed during our first meeting, Reagan took Congress very seriously and was always coming over to the Capitol for meetings. According to what I heard, he instructed his people, "Tell me who you want me to call and I'll take care of it." I would have given my right arm to hear those words from Jimmy Carter.

Reagan had tremendous powers of friendly persuasion. He once secured the votes of four Louisiana Democrats by promising to provide a support program for sugar. When a reporter asked one of them if this meant that his vote could be bought, he replied, "No, but it can be rented."

The president was continually calling members of the House. He didn't always get his way, but his calls were never wasted. He was very effective on the phone, making almost as many calls as Lyndon did.

The members adored it when he called, even when they had no intention of changing their vote. The men and women in Congress love nothing better than to hear from the head guy, so they can go back to their districts and say, "I was talking to the president the other day." The constituents love it too, because they want to believe that their representative is important enough to be in touch with the chief.

Another reason Reagan was so successful in getting his legislation passed was that he had strong, capable people around him, including Michael Deaver, Ed Meese, Jim Baker, and David Stockman, among others. I didn't like their mean-spirited philosophy, but they knew where they were going and they knew how to get there. They put only one legislative ball in play at a time, and they kept their eye on it all the way through. Shortly after the inauguration, for example, when Secretary of State Haig tried to raise the issue of Central America, the White House told him to leave it alone. There was to be only one issue on the agenda—the economy.

Reagan's aides were never parochial, and despite our many disagreements, they never showed any animosity toward me. On a few occasions, when lower-echelon people tried to block programs for my district, I would call the White House, where Mike Deaver or Jim Baker or somebody else on the president's team would always straighten things out.

My relationship with Donald Regan was a little rockier. Regan started out as secretary of the treasury, but in 1985 he switched jobs with Jim Baker, the White House chief of staff. This was one of the president's worst mistakes: Don Regan may have been a financial genius, but he knew nothing about politics.

Like me, Don grew up in a working-class neighborhood of Cambridge. He went to Harvard on a Buckley scholarship, which was established for graduates of Cambridge public schools.

But like the president, Don Regan forgot his roots. He's Harvard, while I'm still Boston College. He made it big, while I stayed with the people. Over the years, he moved a long way from the other side of the tracks.

His cousins still lived in Cambridge, and every now and then I would run into them.

"Do you agree with Don's politics?" I once asked.

"We're very proud of him," they replied, "but we're strictly O'Neill Democrats."

Whenever I saw Don, I used to tease him by asking what was new with his relatives in Cambridge.

Even David Stockman gained my respect, although, as director of the Office of Management and Budget, he was the point man for all of Reagan's cuts in social programs. Stockman was my chief adversary in the White House, but if he had stayed on in Congress he would have played the same role there. Although I despise his philosophy, I've never doubted his talent. He's a good politician, and we were always able to compromise.

But there was no way I was going to swallow the ridiculous notion that supply-side economics would lead to prosperity. The administration tried to market this as a new idea, but the only thing new about it was the name. The policy itself came from the administration of Herbert Hoover, who in my opinion is not the sort of guy whose economic views you want to emulate. But politics is the art of repackaging. The pendulum swings back and forth, and every time it returns, you wrap your philosophy a little differently than the last time you sold it.

The real question wasn't whether supply-side economics was new. It was whether you would really be helping the economy by cutting taxes for the rich so that the benefits would trickle down to the poor. Like many highfalutin concepts, this one works better in theory than in practice.

The idea of supply-side economics had been instilled in the president by so many of his advisers that he honestly didn't think it could fail. But his advisers were wrong. In theory, supply-side economics creates jobs. In practice, it amounts to soaking the poor to subsidize the rich.

So for both of these reasons—the president's willingness to lobby for his own program, and the political skills of his staff—Reagan got off to a strong start. Another factor was Reagan's enormous personal appeal, especially after the attempt on his life. He quickly became a folk hero, and he performed so beautifully on the tube that he could sell anything.

In 1981, I started to receive a tremendous amount of mail—more letters than I had seen in my entire career—asking me to give the president's program a chance. Most of these letters echoed what the press was saying: that America was demanding a change in its fiscal policy. There was one week when I received something like fifty thousand letters a day, including many from my own constituents in a fairly liberal district.

As Speaker, I could have refused to play ball with the Reagan administration by holding up the president's legislation in the Rules Committee. But in my view, this wasn't a politically wise thing to do. Despite my strong opposition to the president's program, I decided to give it a chance to be voted on by the nation's elected representatives.

For one thing, that's how our democracy is supposed to work. For another, I was afraid that the voters would repudiate the Democrats if we didn't give the president a chance to pass his program. After all, the nation was still in an economic crisis and people wanted immediate action.

In early March, I met with the House Republican leadership and agreed to an expedited schedule for consideration of the president's economic program. At the meeting, I promised that his budget and tax cuts would come to a vote in the House before August 1.

I was fully aware of the advantage I was giving the Republicans, as all the votes would take place well within the new president's honeymoon period. But my strategy was to keep in mind the long-term situation. I was less concerned about losing the legislative battle in the spring and summer of 1981 than I was with losing at the polls in the fall of 1982. I was convinced that if the Democrats were perceived as stalling in the midst of a national economic crisis, there would be hell to pay in the midterm elections.

At the time, Jim Jones, the new chairman of the Budget Committee, and Dan Rostenkowski, the new chairman of Ways and Means, were eager to compromise with the administration. Above all, they wanted to avoid defeat in their first tests on the floor as committee chairmen. But I didn't believe that this administration was willing to compromise, and as things turned out, I was right.

The president was not much on the details of legislation, but he was great at fighting for it. He spoke to the American people on television. He pleaded with members of Congress over the phone. He worked through James Baker, his chief of staff, and through an experienced and savvy team of congressional liaison men. All in all, the Reagan team in 1981 was probably the best-run political operating unit I've ever seen.

Some members in my party, including Jack Brooks from Texas, Ted Weiss from New York, John Conyers from Michigan, and Don Edwards from California, thought I was being overly accommodating. Their attitude was "Don't give him anything." But I fully expected that in the long run, the American people would repudiate Reagan's policies.

First, though, we had to get through the short run. I knew it wouldn't be easy, but I still wasn't prepared for what happened in 1981. As part of the Gramm-Latta budget, the administration put all its proposals into one huge package, an eight-hundred-page bill that passed the House so quickly that many members didn't even know what they were voting for. The legislation was so complicated and so enormous that the president could have put us into war and we might not have discovered it for weeks.

Later, we salvaged some of what the president had cut, but the damage done by Gramm-Latta was enormous. By forcing it through in a single package, the Republicans were able to put in Social Security reductions that never could have passed on their own. And that was just the beginning, as a great many Americans were hurt through cuts in various social, health, and education programs. Good-bye to public service jobs under the Comprehensive Employment Training Act, and to college education benefits from Social Security. Medicare payments were lowered, along with student loans. Child nutrition programs were slashed to ribbons. Unemployment compensation was reduced from thirty-nine weeks to twenty-six at a time when more people than ever were out of work. A million food-stamp recipients were struck from the rolls, and the rest had their benefits cut. The administration even repealed the Randolph-Shephard Act, which provided that food concessions in federal buildings be staffed by blind people. And all this from a man who swore that his budget cuts wouldn't hurt anyone!

The Pentagon, of course, made out fine. Reagan had promised to increase military spending, and this was one commitment he kept, as he added $28 billion to the military budget.

Once the bills got to the floor, I screeched and I hollered and I fought his program every way I could, but there are times that you just can't buck a trend. I got clobbered so badly that I felt like the guy in the old joke who gets hit by a steamroller. Somebody runs to tell his wife about the accident.

"I'm taking a bath right now," she says. "Could you just slip him under the door?"

That's what happened to me during the president's first year, except that they didn't bother to slip me under the door. They just left me lying out in the street.

Thank God for Millie. There were mornings when it was hard to go to work, but Millie would fix my tie and I'd give her a kiss, and she'd say, "Do you believe in what you're fighting for?"

"Sure I do."

"Then go out and do your job."

She's a strong woman, and I really needed her help.

In all my fifty years of public life, this was absolutely the lowest point in my career. I have a thick skin, and mean comments roll off me like water off a duck. But when a program I cared about was cut, *that* was hard. In 1981, everything I had fought for, everything I had believed in, was being cast aside.

The most depressing thing of all was the hatred for the poor that developed all across America. Almost overnight, there was a new and widespread hostility on the part of the haves toward the have-nots. I had worked all my life to help create a middle class, and suddenly that middle class was rebelling against the 10 or 15 percent of the population that hadn't yet made it. The administration had people believing that their fellow citizens were getting something for nothing. Millions of Americans who had achieved some success now wanted to pull up the ladder to prevent anyone else from climbing aboard.

Now there's always been an undercurrent of resentment out there, especially among the conservatives, who believe that anybody who really wants to make it in this country can do so. But when that feeling rose to the surface, it turned mean. "To hell with the other guy," people said. "I'm looking out for number one."

I couldn't believe what I was hearing, and it wasn't only from the middle class, either. I remember a lunch on Cape Cod that I gave for thirty New England leaders of industry, all of them millionaires. Like so many Americans in 1981, they were convinced that the president was on the right track, and that previous administrations had been overly generous to people in need.

"Be honest with me," I said. "I'll bet that somewhere along the line, eighty percent of you got help from Uncle Sam. Maybe you went to a community college or a state university. Maybe you were educated through the National Defense Education Act. Maybe you attended a private college with the help of government loans. Or maybe you went to college on the G.I. Bill."

I asked for a show of hands, and it turned out that all but a handful had their college tuition paid by the federal government after coming out of the service. "Where would you have been without that help?" I asked. "Without your free education, would you have been such a success in life? Of course not. Then how can you sit there and say that we shouldn't give the same help to the next guy along the line?"

My question seemed to touch them, so I started asking it whenever I addressed an audience of people in business. In Florida, I once spoke to several hundred executives at a meeting on Marco Island. When I asked how many of them had received some form of government assistance along the line, something like 80 percent raised their hands. I really believe that my question forced many of these people to see the problem in a different perspective.

People don't develop new attitudes out of thin air. These grasping and uncaring views had to come from somewhere, and I blame the president for allowing this kind of selfishness to become respectable.

There's a story that Reagan loves to tell about a black welfare woman in Chicago who lives lavishly and supposedly collects something like a hundred and three welfare checks under different names. Now this anecdote has been checked by a number of different people, including Joe Califano, who has written to the president on three different occasions to tell him that the story is mythical and that this woman doesn't exist. The president *knows* the anecdote isn't true, but he continues to use it.

There are a hundred urban legends just like it, such as the one about the fat lady getting out of a taxi and buying liquor with her food stamps. Now, I know there are abuses in our welfare and entitlement systems. In a system that large, abuses are inevitable. But listening to Reagan, you'd think they were the rule rather than the exception.

There are abuses in the military, too, but I haven't noticed anybody calling for the government to shut down the Defense Department. And yet the sheer waste that goes on in the Pentagon is an outrage. By now, of course, this story is well known. In Congress, though, I would run up against another dimension of the problem. When the generals come over to address the Appropriations Committee, they've got nine colonels carrying their bags. I would look out in the corridor and see a million dollars' worth of talent, just holding the bags. At least *my* spending does some good.

There's no getting around the fact that Reagan has been a rich man's president. He has shown no care or compassion for the poor, or for the working person. But when it comes to giving money to the Pentagon or tax breaks to the wealthy, the guy has a heart of gold.

It comes down to one word—fairness. The president's program wasn't fair. It made the rich richer and the poor poorer, and it did nothing for the middle class. On the contrary: it took from the truly needy and gave to the truly greedy.

I certainly hadn't become Speaker to dismantle the programs I had fought for all my life. When the Reagan plan got going in 1981, I saw myself as Horatio at the Bridge. Somebody had to stand out there and maintain the basic creed of the Democratic party, which has always believed that we are responsible for the welfare of our fellow Americans.

After all, the Constitution begins with the words "We, the people." It does not begin, "I, the individual." Prosperity and opportunity should exist for everybody, and now that this philosophy was out of fashion, somebody had to speak out. I refused to act as an apologist for this new heartlessness, as many in our party were starting to do.

For months, I stood on the floor of the House and said exactly what I thought of the president and his program. That Ronald Reagan was Herbert Hoover with a smile. That he was a cheerleader for selfishness. That he had no compassion. Yes, I was tough on the president, but not nearly as tough as his programs were on the American people.

From time to time, Reagan would strike back. He would charge that all the Democrats wanted to do was raise taxes. Or he'd get a little more personal and tell reporters that he liked to keep in shape by jogging three times a day around Tip O'Neill.

For a while, I was a solitary voice crying in the wilderness. To my distress, some of the weak-kneed members of my party were willing to desert our basic principles and vote with the Republicans. A few of them at least came to me and explained that the people back home really wanted them to support the president—which was undoubtedly true. But I had hoped that members would educate their constituents and let them know what the president was doing. Many Democrats were scared stiff at the prospect of being out of step with the mood of the country. And for a while there, we *were* out of step.

Times may change, but the basic moral truths of life remain constant. Even in 1981, I knew that the philosophy I had stood for all my life was still correct. Although the situation looked hopeless, I was confident that the American values I've always believed in would come back. The challenge was to keep calm and hold on to my temper.

We did manage some modest success against the tidal wave of change. We succeeded in saving programs for the handicapped. We stopped the Republicans from lacerating education. We protected the summer lunch programs and the milk programs. And we stood up to the president when he tried to cut Social Security.

He had proposed a 40 percent cut for those retiring at sixty-two, and a 23 percent reduction in benefits for all future retirees. This was a rotten thing to do, especially for a man who had promised in 1980 to *strengthen* Social Security. The Republican-controlled Senate gave him a clear message by turning him back on that plan, 96–0. And the House voted 404–20 to restore the minimum benefit, although even that was cut by the administration.

But for the most part the president had his way, and some of my fellow Democrats started saying I was old and out of touch. Les Aspin from Wisconsin wrote in a newsletter to his constituents that I was reeling on the ropes. "Tip doesn't understand the explosions that have been going off since November," he observed. "He's in a fog."

Wrong, Les. I understood those explosions all too well. But I'd be damned if I was going to go along with them.

A few of the younger fellows actually called on me to resign as Speaker, although nobody ever said so to my face. But I had no intention of giving up—not for a minute. Anybody who wanted Tip O'Neill out of office would have to vote me out.

Still, there were rumblings of dissent, and Dave McCurdy from Oklahoma led a small band that wanted to run somebody against me for Speaker in 1982. The candidate they preferred was Richard Gephardt of Missouri, but Dick came in to tell me he had nothing to do with this plan. Looking back, I don't think McCurdy actually expected to dump me. More likely, he was opposing me for home consumption, figuring that in 1981 Tip O'Neill wasn't too popular in Oklahoma.

Even the press turned against me in 1981. The editorial writers and the cartoonists were merciless. The low point was a full-page article in *Time* Magazine (May 18, 1981), shortly after the first Gramm-Latta budget vote. "At that moment," noted Robert Ajemian, who wrote the piece, "it was clear that the nation's most powerful Democrat had been badly, perhaps even fatally, wounded." And later in the article, "O'Neill is beginning to show an uncharacteristic passivity, as if events are already intimidating him." And finally, "It was obvious that he still had an emotional hold on the House. But the hold is loosening now, and it looks very much as if the job Tip O'Neill has worked a lifetime for is offering challenges he cannot meet."

On another occasion, when the Republicans defeated my Rules Committee resolution and voted to cut minimum benefits for Social Security, an article in the *New York Times* speculated that after the 1982 congressional elections I might find myself in the unwelcome position of minority leader in the next Congress.

Nobody enjoys being criticized in the press, but it's something you learn to live with in politics. What I had to get used to in 1981 was being criticized not only by the press but by the man on the street—or, to be more precise, the man in the airport. I don't know why it happens, but air travelers are often in a foul mood, and during my various trips around the country, as I trudged through the passageways and terminals of the nation's airports, I was harassed by a continual stream of disgruntled people. Some shouted insults like "Leave the president alone, you fat bastard." Now and then somebody would be supportive, but friendly voices were all too few.

When I flew into Chicago with Dan Rostenkowski, a fellow in the airport was so hostile that Danny had to grab the guy and push him aside. From then on, every time I came to Chicago, Danny made sure the police were there to escort me from the terminal.

The Lyndon LaRouche people were the worst. Most of the country learned about this group only in 1986, after they made problems for Adlai Stevenson in Illinois, but I've had the dubious pleasure of knowing them for years. I don't mind being their favorite target, but I have no use for the way they make their points. They're a vicious bunch, and they've always got time for a rude insult or a nasty gibe.

I escaped from this predicament quite by accident. An air force colonel was in the office one day, and he happened to ask Leo how I traveled to various meetings and speaking engagements.

"The Speaker takes commercial flights," said Leo. "Why do you ask?"

"He doesn't have to, you know," said the colonel, who informed us that the Speaker of the House, just like the vice president, has the right to use a private government plane whenever he wants to, provided that the trip is not being made for purely political reasons. For some reason, nobody had ever told us about this before, and I don't recall that Carl Albert ever used one of these planes. (McCormack and Rayburn rarely traveled, except between Washington and their districts.) A private plane is a lot more convenient, of course, but the real reason I started using them was to avoid the LaRouchites and other hostile types.

There were also more death threats than usual during this period. Often, when I'd arrive at the Capitol, the police would be waiting to escort me inside. There were nights when the police stood guard outside my house, in suburban Maryland, where we lived, or in

Cambridge. On winter nights I would invite them in for coffee, but they refused to leave the beat.

To my amazement, I even had problems in Boston. At one point, to help the Boston Symphony in a fund-raising drive, I agreed to let them auction off a private lunch with the Speaker of the House. The fellow who won paid something like fifteen hundred dollars for that privilege. When he and his wife came to my office in the Capitol, I could see that she was very nervous. "Not now, dear," she kept whispering to her husband.

At the end of the meal, I said to them, "I'm delighted that you came here today. Tell me, how did you happen to bid on this lunch?"

The man looked at his wife for a moment, and then he turned to me and said, "Because I wanted to tell you to your face that you're a son of a bitch for being so tough on the president."

"Well," I said with a smile, "if you paid good money just to say that, it's all right with me."

A few days later, I received a thank-you letter from his wife, saying that I had been gracious and charming, and apologizing for her husband's rude behavior. But that's the kind of year I had in 1981.

And I haven't even mentioned the Republicans. As if I wasn't having enough troubles, a small group of young, ultraconservative Republicans saw it as their patriotic duty to antagonize and insult me. These people believed that all government was evil, that the poor deserved to be poor, and that the American way was to look out for number one.

Although I'm about as loyal a Democrat as you'll ever see, I've always enjoyed good personal relations with Republican members, no matter how conservative they were. But these guys were different. They were the real weirdos of the Republican party who wanted to turn back the clock to the days when there were only two groups in America—the rich and the poor. But it wasn't only their philosophy that was mean; it was their whole style of operating. There are always young guys coming down the pike who want to make their reputation by pulling down the leaders, but it was unusual to have so many of them in the House at the same time.

The worst one was John LeBoutillier, a wealthy young fellow who more or less bought himself a seat in Congress and was elected in 1980 from Long Island. He had gone to Harvard, and had written a book in which he charged that the university was filled with hypocritical, bleeding-heart leftists. At twenty-seven, he was the youngest member in the House—and possibly the most obnoxious.

He was a real wise guy with an abusive phrase for just about every leading Democrat. Jimmy Carter was a "complete birdbrain." George McGovern was "scum." Pat Moynihan was a "drunken bum." And Tip O'Neill was "big, fat, and out of control—just like the federal government."

He actually tried to begin a national crusade to "Repeal O'Neill," and he even flew up to my district to campaign against me. Twenty members from the press showed up, and they constituted the entire audience—except for a group of pickets and hecklers protesting his visit.

I had never been introduced to John LeBoutillier, and he had never participated in debate on the floor of the House. So when reporters asked me about him, I answered, truthfully, that I wouldn't know him from a cord of wood.

But when he ran for reelection in 1982, Leo Diehl, my special assistant, went out to his district to raise money for his opponent. It was a close race, but Bob Mrazek won in an upset. So much for LeBoutillier.

But there were several others of his kind who did their best to undermine the dignity of the House, including Newt Gingrich of Georgia, Robert Walker of Pennsylvania, and Bruce Caputo of New York. Caputo was only congressman I've ever known who actually wanted to be on the Ethics Committee, where members pass judgment on their peers who may be guilty of wrongdoing. But he had lied about his military record, which didn't play too well during his campaign for the Senate.

Toward the end of Reagan's first term, several of these right-wing Republicans started taking advantage of a procedure known as "special orders" to attack their Democratic colleagues. After the House has finished its business for the day, a member is entitled to take the floor and to speak for up to an hour on any subject of his choosing. By then the House chamber is empty, and these special-orders speeches have traditionally been made strictly for home consumption. But in recent years there's been a whole new national audience on the C-Span cable TV network.

What really infuriated me about these guys is that they had no real interest in legislation. As far as they were concerned, the House was no more than a pulpit, a sound stage from which to reach the people at home. If the TV cameras were facing the city dump, that's where they'd be speaking.

I happened to be watching in my office one afternoon as Newt Gingrich was taking advantage of special orders to attack Eddie Boland's voting record and to cast aspersions on his patriotism. The camera focused on Gingrich, and anybody watching at home would have thought that Eddie was sitting there, listening to all of this. Periodically, Gingrich would challenge Boland on some point, and would then step back, as if waiting for Eddie to answer. But Boland had left hours ago, along with everybody else in the place.

The next day, when Robert Walker of Pennsylvania tried something similar, I called Charlie Rose, the member in charge of television in the House, and told him I thought the cameras should pan the entire chamber. Charlie informed the camera crew, and when they showed the empty hall, Walker looked like a fool.

The Republicans went wild when we did this, especially since I didn't consult them. They were right about that; I should have issued a warning before going ahead. But I wasn't going to tolerate members making charges in front of an empty hall when there was nobody around to refute what they were saying. I couldn't stop them from speaking, but I could certainly prevent the cameras from helping them stage their cynical charade.

A few days later, I rebuked Newt Gingrich on the floor of the House: "You deliberately stood in that well before an empty House and challenged these people when you knew they would not be there," I said. "It is the lowest thing that I have ever seen in my thirty-two years in Congress."

Trent Lott, the Republican whip, objected to my language, and on the advice of the House parliamentarian, the word "lowest" was ruled out of order and stricken from the record. I had done my best to control my temper, but much harsher thoughts were on my mind.

Congress has always been an exceedingly polite society, where even my justified rebuke of Newt Gingrich constituted unacceptably bad conduct. Because the House of Representatives includes 435 members from all regions of the country who hold a wide range of political philosophies, it's critical that members treat each other with respect. Attacking another member when he's not there to respond, while pretending that the House was in session, is a gross violation of our code of behavior.

Fortunately, the debacle of 1981 did not last forever, and in the 1982 congressional elections we gained twenty-six seats. Why did we do so well? Because we had succeeded in framing the issues—unemployment, fairness, and especially Social Security. In addition, our campaign committee targeted the Republican class of 1980 for defeat. We called them Reagan Robots and gave them a merciless pounding for their voting records—with a special emphasis on Social Security. The strategy worked, as thirteen of them were defeated. In all, twenty-four Republican incumbents failed to get reelected.

As a result, we once again had working control of the House, with enough votes to defeat the traditional alliance of Republicans and conservative Democrats. We had been slaughtered in the Reagan victory only two years earlier, but I had learned long ago that the horse that runs fast doesn't always run long.

I had gambled that the meanness of America in the first two years of Reagan's administration was a fad that wouldn't stick, and that you couldn't hurt people for long without there being a reaction. So our strategy in 1982 was simple: we talked about fairness.

Specifically, we hammered away on what the administration was doing to senior citizens, to poverty programs, and to education. We put a special emphasis on Social Security, reminding people that Reagan had promised in 1980 that he would never cut Social Security, but that in 1981, as part of the Gramm-Latta budget, he had cut minimum benefits, student survivor benefits, and death benefits—cuts that affected five million people. He had proposed cutting the benefits of early retirees from 80 percent to 55 percent, and had wanted to reduce cost-of-living adjustments over the next four years, but the Democrats in Congress had refused to go along with him on these proposals.

The Republicans had expected to beat the hell out of me in the 1982 elections. I say "me," rather than the Democrats, because they decided to make Tip O'Neill the issue. Their strategy was to take Mr. Smooth and run him against Mr. Old Pol, who was fat and out of shape and a big spender. Two years earlier, they had even produced TV ads that featured an actor who allegedly looked like me. He was driving along and laughing off warnings that his car was low on fuel—until it finally slowed to a halt as a voice announced that the Democrats were running out of gas.

After the 1982 election, I regained a good deal of support from Democrats who had opposed my leadership only a year earlier. In retrospect, they could see that we had been right to put the president's program on the fast track so that he could not blame the Democrats for the downturn in the economy.

But despite what I saw as the country's partial repudiation of his policies, Ronald Reagan's personal popularity continued to be immense. Two years later, in the 1984 elections, he was, of course, reelected in a landslide, defeating Mondale in every state but Minnesota.

I've always been proud of my ability to read the political map, but in Reagan's case my record is pretty bad. Two years before the 1984 election, I was convinced that he wasn't going to run for a second term. I remember a conversation I had with Mike Deaver in 1982 at a party at the house of the columnist Mary McGrory.

"He's not going to run again," I said.

"You've got to be kidding," said Deaver.

"Come on," I said. "I don't have to tell you about his limitations. He doesn't even know what's going on in his own programs! Believe me, by the time his first term is over, you'll be so grateful that the public doesn't realize how little this guy knows that you'll want to get him out of office while he's still a hero."

"Tip, you've got the guy wrong," said Deaver. "Ronald Reagan is one of the smartest pols that ever came down the pike. He's going to win so big in eighty-four that you won't believe it."

Maybe we were both right. Reagan did win big in 1984. But he would have looked a lot better in history if he had left office after the first term.

Despite Reagan's tremendous victory in 1984, the Republicans gained only 14 seats in the House, which was not enough to revive the conservative coalition of 1981. Although Reagan won the general election by sixteen million votes, in the congressional races the Democrats received a total of five and a half million more votes than the Republicans. To me, that said that although the people loved Reagan, they wanted Congress to continue acting as a check on the president and his policies. In other words, the American people supported this president without necessarily endorsing his programs.

The public's double vision of Reagan was brought home to me one day by a construction worker who came to see me at my district office in Boston. He was a strong, husky fellow who had fallen off a roof and had suffered a spinal cord injury that meant he would never walk again. He was angry because the administration wanted to tax workman's compensation benefits, and he wanted to see if anything could be done.

But while he was in, he decided to register another complaint: "Tip," he said, "I've voted for you all my life, but I think you're too tough on the president."

I was stunned. "Who do you think is cutting your benefits?" I asked.

"Not the president," he replied confidently. "He's got nothing to do with it. It's the people around him."

I couldn't believe my ears. But that's the amazing thing about Ronald Reagan. People just wouldn't believe he would do anything to hurt them. Even while he was cutting the heart out of the American dream to own a home, they continued to support him. The only way I can explain it is that the public just didn't connect this man with his own government—at least not until the Iran arms scandal at the end of 1986.

As far as I'm concerned, just about the only good thing that happened in the 1984 election was the nomination of Geraldine Ferraro. And despite all that's happened to her since, I'm still proud to take some of the credit for having Gerry be the first woman on a national ticket. I first got to know her in 1978, when she beat the party regulars in her district and defeated Tom Manton in the primary. Because Manton had been the choice of the party leaders in her area, Gerry was afraid that they wouldn't support her in the November election, and she called to ask if I would appear at a fund-raiser on her behalf in Queens. I was highly impressed with this bright, attractive woman who believed in the same principles as I did.

A few weeks before the convention, I was having lunch with Walter Mondale. "You've got the nomination sewed up," I said, "and it's time to start thinking about a running-mate. I've got just the candidate for you—Geraldine Ferraro from Queens. She's talented, she's a hard worker, she's articulate, she understands politics, and she's extremely popular in the House. She'd also give the ticket a great balance, because she's an Italian Catholic woman from the Northeast."

"I've never really thought about her," said Mondale.

Later, after I went public with my support of Geraldine, several of the other women in the House, including Lindy Boggs of Louisiana, Patricia Schroeder of Colorado, and Barbara Mikulski of Maryland, were upset with me for not endorsing *them*. I couldn't believe that they all saw themselves as candidates for vice president, but apparently they did. They're all fine and talented people, but none of them, in my view, would have been right for the ticket.

When Geraldine was being considered, I said to her, "There's nothing in the woodwork, is there?"

It was the same question I had asked Peter Rodino during the Watergate hearings, and I wasn't surprised to hear a similar response from Geraldine. She assured me that everything was fine, and I had no reason to doubt it. But of course everything *wasn't* fine, and all the things that happened to Geraldine and her family after her nomination added up to a sad derailment of a brilliant political career.

Along with a number of other candidates, Geraldine went out to Minnesota to be interviewed by Mondale. She called me as soon as she returned. "I didn't go over too well," she said. "I don't think his staff liked me."

"Listen," I said, "just sit tight and keep your mouth shut. Don't make any statements. They've got no other alternative. You're the one they'll choose. Again, are you absolutely sure there's nothing in the woodwork?"

Famous last words.

But Geraldine Ferraro's historical importance must not be underestimated. The night she was nominated, my daughter Susan turned to me with tears in her eyes and said, "Dad, do you realize what this means? When we were young, you used to tell Tommy,

Kip, and Michael that someday they could be president of the United States. You never said that to Rosemary, and you never said it to me. But now all that has changed, and I'll be able to say it to *my* daughter."

In almost any other year, Walter Mondale would have been the ideal Democratic candidate. But in 1984, he had the misfortune to be running against an incumbent president with whom the nation was infatuated—just as four years earlier, Ronald Reagan had the good fortune to be running against Jimmy Carter. There's so much in politics that you can never control.

A couple of scenes from that campaign remain with me. On Labor Day, I went down to an Italian street festival in East Cambridge, which has always been as solid a Democratic neighborhood as any in the country. But in 1984, people were saying, "Tip, we love you, we've always voted for you, but lay off the president."

A few days later I was campaigning for Mondale in New Jersey. We toured a sausage factory, and a woman who worked there came up to me and said, "I love Mr. Reagan. Why don't you leave him alone?" I was disheartened by that remark, because whenever you have people supporting a Republican while they're working for the minimum wage, the Democrats don't have a prayer.

I did hear one dissenting view during the campaign. I was campaigning for Nicholas Mavroules, a member of Congress from Lynn, just north of Boston. As I was coming out of a hall after addressing a group of senior citizens, a little nun came up to me. "Stop calling the president a decent man," she said. "After what he's done to old people and to handicapped children, how can you go around saying that?"

Mondale couldn't have won no matter what he did, but he certainly didn't help the cause by calling for higher taxes during his acceptance speech at the convention. I was sitting in a broadcast booth with Dan Rather, and I couldn't believe my ears. It was a terrible mistake, which played right into the hands of the Republicans. It gave Reagan the opening he was looking for, and allowed him to use his favorite line on the Democrats: "There they go again, tax and spend, tax and spend."

Ronald Reagan would never say that we had to raise taxes because he always shied away from the bad news. He let the voters believe that the answer to our economic problems was to cut their taxes—along with other people's benefits. He preferred happy talk, and always told people what they wanted to hear.

The outcome of the election was a foregone conclusion, although the Democrats did have a brief moment of hope after the first Reagan-Mondale debate, when the president was clearly befuddled. If he hadn't recovered in time for the second debate, he would have been in big trouble.

Many people were shocked by how poorly the president performed during that first debate, but to me, that was the real Ronald Reagan. I've said it before, but this book is my political testament, and I'll say it again here. Ronald Reagan lacked the knowledge he should have had in every sphere, both domestic and international. Most of the time he was an actor reading lines, who didn't understand his own programs. I hate to say it about such an agreeable man, but it was sinful that Ronald Reagan ever became president.

I'm not playing politics when I say these things. I have no more elections left, and Reagan doesn't either, so the Democrats have nothing to gain by these comments. But I've known every president since Harry Truman, and there's no question in my mind that Ronald Reagan was the worst.

He wasn't without leadership ability, but he lacked most of the management skills that a president needs. But let me give him his due: he would have made a hell of a king.

We're talking about a man who went into meetings reading all his remarks from three-by-five cue cards. A couple of years ago, a prominent auto executive told me that just before the president flew to Japan, he met with the heads of the Big Three car companies. For the first few minutes of the meeting, Reagan was reading from cue cards—*but they were the wrong cards.* His guests were so embarrassed that no one could bring himself to mention the mistake. Eventually, the president realized he was barking up the wrong tree.

When Nixon and Carter used to meet with the congressional leaders, they would explain their legislative proposals in great detail. Ronald Reagan explained nothing. Whenever there was an issue of substance, he called on somebody else to discuss it for him. Now I myself have never been an expert on the specifics of legislation, but compared with this guy, I was a stickler for detail.

All the stories about Reagan's working only three or four hours a day made me wonder who was really in charge in the White House. I'll never forget that summer day in 1983 when Flight 007, the Korean airliner, was shot down by the Soviets. I was on Cape Cod, where Secretary of State George Shultz called me at seven in the morning. After telling me what had happened, he said he was sending down a plane to bring me to Washington for an emergency meeting at the White House.

"I'll be ready," I said. "But what does the president think about this?"

"He's still asleep," said Shultz. "He doesn't know about it yet."

"You've got to be kidding," I said. "You mean you're calling me before you've even notified the president?"

"We'll tell him when he wakes up," said Shultz. To me, that comment spoke volumes.

But my biggest disappointment with Ronald Reagan's presidency is that he didn't grow in office. Back in 1981, I told him a disturbing story I had recently heard about a girl who had just graduated from high school with top honors. Both of her parents had died, and she was receiving a small Social Security check. But the Reagan budget had wiped out her college benefits, and she was stuck.

"That's terrible," said the president. He called in Ed Meese and asked me to repeat the story. "Ed," he said, "let's see if we can take care of this girl."

"Mr. President," I said, "I'm not here to talk about one girl. I'm using her as an example. There are *thousands* of people in that situation."

I still don't think he understands the point I was making. Ronald Reagan is a pushover for an individual hard-luck story, and he really did want to help that girl—as long as it could be done through the private sector. At the same time, he also wanted to eliminate the program whereby she and thousands like her would have been helped.

There have been a number of similar situations. On several occasions, President and Mrs. Reagan have made personal appeals to help people in urgent need of organ transplants. But in January 1987, the president submitted a budget that cut out the recently created Office of Organ Transplantation, as well as the national computer network that matched organ donors with waiting recipients. Both of these were low-budget programs that accomplished, fairly and effectively, what the president had tried to do on an ad hoc, personal basis.

One of my most unpleasant confrontations with Reagan came in January 1986, at a bipartisan meeting at the White House that included a discussion of the unemployment problem. At the time, the unemployment rate was 7 percent, although in some areas of the country it was considerably worse.

When I complained that 7 percent was still too high, the president replied that the figure would be lower if members of the armed services were counted in the work force. While this was true enough, it had *always* been true—and had nothing to do with the topic at hand.

Then he started singing a familiar song. "Those people out there can get jobs if they really want to," said the president. "I'm told about the fellow on welfare who makes phone calls looking for work. On the third call they offer him a job, and he hangs up. These people don't *want* to work."

I couldn't believe he was still spouting this nonsense, and I exploded. "Don't give me that crap!" I said. "The guy in Youngstown, Ohio, who's been laid off at the steel mill and has to make his mortgage payments—don't tell me he doesn't want to work. Those stories may work on your rich friends, but they don't work on the rest of us. I'm sick and tired of your attitude, Mr. President. I thought you would have grown in the five years you've been in office, but you're still repeating those same simplistic explanations."

He started to sputter, but Alan Simpson, the assistant majority leader in the Senate, jumped in and intervened: "This is awful," he said. "You fellows are always bickering. The leader of the free world and the leader of the opposition shouldn't be fighting like this. It isn't right."

"I'm sorry," I said, "but I just can't sit here and listen to him talk like that. I don't want my silence to be regarded as acquiescence. You know I have nothing but the greatest respect for the presidency."

"With the exception of this incumbent," said Reagan.

When I left the White House that morning I was still genuinely angry at this man, who seemed blind to the suffering of so many people. This, without a doubt, was Ronald Reagan at his worst.

Later that same day, I saw Ronald Reagan at his best. Shortly after our meeting ended, the space shuttle *Challenger* exploded just after takeoff, killing all seven of the crew. That evening, the president went on television to address the nation. As he spoke, even his most severe critic had to acknowledge that his tribute to the *Challenger* crew was a masterly speech that touched the hearts of us all.

As I listened to him, I had a tear in my eye and a lump in my throat. It was a trying day for all Americans, and Ronald Reagan spoke to our highest ideals. He may not be much of a debater, but with a prepared text he's the best public speaker I've ever seen. With age, I'm beginning to think that in this respect he dwarfs both Roosevelt and Kennedy.

During my six years as Speaker in Reagan's presidency, we fought hard on domestic issues. But his foreign policy was equally misguided, and I struggled with him on that front as well.

After the Korean airliner went down on September 1, 1983, and Shultz brought me back to Washington, there was a high-level meeting at the White House. After a discussion of the airliner incident, the president changed the subject to Lebanon. Robert McFarlane, who at that point was deputy national security adviser, had just returned from Beirut, where he had arranged a brief cease-fire among the various factions. He spoke of an agreement under which the Israelis and the Syrians would remove their troops, and the prime minister of Lebanon would put together a new, broader cabinet. As part of this new arrangement, we would keep our marines in Beirut as the symbol of American power and prestige.

Put that way, the presence of the marines made sense. But at the time, nobody mentioned that their real mission was to protect the highly exposed Beirut airport. When neither the Syrians nor the Israelis withdrew, our boys became increasingly vulnerable. Not knowing the real purpose they would be serving, I supported the president's decision to keep the marines in Beirut.

In the House, I delivered enough Democratic votes to give us a bipartisan policy with regard to Lebanon. But on October 23, 1983, everything changed when 241 marines were killed by a Moslem terrorist who drove a truck full of explosives into their compound.

Following the explosion, and the publication of the Long Committee report, I became convinced that the president should withdraw
the marines completely—and I said so publicly.

One night, at a social event, I ran into a White House official who
said, "Isn't it great that the president is planning to bring home the
marines?"

He must have assumed that I knew the decision had already been
made, but it was news to me.

The next day I seized the initiative and came out with a statement
demanding once and for all that the president bring the boys home.

The president's response was to try to make me the villain. "Tip
O'Neill may want us to surrender," he told the *Wall Street Journal*
on February 3, 1984. "But I don't." Four days later, however, he
started bringing home the marines, calling the move a "redeploy-
ment" rather than a withdrawal. I still don't understand how he got
away with it.

The day after the Beirut bombing back in October I held a previously scheduled meeting with Kenneth Dam, the deputy secretary
of state, and a special House task force on Lebanon. But because of
the tragedy, both George Shultz and Caspar Weinberger, the secretary of defense, came to the meeting.

Congress was in an uproar. During the meeting, the administration's views on Lebanon were strongly challenged, and Shultz and
Weinberger were peppered with hard questions.

The meeting was still going on at 6:45 in the evening when Kirk
O'Donnell, my general counsel and top adviser, came in and motioned to me to step outside. In a whisper, he told me that Jim Baker,
the White House chief of staff, was down the hall and needed to
speak to me in confidence.

Jim got right to the point. "There's a highly confidential meeting
with the president at eight o'clock tonight," he said. "The Secret
Service will pick you up and take you there."

"Don't give me that malarkey," I said. "Just tell me where it is
and I'll show up."

Baker told me to report to the side door of the Executive Office
Building at ten minutes to eight. On the way over, I said to Kirk,
"I don't know what this is about, but I bet we're invading Grenada."

"Grenada? You can't be serious."

"I am," I replied. "I just have a feeling about it. The administration has been wanting to go in there for a long time. I heard on the radio that one of our ships on its way to Lebanon has been turned around, and that got me thinking. Besides, the prime minister down there has been killed, so they have the perfect excuse."

"Then you don't think the meeting is about Lebanon?"

"Sure I do," I said. "They're invading Grenada so people will forget what happened yesterday in Beirut."

Kirk said that was incredible, but I couldn't imagine any other scenario. "We'll know soon enough," I said as I climbed out of the car.

From the Executive Office Building, I was taken to a basement room at the White House, where coffee was served. When everybody had assembled, I could see that something big was in the works. Shultz and Weinberger were there, along with Robert McFarlane (who had recently been promoted to national security adviser), Edwin Meese, General John Vessey (chairman of the Joint Chiefs of Staff), Mike Deaver, and a handful of leaders from the House and Senate. Jim Baker brought us upstairs to the president's living quarters.

The president opened the meeting by announcing that he had made the decision to go into Grenada. He then gave the floor to McFarlane, who provided a short history of the island. As we all knew, Prime Minister Maurice Bishop had been killed in an army uprising. McFarlane also said there were six hundred Cubans in Grenada, building an airport, and that Cuba had several hundred armed troops there as well. He added that some of Grenada's neighbors were afraid the island was being used for training terrorists. But the most pressing reason we were going into Grenada was to protect approximately a thousand Americans, most of whom were medical students.

The invasion was already under way, so even if we opposed it there was nothing any of us could do. I had some serious reservations, and I'm sure that my Democratic colleagues did as well, but I'd be damned if I was going to voice any criticism while our boys were out there.

During the course of the meeting, a very odd thing happened.

While McFarlane was answering a question, the president broke in and said, "You know, I remember the greatest speech I ever heard. It was in Los Angeles, quite a few years ago. The speaker was Ambassador Carlos Romulo from the Philippines, and he was describing the scene on July 4, 1946, the day we returned his country to its people after the war. As our soldiers and marines were leaving, a quarter of a million Filipinos were standing on the shore, waving American flags, throwing garlands and flowers, and cheering our men. As he painted that scene for us, there wasn't a dry eye in the place."

I didn't see how any of this was relevant to our discussion, but later the president took me aside and said, "I can see the day, not too many weeks from now, when the Lebanese people will be standing at the shore, waving and cheering our marines when they depart."

God save us all, I thought. This really *is* about Lebanon.

I asked a number of questions that evening, which were answered by McFarlane, Shultz, and Weinberger. One of the points I raised turned out to be rather embarrassing.

"Grenada is part of the British Commonwealth," I said. "What does Mrs. Thatcher think about all this?"

"She doesn't know about it," said the president.

That didn't sound right to me. Mrs. Thatcher was our closest ally, so how could we go into Grenada without informing her? Clearly, in all their excitement about the invasion, the White House had overlooked the British connection.

Sure enough, as we left the meeting, Bob Michel, the House Republican leader, told me that the president was already on the phone with Margaret Thatcher. We could hear Reagan's side of the conversation, and from his fumbling and his apologies it was obvious that she was enraged.

I took notes that night, and not long ago I read them over. The last line I wrote was: "I left the meeting with a great concern for my country."

Today I feel even more strongly that we should not have invaded Grenada. Despite what the administration claimed, the students were never in danger. None of the students trapped in the second campus of the medical school for nearly two days after the invasion were harmed, and neither were any of the American residents on the island. But over a hundred American troops were killed or wounded in that operation. We were supposed to be out within forty-eight hours, but our combat troops stayed on for weeks. And as far as I can see, it was all because the White House wanted the country to forget about the tragedy in Beirut.

It was bad enough that Grenada was really about Lebanon. Unfortunately, that's not all it was about. My greatest fear about Reagan's foreign policy is that ten years from now we'll look back on the Grenada incident as a dress rehearsal for our invasion of Nicaragua.

From the beginning, I fought against the administration's support of the contras. The CIA is great at analysis, and if the president had read the national intelligence estimates he was getting from them, he would never have kept the marines in Beirut as long as he did. Back in 1967, Lyndon Johnson was in a similar position: if only he had invited a few CIA analysts to the White House, he might have saved a great many American lives. Our nation certainly needs a major intelligence agency like the CIA if we are to protect our interests in the world. But we do not need an agency to conduct secret wars—especially against a nation with which we have full diplomatic relations and are officially at peace.

Although President Reagan's reelection in 1984 carried no mandate for funding the contras, he wasted no time in trying to secure more money for them. In 1985, his first major television address from the Oval Office was directed at this effort. I was surprised that a man who had had his finger on the pulse of America in 1981 could be so far from the popular will in 1985. But instead of making the budget deficits the top priority of his second term, he decided to give that honor to a sorry group of mercenaries.

Even so, it took over a year for the president to get Congress to go along with him in supporting aid to the contras. On the first vote, in March 1985, he was easily defeated. A month later, both he and I fought considerably harder to gather support for our respective positions. An hour before the vote in the House, the president called me to complain that I was twisting arms and violating my well-known belief that foreign policy should be a matter of individual conscience. He also told me that if he were to lose this vote it would diminish the office of the presidency in the eyes of the world. I responded that I had no desire to harm the prestige of the president, and I denied that I was putting pressure on Democratic members.

At the same time, I let him know once again that I was strongly opposed to his policy in Nicaragua, and that if he wanted to see a good reason to vote against contra aid he should look at the current issue of *Newsweek*, which ran a photograph of a man lying in an open grave with his throat slit—a victim of contra terror.

"I saw that picture," replied the president, "and I'm told that after it was taken, the so-called victim got up and walked away."

It was clear to me that this conversation was leading nowhere. At the same time, I did offer to delay the vote for a few days. After all, there was some legitimacy to the president's concern for the image of the presidency, and I recalled that Jimmy Carter had never lost a major foreign policy vote.

The president said he would think over my offer and call me back, but in the end he decided not to have the vote postponed. The president lost that vote, but a few days later, Daniel Ortega left Nicaragua for an official visit to Moscow. When that happened, it was only a matter of time before the House would rally behind President Reagan and vote with him to fund the contras.

If Reagan does bring us into Nicaragua, we will look back to June 25, 1986, as the day Congress passed the Central American equivalent of the Gulf of Tonkin Resolution. For that was when the administration was finally successful in getting the House to approve $100 million in aid to help the contras overthrow the government of Nicaragua.

At the time, the president's popularity was at its peak. But I think it's significant that even so, the aid package to the contras passed the House by only a dozen votes—221 to 209.

In order to win that one, the administration pulled out all the stops and used one tactic that was unprecedented in its arrogance. Three days before the vote, a messenger tracked me down on the eighth hole of a golf course to say that the White House was looking for me.

As instructed, I called Operator 29 at the White House, who put me through to Don Regan.

"This better be important," I snapped, "because you're getting me off the golf course."

"The president would like to address the Congress tomorrow," he said.

"No problem. We'll schedule a joint session. What time do you want it?"

"We don't want a joint session," he replied. "The president wants to address the House on Central America."

"I see," I said. "In other words, he wants to *lobby*. I can't allow that; it violates the separation of powers. A joint session would be fine, but he can't address the House."

"Nixon did," said Regan.

"I remember that," I replied. "But I also remember that John McCormack invited him. It was in 1969, and the president wanted to thank Congress for supporting his policies in Vietnam. First, he was invited. Second, he addressed both the House and the Senate on successive days. And third, he wasn't there to lobby."

The administration publicly claimed to be "flabbergasted" at my refusal, but Don Regan knew in advance that I would rule against his proposal. Before he reached me, he had already called Representative John Murtha of Pennsylvania, a Democrat who supports the president on the contras, and a powerful, behind-the-scenes player. Murtha assured Regan that I would never go along with the plan. The White House was only trying to embarrass me, and the entire episode was a cheap political trick.

But the administration was willing to try almost anything to help the contras—including, as we learned later, sending them the profits from the secret Iran arms sale—and the lobbying before the June 25 vote was fierce. One member told me that he had never spoken to a president before, and that he was awed and overwhelmed by the experience. It's always hard to turn down the man in the White House, and if that man is Ronald Reagan, it's even harder.

I've been suspicious of the Reagan administration with regard to Central America ever since they came into office. Alexander Haig hadn't been secretary of state more than three weeks when he told me over breakfast that we ought to be cleaning out Nicaragua. In 1983, the administration found a pretext to invade Grenada. I'm afraid they won't be satisfied until they get us into Nicaragua as well.

I'm not crazy about the Sandinistas, but their country was ravaged by the Somozas and their cronies for forty-five years, when we virtually forced their people into servitude through our corporations. We're not responsible for all of their problems, but we certainly played a part.

This doesn't mean that I like or approve of President Daniel Ortega, either. As far as I'm concerned, he can move to Cuba and smoke cigars with Castro. He embarrassed a lot of his American supporters when he flew to Moscow in 1985. But does that mean we should be giving military aid to the contras?

The president calls them "freedom fighters," but that's ridiculous. In reality, they're a small ragtag army of racketeers, bandits, and murderers who are led by some of the same people who ran the national guard under Somoza. They were thrown out of office, and now we're trying to put them back in.

People often ask me where my passion about Central America comes from. In fact, I have a special source—the Maryknoll priests and nuns, who are there as missionaries and health care workers. These people don't care about politics; their only concern is the welfare of the poor. And I haven't met one of them who isn't completely opposed to our policy down there.

My earliest connection to the Maryknoll Sisters of St. Dominic came through my aunt Ann, who was known as Sister Eunice. She entered the order in 1920, only eight years after the first Maryknoll community was established, and she served in China and several other countries. But no matter where she was, we were always in touch. She remained a Maryknoll sister all her life—until her death in 1983 at the age of ninety-one. She's no longer in this world, but I continue to be inspired by her convictions.

Except as a last resort, the military route is the wrong way to go. Ever since World War II, our greatest successes on the international front have been achieved through economic, diplomatic, and political means. We saved Europe through the Marshall Plan. We saved Greece and Turkey through the Truman Doctrine. We turned the tide in places as far apart as Egypt and Indonesia.

Even in the Reagan years, we've used our political skills overseas to great advantage. For all my differences with the administration on Central America, I was tremendously impressed with the way it handled complex and difficult situations in the Philippines and Haiti. It shouldn't be too hard to figure out a diplomatic solution to our differences with the government of Nicaragua.

But if we don't seek a peaceful solution, that hundred million dollars, together with our previous grants to the contras, will come to represent a small down payment in a conflict where our best hope is a long and bloody stalemate.

In other words, Nicaragua really *could* be another Vietnam. It certainly won't be another Grenada, where it was all over in a matter of days. If we ever go into Nicaragua, all Americans will come to regret it.

Early in 1984, I started thinking about retiring from the House. I could have stayed on indefinitely, but I had no great desire to end up as a tottering old congressman. In my younger days, I used to feel that both Rayburn and McCormack had remained on the job too long, and this was one mistake I was determined to avoid. Besides, after fifty years with too little time for my family, I thought they deserved more of my time and attention. Finally, there was Jim Wright to consider: he had been the loyal majority leader since 1977, and a member of the House since 1954. He was clearly going to be the next Speaker, and he deserved his day in the sun, too.

Unfortunately, the announcement of my retirement came out before I was ready. On the afternoon of February 29, Martin Tolchin, who covered Capitol Hill for the *New York Times*, popped his head into my office, saw that I was free, and came in to shoot the breeze. Gary Hart had just upset Walter Mondale in the New Hampshire primary, so there was plenty to talk about. As our conversation came to an end, the talk became more personal.

"How long are you planning to stick around?" Tolchin asked.

"If we can elect a Democratic president in November," I replied, "I might leave at the end of the year. Otherwise, I'll probably stay one more term."

"What would you do if you left this place?" he asked.

"I'm not sure," I said. And then, because Marty was a friend, I told him that I harbored a wistful fantasy about being named ambassador to Ireland by a Democratic president.

I had casually assumed that all of these comments about my future plans were off the record, but I should have realized that you're *never* off the record with a reporter unless you explicitly say so at the time.

I didn't give the matter another thought, but rumors spread quickly on Capitol Hill, and within an hour or two, Robert Healy of the Boston *Globe* and David Rogers of the *Wall Street Journal* sensed that something was up and started working on their own stories about my plans to step down. When he reached me by phone, Healy was especially upset. "What kind of friend are you," he asked, "telling Tolchin that you're leaving and that you want to become an ambassador?"

It was only then that I realized that I had inadvertently given Tolchin a big scoop. Under the circumstances, I could certainly understand how Healy felt. Not only was he a close friend, but the *Globe,* after all, was my hometown paper.

The following day, all three papers carried the story. The article in the *Times* was the most complete, and it ran on the front page with the headline O'NEILL HOPES TO RETIRE SOON, TO ANOTHER JOB.

I immediately called in Jim Wright, the House majority leader and the obvious choice to succeed me as Speaker. "I'm sure you read the *Times* this morning," I said, "and I want to apologize to you. I didn't mean for it to come out like that. I would have let you know in advance if I had any idea they would print it."

Still, after half a century in politics, I should have done a better job at stage-managing my own retirement.

Two years later, just before I stepped down as Speaker, the Iran-contra affair became public. In my view, nothing like this could have happened if Reagan's first-term staff—including Jim Baker, William Clark, and Mike Deaver—had still been around. Nobody at the White House or the National Security Council could have gotten away with acting behind the scenes, because one of them would have caught it. These men were master image-makers who would never have permitted a situation to develop that made the president look so bad.

But Don Regan is another story. When you have a president who likes to delegate, assisted by a White House chief of staff who likes to amass power, it's a formula for disaster.

This whole thing happened, in my view, because people around the president were willing to do almost anything to bring the Beirut hostages home before November 4, 1986, the date of the midterm elections. The Republicans were desperate to maintain control of the Senate, which was essential if the president was to get his legislation passed. If they could deliver the hostages, it would translate into a rush of support for the president, and for his allies in the Senate who were running for reelection.

Until the Iran-contra scandal broke, President Reagan was running on an incredible string of good luck. After six years of success, his staff had grown complacent and arrogant. The president was so popular and so above criticism that his aides came to believe that the administration could do anything it wanted, regardless of Congress and the American people.

I took no pleasure from the fact that I had been saying these things about Ronald Reagan all along.

From my point of view, the one bright spot in Reagan's second term was tax reform. At first I was skeptical. Tax reform was a fine and necessary idea, but I had seen Franklin Roosevelt, Jack Kennedy, and Jimmy Carter all fail in their attempts to change the tax code. Still, I had strongly endorsed the Gephardt-Bradley plan when it was first developed in 1983, and I didn't want anyone to think I was unwilling to try something new.

The president's men believed that tax reform would bring middle-class Americans so solidly behind the Republicans that it would actually realign the political parties. With that in mind, I picked Dan Rostenkowski to respond to the president's speech unveiling tax reform in the spring of 1985. Dan did a masterly job by promising Democratic support for the plan while pledging to make the president's program even more fair.

As things turned out, the president had to drag the Republican House members along kicking and screaming, as the interests of their business associates and contributors were apparently more important to them than the fate of their party—not to mention the state of the nation. When the legislation came to the House floor in November, both the president and I were shocked as the Republican minority voted overwhelmingly against even considering the bill.

I had produced 180 Democratic votes, but the president could not muster even 20 on his end. Many House Democrats wanted me to let the tax bill die and have the Republicans take the blame for killing it.

I'm as political as the next guy, but there are times when you have

to take a longer view. The day after the vote I met with Rostenkowski and Jim Baker, secretary of the treasury. I told Baker that if the
president could round up 40 Republican votes for consideration of
the bill, I would report it out once again.

As soon as they read the papers, some of the House Republicans
realized their mistake in voting against the president on tax reform.
And, not surprisingly, the president got on the phone and started
chasing votes. He also attended a meeting of all House Republicans
on Capitol Hill and appealed for their support. With his tremendous
persuasive abilities, he was able to round up his 40 votes.

After the vote, I was struck by how much could be accomplished
when the president and the Speaker, coming from opposing parties
but working together, could agree on specific legislation. Only a few
months earlier, none of the lobbyists had given tax reform a chance,
especially in view of the millions of dollars of special-interest contributions that seemed to stand in its way. But tax reform eventually
passed, and it shifted $120 billion in tax burdens from individuals to
corporations. This was one case where leadership made all the difference.

All along, I was confident that the 1986 congressional elections
would go well and that I would be able to give a strong Democratic
House majority to Jim Wright. Four years earlier, in 1982, the election boiled down to control of the House. This time we concentrated on the Senate, where the Republicans were most vulnerable.
As we had done in the House elections in 1982, the Democrats
concentrated on the freshman senators who had come in with Reagan in 1980 and who, in our view, were just as vulnerable as the
Reagan Robots had been in the House.

The president recognized that his Senate majority was in trouble,
and in the weeks before the election he went all out to save it. As
in the past, he attacked me personally during the campaign. Fortunately, my popularity ratings were a lot higher in 1986 than they had
been in 1981, and according to the pollsters I was almost as well-liked
as the president. As a result, my House colleagues who were running for the Senate did not have to worry about being tied to Tip
O'Neill.

During the final weeks of the campaign the president tried to make the election a referendum on Star Wars. But this was not enough to stop the Democratic momentum, and on election day the president lost the Senate more decisively than anyone had thought possible.

As soon as the results were in, the press asked me for a statement. "The Reagan Revolution is over," I told them.

And so, for all practical purposes, was my tenure as Speaker. A lot of Americans had been hurt by Ronald Reagan's policies over the past six years, but I took some comfort from the knowledge that without Tip O'Neill, the damage would have been a lot worse.

Epilogue
What I Believe

I BEGAN my political career in 1936, on a slogan of "work and wages." Today, more than half a century later, I'm still a bread-and-butter liberal who believes that every family deserves the opportunity to earn an income, own a home, educate their children, and afford medical care.

That is the American dream, and it's still worth fighting for. In my view, the federal government has an obligation to help you along the line until you achieve that dream. And when you do, you have an obligation to help out the next group that comes along.

In recent years, this idea has fallen out of favor. Today, there are those who argue that the way to achieve the American dream is to go it alone. This new morality claims that the young should forget about the old, that the healthy should ignore the sick, and that the wealthy should abandon the poor.

But this is an alien philosophy in our country. While we Americans certainly believe in getting ahead through education, sacrifice, and hard work, we also believe in looking out for the other guy. From our earliest beginnings, we have insisted that the individual human being is of fundamental value, and that even the humblest, meekest person has the right to be treated with dignity and respect.

I often hear successful people talking about the "good old days." Their message is always the same: how wonderful life used to be when we had less government and fewer social programs and people were left to fend for themselves.

But I came of age in those good old days, and I remember very clearly what they were like. When I first entered politics, 50 percent of the population were living in poverty. A full 25 percent of Americans were out of work.

Even if you were fortunate enough to have a job, life was still pretty tough. A policeman worked twelve hours a day, seven days a week. If you were a fireman, you were on duty even longer, and you worked a hundred and four hours a week. The postman delivered mail on Christmas Day. For most people, the work week was six days long—and those were six long days. The only time you saw your family was on Sunday.

For the majority of Americans, health insurance was out of the question. If you became sick, your world collapsed. For the elderly, life was filled with uncertainty and fear. Only a lucky few had pensions, and Social Security was a brand-new idea.

In those days, there was virtually no middle class in America—only a handful of rich people at the top, and millions of poor people at the bottom. Between the two groups stretched a huge and sparsely populated wilderness. The best way to close that gap was to attend college, but only a small percentage of the population could afford to go.

That was the America I knew in 1936. And despite all the problems we now face, I can never forget how far we have come in fifty years. Today, everyone goes to high school, and close to two-thirds of our young people pursue some form of higher education. And although poverty has certainly not been eliminated, we were able to get the poverty rate down to 10 percent in 1980. Today, virtually all workers have some form of health insurance. Social Security has made it possible for people to retire with a small but steady income. Without this protection, half of the elderly would be living in poverty.

As a result of these changes, our country now has a thriving middle class. We have many other things, too, including housing and job programs, a thriving system of state colleges and universities, and a farm program that has helped make us the greatest agricultural nation in the world.

Even those who are not yet part of the middle class are better off than they used to be. Through the years, our society has accepted a strong role in taking care of those who can't take care of themselves, including the sick, the handicapped, and the elderly.

We have provided a safety net for those who need protection.

My critics like to refer to me as the last of the big spenders. Maybe so, but I've always believed in our responsibility as a nation to pay for the health and welfare of the American people. Yes, I've supported higher taxes, but it's those taxes that made possible the tremendous progress we've seen.

Over the years, I've witnessed some miraculous improvements in this country. And above all, I'm proud that I had the opportunity to play a part in helping them along.

Even so, politics wasn't always easy, and there were several critical moments of truth—the teachers' oath bill in 1937, the Vietnam War in 1967, and the Reagan legislative locomotive in 1981—when I felt especially alone, and when even most Democrats stood against me. At those moments, my political future looked bleak. But today I look back at those times with the pride that comes from knowing I did the right thing.

I also look back to that summer day in 1927, when I stood outside the canvas tent at Harvard University. As I watched the privileged sons of America drinking their champagne, I dreamed of bringing my own people—and *all* Americans who weren't born to wealth or advantage—into the great American tent of opportunity.

And while some of the work remains to be done, I must be a lucky man, for so much of my dream has already come true.

Index